D1003353

SHANGHAI MODERN

·Leo Ou-fan Lee·

SHANGHAI MODERN

THE FLOWERING OF A NEW URBAN

CULTURE IN CHINA, 1930–1945

· Harvard University Press ·

Cambridge, Massachusetts

London, England

Second printing, 2001

Library of Congress Cataloging-in-Publication Data
Lee, Leo Ou-fan
Shanghai modern : the flowering of a new urban culture in China,
1930–1945 / Leo Ou-fan Lee.
p   cm.
Includes bibliographical references and index.
ISBN 0-674-80550-X (alk. paper.)
ISBN 0-674-80551-8 (pbk.: alk. paper)
1. Popular culture—China—Shanghai.
2. Shanghai (China)—Social life and customs.
3. China—Civilization—1912–1949. I. Title.
DS796.S25L43   1999
306'.0951'132—dc21   98-32318

FOR PAUL ENGLE (1908–1991) AND HUALING NIEH ENGLE

CONTENTS

ILLUSTRATIONS

Advertisement for Golden Dragon cigarettes (*Liangyou*, no. 1, February 1926).

Advertisement for Momilk (*Liangyou*, no. 14, April 1927).

Calendar poster from Hatamen cigarettes.

Movie theaters in Shanghai (*Liangyou*, no. 62, October 1931).

More movie theaters: the Carlton and the Odeon
(*Liangyou*, no. 62, October 1931).

Dai Wangshu's wedding, circa 1930.

Shi Zhecun.

Liu Na'ou.

Mu Shiying.

Portrait of Shao Xunmei by the famous artist Xu Beihong.

Ye Lingfeng in his later years.

Eileen Chang in a theatrical pose.

The cover design of Eileen Chang's story collection, *Chuanqi* (Romances).

PREFACE

This is a book about the city of Shanghai in the 1930s as a cultural matrix of Chinese modernity. In contrast to popular Western lore about the city, I take an insider's point of view by reading primarily Chinese materials—literary journals, newspapers, as well as works by individual authors and scholars—in order to construct a picture of Shanghai's urban culture at the height of its splendor. Such a topic would seem natural for a scholarly research project, but it proved more difficult than I first expected. When I first began exploring the subject some twenty years ago, I realized that it was all but an ideological taboo in China, while scholarship in modern Chinese studies in Western academia was preoccupied with rural villages.

This rural preoccupation is perfectly understandable, for China is still a predominantly rural country. In the modern Chinese literary imagination ever since the May Fourth period (1917–1923), patriotic sentiments invariably stemmed from, and were envisioned as, an ethos of the countryside, with the country (*guojia*) symbolically invoked as the "native land" of villages (*xiangtu*). Shanghai, the largest city in China and, as the hub of the publishing industry, the place where most of this literature was produced and circulated to the country at large, was cast in a negative light as a bastion of decadence and evil—the consequence of a long history of Western imperialism. As the treaty port par excellence—the largest of a dozen treaty ports on the Chinese coast—Shanghai became a constant reminder of a history of national humiliation.

Although the unequal treaties with the Western powers had been largely abolished by the mid-1940s, the Chinese Communist Party (CCP), which had been founded in Shanghai in 1921, perpetuated this negative image and made it into a major target by leading a revolution that sought to "mobilize the countryside to surround the cities." Since Shanghai was also the financial headquarters of the Nationalist (Guomindang) regime, it became, in a way, the CCP's worst enemy. After the establishment of the People's Republic in 1949, the material conditions of Shanghai deteriorated as its population continued to grow. Politically the city had always played second fiddle to Beijing, the nation's new capital. And for all the talk in literary circles about the "competition" between the Beijing school (Jingpai) and Shanghai school (Haipai) before Liberation, the culturally and politically hegemonic status of Beijing remained unchallenged—at least until recently.

This said, I must confess that Shanghai is a city for which I cherished few fond memories. I first visited the city in 1948 as a child and a refugee from the advancing troops of the People's Liberation Army on the eve of its victory. My strongest impression then was of its streetcars and neon signs lit by electricity. (Born in the rural region of Henan, I had never even seen an electric bulb!) I was also scared of the revolving doors in the hotel where my maternal grandfather lived. One morning I ventured out to buy some meat dumplings at a nearby food stand. On my return I got my ears caught in the fast-moving revolving door, and in a panic I lost all my dumplings—such being my first exposure to Shanghai modernity! The path toward my rediscovery of Shanghai's literary renown was paved in Taiwan and America—an intellectual journey which took nearly thirty years.

In 1949 my family moved to Taiwan, where I grew up and became interested in Western literature. As a sophomore in college I was involved in establishing a small literary journal, *Modern Literature* (Xiandai wenxue), which launched Taiwan's "modernist" movement in the early 1960s. When our first issue featured the works of Franz Kafka, I had no idea who he was, and I proceeded to translate a learned article on

Thomas Mann for another issue without the vaguest idea of his literary stature. Some twenty years later, when I was asked to write an article on modernism in Taiwanese literature, I began to reflect on this curious state of affairs: How could this brand of "modernism" have been produced in the corridors of an old university building in Taipei by a small group of college sophomores and juniors who could barely read English or any other Western language? Where did we find the works of Kafka, Mann, Joyce, Faulkner, and Hemingway? (Answer: in the small library of the Department of Foreign Languages and Literatures at Taiwan University.) We had made what we considered to be a major "discovery" at a time when High Modernism had already passed its creative prime and entered the American classroom as classics. Did Chinese writers of an earlier generation know about these modern masters when they were still alive—that is, in the period between the two World Wars? My curiosity led me back to Shanghai in order to trace these and other possible antecedents in modern Chinese literary history.

In fact, it was through the timely advice of a former Shanghai resident, C. T. Hsia, that I learned about another literary journal published in the 1930s with a similar name, *Xiandai zazhi* (Modern magazine; translated by its editor, Shi Zhecun, into French as *Les Contemporains*). Thus began my long journey toward retracing the footsteps of our literary predecessors—a *recherche du temps perdu* which brought me back to Shanghai in 1981. I have visited the city half a dozen times since, and each time I was privileged to meet and interview Shi Zhecun himself at his home, and at the Shanghai Municipal Library I was able to plumb the rich collections of literary journals and other rare collections which are not found anywhere abroad. For instance, I took out a copy of Liu Na'ou's *Dushi fengjingxian* (Scenes of the city) surreptitiously during lunch break (as no material was allowed to leave the library) and had the entire volume photocopied at a nearby copy shop that had just opened—a peculiar form of revenge on my fiasco at the revolving door some thirty years earlier: if I had once lost the dumplings, I now had a copy of a rare book!

Through these early research ventures I became obsessed with an old Shanghai I had remembered as a nightmare but which now emerged on thousands upon thousands of printed pages as a city of great splendor—the very embodiment of Chinese modernity. During my research I also learned that not only had the very English word "modern" entered the modern Chinese vocabulary as a transliteration, *modeng*, coined of course in Shanghai, but, more importantly, the whole gamut of Western literary modernism was known in the 1930s, and was even made quite popular by a number of writers who published translations, essays, and their own creative writings in scores of literary journals. The ways in which they managed to start their small publishing ventures had been quite similar to ours many years later—unplanned haphazard enterprises driven by intellectual curiosity and boundless energy, though not many financial resources, on the part of a small coterie of young novices. (For a detailed description, see Chapter 4.) But the names of these modern writers were either consciously erased or largely forgotten—Shi Zhecun (b. 1905), Liu Na'ou (1900–1939), Mu Shiying (1912–1940), Shao Xunmei (1906–1968), Ye Lingfeng (1904–1975), Eileen Chang (1920–1995), to mention the few who will enter into the present book as primary protagonists. By a happy coincidence, my own research project came at precisely the moment when a few Chinese scholars were beginning to rediscover these writers. Thus I was able to escape possible ideological censure (for doing research on "bourgeois decadence") and join their scholarly ranks as a pioneer.

But this pioneering status in the early 1980s was soon challenged by a spate of research publications all focused on Shanghai's urban history and by a resurgence of American scholarly interest in this city. Despite its early start, my research now may seem to lag behind and follow a well-trodden trail of books on various aspects of Shanghai—although I maintain that not much has been written on Shanghai's urban culture. The real reason for the delay of this research project was the crisis in Tiananmen Square in the spring of 1989. As a result of the massacre of demonstrators on June 4, I all but decided to abandon it in order to focus my energies on the more urgent issues of contemporary Chinese culture over the next few years. But this delay has also been, in scholarly terms, a blessing in disguise, for the publications of other scholars working on similar topics have fertilized the field which once looked so barren when I first ventured into it. Their work has also helped me to rethink some of my earlier ideas and to form my own framework. Still, thorny interpretive problems remain, which have been complicated by the recent "theoretical" turn in modern Chinese literature and cultural studies, in which the display of textual strategies, virtuoso readings, and other forms of interventions and subversions—all based on recent Western theories—seem to have taken over the task of research itself. All a scholar needs to do, it seems, is to read a few "privileged" texts!

I am by no means averse to theory; in fact I welcome it as intellectual challenge. The work of Walter Benjamin has proved especially relevant to my endeavor, as my final reflections in Chapter 1 clearly show. But I still prefer to do my work "from the ground up" by establishing first a context of Shanghai's urban culture before I attempt to reconfigure the texts into a meaningful set of readings. Owing to the rich materials I have gathered (both written and visual) and present to my intended readers—both academics and non-academics—I have chosen to write in an essay-like style and in a language that is not burdened with theoretical density. Contrary to the usual practice of laying out my theoretical arguments in the first chapter, I instead lay out Shanghai's urban background by a method that combines factual description with my own narration. Each of the other three chapters in Part I takes up an area of "cultural production"—print culture, cinema, and literary journals—which is illustrated with more materials and approached from different interpretive angles. My purpose is to construct an urban cultural context in which the various literary texts discussed in Part II might make more sense. Since most of these texts are not yet translated, hence new and unfamiliar to Western readers, I have included a few long paragraphs of my own translations. In the final part of this book I offer some general reflections and arguments that serve to round off my picture and bring my story into the late 1990s—to Hong Kong at the time of its "return" to the motherland. If it can be said that 1930s Shanghai has been reincarnated in Hong Kong since the 1950s, I believe that Hong Kong will in turn contribute to the rebuilding of Shanghai into a cosmopolis for the twenty-first century.

In the long and protracted course of research and writing, I have incurred more intellectual debts than I can ever list in the usual acknowledgments section. Still, I would like to thank the following foundations and institutions for their generous support: the Guggenheim Foundation, the Wang An Fellowship in Chinese Studies, the Committee on Scholarly Exchange with the People's Republic of China, as well as various faculty research grants from the University of Chicago, UCLA, and Harvard. The East Asian Library at the University of Chicago, the Harvard-Yenching Library, the Hoover Library at Stanford University, and above all the Shanghai Municipal Library and the libraries at East China Normal University, Fudan University, and the Shanghai Writers' Association have provided a wealth of materials for a literary scholar who loves to play archival detective. A number of scholars and friends in China have been especially helpful in spite of the considerable difficulties I have inadvertently caused them: Shi Zhecun, for his generosity of spirit and intellectual guidance; Xu Chi (1914–1996), poet and self-styled modernist, for his invaluable reminiscences and his precious photographs; Wei Shaochang, Ying Guojing, and Chen Zishan, for leading me through the material and human maze of doing research in Shanghai and for introducing other young scholars to me; and Yan Jiayan, for compiling the first collection of *Xin ganjuepai xiaoshuo xuan* (Selected stories of the neo-sensationalist school), published in time to provide me with a much-needed primary source. The names and works of numerous other Chinese and American scholars on Shanghai whom I have consulted I gratefully list in the notes. But I must single out Sherman Cockran, Arif Dirlik, Po-shek Fu, Bryna Goodman, Benjamin Lee, Lydia Liu, Frederic Wakeman, Wen-hsin Yeh, and Yingjin Zhang for their comments, suggestions, and research assistance, and the two anonymous readers who approved this manuscript for publication. I am especially grateful to the many graduate students I have had the good fortune to teach and to learn from in the seminars, workshops, and courses given at Chicago, UCLA, and Harvard; in particular I have benefited greatly from the research assistance and writing of Heinrich Fruehauf, Chen Jianhua, Robert Chi, Xincun Huang, Meng Yue, Ming Feng-ying, Daisy Ng, Emanuel Pastreich, Shu-mei Shih, and Ban Wang. Chapter 3 was further enriched by the timely assistance of Andrew Field of Columbia University and by hard-to-find materials from Po-shek Fu and Sheng Changwen. Two undergraduate students at Harvard, Ezra Block and Anthony Greenberg, valiantly took on the task of checking rather obscure Western sources, such as the stories of Paul Morand, at Harvard's Widener Library. Chen Jianhua, my chief research assistant, has been involved with this manuscript at every step of its preparation, including the arduous task of compiling the glossary and locating the photographs.

A much-shortened version of Chapters 1 and 9 appeared as a paper in a special issue of *Public Culture*. An earlier version of Chapter 3 appears in *Cinema and Urban Culture in Shanghai, 1922–1943* (Stanford University Press, 1999), edited by Yingjin Zhang. A revised version of Chapter 2 is included in a collection of conference papers titled *Becoming Chinese: Passages to Modernity and Beyond, 1900–1950* (University of California Press, 1999), edited by Yeh Wen-hsin. Both are used with the permission of the publishers.

This book is dedicated to the memory of the late Paul Engle (1908–1991), American poet and founding father of the Writers' Workshop at the University of Iowa, who taught me how to read Eliot and opened my eyes to true literary cosmopolitanism; and to Hualing Nieh Engle, his beloved wife and co-founder of the International Writing Program at Iowa and herself a distinguished novelist, whose love and concern have sustained me through all these trying years.

SHANGHAI MODERN

part one

THE BACKGROUND OF URBAN CULTURE

REMAPPING SHANGHAI

The sun had just sunk below the horizon and a gentle breeze caressed one's face . . . Under a sunset-mottled sky, the towering framework of Garden Bridge was mantled in a gathering mist. Whenever a tram passed over the bridge, the overhead cable suspended below the top of the steel frame threw off bright, greenish sparks. Looking east, one could see the warehouses of foreign firms on the waterfront of Pootung like huge monsters crouching in the gloom, their lights twinkling like countless tiny eyes. To the west, one saw with a shock of wonder on the roof of a building a gigantic NEON sign in flaming red and phosphorescent green: LIGHT, HEAT, POWER![1]

So begins Mao Dun's famous novel *Midnight* (Ziye), subtitled *A Romance of China in 1930*. The city in the background is of course Shanghai. By 1930 Shanghai had become a bustling cosmopolitan metropolis, the fifth largest city in the world[2] and China's largest harbor and treaty port, a city that was already an international legend ("the Paris of Asia"), and a world of splendid modernity set apart from the still tradition-bound country-side that was China. Much has been written about Shanghai in the West, but the corpus of popular literature which contributed to its legendary image bequeathed a dubious legacy. For aside from perpetuating the city's glamour and mystery, it also succeeded in turning the name of the city into a debased verb in the English vocabulary: "to shanghai" is "to render insensible, as by drugs [read opium], and ship on a vessel wanting hands" or "to bring about the performance of an action by deception or force," according to *Webster's Living Dictionary*.[3] At the same time, the negative side of this popular portrait has been in a sense confirmed by Chinese leftist writers and latter-day communist scholars who likewise saw the city as a bastion of evil, of wanton debauchery and rampant imperialism marked by foreign extraterritoriality, and a city of shame for all native patriots. It would not be too hard to transform this narrative theoretically into a Marxist, Maoist, or even postcolonial discourse by focusing on the inhuman exploitation of the urban underclasses by the rich and powerful, both native and foreign.

Although I am naturally drawn to the "political correctness" of such a line of interpretation, I am somewhat suspicious of its totalizing intent. Mao Dun, an avowed leftist writer and an early member of the Chinese Communist Party, inscribes a contradictory message on the very first page of his novel. Whereas Shanghai under foreign capitalism has a monstrous appearance, the hustle and bustle of the harbor—as I think his rather purple prose seeks to convey—also exudes a bound-less energy: LIGHT, HEAT, POWER! These three words, together with the word "NEON," written originally in capital letters in English in the Chinese text, obviously connote another kind of "historical truth": the arrival of Western modernity, whose consuming power soon frightens the protagonist's father, a member of the traditional Chinese country gentry, to death. In the first two chapters of the novel, Mao Dun in fact gives prominent display to a large number of *material* emblems of this advancing modernity: cars ("three 1930-model Citroëns"), electric lights and fans, radios, "foreign-style" mansions (*yang-fang*), sofas, guns (a Browning), cigars, perfume, high-heeled shoes, "beauty parlors" (he uses the English), jai alai courts, "Grafton gauze," flannel suits, 1930 Parisian summer dresses, Japanese and Swedish matches, silver ashtrays, beer and soda bottles, as well as all forms of entertainment, such as dancing (fox-trot and tango), "roulette, bordellos, greyhound racing, romantic Turkish baths, dancing girls, film stars."[4] Such modern conveniences and articles of comfort and consumption were not fantasy items from a writer's imagination; on the contrary, they were part of a new reality which Mao Dun wanted to portray and understand by inscribing it onto his fictional landscape. They are, in short, emblems of China's passage to modernity to which Mao Dun and other urban writers of his generation reacted with a great deal of ambivalence and anxiety.[5] After all, the English word "modern" (along with the French *moderne*) received its first Chinese transliteration in Shanghai itself: the Chinese word *modeng* in popular parlance has the meaning of "novel and/or fashionable," according to the authoritative Chinese dictionary *Cihai*. Thus in the Chinese popular imagination Shanghai and "modern" are natural equivalents. Therefore the beginning point of my inquiry will have to be: What makes Shanghai modern? That is, what constitutes its modern qualities in a matrix of meaning constructed by both Western and Chinese cultures?

The question may be posed to different audiences and may receive different responses. Westerners in Shanghai in that period would have taken the answer to such questions for granted: their presence in their privileged treaty port environs was what made this urban modernity possible. For the Chinese residents, by contrast, the responses would have been much more complex. Politically, for a century (from 1843 to 1943) Shanghai was a treaty port of divided territories. The Chinese sections in the southern part of the city (originally a walled city) and in the far north (Chapei district) were cut off from each other by the foreign concessions—the International Settlement (British and American) and the adjacent French Concession—which did not come to an end until 1943, during the Second World War, when the Allied nations formally ended the concession system by agreement with China. In these extraterritorial zones, Chinese and foreigners lived in mixed company (huayang zachu) but led essentially separate lives.[6] The two worlds were also bound together by bridges, tram and trolley routes, and other public streets and roads built by the Western powers that extended beyond the concession boundaries. These boundaries were marked by stone tablets, which were hardly noticeable in the labyrinth of streets and buildings that signaled the Western hegemonic presence: bank and office buildings, hotels, churches, clubs, cinemas, coffeehouses, restaurants, deluxe apartments, and a racecourse. They not only served as public markers in a geographical sense, but also were the concrete manifestations of Western material civilization in which was embedded the checkered history of almost a century of Sino-Western contact.[7]

The Sino-Western contact had in no small way shaped modern Chinese history since—even before—the Opium Wars, as it brought about not only Western invasions and imperialism but also successive reform efforts by the Chinese elite at the national and regional levels. This is of course a familiar narrative. What has not received sufficient scholarly attention until recently are the *material* aspects of Western civilization, which the more reform-minded Qing officials and intellectuals in the second half of the nineteenth century apparently appropriated as part of the "utility" component of their reform discourse, as summed up in the famous motto first coined by Governor Zhang Zhidong: "Chinese learning as essence, Western learning as utility." These material aspects of Western modernity, according to Tang Zhenchang, a leading scholar on Shanghai history, proved easier to accept than the "spiritual" aspects, and the response of Shanghai natives to these material forms of Western modernity followed a typical pattern of shock, wonder, admiration, and imitation.[8] In fact, most of the facilities of modern urban life were introduced to the concessions soon after the mid-nineteenth century: banks (first introduced in 1848), Western-style streets (1856), gaslights (1865), electricity (1882), telephone (1881), running water (1884), automobiles (1901), and trams (1908).[9] Thus, by the beginning of the twentieth century, the Shanghai concessions already had the infrastructure of a modern city even by Western standards. By the 1930s, Shanghai was on a par with the major cities of the world.

What made Shanghai into a cosmopolitan metropolis in cultural terms is difficult to define, for it has to do with both substance and appearance—with a whole fabric of life and style that Marxists used to call "superstructure." While obviously determined by economic forces, urban culture is itself the result of a process of both production and consumption. In the case of Shanghai, the process involved the growth of both socioeconomic institutions and new forms of cultural activity and expression made possible by the appearance of new public structures and spaces for urban cultural production and consumption, mostly in the concessions. Aspects of the former have been studied by many scholars,[10] but the latter remains to be fully explored. I believe that a cultural map of Shanghai must be drawn on the basis of these structures and spaces together with their implications for the everyday life of Shanghai's residents, both foreign and Chinese. In this chapter I therefore map out some of what I consider to be the significant public structures and spaces which had a crucial bearing on the figures and texts I shall study later in this book.

Architecture and Urban Space

"There is no city in the world today with such a variety of architectural offerings, buildings which stand out in welcome contrast to their modern counterparts," wrote an old Shanghai hand.[11] The statement implies that Shanghai itself offered a contrast of old and new, Chinese and Western. This does not mean, however, that the Chinese occupied only the old sections of the city and the Westerners the modern concessions. The notorious regulation that barred Chinese and dogs from the Westerners' parks was finally abolished in 1928, and the parks were open to all residents after 1928.[12] In fact, the population in the foreign concessions was largely Chinese: more than 1,492,896 in 1933 in a total city

7

population of 3,133,782, of which only about 70,000 were foreigners.[13] But the contrast nevertheless existed in their rituals of life and leisure, which were governed by the ways in which they organized their daily lives. "The Chinese and foreign residents of Shanghai might mingle at work when it was mutually beneficial, but almost invariably they spent their leisure hours separately."[14] For the Chinese, the foreign concessions represented not so much forbidden zones as the "other" world—an exotic world of glitter and vice dominated by Western capitalism as summed up in the familiar phrase *shili yangchang* (literally, "ten-mile-long foreign zone"), which likewise had entered into the modern Chinese vocabulary.[15]

The heart of the *shili yangchang* was the Bund, a strip of embankment facing the Huangpu River at the entrance to the harbor. It was not only the entrance point from the sea but also, without doubt, the seat of British colonial power. The harbor skyline was dotted with edifices, largely British colonial institutions, prominent among which were the British Consulate (the earliest building, 1852; rebuilt in 1873), the Palace Hotel, the Shanghai Club (featuring "the longest bar in the world"), Sassoon House (with its Cathay Hotel), the Customs House (1927), and the Hong Kong and Shanghai Bank (1923).[16] The imposing pomposity of the last two buildings, in particular, perfectly represented British colonial power. The massive headquarters of the Hong Kong and Shanghai Bank was the second largest bank building in the world at the time, designed in the neo-Grecian style by the architectural firm of Palmer and Turner.[17] "A 62-foot-wide flight of steps, originally flanked by a pair of bronze lions, one in a roaring posture, the other in repose, led from the street to the main entrance"[18]—"their noses and paws rubbed bright by passing Chinese hoping to improve their 'joss' or luck."[19] The reference to capitalist desire in this often-reported ritual of "petting the lions" is obvious: as the designated emblem of the British Empire, the bronze lions were rubbed a bright gold—symbolizing the accumulated wealth of British imperialism—and the "lucky" talisman was but another inducement to native greed.[20] The newly built Customs House, another building in the neo-Grecian style, was described by the *Far Eastern Economic Review* in 1927 while still under construction:

> The entrance portico follows a pure Doric Style, the inspiration being taken from the Parthenon at Athens. Ships and gods of the sea will be portrayed in the metopes of the frieze and much of the ornamentation will be symbolical. Vertical lines predominate from the 3rd to the 7th floor to accentuate the height, in contrast to the long, horizontal lines of the Hong Kong and Shanghai Bank, which has a frontage to the Bund of much greater length. The major portion of the tower is simple masonry in order to give prominence to the clock.[21]

Adding a final touch to this landscape of colonial economic power, the clock was a replica of London's "Big Ben"; it has struck every quarter hour since 1893, except during the Cultural Revolution.[22]

From this description it is clear that most of these British edifices on the Bund were built or rebuilt in the neoclassical style prevalent in England beginning in the late nineteenth century, which replaced the earlier Victorian Gothic and the "free style" of the arts and crafts movement. It was essentially the same style that the British imposed on their colonial capitals in India and South Africa. As the dominant style in England's own administrative buildings, it consciously affirms its ties to imperial Rome and ancient Greece. As Thomas Metcalf has stated, "The use of classical forms to express the spirit of empire was, for the late-Victorian Englishman, at once obvious and appropriate, for classical styles, with their reminders of Greece and Rome, were the architectural medium through which Europeans always apprehended Empire."[23] At the heart of this revived classicism was a celebration of empire and prosperity as symbolized in the 1897 Jubilee celebration of the sixty-year reign of Queen Victoria. By the 1930s, however, the era of Victorian glory was over: England was no longer the unchallenged master of world commerce. A new power, the United States of America, began its imperial expansion into the Pacific region following its conquest of the Philippines. The merger of the British and American concessions into one International Settlement had occurred earlier, at a time when American power was still dwarfed by the might of British imperialism. But by the 1930s, Shanghai's International Settlement was the site of competing powers and architectural styles: whereas British neoclassical buildings still dominated the skyline on the Bund, other structures in a more modern style had also appeared which exemplified the new American industrial power.

Since the late 1920s, some thirty multistory buildings taller than the colonial edifices on the Bund had begun to rise as a result of the development of new construction materials and techniques in America.[24] These were mainly bank buildings, hotels, apartment houses, and department stores—the tallest being the twenty-four–story Park Hotel designed by the famous Czech-Hungarian architect Ladislaus Hudec, who was first associated with the American architectural firm of R. A. Curry before opening his own offices in 1925.[25] Hudec's "innovative and elegant style added a real flair to Shanghai's architecture," as evidenced by the many buildings he designed: in addition to the Park Hotel, the twenty-two–story building of the Joint Savings Society, the Moore Memorial Church, several hospitals and public buildings, and three movie theaters, including the renovated Grand Theater.[26] The exteriors and interiors of some of these modern buildings—the Park Hotel, the Cathay Hotel and Sassoon House, new cinemas such as the Grand, the Paramount Ballroom and Theater, and the Majestic Theater, and many apartment houses—were in the prevalent Art Deco style. According to Tess Johnston, "Shanghai has the largest array of Art Deco edifices of any city in the world."[27] The combination of the high-rise skyscraper and Art Deco interior design thus inscribed another new architectural imprint, that of New York City, with which Shanghai can be compared.[28]

New York remained in many ways the prototypical metropolis for both the skyscraper skyline and the Art Deco style. Its tallest buildings at the time—Rockefeller Center, the Chrysler Building, and above all the Empire State Building—were all constructed only a few years before

Shanghai's new high-rise buildings. While dwarfed by their height, the Shanghai skyscrapers bore a visible resemblance to those in New York. This American connection was made possible by the physical presence in Shanghai of American architects and firms. Another likely source of American input was Hollywood movies, in which silhouettes of skyscrapers and Art Deco interiors had become hallmarks of set design in musicals and comedies.[29] The Art Deco style may be said to be the characteristic architectural style of the interwar period in Europe and America; it was an architecture of "ornament, geometry, energy, retrospection, optimism, color, texture, light, and at times even symbolism." When transplanted into the American cities, New York in particular, Art Deco became an essential part of "an architecture of soaring skyscrapers—the cathedrals of the modern age."[30] The marriage between Art Deco and the skyscraper lent a peculiar aesthetic exuberance that was associated with urban modernity, as they embodied the spirit of "something new and different, something exciting and unorthodox, something characterized by a sense of *joie de vivre* that manifested itself in terms of color, height, decoration and sometimes all three."[31] When "translated" into Shanghai's Western culture, the lavish ornamentalism of the Art Deco style became, in a sense, a new mediation between the neoclassicism of British imperial power, with its manifest stylistic ties to the (Roman) past, and the ebullient new spirit of American capitalism.[32] In addition to—or increasingly in place of—colonial power, it signified money and wealth. The Art Deco artifice also conveyed a new urban lifestyle: the image of men and women living in a glittering world of fashionable clothes and fancy furniture was, to Chinese eyes, very much part of its exotic allure. The American magazine *Vanity Fair*, perhaps the best representation of this image in print, was available in Shanghai's Western bookstores and became the favorite reading of several Shanghai writers—Shi Zhecun, Xu Chi, and Ye Lingfeng in particular—which in turn lent itself to the construction of a *modeng* fantasy for the Shanghai bourgeoisie. One need only glance through a few issues of the magazine to discover how its visual (Art Deco, of course) and written contents (articles by Paul Morand, for instance) were readily transplanted into Chinese and reappeared in a different guise in the *modeng* magazines of Shanghai.

Whereas this gilded decadent style may be a fitting representation of the "Jazz Age" of the "Roaring Twenties" in urban America, as glorified in the fiction of F. Scott Fitzgerald, it remained something of a mirage for Chinese readers and filmgoers, a world of fantasy which cast a mixed spell of wonder and oppression. The Chinese term for skyscrapers is *motian dalou*—literally, the magical big buildings that reach the skies. As a visible sign of the rise of industrial capitalism, these skyscrapers could also be regarded as the most intrusive addition to the Shanghai land-scape, as they not only towered over the residential buildings in the old section of the city (mostly two- or three-story structures) but also offered a sharp contrast to the general principles of Chinese architecture, in which height was never a crucial factor, especially in the case of domestic architecture. No wonder they elicited responses of heightened emotion: in cartoons, sketches, and films, the skyscraper is portrayed as showcas-ing socioeconomic inequality—the high and the low, the rich and the poor. A cartoon of the period, titled "Heaven and Hell," shows a sky-scraper towering above the clouds, on top of which are two figures apparently looking down upon a beggar-like figure seated next to a small thatched house.[33] In another by the famous artist Zhang Guangyu, two country bumpkins are talking against the backdrop of the Park Hotel, their dialogue peppered with local dialect expressions:

> *Country bumpkin A:* "Such a tall building, what's it for?"
> *Country bumpkin B:* "You sure know nothing, this is for the time when the water of the Huangpu River swells up!"[34]

A book of aphorisms about Shanghai includes the following entries: "Shanghai has big foreign buildings of twenty-two stories high; it also has thatches like coffins. Only with this [combination] can it manifest the 'Oriental color' of this 'Paris of the East'"; "The neurotic thinks that in fifty years Shanghai will sink beneath the horizon under the weight of these big, tall foreign buildings."[35] These reactions offered a sharp contrast to the general pride and euphoria expressed by New Yorkers, as described by Ann Douglas.[36]

To the average Chinese, most of these high-rise buildings were, both literally and figuratively, beyond their reach. The big hotels largely catered to the rich and famous, mostly foreigners. A Chinese guidebook of the time states: "These places have no deep relationship to us Chinese . . . and besides, the upper-class atmosphere in these Western hotels is very solemn; every move and gesture seems completely regulated. So if you don't know Western etiquette, even if you have enough money to make a fool of yourself it's not worthwhile."[37] This sense of alienation from Western places does not prevent the author of the guidebook, Wang Dingjiu, from waxing ecstatic about the *modeng* cinemas and dance halls and, in the section on shopping, about all the stylish clothes, foreign-made shoes, European and American cosmetics, and expensive furs for sale in the newly constructed department stores. It seems as if he were greeting a rising popular demand for consumer goods by advising his readers how to reap the maximum benefit and derive the greatest pleasure.

Department Stores

Whereas the deluxe Western hotels catered mainly to a Western clientele (although a Chinese crowd of thousands greeted the opening of the Park Hotel), a number of multistory department stores in the International Settlement—in particular the "Big Four" of Xianshi (Sincere), Yong'an (Wing On), Xinxin (Sun Sun), and Daxin (Sun Company), all built with investment from overseas Chinese businessmen—had become great attractions for the Chinese. With their escalators leading to variegated merchandise on different floors, together with dance halls and rooftop bars, coffeehouses, restaurants, hotels, and playgrounds for diverse entertainments, these edifices of commerce combined the functions of consumerism and recreation. (The playground design may have been influenced by the famous "Da shijie," or "Great World," which may be considered a department store of entertainment, with its six floors of local variety shows, food shops, and later cinemas in a carnival atmosphere.)[38] An article on Shanghai department stores in the *China Weekly Review* gave a "unique history of their founding" by using Sincere as a typical example. The idea came from an overseas merchant from New South Wales, Australia, Ma Ying Piu, who returned to Hong Kong and "inaugurated a business which was to proclaim the introduction of the 'fixed price' system by which protracted bargaining, so traditional among Chinese merchants at that time, would be eliminated. The public were to be assured of perfect fairness and sincerity in trading"—"thus the name 'Sincere,' or more complete, 'The Sincere Co., Ltd.'"[39] From its first six-story department store in Hong Kong, the company soon opened branches in other cities. The article ends with a most fantastic comment:

> The average Occidental is inclined to think of Shanghai as something primitive if not semi-civilized. Very often the city is associated with wheelbarrows and junks and that sort of progress . . . What a surprise it then is to be [sic] new arrival upon seeing the latest model of the Rolls-Royce whirring up Nanking Road and stopping in front of stores whose size and appearance compare most favorably with those on Oxford Street, Fifth Avenue, and the Rue de la Paix! The tourist steps ashore and finds that all "home side" brands are advertised and sold in the department stores of Shanghai. The "Jaeger" pullover is displayed side by side with the B.V.D. underwear, and "Houbigant" perfumes are sold in a department just above that where "Florsheim" shoes attract their attention. Shanghai with its cosmopolitan department store supplies can well boast of its foreign and Chinese stores as "universal providers." . . . Who can say that the department store is not doing its part to make "Greater Shanghai" all the greater?[40]

Any Occidental tourist who entered Sincere or Wing On (opened in 1917 and 1918, respectively), situated across from each other on the city's major thoroughfare, Nanking Road, would surely experience another form of excitement: the fierce competition to attract customers. Sincere initiated the new mass-consumer design for offering diverse merchandise. It was also the first store to employ salesgirls.[41] Wing On duplicated all of Sincere's attractions in its seven-story building; then in 1932 it erected a new nineteen-story skyscraper of triangular shape, complete with all the latest conveniences: fast elevators, central heating, air-conditioning.[42] The third department store, Xinxin, or "Sun Sun," opened in 1926 and advertised itself as "the only IDEAL STORE in the town offering High Quality, Good Service, Reasonable Price."[43] To compete for business, it devised a new advertising gimmick by installing on its sixth floor a radio studio in a glass cage so that customers could watch famous singing stars perform.[44] The fourth largest department store, Daxin, was opened in 1936 in another brand-new building.

That all these department stores were located on or near Nanking Road, the main thoroughfare of the International Settlement, was no surprise. If the Bund was the seat of colonial power and finance, Nanking Road, which stretched westward from the Bund, was its commercial extension: "Nanking Road was Shanghai's Oxford Street, its Fifth Avenue."[45] The natives still called it Damalu—the Number One Street (with a premodern reference to its days of horse-drawn carriages, or *malu*)—in honor of its privileged status. In 1908 the first tram line on Nanking Road was completed; it extended from the Bund to Tibet Road, beyond which it switched onto the equally famous Bubbling Well Road. The tram quickly became one of the most frequently used forms of public transportation in the city, together with the trackless trolley and bus. Land values along the thoroughfare skyrocketed. Since the late 1910s, its eastern portion had already become the most prosperous of Shanghai's commercial area. A 1920 handbook on Shanghai written by a Reverend Darwent describes the street:

> Nanking Road is certainly one of the most interesting streets in
> the world . . . The visitor will be surprised—I think this will be
> his first impression—how thoroughly *Chinese* the road is . . .

There are 1,000,000 Chinese to fewer than 15,000 western foreigners. This will explain what is to a newcomer the amazing fact that he hardly ever meets a foreigner of whom he can ask the way. Foreign men are in offices. Women are at home or in carriages. He will realize that powerful as foreign influence is, this is China and the vast overwhelming majority of people in the streets are Chinese.

The next thing that will strike a visitor may be the traffic . . . Here are the figures from the Municipal Council returns, of the "Average census of traffic passing at the junction of Nanking Road and Kingsu Road on Feb. 25, 27, 28, 1918, from 7 A.M. to 7 P.M.": "rickshaws 14,663; pedestrians 30,148; carriages 942; motor-cars 1,863; wheel-barrows 2,582; hand-carts 527; bicycles 772; pony-carts 129; tram-cars 754."[46]

The street's legendary reputation could only be further enhanced by the addition of the new department stores—this "extraordinary type of semi-foreign and gorgeous shop" where "Chinese and foreign elements meet . . . Silver ornaments, silks, satins, furs may be purchased in rich variety. It is commonly reported that on the first day that one of these stores opened it took $100,000 in cash across the counter, which is likely enough."[47] For out-of-towners visiting Shanghai, shopping for modern luxury items at the department stores on Nanking Road had become a necessary and desirable ritual. If they chose, they could stay in the Sincere Hotel, with 114 rooms "in Chinese style from $1 to $2.5 a day; in foreign style from $2 to $6 a day."[48]

An index to the role of material consumption in Shanghai's modern life can be found in the omnipresent advertisements, which appeared as signs lit up with neon lights, as billboards in front of street-level stores, and above all as printed words and pictures in the newspapers and journals. They add up to what may be called a semiotics of material culture. We can easily compile a list of daily necessities and luxuries for the modern urban household, gathered from the ubiquitous ads in

Liangyou: sundry food products (Quaker Oats, Momilk), laundry detergent (Fab), medicine and health products ("Dr. Williams' Pink Pills for
Pale People"), electric cooking pots and gas burners, medicine, perfume,
cigarettes, cameras, gramophone and records (Pathé, RCA), and many
more. Needless to add, advertisements for automobiles are everywhere;[49]
the number of privately owned automobiles more than doubled between
1922 and 1931 from 1,986 to 4,951.[50] Reportedly the Sincere department store even transported its favored customers in automobiles. Such
a picture of modern consumption set in urban Shanghai must have struck
any Chinese of the time who lived in the rural hinterland as nothing
short of a wonderland—a brave new world overflowing with foreign
goods and foreign names. In fact, it became the target of Shen Congwen's famous satirical novel *Alice's Travels in China (Ailisu Zhongguo youji)*, in
which the foreign Alice feels right at home in this faraway city.

Consumption was also linked with leisure and entertainment,
whose institutions deserve equal attention: in particular, cinemas, coffeehouses, theaters, dance halls, parks, and the racecourse. Whereas Western-style hotels were beyond the pale of Chinese life, cinemas, cafés, and
dance halls were an entirely different matter. In a way, they provided an
alternative to the traditional places of leisure and entertainment for
native residents, the local opera houses, the restaurants and teahouses in
the old city, as well as the houses of prostitution, which continued to
hold sway in the Chinese sections of the city. Together these places of
leisure and entertainment which sprang up in the foreign concessions
became the central sites of Shanghai's urban culture, and they in turn
served frequently as background settings for the literary works discussed
later in this book. (Because of its special significance, I shall deal with
Shanghai's cinema culture separately, in Chapter 3.)

Coffeehouses

As a public place fraught with political and cultural significance in
Europe, especially in France, the coffeehouse proved likewise extremely

popular in 1930s Shanghai. Like the cinema, it became one of the most popular leisure spots—decidedly Western, to be sure—a necessary site for men and women sporting a modern lifestyle, particularly writers and artists. The coffeehouse habit and style flourished primarily in Shanghai's French concession. While the British-dominated International Settlement was the site of skyscrapers and deluxe mansions and department stores, the scenery underwent a sudden transformation in the French Concession. The farther one followed the tram route into the concession along its main street, Avenue Joffre (named after the French general who stemmed the German invasion during the First World War), the more serene and atmospheric the place became. Trees imported from France (the Chinese called them French *wutong*) flanked the street, along with fine "suburban" residences built in various styles. According to an English guidebook of the time, "the peace and quiet was made possible by French policy," since "the French authorities have always taken a stronger line than those of the International Settlement. They refuse to allow businesses and factories to be established in residential roads."[51] Instead, one found churches, cemeteries, schools (including the famous Aurora University, where Shi Zhecun, Liu Na'ou, and Dai Wangshu studied), the French Park, as well as cinemas (including the Empire, Cathay, and Paris, the setting for Shi's story "At the Paris Cinema") and coffeehouses or cafés. As one local aficionado observed, on Avenue Joffre "there are no skyscrapers, no especially large structures," but "every night there are the intoxicating sounds of jazz music coming from the cafés and bars that line both sides. This is to tell you that there are women and wine inside, to comfort you from the fatigue of a day's toil."[52]

It is interesting to note that whereas the International Settlement seemed to showcase the hustle and bustle of high commerce, the French Concession always conjured up an aura of culture—both high and low, but definitely French, and even more exotic than the British and American. The special allure of French culture was perpetuated by a number of Chinese Francophile writers, notably the Zengs, father and son—Zeng Pu and Zeng Xubai. Together they founded in 1927 the publishing house of Zhen Mei Shan—literally, "True, Beautiful, and Good"—the name directly inspired by their image of the French Romantic writers whom Zeng Pu once studied with the legendary Chinese general Chen Jitong, who had spent many years living and writing in France. Although Zeng Pu, author of the famous late Qing novel *Niehai hua* (A flower in a sea of retribution, 1905), had never set foot on French soil, he lost no time in creating his own French world in his bookstore-residence at 115 rue Massenet in the heart of the French Concession. The following quotation is a good example of his effusively imaginative identification with all things French:

> Massenet is the name of a modern French composer, and as soon as I step out on the street, his operas *Le roi de Lahore* and *Werther* come to my mind. Late in the afternoon when I stroll over the tightly knit shadows of the tree-lined walk, the tragic scenarios of *Le Cid* and *Horace* unfold on my left, vis-à-vis the rue Corneille. And on my right, from the direction of the rue de Molière, the cynical laughter of a *Tartuffe* or a *Misanthrope* seems to enter my ears. Horizontally in front of me stretches the Avenue de La-fayette . . . which evokes the scenery depicted in . . . *La princesse de Clèves* and the historic sites described in *Mémoires Interessants*. The French Park is my [Jardin du] Luxembourg and the Avenue Joffre my Champs-Elysées. My steadfast determination to stay in this area is solely rooted in this eccentric *exotisme* of mine.[53]

Zeng Pu intended to make his publishing house not simply a library of French literature but a cultural salon, in which he would gather his guests and disciples around him and discuss his favorite French authors: Victor Hugo, Anatole France, Leconte de Lisle, George Sand, and Pierre Loti. As Zeng's son, Zeng Xubai, vividly recalls:

> There was hardly an evening when the lights of our guest room didn't glow until very late at night. My father was not only extraordinarily hospitable, but he also exuded an intoxicating

fascination which caused every guest to be drawn deeply into the stream of his conversation . . . Whoever came, came, and whoever felt like leaving, left, always without the exchange of notable formalities. My father cherished this free and unconstrained atmosphere; only in this manner, he believed, would everything resemble a genuine French salon.[54]

The guests and friends at Zeng's bookstore-salon had all become Francophiles themselves. A few of them—Li Qingya, Xu Xiacun, Xu Weinan—became famous translators; most others were writers, poets, and publishers, such as Shao Xunmei, Xu Zhimo, Tian Han, Yu Dafu, Lu Mengshu (editor of the movie magazine *Yinxing*, or "Silver Star"); and three aestheticians—Fu Yanchang, Zhu Yingpeng, and Zhang Ruogu—who went a step further than Zeng and incorporated French and Western exoticism into a nationalist argument: they "considered the special status of Shanghai as a circumstance that would eventually benefit the aesthetic outlook of the whole nation. Shanghai, because it was so 'exotic,' so different from the rest of China, could become a cultural laboratory where *in vitro*, the experimental restoration of Chinese civilization would be undertaken."[55]

It is doubtful that the Chinese Francophiles had succeeded in turning their literary salon into something approaching Jürgen Habermas's notion of the "public sphere." But there is no denying that Shanghai writers used the coffeehouse as a place for friendly gatherings. From both contemporary accounts and latter-day memoirs, we discover that this French institution was combined with the British custom of afternoon tea to become a highlight in their daily rituals. The choice of the hour for taking tea was often necessitated by economic considerations, since some of the cafés most frequented by impoverished writers and artists were housed in restaurants which offered reduced afternoon prices for coffee, tea, and snacks. Zhang Ruogu, an avid Francophile, named several spots as his favorites: Xinya (Sun Ya) on Nanking East Road across from the Xinxin department store (for tea and snacks); Sullivan's, a justly famous chocolate shop (for coffee, Coca-Cola, chocolate, and ice cream); Federal, a German-style café on Bubbling Well Road (for coffee and cake); Constantine's, a Russian café (for "pure Arabian black coffee"); and Little Man (Xiao nanren), across the street from the Cathay Theater (where "the decor is splendid and the waitresses young and pretty").[56] But Zhang's favorite spot was apparently the Balkan Milk Store, another Russian-run café in the French Concession, which offered coffee at cheaper prices than the more aristocratic Marcel or Federal, and where he and his friends could spend long hours undisturbed by the waiters.[57] In a collection of his essays appropriately titled *Kafei zuotan* (Café forum), Zhang comments:

> Aside from sitting in the office and browsing in the bookstores, I spent practically all my leisure time in the cafés on Avenue Joffre. I was interested only in sitting and talking with a few close friends in a café. This kind of enjoyment was more effortless and freer than discussing issues painstakingly in writing, and the pleasure of talking could be had only from a gathering of intimate friends, not from meeting with a multitude. Come late afternoon, all of us would gather, without prior arrangement, at a few of our usual cafés, and as we drank the strong and fragrant coffee to enhance our fun, we would gently talk our hearts out. This kind of natural and carefree pastime—it really could not be shared with outsiders.[58]

Zhang writes that there were three kinds of pleasures that could be derived from going to the coffeehouse: first, the stimulus of the coffee itself, with an effect "not inferior to that of opium and wine"; second, the opportunity provided by the coffeehouse for long talks among friends, "the most pleasurable thing in life"; and last but not least, the charming presence of the coffeehouse waitress, a literary figure first introduced to Chinese writers by Yu Dafu's translation of a story by George Moore,[59] and made more famous by their knowledge of Japanese waitresses in Toyko bars and coffeehouses before the 1923 earthquake.[60] Zhang, however, did not take the coffeehouse merely as a "decoration of modern urban life" or "a good place for rendezvous"; instead it was one of the crucial symbols of modernity, together with the cinema and the automobile; more than the latter two, it had an enormous impact on modern literature. He proudly mentions some of his favorite French writers—Jean Moréas, Théophile Gautier, Maxime Rudé, and Henri de Régnier—as diehard café addicts.[61]

For Xu Chi, who was a young poet and a budding modernist in the early 1930s, the Sun Ya was a favorite place, though fairly expensive, and not strictly speaking a coffeehouse but rather a restaurant. Its second floor became a popular spot for tea and snacks between four and six in the afternoon. Sometimes such gatherings would draw as many as thirty writers and artists, who would be seated at five or six tables, and people would move from one table to another to chat with acquaintances.[62] They all had to leave at six so the waiters could prepare the tables for dinner. There were about half a dozen popular spots known to writers, artists, and journalists, according to Xu, whose own favorites were, in addition to the Sun Ya, D.D.'s Café on Bubbling Well Road and Café Renaissance on Avenue Joffre, both of which were run by White Russian émigrés. Zhang Ruogu even devotes an entire essay to Café Renaissance, in which he constructs a scenario involving three well-dressed young men, "three musketeers of the metropolis," who bring with them a fashionable "modern girl" in an automobile—"a southern maiden whose face looks like the beauty on Lucky cigarette ads—adorned with a pair of big black eyes with long eyelashes and long Cutex-painted fingernails."[63]

At the time of Zhang Ruogu's writing (1929), literary Shanghai seemed to be caught in a coffeehouse craze, celebrated not only in Zhang's essays and Yü Dufu's translations but also in Tian Han's play *One Night in a Café* (Kafei guan de yiye) and numerous works of fiction. Tian Han also advertised a new bookstore run by his Nanguo (Southern China) dramatic society with a coffeehouse attached, where "waitresses trained in literature will let the customer enjoy the pleasure of good books and good conversation over drinks." All this Occidental exotica naturally converged on a bohemian self-image. Visiting the painter and poet Ni Yide in his small attic room, Zhang Ruogu jokingly remarked, "This room has the atmosphere of the painter Rodolfo's room, but regrettably you don't have a Mimi to be your companion."[64] Tian Han went so far as to incorporate the characters of La Bohème into the first part of a film he scripted, Fengyun ernü (Heroic youths, 1935), which ends with a call to war accompanied by the film's theme song, "The March of the Volunteers," which eventually became the national anthem of the People's Republic.

Dance Halls

Another public institution, somewhat lower in cultural prestige than the coffeehouse, was the ballroom/cabaret and the dance hall (wuting or wuchang): the former refers to places with a more deluxe decor and often featuring cabaret performances, patronized mostly by foreigners, whereas the latter had only a small band and "taxi dancers" or dance hostesses. By 1936 there were over three hundred cabarets and casinos in Shanghai.[65] The foreigners and the wealthy Chinese patronized the leading high-class ballrooms and cabarets, which offered floor shows and performances: the Tower atop the Cathay Hotel, the Sky Terrace at the Park Hotel, the Paramount Theater and Ballroom, Del Monte's, Ciro's, Roxy's, Venus Café, the Vienna Garden Ballroom, the Little Club, and so on. The very foreignness of these names seems to invoke an alienating effect similar to that of the high-class Western hotels and served as a pronounced reminder of their Western colonial-metropolitan origins: New York, London, Paris, Vienna. Still, the Chinese clientele managed to domesticate them to some extent by translating these exotic names into Chinese equivalents with native allure: thus Ciro's became Xianluosi, or "fairy land of pleasures," and Paramount became Bailuomen, or "gate to a hundred pleasures"; the legendary fame of the latter, in particular, has left an enduring mark on the Chinese literary imagination.[66] Although social dancing, like horse racing, was decidedly a Western custom, first introduced by Shanghai's foreigners in the mid-nineteenth century, that did not stop the Chinese from embracing it as a vogue. Shanghai natives reportedly flocked to the first dance halls in droves as soon as they were opened in the early 1920s.[67] By the 1930s, dance halls had become another famous—or infamous—hallmark of Shanghai's urban milieu. Frederic Wakeman, Jr., has provided some interesting information about Shanghai's dance scene:

> The tea dance was one of the first cultural events to bring the Chinese and Western elites together. As Western dancing became more popular, it spread among Shanghai's "petty urbanites" (*xiao shimin*) and dancing schools appeared, in some cases licensed by the authorities . . . Public dancing had been more or less monopolized by White Russian women, but around 1930 dance halls on the Western model began to open up in Shanghai and other Chinese port cities with Chinese *wunu* (dance hall girls). By the end of the '30s, fly-by-night dancing schools were little more than glorified brothels—which led the regularly licensed cabarets and dance halls to complain bitterly to the police that they were being forced out of business.[68]

One such school, started by Li Jinhui, a composer known for his "lascivious" tunes, even staged dancing by nude women.[69]

According to a report by two Western insiders, a low-class Chinese dance hall

> is usually decorated to the most remote corner, with perhaps half a dozen incongruous and clashing types and styles of Western ornamentation fighting for honors. The orchestra, invariably Filipino, pumping away at a tune-a-minute rate continuously between the hours of eight and two or three or four o'clock, rather lackadaisically ensconced on the bandstand . . . The guests, mostly male, very blasé, apparently quite unaware of the dancing girls, or *"woo niubs"* who sit but an arm's-length away from them, noisily eating watermelon seeds, a dish of which are

[sic] placed on each table by the management as a gratuitous gift. And last but most important, the *woo niubs*, slim, nonchalant and self-possessed and self-sufficient to the nth degree, cuddling their miniature hot water bottles if it is winter time, and acting for all the world as if they were really just waiting for a street car and no amount of dance tickets could tempt them onto the floor.

The same report discloses that the price of dance tickets varied from three for a dollar at the best places to eight, ten, and even fifteen at some of the dives, and it was not uncommon to use several tickets for one dance.[70]

It was presumably at one such dance hall, called Moon Palace, that the writer Mu Shiying spent most of his time in dedicated pursuit of a dance hostess who eventually became his wife. A talented writer whose meteoric rise to literary fame in the early 1930s was cut short by gambling and death (probably by assassination) in Japanese-occupied Shanghai in 1940, Mu in many ways embodied the temper and spirit of a truly urbanized writer. Together with Liu Na'ou, he attempted to capture in his fiction the frenzied sensations of urban life by experimenting with a prose style which imitates the technique of cinematography. The central setting of Mu's fiction is invariably the dance hall—a setting drawn from personal observation and experience, to be sure, but also intended by Mu as the perfect backdrop for a kind of dark parable of human alienation. (See Chapter 6.)

Mu's case—that of a talented writer who consciously sought inspiration for his art in the dance hall—may have been the exception to the rule. But his lifestyle as a Shanghai urbanite, as projected in his stories, was by no means a mere fictional construction. In terms of the number of customers, the popularity of dance halls in Shanghai clearly surpassed that of the coffeehouses. Whereas the coffeehouses remained the haunt of upper-class Chinese and foreigners as well as writers and artists, the dance hall reached out to people of all classes and soon became a fixture in the popular imagination. This is evidenced by the numerous reports, articles, cartoons, drawings, and photographs in the daily newspapers (especially the so-called mosquito press) and popular magazines. In fact, some of the leading Shanghai artists—Ye Qianyu, Zhang Yingchao, Zhang Leping—used the dance hall and dance waitresses as the subjects of their cartoons. These typically consist of variations on a man and a woman (or occasionally two women) dancing: the man can be young or old, wearing a long Chinese gown or a Western suit, but the woman is invariably dressed in a qipao, a gown of "Manchu cut" widely popular at the time. The portrait unwittingly conveys a gendered differentiation: of the woman as a fixed object of desire for men of various classes, her qipao revealing the contours of her body. These variations on the dancing couple are all apparently drawn from the model of dance hostess and her various clients. This impression receives written confirmation in the accompanying articles, in which the authors describe and comment on the dance hostess and the allure of female flesh as commodity. Most of the articles tend to focus on the small lower-class dance halls, which were more numerous than the large renowned cabaret clubs. According to one such article,

> the dance space is small, its environs also small, and the price is cheap (one dollar can buy five or six dances) . . . A cup of tea costs twenty cents, no matter how long you want to stay, five or six hours . . . Because the dance space is small, when you dance you feel the tension of the flesh even more . . . In the large dance halls we are always [made to feel] like gentlemen and all but lose the intention of seeking the taste of women. As we follow the music we must dance the fox-trot or waltz or blues, as if a wrong step would elicit the shaming laughter of the whole audience. But in a small dance hall, you can dance as you wish; you need not coordinate the movement of your steps, and you can step out of the rhythm of the musicians as they play either a "Peach Flower River" or a "Vienna." You do as you like . . . Also in a small dance hall, the duration of each dance is twice as long as in a big ballroom, and the scattered lights of green or red or purple are

turned off many times. This is to make you more eager, because you can touch the dance hostess's breasts, kiss her cheek or mouth; you can do as you wish.[71]

In these small dance halls both the hostesses and their customers were mostly Chinese, and the latter seem to have been more exploitative of their own kind. It does not take much leftist sympathy to voice a moral concern for the economic plight of the dance hall hostesses. Here is a rough estimate of the monthly income and expenses of an average dance hostess.

Expenses:

Room rent	25 yuan
Board	30 yuan
Social expenses (including movies)	20 yuan
Clothes	54 yuan
Family support (note: this may be unreliable)	200 yuan
Deposit to savings	25 yuan
Total monthly expenses:	354 yuan

Income:

Based on five hours of work per day (ten dances per hour) for a total dance fee of 8.50 yuan.

Her monthly income is 255 yuan, hence 99 yuan in debt.

(Note: How such a debt is settled remains a riddle)[72]

This sample may not be reliable, but it is nevertheless revealing. On the basis of these figures, the only way for a hostess to keep a positive monthly balance was to cut back on the "unreliable" sum of 200 yuan for family support. A single hostess with no family burden might net about 100 yuan per month after expenses; but those with poor families in rural areas who depended on their support would certainly be in deep financial trouble. Aside from money sent back home, the biggest estimated expenditure is for clothing: 54 yuan. The cost of clothing and cosmetics can be gauged from this itemized chart of "Estimates for Spring Clothing: the lowest expenditures for a modern woman," a total of sixteen items, including one of each of the following: shoes, stockings, bra, gown, short coat, gloves, face powder (such brands as "Face Friend" and Coty), rouge, lipstick, leather bag, permanent wave rod, pencil, and honey, for a total of $52.05 in silver dollars.[73]

The high cost of clothing gives another indication not only of the general trend toward commodification in Shanghai's urban life but also of the issue of fetishization—the purposeful flaunting of a woman's body as commodity and material object of male gaze and desire. If we compare the descriptions of coffeehouse waitresses and dance hall hostesses by modern Chinese writers, it would seem that while the former were celebrated by the Francophile writers as romantic figures in their ideal-ized vision of a bohemian life, the latter were seen as miserable, though still alluring, creatures. There was no attempt to construct a literary pedigree for hostesses in small dance halls (whereas the Western cabaret hostesses came to be romanticized in films, such as Marlene Dietrich in *The Blue Angel*). In this regard, Mu Shiying's fictional portrait of the dance hostess does serve a literary purpose. As I shall discuss in Chapter 6, the dance hostesses in Mu Shiying and Liu Na'ou's fiction are often por-trayed as larger than life, and they take a more active, even dominant, role over men; as objects of male desire they also defiantly return the erotic gaze of men. Such portrayals of the emerging femme fatale in the world of the café, the ballroom, and the racecourse may be interpreted as fictional projections of the author's male fantasy, or they can be seen as a mere embodiment of the city's material glamour, hence further reinforc-ing the inevitable process of commodification.

I would argue a slightly different thesis, however. The popularity of the dance halls in Shanghai's urban life seems to have served ironically as the necessary, albeit negative, backdrop for the emergence of a new public persona for women. If we combine the descriptions of dance hostesses with earlier portraits of courtesans and movie stars and read them symbolically as marking different facets of a cultural genealogy, we can recall a long tradition of literary tropes which in varying ways center on figures of women in the public arena. Before leftist critics in the 1930s began to see all such women as oppressed and downtrodden, some Shanghai writers—particularly those of the "neo-sensationalist" school (Xin ganjue pai)—had chosen to "modernize" such a long-standing trope in traditional Chinese popular literature by making these female figures, even as embodiments of urban material culture, more dynamic and ironically more confident in their own subjectivity as women—to the extent that they can play with men and make fools of them in such public places of leisure as the dance hall, the coffeehouse, and the racetrack.[74]

Public Parks and the Race Club

It remains for me to discuss briefly the two public sites which were clearly derived from the British colonial legacy: public parks and the Shanghai Race Club (Paomating).

A humiliating reminder of the Western imperialist presence was, of course, the notorious sign of exclusion that reportedly hung at the gate of the Public Gardens in the International Settlement: "No Chinese or Dogs Allowed." The real sign, though no less humiliating to the Chinese, did not exactly read this way. It was a bulletin listing five regulations first decreed in 1916. The first regulation reserved parks for the use of foreign residents. The second stipulated that "dogs and bicycles are not admitted," and was followed by the third: "Chinese are not admitted" except "in the case of native servants accompanying their white employers." The fourth and fifth regulations excluded Indians (except for those in dignified attire) and Japanese (except for those wearing Western clothing).[75] These posted regulations finally came down when the Nationalist forces under Chiang Kai-shek assumed control of Shanghai in 1927. In Betty Wei's vivid account, on April 12, "as if symbolic of the new state of affairs in Shanghai, the Ratepayers' Meeting in the International Settlement passed a resolution: 'Jessfield and Hongkew Parks, the Public Gardens, the Bund Lawns and Foreshore, Quisan Gardens, and Brenan Piece be opened to the Chinese on the same terms as foreigners.'"[76] Although there was still an admission charge, "the people of Shanghai responded to this opening of facilities with great enthusiasm. Admittance figures kept by municipal authorities show an impressive number of visitors to the public parks"—up from 1,625,511 in June–December 1928 to 2,092,432 in 1930.[77] Aside from the half-dozen parks in the International Settlement, there were, of course, parks and gardens in the French Concession and in the Old City: a guidebook of the period lists nearly forty public and private parks and gardens.[78] Of these a particular favorite of the writers was the new amusement park, Rio Rita's, run by Russian émigrés, which became a literary legend with the publication of Mao Dun's novel *Midnight,* in which a minor decadent character describes the place: "They've got good wine and good music, and there are White Russian princesses, princes' daughters, imperial concubines and ladies-in-waiting to dance attendance on you. Green, shady trees and lawns as smooth as velvet. And then there's a little lake for boating . . . ah, it reminds me of the happy hours I spent on the banks of the Seine."[79]

Obviously, this "pleasure garden" combined the functions of dance hall, café, restaurant, and park. There was in fact an open-air dance hall, which was a popular spot for "nocturnal entertainment in summer."[80] Thus it seems that for the Chinese, parks and gardens served the purpose not only of relaxation—a place for taking a leisurely stroll on Sundays or holidays (when a British band would play in one of the parks, according to Xu Chi), as the foreigners would do—but also of pleasure-seeking recreation. They also provided a public place for romantic trysts and rendezvous. In the films of the 1930s, such as *Crossroads* (Shizu jietou), romantic rendezvous or chance encounters in the park became almost a new plot convention.

The history of horse racing has been fully documented by Austin Coates in *China Races* (1983), which was commissioned, appropriately enough, by the Royal Hong Kong Jockey Club to mark its centenary in 1984. Hong Kong held its first race in 1845, possibly a year or so earlier than Shanghai.[81] The Shanghai racecourse was rebuilt at least three times. In 1862 the Shanghai Race Club was established, soon overtaking

Hong Kong as the leading racecourse in East Asia. This British sport became immediately popular with the Chinese, who participated eagerly from the very beginning and also founded their own race clubs. In Coates's succinct words, "Chinese always claimed they went to the races for the sheer enjoyment of it, which means they were betting."[82] Even in the late nineteenth century, "Chinese, in fact, were infiltrating the proceedings. Respectable Chinese, as they were called, had always been allowed into the enclosure on payment . . . and there were two incredible Stands, known as the 'Grand' and the 'Little Grand,' the perilous edifices crammed with Chinese—crazy-looking erections which somehow never fell down."[83] Despite sharing the stands as spectators during race days, however, the Chinese were not allowed to enter the club grounds or to become formal members of the Shanghai Race Club.[84] The club building itself, constructed in 1933, was a "massive six-story building with an imposing clock-tower twice as high," which became "one of the landmarks of downtown Shanghai."[85] The club grounds "covered sixty-six acres of the choicest property in the city" and "constituted an extravagant spatial intervention of Western culture and capital in the Chinese city space."[86] While it brought a touch of English-style countryside into the modern metropolis, "once one's gaze transgressed the boundaries of the illusory spectacle, one would find that the city encroached on this countryside idyll," for "the vast lawn could not conceal the proximity of the city," with its crowded streets and the high-rise buildings of the British Concession.[87] This jarring cityscape, "suspended between countryside scenery and urban construction," provided a fantastic setting, a visual spectacle, for Liu Na'ou's story "Two Men Impervious to Time" (Liangge shijian de buganzheng zhe), in which the heroine plays an elaborate game of tease and seduction with the hero in the grandstand. Gambling—betting on the horses—became a fitting incentive in the "economy" of "exchanging one currency of desire for another."[88]

As the Shanghai racecourse illustrates, the contrast between East and West in Shanghai's urban space could not have been greater. It was a contrast in both space and style: the Western buildings flanking the Bund and along the major thoroughfares in the concessions clearly dominated Shanghai's landscape and visibly marked the hegemonic presence of the foreign powers. We can see a clear colonial imprint in the concession areas, on which were inscribed parts of Paris, London, and New York. Thus the mixture of architectural styles, while lending a cosmopolitan flavor to the city, also betrayed the ignoble origins of Western intrusion into China. How did the Chinese residents cope with such an environment? Did it signify that the hegemonic Western presence had turned Shanghai into a Western colony in both name and fact? How could Chinese writers in Shanghai still carry on their lives and write and publish their works in what Harold Isaacs called the "chaotic sea of Chinese lawlessness" dominated by Western racial inequality? In Isaacs's account, the treaty port offered few advantages to the modern Chinese writer except for "some limited freedom of movement, and even of publication."[89] What was it like for Chinese writers and artists to live and work in this heavily Westernized metropolis that was unlike any other Chinese city?[90] To pave the way for more in-depth analysis and assessment, some description of their daily existence is necessary.

Life in the "Pavilion"

While most foreigners and some wealthy Chinese in Shanghai lived in high-rise apartment buildings or mansions, most natives—including writers—lived in a totally different world of *linong* (alley compounds) or *nontang* (alley courtyards), consisting of clearly defined residential units, rows of plain-looking two- or three-story houses enclosed in a compound with narrow alleys, small front yards, and a front gate—hence called *shikumen*, or "stone-gate" houses. Some of these housing modules were designed also as shop-houses with one side facing the main street. Thus they served to modulate the street pattern and shaped the general character of Shanghai's urban form.[91] With the exception of Nanking Road and a few major thoroughfares, most of Shanghai's streets were flanked or backed by such residential compounds, whose omnipresence suggested not only the density of the Chinese residential population but also the close proximity of dwellings to public buildings and spaces—so much so that the two worlds, Chinese and foreign, could easily be crisscrossed. Whereas Westerners shied away from the *linong* world, the Chinese residents seem to have had no qualms about moving back and forth between their residential compounds in the back alleys and the open public spaces, and they took full advantage of the recreation and entertainment offered by the latter. As the previous section of the chapter suggested, writers seem to have been particularly adept at negotiating such traffic.

A poor Shanghai writer might live and work in the so-called *tingzi-jian* (pavilion room), usually a small room upstairs in the passageway between the front and back sections of a typical Shanghai townhouse, often just above the kitchen. The room was hot in summer and cold in winter, owing to its poor ventilation and year-round lack of sunshine (its windows faced north). Consequently, the rent was cheap: for less than four yuan per month, two or three writers could squeeze into a space no larger than ten square meters.[92] For the residents of the stone-gate houses, most of whom belonged to the middle or lower-middle class, subletting a pavilion room was an economic necessity. According to one study, the average monthly income for a typical office clerk was forty to sixty yuan, and the monthly expenses for a five-member middle-class family came to sixty-six yuan.[93] Thus rentals and sub-rentals were extremely popular. (A famous film, *Crows and Sparrows*, used such rented spaces as its entire setting.) The pavilion room became a fixture of Shanghai literary life; it was so popular that the phrase became an epithet, *tingzijian wenren*, or "writers from the pavilion room." The realities of living offer a key index not only to the socioeconomic conditions of Shanghai writers but also to their lifestyle.[94]

In their own self-parodies, getting "squeezed into a pavilion room" (*jishen tingzijian*) was to find temporary shelter, a stopgap measure before one could afford to move to a more comfortable dwelling. This was due to the fact that most of the modern writers who congregated in Shanghai in the early 1930s were newcomers—those who had either escaped from warlord-torn Beijing or sought refuge in Shanghai's concessions after Chiang Kai-shek's 1927 coup—who were yet to feel at home, for the city was not theirs, and to find one's bearings in the big city took great effort. Gradually, however, as they tried to make ends meet, they also created a half-inflated and half-parodied self-image of their bohemian existence as "life in the pavilion room." The famous writer Ba Jin once led such a pavilion existence and wrote his own experience into his novel *Miewang* (Destruction), as the author lies in bed listening to his landlord fighting with his wife downstairs.[95] Ye Lingfeng signed off his novels with the phrase "written in the Studio of Listening to Tram Cars," so named because of the proximity of his pavilion room to a tram line. Even Chairman Mao saw fit to criticize Shanghai's "pavilion" writers as being too arrogant and self-satisfied and therefore unsuited to the new revolutionary surroundings in Yan'an.[96] The term later became synonymous with Shanghai's writers.

Thus, a private lifestyle began to take on the quality of literary representation. Especially among leftist writers, the pavilion became also an ivory tower, in which as bohemian artists they could turn their poverty-stricken existence into a source of romantic inspiration. But the sociopolitical reality outside compelled them to break out of their self-centered ivory towers to form like-minded groups in order to "serve society" or engage in more radical activities.

Even for writers who were not so engaged politically, the contrast between their private space in the pavilion and Shanghai's public spaces could not have been greater. Yet it was precisely this discrepancy that induced them to take advantage of some of the city's public spaces and appropriate its Western material culture. They shunned the more expensive restaurants and cabarets in the big hotels, but the relatively inexpensive cafés run by exiled Russians became their favorite gathering places. Cinemas showing first-run Hollywood movies were another popular site, as were dance halls. Even Shanghai's racecourse and jai alai courts were not beyond their reach: Liu Na'ou, Mu Shiying, and Hei Ying used them as settings for introducing the most outlandish and adventurous of their fictional heroines.

This process of appropriation was not one of material possession, but it nevertheless extended the imaginary boundaries of their lives. Not only did the writers feel that they had every right to share such an urban space with Shanghai's foreign residents, but also their imaginary occupation of it in turn forged a link with an even larger world. As Zeng Pu walked along rue de Massenet or rue de Corneille in the French Concession, he was literarily transported to the world of French culture. Other writers, such as Zhang Ruogu, had similar experiences at Shanghai's coffeehouses. Both Shi Zhecun and Xu Chi told me during interviews that their most exciting experience while cruising Shanghai's foreign quarters was to buy books, new or used, in a number of Western bookstores (see Chapter 4). In his reminiscences Ye Lingfeng recounts how his mind was fired up when, as he peered through the display window of one such bookstore, he spotted a copy of Joyce's *Ulysses* published by the Shakespeare and Co. bookstore in Paris; he immediately bought the book, which cost U.S. $10, at the unbelievable price of 70 cents.[97] Clearly, the treaty port concessions made it possible for writers like Ye and others to partake of the goods—and to participate in an imagined community—of world literature. It was through such imaginary acts that they felt connected to the city and to the world at large.

Of course, writers and artists did not belong to either the wealthy upper class or the great mass of the urban poor. They may seem as Westernized as the compradorial class, but perhaps more so in their intellectual predilections than in their lifestyle (although, as I mentioned earlier, some adopted Western public postures as café aficionados or Hollywood movie buffs). They bought and read foreign books and journals, from which they extracted materials for translation. In their works they were constantly engaged in an imaginary dialogue with their favorite Western authors. As I shall demonstrate later on, even their writings were dialogically engaged in a kind of intertextual transaction in which the Western textual sources were conspicuously foregrounded in their own texts. What Isaacs fails to take into account are these real or imaginary cultural relationships with the West which coexisted with the obvious inequalities in real life.[98] Thus in discussing the writer's creative relationship with the city we must turn to an interpretive model which may prove more relevant.

The City and the *Flâneur*

Walter Benjamin's unfinished but incomparable cultural commentary *Charles Baudelaire: A Lyric Poet in the Era of High Capitalism* has been a source of inspiration for many scholars. Benjamin's genius lies in defining a critical role and an allegorical space for the writer in the city. "With Baudelaire, Paris for the first time became the subject of lyrical poetry. This poetry is no local folklore; the allegorist's gaze which falls upon the city is rather the gaze of alienated man. It is the gaze of the *flâneur*."[99] A man of leisure, the *flâneur* moves along the Parisian streets and arcades and interacts with the city crowd in an unending and curiously ambivalent relationship.

> The *flâneur* still stood at the margin, of the great city as of the bourgeois class. Neither of them had yet overwhelmed him. In neither of them was he at home. He sought his asylum in the crowd. The crowd was the veil from behind which the familiar city as phantasmagoria beckoned to the *flâneur*. In it, the city was now landscape, now a room. And both of these went into the construction of the department store, which made use of *flânerie* itself in order to sell goods. The department store was the *flâneur*'s final coup.[100]

This new, increasingly commodified urban world—"the world of boulevards, cafés, bars, brothels, the Folies, and above all the comfort of the crowd, and the *flâneur*"—had been the object of French avant-gardist representation since Baudelaire; it also provided the essential condition for the "dawn of modernism."[101]

It was with Benjamin's text in mind that I first tried to "remap" Shanghai from a literary angle. In my attempt to conceptualize Shanghai along a Benjaminian trail, however, several problems immediately arose as I tried to cross the cultural boundaries between Paris and Shanghai. The discrepancies between the cities are obvious: although Shanghai was often called the "Paris of the Orient," owing in part to its French Concession, there was no Chinese concession in Paris. Thus, in a sense, the Paris of Baudelaire's time was less diversified and cosmopolitan than Shanghai, and far more monolithic and imperial in its architectural style; in fact, the French metropolitan capital had itself become the model for French colonial cities.[102] By contrast, with its mixture of Western and Chinese residential and commercial spaces, Shanghai presented a more "vernacular" landscape. Unlike in Paris, there was a widening gap between the still traditional Old City, with its narrow alleys, small shops, restaurants, and teahouses, and the highly modernized International Settlement, with its high-rise apartment buildings, department stores, and movie palaces, and the French Concession, with its tree-lined streets leading to fanciful Western-style residences. Paris also had a much longer history than Shanghai, and by Baudelaire's time it had reached a high point of capitalist development—such that French writers and artists began to adopt a critical attitude toward the city's increasingly philistine bourgeois crowd. By comparison, Shanghai developed into a modern metropolis in only a few decades in the early twentieth century, a city whose material splendor seems to have so dazzled its writers that they had not yet developed the detached and reflective mentality characteristic of the Parisian *flâneur*. Nevertheless, whereas the Paris of Baudelaire was still a city of carriages, Shanghai in the 1930s was already a modern city in a country yet to be fully modernized—a city of trams, buses, automobiles, and rickshaws. Earlier in the century, the sight of carriages carrying famous courtesans on an outing from the Old City to the Bund was a familiar one. But by the 1930s, carriages were rapidly disappearing—so much so that in one of Ye Lingfeng's stories, when the male protagonist sees a beautifully clad woman stepping down from a carriage to go into a movie theater, he is greatly surprised, only to realize later that she was a ghost.[103]

In Benjamin's study, the most significant urban space that defines the ambivalent relationship between the *flâneur* and the city is the arcade—and, by extension, the department store. Benjamin's views on the Parisian arcades are by now well known.[104] The arcades, a new invention of "industrial luxury" in nineteenth-century Paris, "are glass-covered, marble-paneled passageways," and "both sides of these passageways, which are lighted from above, are lined with the most elegant shops, so that such an arcade is a city, even a world, in miniature." According to Benjamin, "it is in this world that the *flâneur* is at home; it provides the favorite sojourn of the strollers and the smokers, the stamping ground of all sorts of little *métiers*."[105] But there were no arcades in Shanghai; the traditional amusement halls like the "Great World" (Da shijie) were certainly not equivalents, as they catered largely to a clientele of out-of-towners and the mass of Shanghai's "petty urbanites." The four major department stores provided glass-covered windows for window-shopping. But they were not "lined with elegant shops" and thus were no substitute for the arcades where the *flâneur* could do his leisurely loitering. As we have seen, the department stores soon took up the entertainment functions of amusement halls by installing performance areas and restaurants. They became fitting spaces for the Shanghai middle class, but not necessarily a world where a Chinese *flâneur* would feel at home.

As the Baudelairean prototype implies, the *flâneur's* relationship to the city is both engaged and detached: he cannot live without the city, as he surrenders himself to the intoxication of its commodity world; at the same time, he is also marginalized by the city in which he is condemned to live. Thus he keeps himself at a distance from the crowd, and it is from his distanced gaze that the city is allegorized. His leisured gait is both a posture and a protest: as Benjamin suggests, "his leisurely appearance as a personality is his protest against the division of labor which makes people into specialists. It is also a protest against their industriousness. Around 1840 it was briefly fashionable to take turtles for a walk in the arcades. The *flâneurs* liked to have the turtles set the pace for them."[106] Thus it has been pointed out that the *flâneur* embodied a paradox: a modern artist who rebels against the very circumstances which have made his existence possible—in other words, an embellishment of Baudelaire's famous characterization in "A Painter of Modern Life."[107] Such a paradoxical reaction against modernity was not necessarily shared by the avowedly *modeng* writers of Shanghai, who were much too enamored of the light, heat, and power of the metropolis to engage in any detached reflection.

Benjamin barely mentions the more degraded female counterpart of the male *flâneur*, the woman who walks the streets (i.e., the prostitute). In fact, this familiar sight was equally characteristic of both nineteenth-century Paris and early twentieth-century Shanghai, where the street-walkers were called, derogatively, *yeji*, or "wild chicks."[108] The phe-nomenon becomes an ironic reminder of another exalted posture of the male *flâneur*—the freedom and flair of his walking the streets. In fact, this "street-walking" tradition has been further theorized by Michel de Certeau as a specific form of spatial practice in the modern city, "part of a social process of inhabiting and appropriating urban space."[109] Of course Shanghai's writers and residents traversed the various urban spaces in the course of their everyday lives. But this does not mean that they had made a fine art of urban walking.

To be sure, there is no shortage of literary references to walking (*sanbu*) itself in Chinese poetry and fiction, both traditional and modern. But such literary walks often take place against or amidst a pastoral landscape. The modern writer Yu Dafu was much influenced by Rous-seau's *Rêveries du promeneur solitaire* and cast several of his stories in a similar vein of the solitary traveler.[110] But his fictional alter egos, though sufficiently sensitive and pensive, are not *urban* strollers in the *flâneur* mode. Other Shanghai writers, especially the Francophiles, consciously flaunted a habit of frequenting cafés—but only so that they could meet and chat with friends, not sit alone and gaze at the crowd. If they took a walk, it would be for the sake of going to restaurants, bookstores, or

movie theaters. A seemingly aimless stroll was reserved only for a romantic rendezvous in the public parks, which by this time were mostly open
to the Chinese. In these situations, the act of walking was seldom performed alone and thus does not necessarily contribute to the lofty image
of *flânerie*. Perhaps only on some of the tree-lined streets in the French
Concession, such as rue Massenet, do we find an occasional stroller, such
as Zeng Pu (who also lived there), who could "conjure up the images of
an aesthetically saturated French life."[111] Interestingly, even this most
enthusiastic of Chinese Francophiles makes no mention of either Baudelaire or the *flâneur*.

The Chinese popular press at the time, however, provided a new
satirical twist on the Western style of walking by focusing on an accompanying instrument, the walking stick. As the female street-walker is
associated with prostitution, the carrier of the walking stick is often a
Chinese "fake foreign devil" (*jiayangguizi*), a term made famous by Lu
Xun's story "The True Story of Ah Q." The image, which may have had
more to do with the Johnny Walker Scotch ads than with the *flâneur's*
posture, is of an imitation Western "gentleman," facetiously transliterated as *jiantouman*, or "man with a pointed head," referring specifically to
his fashionably pointed leather shoes. The image better befits a member
of Shanghai's compradorial class than any writer; writers, however, certainly did not shy away from donning such Western emblems as a suit
and tie, together with fashionable white shoes.

The attention to Western clothing leads us to a relative of the
flâneur, the dandy. In Chapter 7 I will discuss the cases of Shao Xunmei
and Ye Lingfeng: the former was hailed as "indubitably the most eccentric urban dandy alive in late-1920s Shanghai";[112] the latter attempted to
carve out a strikingly decadent dandy figure in one of his fictional works.
The dandy in European literature, derived from the protagonist des
Esseintes in Huysmans's novel *À rebours* (1884), can be regarded as an
aristocratic figure who protests against bourgeois modernity by flaunting
his eccentricity and foppish clothing. Shanghai writers of the time were
certainly aware of the dandy figure in Western literature but did not

consciously imitate him; even the flamboyant Shao Xunmei often chose to wear a traditional long gown rather than a garish cape. Rather, they seem to have been more interested in the dandy's connection with artistic decadence, which they tried to evoke in their fiction as a way to impart both an exotic appeal and a degree of eroticism. In some of Shi Zhecun's "gothic" stories (see Chapter 5), one of the sources of his creative inspiration, so he told me, was the French writer of *dandysme*, J.-A. Barbey d'Aurevilly (1808–1889). Thus for Chinese writers the attraction of the dandy and the *flâneur* lies in their being part of a modern image or style of "Occidental exoticism."[113] As such, they are figures more of mythology than of real life.

How should we renegotiate this avowedly Western mythological ideal-type in a Chinese cultural context? One obvious way is through the *fictional* landscape of Shanghai. In his recent study *The City in Modern Chinese Literature and Film*, Yingjin Zhang has demonstrated that indeed the *flâneur* figure can be sited in several creative works, both fiction and poetry. Zhang gives this *flâneur* figure an erotic charge by emphasizing his voyeuristic gaze and his "acting out" of the roles of dandy and reluctant detective in the popular novel *The Whirling Wind* (Feng xiaoxiao) by Xu Xu.[114] But how involved is Xu Xu's hero with the city itself? Insofar as we can find him "strolling aimlessly" in the streets, we do not see much engagement—aesthetic, paradoxical, or erotic—with the urban crowd, except in the ballrooms and at the lavish parties thrown by Japanese generals. Instead of presenting a *flâneur* allegorizing the city with his deeply ambiguous gaze, the author's portrait of the hero is tinged with romance (in the double sense of the word: a story about a romantic hero as well as a story in the genre of romance). His passivity, narcissism, and excessive sentimentality are the hallmarks of a bygone era—a derivation and a popularization of what I once called the "Wertherian" hero in May Fourth fiction.[115] It is certainly a far cry from the fictional heroes of the so-called neo-sensationalist school.

Elsewhere Zhang has cited a story by a member of the school, He Ying's "When Spring Arrives," to show that the narrator, by walking

Shanghai's streets, "acquires his knowledge of the city" and is able to "select for his aesthetic appreciation a number of urban images and icons that provide new ways of perceiving the urban metropolis."[116] Unlike Benjamin's *flâneur*, however, he is not an anonymous loner in the urban crowd; rather, he "prefers to be known," and he enjoys the various aspects of the urban spectacle in the company of a city girl called Suzie, who is likely a prostitute.[117] Obviously, He Ying's narrator-hero, like those in the fiction of Liu Na'ou and Mu Shiying who served as his model, is too enamored of the city and too immersed in the excitements it provides to achieve an attitude of ambivalence and ironic detachment.

As Benjamin has reminded us, "Baudelaire's genius, which drew its nourishment from melancholy, is an allegorical one. With Baudelaire, Paris for the first time became the subject of lyrical poetry."[118] Is it possible for Chinese writers to accomplish a similar feat of aesthetic reflection in a different urban cultural context? In Benjamin's view of Baudelaire, the "allegorist's gaze" turns the city into "the subject of lyrical poetry." It is an aesthetic act that, by "taking stock" of all the sights and sounds and commodities that the city can offer, transforms them into art. Thus, the *flâneur* is a modern artist who cannot exist without the city, and whose object of inquiry, as Susan Buck-Morss reminds us, is modernity itself.[119] In what ways, then, can we expect Shanghai's writers to fulfill a comparable mission at a time when Chinese modernity itself was being constructed as a cultural imaginary? What did modernity mean to modern Chinese writers and intellectuals? It may be appropriate first to address the issue of "Chinese modernity" itself, which is a very complex—and in many ways still incomplete—intellectual and cultural project that has been in the making ever since the beginning of the twentieth century. In the next chapter I discuss some aspects of the project of Chinese modernity as constructed in urban print culture.

THE CONSTRUCTION OF MODERNITY
IN PRINT CULTURE

In the previous chapter I laid out the grounds of my research by mapping the city of Shanghai circa 1930. It is against such an urban background that my narrative of Chinese modernity unfolds. While the problematic of Western modernity has been thoroughly treated—and critiqued—in recent scholarship, that of Chinese modernity remains to be examined. This chapter represents an attempt to do so from one angle: print culture.

The Problematic of Modernity

Modernity in China, as I have argued elsewhere, was closely associated with a new linear consciousness of time and history which was itself derived from the Chinese reception of a Social Darwinian concept of evolution made popular by the translations of Yen Fu and Liang Qichao at the turn of the century. In this new temporal scheme, present (*jin*) and past (*gu*) became polarized as contrasting values, and a new emphasis was placed on the present moment "as the pivotal point marking a rupture with the past and forming a progressive continuum toward a glorious future."[1] This new mode of time consciousness was, of course, a derivative discourse stemming from the Western post-Enlightenment tradition of modernity—an intellectual package now receiving severe criticism by postmodern theorists for the positivistic and inherently "monological" tendencies embedded in its faith in human reason and progress. One could argue further that the very same post-Enlightenment legacy has infused the expansionist projects of the colonial empires, particularly England, and one of its political by-products was the modern nation-state. Once transplanted into China, however, such a legacy served to add a new dimension to Chinese semantics: in fact, the very word "new" (*xin*) became the crucial component of a cluster of new word compounds denoting a qualitative change in all spheres of life, from the late Qing reform movement (*weixin yundong*) with its institutional designations from "new policies" (*xinzheng*) to "new schools" (*xinxue*), to Liang Qichao's celebrated notion of "new people" (*xinmin*) and the slogans such as "new culture" (*xin wenhua*) and "new literature" (*xin wenxue*) of the May Fourth movement. Two terms that gained wide popularity in the 1920s were *shidai* (time or epoch) and *xin shidai* (new epoch), based on the Japanese word *jidai*. This sense of living in a new era, as advocated by May Fourth leaders such as Chen Duxiu, was what defined the ethos of modernity. By the 1900s another Japanese term had been adopted—*wenming* (*bunmei*), or "civilization"[2]—which came to be used with words such as *dongfang* (east) and *xifang* (west) to form the common May Fourth vocabulary of "Eastern" and "Western" civilizations as dichotomous and contrasting categories. The underlying assumption was that "Western civilization" was marked by dynamic progress made possible by the manifestation of what Benjamin Schwartz has called the "Faustian-Promethean" strain that resulted in the achievement of wealth and power by the Western countries.[3]

Schwartz's pioneering study of Yan Fu, however, does not cover the rapid spread of these new categories of value and thought in the Chinese popular press. In newspapers such as *Shenbao* (Shanghai news) and magazines such as *Dongfang zazhi* (Eastern miscellany) published by the Commercial Press, the new vocabulary became a regular feature of most articles. Thus by the 1920s it was generally acknowledged that "modernity" was equated with "Western civilization" in all its spiritual and material manifestations. Whereas conservative or moderate commentators in the *Dongfang zazhi* and other journals voiced concern about the possible bankruptcy of Western civilization as a result of the First World War, intellectuals of a radical persuasion continued to be firm believers in modernity formulated in this manner. The center of cultural production for such ideas about modernity was indisputably Shanghai, where the great majority of newspapers and publishing houses were located—in fact concentrated in one small area around Foochow Road (see Chapter 4.) It is also worth noting that the earliest use of the Western calendar occurred in *Shenbao*, a newspaper originated by a Westerner, which began to print Chinese and Western calendar dates side by side on its front page in 1872. But it was not until Liang Qichao proclaimed his own use of the Western calendar in his 1899 diary of his travels to Hawaii that a paradigmatic change in time consciousness was effected. Typical of his elitist aspirations, Liang simply announced that, as he declared his own transformation from a provincial person to a "man of the world," his use of the Western calendar was in keeping with the general trend toward universalizing the measurement of time.[4] By coincidence, Liang announced his adoption of the calendar on December 19, 1899, as he departed from Yokohama for Hawaii, on the very eve of the new century. By the 1920s, if not earlier, the commercial calendar poster had become a popular promotional item for Shanghai's tobacco companies and a fixture in urban daily life.

It was against such a "timely" background that a Chinese nationhood came to be imagined. Benedict Anderson's widely cited book has led us to believe that a nation is first an "imagined community" before it becomes a political reality. This new "community" is itself based on a conception of simultaneity "marked by temporal coincidence and measured by clock and calendar."[5] The technical means for representing this "imagined community," according to Anderson, are the two forms of print culture—newspapers and the novel—that first flowered in the eighteenth and nineteenth centuries in Europe. Anderson does not go into much depth, however, in fleshing out the complicated process whereby these two forms are used to imagine the nation (aside from citing two Philippine novels).[6] Another theorist, Jürgen Habermas, has likewise pointed to the close connection between periodicals and salons which contributed to the rise of the "public sphere" in England and France.[7] But neither Anderson nor Habermas has seen fit to connect the two phenomena, nationhood and the public sphere. In my view this was precisely what constituted the intellectual problematic for China at the turn of the century, when the intellectuals and writers sought to imagine a new community (*chun*) of the nation (*minzu* or *guojia* but not yet *minzuguojia*) as they tried to define a new reading public.[8] They attempted to draw the broad contours of a new vision of China and disseminate such a vision to their audience, the newly emergent public consisting largely of newspaper and journal readers and students in the new schools and colleges. But such a vision remained a vision—an imagined, often visually based evocation of a Chinese "new world"—not a cogent intellectual discourse or political system. In other words, this visionary imagination preceded the efforts of nation-building and institutionalization. In China, modernity for all its amorphousness became the guiding ethos of such a vision, as yet without the Weberian concerns of "rationalization" and "disenchantment" that the practical workings of "instrumental rationality" inevitably entail.

Thus I would argue that the nation as an "imagined community" in China was made possible not only by elite intellectuals such as Liang Qichao, who proclaimed new concepts and values, but also, more important, by the popular press. It is interesting to note that the rise of commercial publishing—particularly the large companies such as the Commercial Press (Shangwu yinshu guan, literally, the shop which printed books for commercial purposes) and China Bookstore (Zhonghua shuju)—also predated the establishment of the Republican nation-state in 1912. (In this regard we might give Homi Bhabha's term in the context of nationalism another twist in meaning: "dissemi-Nation,"[9] indicating, more literally and less ironically, that knowledge about the new nation must first be *disseminated*.) As I will show in detail in this chapter, these commercial ventures in publishing were all undertaken in the name of introducing "new knowledge" (*xinzhi*), the "textual" sources of modernity, of which general journals such as *Dongfang zazhi* and *Xiaoshuo yuebao* (Short story monthly) served as showcases. In a way they are comparable to the eighteenth-century French "business of Enlightenment," as described by Robert Darnton, in which the ideas of the philosophes were popularized and vigorously disseminated by a network of printers and booksellers.[10] In the name of promoting new culture and education, however, books in China were sold quite cheaply as a study aid for students in new-style schools and other readers who were deprived of schooling. In short, from its beginnings Chinese modernity was envisioned and produced as a cultural enterprise of "enlightenment"—*qimeng*, a term taken from the traditional educational practice in which a child received his first lesson from a teacher or tutor. That the term took on the meaning of being "enlightened" with new knowledge in the national project of modernity should come as no surprise.

In this chapter, for obvious reasons, I cannot survey the whole "enlightenment industry." I focus instead on the textbook production of the Commercial Press, as seen in the advertisements of the press's leading journal, *Dongfang zazhi*, in order to throw some new light on this little-studied area of China's modern print culture.[11] Before I do so, a few words about the journal are in order.

Dongfang zazhi: A Middlebrow Journal

Dongfang zazhi may be considered a "middlebrow" publication under the aegis of the Commercial Press, intended for the urban readership. Begun in 1904 as a monthly, it was changed to a fortnightly and continued publication until 1948. Sales for each issue ran as high as fifteen thousand copies.[12] Its table of contents shows its eclectic quality, combining jour-nalistic reports, political commentary, and cultural criticism with transla-tions and learned articles. The journal's miscellaneous contents may have lacked a distinct character, but therein lay its purpose and appeal. A lead article in volume 16, number 7 (1919), of the journal spells out clearly the functions of this general-interest magazine. Whereas, on a lofty level, the magazine claims to live up to three purposes—scholarly pur-suit (*yanjiu xueli*), enlightenment of thinking (*qifa sixiang*), and correction of customs and mores (*jiaozheng xisu*)—its real function, on a mundane level, is like that of a grocery store (*zahuo dian*): the goods are diverse and mundane, seldom precious and valuable, but they are nevertheless daily necessities. The article also sets three more goals for the magazine of the future: to keep abreast of world trends, to be adaptable to present condi-tions, and above all to be suitable for practical life.[13] As an indication of its "world trends" orientation, the journal devoted considerable attention to the European war—with photos, chronology of events, articles, and translations. The writings of Du Yaquan, its editor, and other authors reveal an obvious disillusionment, which led them to caution against excessive Westernization. At the same time, however, the journal con-tains extensive coverage and discussion of postwar European political, intellectual, and cultural trends and gives much attention to discussions of nationalism and socialism (the latter especially after 1919). Conscious of the continued impact of knowledge from the West, the journal's editors and leading authors can be seen groping toward a moderate position by mediating and seeking compromises between Western mod-ernity and Chinese tradition, which they considered to be still relevant.

During the period 1915–1920, the journal gave voluminous cover-age to subjects related to science and technology. A large number of articles describe new weaponry used in the European war, in particular the submarine and the dirigible (thus continuing a fascination with un-derwater and air gadgetry in late Qing fiction). But it also carried learned articles on evolutionary theory, on Freud's theory of interpreting dreams as a form of science, and on various technological inventions that were already shaping and transforming human life: not only the telegraph, trolley, telephone, and automobile, but also typewriters, gramophones, and movies. The sum total of the articles (some were translations from British, American, and Japanese popular journals and textbooks) conveys a continuing obsession with what in the late Qing discourse was referred to as the four major categories of modern technology—sound (*sheng*), light (*guang*), chemistry (*hua*), and electricity (*dian*)—a discourse that was later fleshed out in Mao Dun's novel *Midnight*. At the same time, however, some of the journal's articles convey a worried tone. If the triumph of modern civilization is inevitable, they seem to argue, the Chinese should nevertheless be wary and cautious. In one article, "Machines and Life" (paraphrased from an article in the British journal *Contemporary Review* by Arthur Ponsonby), the author warns about the danger of the rapid progress of all the new mechanical inventions, which should not be equated with the progress of civilization.[14] Thus, behind the journal's surface attitude of compromise and moderation lurks a sense of ambiguity and ambivalence, if not anxiety, toward the civilization of Western modernity, an anxiety caused, ironically, by the journal's successful record of introducing it.

Although *Dongfang zazhi* was the flagship of the periodicals published by the Commercial Press, it still vied for attention with at least eight others within the same company. An advertisement lists the nine in the following order: *Dongfang zazhi, Jiaoyu zazhi* (Education magazine), *Xuesheng zazhi* (Student magazine), *Shaonian zazhi* (Young magazine), *Funü zazhi* (Women's magazine), *Yingwen zazhi* (English magazine), *Yingyu zhoukan* (English language weekly), *Xiaoshuo yuebao* (Short story monthly), and *Nongxue zazhi* (Agricultural study magazine). The *Short Story Monthly,* in particular, has received wide notoriety in post–May Fourth accounts as a bastion of the "Mandarin Ducks and Butterflies" school of fiction (so called owing to its preoccupation with traditional-style love stories) until Mao Dun assumed editorship in 1920 and turned it overnight into a journal of New Literature. Still, the imposition of a May Fourth interpretation has certainly not done full justice to this and other journals of the

Commercial Press. Even reading the advertisement can reveal a common purpose and agenda: simply put, it is to provide readers with a certain practical knowledge for their everyday lives. The nine magazines also represented a new way of categorizing this practical knowledge. Whereas *Dongfang zazhi* offered the most comprehensive coverage—from politics, literature, science, business, and news to "encyclopedic learning" (*baike zhi xue*), according to the explanation in the advertisement—each of the other journals clearly catered to a specific category of readership: teachers, college and high school students in the new school system, youth, women, students enrolled in agricultural schools, and, most interestingly, those readers who were "self-learners" outside the school system. As the Commercial Press's only literary journal, the *Short Story Monthly* intended originally for such "self-learners." Another full-page advertisement for the journal mentions not only its increasing sales (six thousand copies per issue), its inclusion of color pages, and the translations of Lin Shu—China's most productive translator, who had rendered more than a hundred Western novels into classical Chinese—but also that its chosen contents were meant to provide "entertainment for the family, and the new knowledge is particularly good for daily use, hence [the journal is] a must-read for household residents *(ju jiazhe)*," a term which in all likelihood referred to urban housewives. [15] No wonder the enormously popular genre of Butterfly fiction became useful content. Still, the fact that the magazines offered entertainment does not detract from their seriousness of purpose: the words *xin zhi* or *xin zhishi* (new knowledge) and *chang shi* (common knowledge) are ubiquitous in the advertisements. Even the two English journals were geared to a practical purpose, as they provided "how-to" lessons in composition, grammar, translation, and letter writing, as well as literature for easy reading. They were also connected with the dictionary projects (*Webster's*) and correspondence schools sponsored by the Commercial Press and by an American company in Pennsylvania. [16] In one ad, the Berlitz method is highlighted.

In accordance with the stated purpose of the Commercial Press magazines, the *Women's Magazine* was seen as an educational mission, designed as an aid to women's education (*nüxue*). The history of women's education in this transitional period deserves a long monograph and is too important to be summarily treated here. It is noteworthy, however, that a distinctly modern attitude is underscored by the ads and articles in the magazine. In an advertisement for the "big improvement" of the *Women's Magazine*, published in 1916, the name of the new editor is prominently mentioned, a Mrs. Zhu Hu Binxia from Wuxi, a modern woman who had been educated in a women's school in Tokyo and then went to America for further education for a total of seven years, including a B.A. from Wellesley and research experience at Cornell.[17] The credential of an American degree (printed in block characters in the ad) thus was seen as a clear asset, one that May Fourth leaders such as Hu Shi also played to their own maximum advantage. The magazine's ads marked a transition of cultural capital: whereas the prime movers of the late Qing reform movement were scholars and officials who did not know any foreign language and had to rely on translations, mostly from the Japanese, the new generation of elite intellectuals were largely Western educated—some in fact contributed articles from abroad to *Dongfang zazhi*—and the countries and educational institutions where they studied were also prominently attached to their names (an editorial practice continued to the present day by some journals in Hong Kong and Taiwan).

Dongfang zazhi carried a number of articles about Western universities, particularly in the United States; it also featured or reprinted from other newspapers and journals accounts of Chinese universities, including the curriculum of Beijing University. But the main goal and market of the educational enterprise of the Commercial Press, insofar as we can gather from its advertisements, was primary and secondary education. Almost every issue is filled with advertised lists of textbooks of various sorts, revealing a feverish publishing activity which was closely geared to the educational policies and laws of the government from the magazine's founding in 1897 until its closing some forty years later. Thus we can safely say that the Commercial Press played a seminal role in the modernization of the educational system: it was a gigantic task which fulfilled a national need after the abolition of the civil service examination system in 1905.

The Business of Enlightenment: Textbooks

The Commercial Press was not the first to publish textbooks. Two smaller companies—Wenming (Civilization) and Guangzhi (Expanding wisdom)—had published a set of textbooks by four Wuxi schoolteachers sometime before 1903.[18] Their textbooks were called Mengxue duben, or texts for "primary studies"; the term refers to the traditional notion of *tongmeng*, or children whose "beclouded" minds need to be cleared by the instruction of moral texts (according to the Confucian injunction), which in turn leads to the notion of *qimeng*, that is, *qifa mengmei*, or opening up the children's state of ignorance, hence "enlightenment." By 1903 the Commercial Press, together with its chief rival, the China Bookstore, began to dominate the textbook market when it started its own textbook enterprise in a big way by setting up a new printing plant, hiring three Japanese advisers, and appointing an editorial board headed by Jiang Weiqiao, of which Wang Yaquan was also a member in charge of science textbooks.[19]

The founding of the Republic was enthusiastically promoted by the Commercial Press: it capitalized on the event of the Wuchang Uprising in 1911 with a detailed account in *Dongfang zazhi* and the publication of thirteen volumes of photos and pictures as well as more than three hundred postcards. Predictably, the press also began to issue in 1912 a new set of textbooks, appropriately titled "Textbooks of the Republic" (*Gongheguo jiaokeshu*). The advertisement in *Dongfang zazhi* was headed by a solemn announcement:

> With the founding of the Republic, the political polity has been changed to that of a republic. The educational policy is consequently changed . . . In view of the present changing circumstances, [this press] respectfully observes Decree no. 7 of the

Ministry of Education, and begins with the revisions of the various textbooks of the primary school level. All the necessary knowledge that a national citizen of the Republic should possess as well as the origins of this Revolution have all been narrated in detail in them, so as to cultivate the complete Republican citizen.[20]

The subject of the national citizen—the Chinese word is *guomin*—thus formally entered the new textbooks. A special *Primer for a National Citizen of the Republic* (Gonghe guomin duben) was issued, clearly a revision of the original *Primer for the National Citizen of the Constitutional Era* (Lixian guomin duben, referring to the late Qing constitutional period of 1910–11). It also became a topic in the brand-new primary school textbooks on *xiushen*, or "cultivation"—a term preserved from premodern primers on Confucian teaching. The new textbooks not only included the major subjects of Chinese (*guowen*), arithmetic (*bisuan*), history (*lishi*), geography (*dili*), and English but also extended to a large number of other subjects: abacus, singing, physical exercise, brush drawing, sewing, science, agriculture, commerce, and handicrafts (for the primary levels). Under the history category we find Chinese history, East Asian history, and Western history; under geography, Chinese geography, foreign geography, and human geography. In addition, there were textbooks on botany, biology, mining, physiology, physics, chemistry, arithmetic, geometry, trigonometry, algebra, general physical exercise, military exercise, and several others.[21] This is a most impressive list, which was apparently intended to fit an equally impressive curriculum.

I do not mean to discuss the pedagogic contents of the textbooks and the curriculum. Rather, I want to show how, through concerted effort, a publishing company succeeded in its self-assigned task of "enlightenment." In so doing, it also aided in the nation-building effort of the Republican government. The compilation of textbooks for the education of its new *guomin* was definitely a priority in the government agenda; the Ministry of Education publicized, as early as 1912, a set of provisional guidelines for general education. The old term for schools, *xuetang*, was changed to *xuexiao*, and coeducation was allowed at the primary level; reading the classics was abolished, as were some of the Qing dynasty legal codes.[22] In particular, it established two bureaus for compiling and censoring textbooks. To be sure, the practice had already started in the Qing period, but the new guidelines made some specific points about how textbooks should be written, together with procedures for examination and approval.[23] The Commercial Press turned this new government policy to its own advantage by citing in its textbook ads the seal of approval of the Ministry of Education (Jiaoyu bu shending) together with the ministry's comments on particular texts. Most of the quoted comments are of a practical nature: for instance, "the choice of materials is excellent, the divisions clear; [the textbook] can be used for the physical sciences in higher primary schools." But occasionally a vaguely ideological phrase or sentence enters: "The wording is clear and succinct, and contains rather lively interest; extremely well equipped with the knowledge and morality for the national citizen" (in reference to *Jianming guowen jiaokeshu*, or *The Concise Textbook of Chinese Literature*). All these endeavors pointed to the overriding objective that the task of education is to train the nation's people to be good citizens.

How should the people of a new nation be properly trained? The decrees issued by the Ministry of Education underwent many changes. Whereas the 1912 decrees seem to have focused on practical education (the primary school curriculum must include handicrafts, physical exercise, abacus, and so on), the 1914 decrees, reflecting the power of the then-president, the conservative warlord Yuan Shikai, restored the classics and honored the words of Confucius, with the special injunction that the curriculum in education must "emphasize the special national character of the people of this nation."[24] In 1919, two years after the Literary Revolution, the ministry formally decreed the use of the modern vernacular and new punctuation in all textbooks for the first two primary school grades.[25]

Given the turmoil of the period, we cannot be sure whether these changes in policy were followed strictly by the publishing companies. The Commercial Press, being the largest, may have developed its own views on education, which, while not contradicting government policy, perhaps extended the prescribed curriculum. The advertisements give the impression that the textbooks were meant not only for the school curriculum but for extracurricular activities as well; some books were clearly aimed at the urban cultural arena outside the schools. For such "outside" needs, the press seems to have paid special attention to children and young adolescents with massive publication of fables, translated stories, picture books, cartoons, color postcards, maps, simple "how-to" primers in arithmetic, and games and toys. Such marketing obviously reflected a commercial effort to seize a new segment of the urban market: children (together with their mothers). At the same time, the extracurricular publications also went far beyond the confines of the school system to the world of the literate adults who for various reasons could not attend the new schools. In my view, it was in this public arena of urban society that the Commercial Press's task of enlightenment performed a crucial role as it served to promote a vision of modernity beyond the ideological confines of government policy.

The Business of Enlightenment: Repositories

How to provide basic knowledge in a way that can make it accessible to everyone in society? In addition to school textbooks, the Commercial Press also launched two well-known "repositories" (wenku): Dongfang wenku (Eastern repository, 1923–1934) and Wanyou wenku (All-comprehensive repository, 1929–1934). Dongfang wenku, in which some of the major articles printed in Dongfang zazhi were collected (together with other treatises and translations which did not appear), totaled more than 120 pamphlet-sized volumes—a device clearly intended for the task of inculcating new knowledge. Its roster of authors is distinguished and includes both academic and non-academic intellectuals representing a wide spectrum of backgrounds and positions. The subjects and titles (mostly translations) are even more impressive, as they cover an immensely wide range. I can give only a rough breakdown of the subjects covered: literature (19 titles), philosophy (17), sciences (13), society (9), economy (7), politics (6), foreign countries (6), diplomacy (6), history (5), geography (5), art (5), women (5), culture (4), psychology (3), law (3), scholarship (3), education (3), military affairs (2), migration (2), and journalism, language, archaeology, religion, and medicine (1 each). This rundown gives only a general impression, and does not reveal the specific contents of the volumes. It suggests a fairly heavy concentration on the humanities (literature and philosophy), followed by the natural and social sciences, and a considerable number of titles are concerned with diplomacy and foreign countries. Among the titles in literature, six are collections of stories from foreign countries: Anglo-American, French, Russian, European, Japanese, and Indian (the works of Tagore). But a more intriguing feature is the diversity of some of the other titles. To give one small example, a pamphlet written by Du Yaquan titled *Chushi zhexue* (A philosophy to cope with the world) turns out to be based on a Japanese translation of a work by Schopenhauer. It is collected in a box (volumes 32–50) which also includes works on journalism, East-West cultural criticism, Chinese society and culture, ethics, psychology, contemporary philosophy (mainly Dewey), Bergson and Eucken, Kropotkin, Gandhism, the philosophy of war, two volumes of Bertrand Russell's essays, and a volume on the fundamentals of science.

Still, *Dongfang wenku* is dwarfed by comparison with its sister repository, *Wanyou wenku,* which was conceived even more ambitiously, for it was designed to constitute nothing less than a modern library. This is clearly what its chief editor, Wang Yunwu, had in mind when he embarked on the two gigantic series of *Wanyou wenku,* each containing more than a thousand volumes. In this way a basic collection could easily be built up by any newly established library in both the most economical and systematic fashions, the former achieved by cost savings through modern printing techniques, the latter by the new index system based on Wang's own four-corner system.[26] This may have been the most ambitious effort in the categorization and dissemination of knowledge for the general public during the Republican period.

From his own preface about the origin of the repository project, we see that Wang's basic design derives from the traditional *congshu* (collectanea) formula, but he had seen fit to add a considerable number of new collections to the "Basic Collectanea of National Learning" (*Guoxue jiben congshu*). We find such collections as *Baike xiaocongshu* (Mini-collection of encyclopedic knowledge) and *Xinshidai shidi congshu* (History and geography of the new era), as well as separate *congshu* for agriculture, industry, commerce, normal school education, arithmetic, medicine, and athletics, all of which were meant to be "disciplinary tools."[27] By the time Wang was editing the second series, he had further enlarged the collections of both Western translations and "national learning," but instead of the disciplinary texts he added two new collections: a collection on natural sciences (*Kexue xiaocongsu*) and a collection on "modern problems" (*Xiandai wenti congshu*); the most complex task, he admitted, was the compilation of the latter because "there were few precedents in publications in the nation and abroad."[28]

A glance through the catalogue of the two series is sufficient for some revelations. The editorial board for Series I lists Wang Yunwu as chief editor and a dozen other editors. At the end of the preface Wang also acknowledges the help of such "friends"—all intellectuals of great renown—as Cai Yuanpei, Hu Shi, Li Shizeng, Wu Zhihui, Yang Xingfo, and others. The editorial guidelines list four basic goals: (1) the repository is intended to "inculcate in the general reading public the knowledge that is necessary for human life"; (2) "the standard of collection is based on necessity"; (3) "the whole collection is clearly systematic and complete in all categories; [the contents] have the effect of mutual enlightenment and do not have the blemish of duplication"; and (4) "what is deemed most necessary for all categories [of knowledge] is provided for the library or individual collector at the cheapest price;

students of the middle school or below or primary school teachers can establish a rudimentary library when they purchase a complete set of this repository."[29] To facilitate such purchases, a cleverly designed mail order scheme, with payment in installments, was offered with a pamphlet which announced the series. It is evident that this massive project surpassed the textbook project in its ambition to spread the "knowledge of human life" to a reading public created by the publishing market.

In its own way the project is certainly comparable to that of the French Encyclopedists and their disseminators.[30] The crucial difference, however, lies in the systems and contents of categorization. Let us leave aside the 400 titles of "Chinese learning" in the two series (100 in the first series and 300 in the second) and look into the 250 translations of "world classics" (100 in the first series, 150 in the second) as well as the 200 titles of "natural science" and 50 titles of "modern problems"—a total of 500 titles of what might be called "Western learning." Even at a glance, the catalogues are most impressive. Here is a selective listing of the categories and the significant Western authors and titles contained therein. There are fifteen categories of translations in Series I:

1. Philosophy (Descartes's *Discourse on Method*, Spinoza's *Ethics*, Hume, Kant's *Critique of Pure Reason*, Schopenhauer, William James, Kropotkin, Nietzsche's *Thus Spoke Zarathustra*, Eucken, Bergson, Dewey, and Westaway's *Scientific Method*).
2. Psychology (William James's *Psychology: Briefer Course*, Freud's *Psychoanalysis*, J. B. Watson's *Psychology from the Standpoint of Behaviorism*, K. Koffka's *Growth of the Mind*).
3. Sociology (Herbert Spencer, Kropotkin, Durkheim).
4. Political science (Plato's *Republic*, Aristotle's *Politics*, Hobbes's *Leviathan*, Bentham's *Introduction to the Principles of Morals and Legislation*, J. S. Mill's *On Liberty*, Bagehot's *Physics and Politics*, Jenks's *History of Politics*, Laski's *Grammar of Politics*).
5. Economics (Adam Smith's *Wealth of Nations*, Proudhon, Marx's *Value, Price, and Profit*, Ingram, Hobson's *Modern Capitalism*, Sidney and Bea-

trice Webb's *History of Trade Unionism*, D. S. Kimball's *Principles of Industrial Organization*, A. L. Bowley's *Elements of Statistics*).

6. Law (Gropius, Montesquieu, Maine, Dicey, Lombroso, Duguit).

7. Education (Rousseau's *Émile*, Spencer, Dewey's *Democracy and Education*).

8. Natural sciences (Newton, Lamarck, Faraday, Darwin, Huxley, Pasteur, Russell, Einstein).

9. Anglo-American literature (Shakespeare's *Hamlet*, Milton's *Paradise Lost*, Defoe's *Robinson Crusoe*, Swift's *Gulliver's Travels*, Benjamin Franklin's *Autobiography*, Goldsmith's *Vicar of Wakefield*, Walter Scott's *Ivanhoe*, Dickens's *David Copperfield*, Washington Irving's *Tales of Alhambra*, mostly translated by Lin Shu; G. B. Shaw).

10. French literature (Rousseau's *Confessions*, Molière's *The Miser*, Hugo's *Les Misérables*, Dumas père's *The Three Musketeers*, Dumas fils's *La Dame aux Camélias*, mostly translated by Lin Shu; Maupassant's *The Heritage*).

11. German literature (Goethe's *Egmont*, Schiller's *Wallenstein*, Hauptmann's *Der rote Hahn*).

12. Russian literature (Gogol's *The Reviser* or *Inspector General*, Turgenev's *Fathers and Sons*, Ostrovsky's *Poverty No Vice*, Tolstoy's *Childhood, Boyhood, and Youth*).

13. Literature of other countries (Homer's *Odyssey*, Cicero's *Orations*, *The Arabian Nights*, Dante's *Divine Comedy*, Cervantes's *Don Quixote*, Ibsen's plays, Bjornson's *In God's Way*, Maeterlinck's *Blue Bird*, Tagore's *Crescent Moon*, a collection of Japanese stories translated by Zhou Zuoren).

14. History (Robinson's *New History*, Wells's *Outline of History*).

15. Geography (Huntington and Cushing's *Principles of Human Geography*, Bowmen's *The New World*).

In Series II the translations of Western titles are divided into the following categories:

Culture and cultural history
Philosophy (Bacon, Leibnitz, Comte, Nietzsche)
Psychology

Logic (Aristotle's *Logic*)

Ethics

Sociology (Durkheim, Morgan, Malthus)

Statistics

Political science (Rousseau's *Social Contract*, Moore's *Utopia*)

World diplomacy

Economics and finance

Law

Military affairs

Education

Industry

Family and marriage

General science

Mathematics

Biological sciences

Physics

Applied sciences (more specialized than in Series I)

General literature

National literatures—collections (including Japan, India, America, England, Germany, France, Italy, Spain, Russia, Poland, Denmark, Hungary, Norway, Sweden, Romania)

National literatures—individual authors (Carlyle, Thackeray, Charlotte Brontë, J. M. Barrie, Drinkwater, Hardy, Galsworthy, Hawthorne, O. Henry, Wedekind, J. Freytag, Theodor Storm, Zola, Romain Rolland, Balzac, Octave Mirabeau, Paul Geraldy, Anatole France, Andreyev, Dostoevsky, Gorky, Dante, Euripides, Sophocles, Aeschylus, Knut Hamsun, Sienkiewicz, Ibañez, K. Palamas)

Geography and travel

Biographies (of Napoleon, Bismarck, Hindenburg, Tolstoy, and autobiographies of J. M. Mill, Edison, Andrew Carnegie)

Historiography

History of Europe and America

History of Asia

To these we may add the 200 titles of "natural sciences" in Series II, divided into 10 categories: general discourses on science, astronomy, physics, chemistry, biology, zoology and anthropology, botany, geology/mining/geography, biographies of famous scientists, and other. Almost all of the titles are translations (with Zhou Jianren, Lu Xun's younger brother, and Zhang Ziping, otherwise known as a popular novelist, taking a prominent share). This collection carries an enormous weight in the repository, but to it we must also add the 70 titles in the natural sciences section and the 30 titles in the applied sciences section of the "mini-encyclopedia" collection of Series I. Thus the sum total of titles related to the sciences alone (excluding subjects such as industry, statistics, psychology, and so on) in the two series comes to 336—roughly the same as the "Chinese learning" collection. If we then add to this the other titles in the translation collections, the balance definitely tilts in favor of "scientific learning." Perhaps a majority of the science titles bear on practical aspects of modern life. (By comparison, titles on the "pure" sciences were apparently included in the textbooks.) This is not surprising, given the practical nature and goals of the repository.

What ultimately seems most relevant are the 50 titles in Series II under the category of "modern problems." What can be categorized as "modern problems" (which is itself a "problematic")? From the Series II catalogue we find the topics divided into two parts: China (24 problems) and the world (26 problems). A mere listing of the titles tells a story of nationalism as conceived and categorized in the popular imagination. Given the background of the Commercial Press, we do not expect such a story to have a radical revolutionary projection. Rather, the problems listed under "China" are clearly applicable to the recently established nation-state: constitution, local self-government, village reconstruction, land, water conservancy (shuili), transportation, finance, taxation, international trade, cotton, silk, tea, compulsory education, adult education, women, labor, consular jurisdiction, recovery of the Northeast, development of the Northwest, Mongolia, Tibet, Sino-Japanese relations, Sino-Soviet relations, and overseas Chinese. The problems represent a preoccupation with issues of social and economic development, while territorial and diplomatic issues also seem to demand attention. The latter are clearly reflected in the second group of titles, problems concerned with "the world," with Japan, Soviet Russia, America, India, and the Philippines (independence) occupying the center of attention. But an overwhelming weight is placed on international issues, above all the reform of the League of Nations, international jurisdiction, and national self-determination, but also military weapons, food, fuel, unemployment, migration, monetary regulations, eugenics, and the sale of narcotics and "rationalization" (belihua). Together they suggest a political context that reflects closely the situation of the world between the two wars, in which the Republic of China took its place as a new nation concerned with territorial sovereignty and domestic development.

If we compare the titles with the revolutionary programs of the Chinese Communist Party, whose activities during the same period (1929–1934) marked a transition from the urban to the rural phase, it is clear that some of the basic revolutionary premises are missing from the "50 modern problems": problems of the urban proletariat, workers' strikes, theories of socialism and revolutionary literature, and above all the peasantry and its revolutionary potential. The discrepancy reveals not just a difference of political orientations (Wang Yunwu's editorial board consisted of moderates and conservatives) but a gap between the urban and rural imaginations. In other words, the entire repository enterprise was both urban based and addressed to an urban public. It deserves our attention because it outlines the basic intellectual material of which the urban conception of Chinese modernity was made. At the very least, the listings should be sufficient to provide a taxonomy of what constituted new knowledge in the early Republican era.

I hope that my narrative centered on the Commercial Press has also conveyed a sense of how its commercial enterprise evolved from an educational enterprise based on textbook production to a cultural enterprise based on journals and repositories. Together these forged a modern trajectory in terms of both time and space: the introduction of new knowledge was animated by a desire to keep China abreast of what was going on around it while at the same time the press sought to support the effort of nation building by providing intellectual resources for both the state and its "people." Its definition of the *guomin* remained vague, however, reflecting a nationalist echo of Liang Qichao's earlier slogan—and unfinished intellectual project—to create a "people made new" (*xinmin*) by renovating their mind and spirit. Whereas elitist intellectuals from Liang to Chen Duxiu and Lu Xun, perhaps following a Confucian precedent, continued to emphasize the question of how to cultivate the intellectual and spiritual "essence" of a people, the less elitist intellectuals were perhaps less driven by such a moral impulse; they may have been more interested in the task of *popularization*, of making knowledge more general and accessible to the "new people" (who were "created," after all, by their textbooks and newspapers), thus infusing urban society with the temper of a new era.

My strategy in the search for a concept of urban modernity is based on the assumption that, contrary to the elitist approach of conventional intellectual history, which tends to discuss only the essential ideas of individual thinkers, the task of a cultural historian is to explore what may be called the "cultural imaginary." Since a cultural imaginary may itself be defined as a contour of collective sensibilities and significations resulting from cultural production, we must also wrestle with both ends of this interpretive strategy—namely, both the social and the institutional context of this cultural production and the forms in which such an imaginary is constructed and communicated. In other words, we must not neglect the "surfaces," the images and styles that do not necessarily enter into the deepest of thought but nevertheless conjure up a collective imaginary. In my view, "modernity" is both idea and imaginary, both essence and surface. I leave the idea part to other scholars—or to another book—and direct my energies to the surface by boldly attempting to "read" a large number of pictures and advertisements in journals and newspapers. For such purposes, I base my analysis on data provided in another journal, a pictorial magazine called *Liangyou huabao* (The young companion, 1926–1945), which was the longest-lasting large-format pictorial journal in modern China. Before I get to the pictorials themselves, I must give a brief background of this cultural enterprise which, though smaller in scale than the Commercial Press, played an equally important role in the history of modern Chinese publishing—and in the shaping of Chinese modernity.

The Pictorial Journal as "Friendly Companion"

The Liangyou tushu yinshua gongsi (literally, the good friend book and printing company), established in Shanghai in 1925, clearly followed in the footsteps of the Commercial Press. Its founder, Wu Liande, an enterprising businessman who once worked for the Commercial Press, was able to enlist such literary luminaries as Zhao Jiabi, Zheng Boqi, Ma Guoliang, and Zhou Shoujuan as its editors. With its flagship journal *Liangyou huabao*, it quickly carved out a market for pictorial journals and other popular magazines. Following the example of the Commercial Press, it also sponsored the publication of collectanea and repositories, of which the most famous were *Liangyu wenxue congshu* (Liangyou's collectanea of literature), *Liangyou wenku* (Liangyu repository), and *Zhongguo xinwenxue daxi* (Compendium of new Chinese literature), the last of which has remained a useful compendium for students of modern Chinese literature.[31] In an advertisement announcing the expansion of the company, it boasts of "the creation of a new era in the field of printing" since it was the first publishing company to specialize in photography. It also sponsored the publication of half a dozen journals: in addition to *Liangyu huabao*, we find a cinema monthly—among the first of its kind—*Silver Star* (Yinxing); *Modern Woman* (Jindai funü); *Yishu jie*, a weekly on the arts edited by four "decadent" aesthetes, Zhu Yingpeng, Zhang Ruogu, Fu Yanchang, and Xu Weinan; and *Tiyu shijie*, a quarterly devoted to the world of athletics. These magazine titles suggest the company's chief commercial direction: arts and entertainment. That such magazines satisfied an urban demand seems self-evident, but it is also likely that such a demand was in part created by the magazines themselves.

At first glance, *Liangyou huabao* immediately impresses the reader with its large size—larger than *Dongfang zazhi*. For a pictorial it contains a fairly heavy dose of written material, but its attraction obviously lies in its visual features. On the cover of each issue is the photograph or portrait of a "modern" woman, with her name printed underneath. This may have been a continuation of a convention established by late Qing courtesan newspapers, in which a number of "famous flowers" (mostly courtesans who were acquaintances of the editors) appeared on the covers. But instead of courtesans, the *Liangyou huabao* covers featured "new-style" women of considerable renown. For instance, Lu Xiaoman, the paramour and later wife of the famous poet Xu Zhimo, appeared on the September 1927 cover. The photograph of the famous actress Anna May Wong (Huang Liushuang) appeared on the cover of the June 1927 issue—a personal gift from her to the editor Wu Liande (her inscription is in English). This public display conveys a sense of both glamour and realism. Beginning in 1927, however, the journal also featured portraits of "fantasy" women. For example, the woman on the June 1928 cover sports not only a pair of chic high-heeled shoes but also, as was apparently the fashion of the period, a fur scarf, prominently displayed on her shoulders. Yet both her dress and her facial features remain "traditional," blending harmoniously with the backdrop of what looks like a traditional Chinese painting. On closer examination, however, we realize that she is not so demurely traditional after all: one of her arms is half exposed and leans against the back of a modern rocking chair, and with the other hand on her crossed legs she strikes a slightly flirtatious pose. Her dress has a more flowery and elaborate pattern than was presumably typical, and she certainly looks rich (or is pretending to be) with her fur scarf and earrings. As in each issue, the title of the magazine appears in both Chinese and English. But whereas the Chinese characters loom large, they are not as artfully designed as the English title, *The Young Companion*. When we read the entire cover, both word and image, a "subtitle" or subtext easily suggests itself: the young, rich, and alluring woman is (made to appear as) a "young companion" to the reader. Thus this fantasy woman is designed to lure the reader into the magazine's written contents, which provide, in a sense, intellectual companionship.

I am not prepared to argue that the women on the covers serve no purpose other than as commodified objects to arouse male desire. The magazine's intended readership may have consisted more of women and school-age youths than of adult men. As a "good companion" to the reading public, the journal could not flaunt a prurient appeal but had to maintain a good reputation in order to sustain its large circulation. This good reputation was established, however, not through any intellectual clout or scholarly depth, but through good-natured gestures of friendliness. The editor's message on the front page of the early issues certainly lends itself to such an impression—that the journal serves as a good and constant companion in the daily lives of its readers. In the third issue (April 15, 1926), the editor, assuming the guise of a spirit (Liangyou zhi shen), greets the readers:

> Good morning, dear good friends:
>
> As you open the first page this morning and meet me, I am really a little abashed, and I don't know what to say. So I'll just say good morning and wish you good health. I was originally an ignorant youth, but thanks to your loving care I have been on friendly terms with you for about two months. I am even more grateful to you for not forsaking me for my ignorance, and from now on I vow to be a good person, a reliable person, and your trusted and loyal friend.

In the second issue (March 15, 1926) the "Words from the Editor" column brings the "friend" even closer to the quotidian life of the intended reader:

> When you are tired from work, pick up a copy of *Liangyou* and read through it; you'll be assured that your energy will be revived

and you'll work better. When you're in a movie theater before the music begins and the curtain is drawn up, pick up a copy of *Liangyou* and read it; it's better than looking around. When at home you have nothing else to do, reading *Liangyou* is better than playing mahjong. When lying in bed, and your eyes are not tired, it's better to read *Liangyou* than to stare and indulge in silly thoughts.

To attribute such messages merely to the ingenuity of the editor would be too easy, since behind the words lurk both a conscious intention and a cultural context. Just as the editors of *Dongfang zazhi* and *Wanyou wenku* capitalized on the obvious need for new knowledge, the editors of *Liangyou huabao* sensed and exploited the public need for a new day-to-day urban lifestyle. Naturally this need was best served by a pictorial magazine. A useful comparison can be made between the journal and its late Qing predecessor *Dianshizhai huabao* (Pictorial from the stone-tablet studio), which heralded the popularity of such a medium. In the late Qing intellectual context, the *Dianshizhai* pictorial, which consisted entirely of drawings in the traditional style, with no photography, was less realistic in content but nevertheless aimed to inform and enlighten the reader by illustrating the wonders of the world. By the time *Liangyou huabao* was published, that educational task was being accomplished by the Commercial Press. At least in Shanghai, modernity, as evidenced by the transliterated term *modeng*, could be seen as an emergent urban style of living. Thus *Liangyou huabao* ushered in a second phase of pictorial journalism which reflected this urban taste for the "modern" life, which became further glamorized by the numerous movie magazines of the early 1930s. It is in this connection that I turn my attention to its coverage of women and children, which I believe unfolds another story of Chinese modernity.

Women and Children

Not only did women grace the front covers of *Liangyou huabao*; they also occupied a central space in the magazine's contents, of which the first and last few pages were entirely devoted to photographs. Other photos and illustrations, including comic sketches (*manhua*), were also scattered among the articles. If the contemporary reader began by looking at the front cover and glancing through the illustrated pages before reading the articles, the sequence would naturally form a chain of visual links. The woman on the cover was expected to lead the reader in: her look and her dress established an initial surface impression which was linked to other pictures inside the magazine. Many of the photos and drawings inside also focused on women; some of them might be variations (more photos or drawings) of the same cover girl as she displayed seasonal fashions. For instance, Yang Aili wears a spring or summer dress on the cover of the May 15, 1926, issue, but inside she wears winter clothing, complete with a large fur piece. As the reader's eyes roam across the other photos (credited by a line in English: "supplied by A. L. Varges, International Newsreel Corp. of New York"), he or she is introduced to various styles of dress. This issue features a full page of six photos of women wearing different fashions, some of whom may have already been familiar owing to their appearance on the magazine's covers. The reader is then drawn into a seasonal fashion "fantasy," in which clothing for different facets of the fantasy woman's social life (ordinary dress for the home, an evening cape for going out to a ballroom, and so on) is featured. Further variations are created by typecasting her in any of several stock social categories, ideological inscriptions borrowed from traditional Chinese culture: for instance, terms such as *miaoling nülang* (young girl at a tender age), *guinü* (young maiden), *dajia guixiu* (cultivated maiden from a well-to-do family), and *yanzhuang shaofu* (gorgeously dressed young lady or housewife) are often used to accompany the fashion photos.

I would argue, however, that fashion consciousness initially played only a small part in these photos and drawings of women. (These were not fashion models, as there was no such profession yet.) Rather, it is a consciousness of *dress* itself which provides an index to a new range of sensibilities in the lives of urban women of the middle and upper classes. I believe that this is what delineates the set of domestic and public spaces in which these categories of "well-dressed women" live and move, from the bedroom to the ballroom, and from the living room to the movie houses and department stores. Thus, it is not surprising that dress consciousness had progressed by 1930 to a consciousness of interior decoration and furnishings. In issue 50 (1930) we find well-dressed women posing in different rooms of "a typical modern home": the parlor with modern furniture; the bedroom, with an emphasis on the colors and tones of the wallpaper; and the children's bedroom with a bed, a chair, and a large drawing of an animal on the wall.

On the basis of these photos, it would seem that woman's place is *still* at home, albeit in a modern space, together with her children. In fact, this domestic link—women and their children—is the most frequently repeated image in the advertisements. At first glance this domestic picture seems to contradict the earlier May Fourth discourse, which centered on the image of an emancipated Nora—a woman who leaves her traditional family to lead an independent life. Still, I would argue that this does not necessarily indicate a conservative retreat from the radicalism of the previous decade. The "narrative" that can be derived from reading through *Liangyou baubao* is one which revolves around women's new roles in a modern conjugal family, into which are woven other aspects of an evolving style of urban bourgeois life. Whereas, as these advertisements suggest, women's new roles are still to be found in the home, it is a home made anew by modern conveniences and interior design. The domestic space of the household is now fully open, "publicized," and as such becomes a public issue.

As the numerous photos and articles in the journal indicate, this new public discourse of domesticity puts a great emphasis on physical health and family hygiene. Some medicine ads are especially revealing in this regard. In a study of the medical ads in the newspaper *Shenbao*, Huang Kewu has concluded that social life in Shanghai was caught up in the problems of contagious and sexually transmitted diseases, and of opium smoking and its prohibition; the ads also indicate some significant changes in women's lives, of which freedom from foot binding was a major phenomenon.[32] My own preliminary findings, drawn from the ads in *Dongfang zazhi* and *Liangyou huabao*, indicate that there were other issues as well. The samples often feature a modern conjugal family of husband and wife, sometimes with one or two children or the occasional grandfather or grandmother. They seem to tell an imaginary story of a modern couple for whom marital happiness based on good health becomes a central element. Read together with Huang's findings, they project an urban lifestyle in which an errant husband is likely to contract sexual diseases outside the home while the wife remains healthily at home. (Of course, he will stay healthy so long as he stays at home with his wife.) In contrast to the implied "evil" space outside, the home is portrayed as a safe, clean place where, in one ad, a woman is seen brushing her teeth with Colgate Dental Cream (when she is not using Colgate's Fab, which "Safely Washes Fine Fabrics"); and in another, a mother holding her baby stands behind a can of Momilk, from American Brewer & Company, beside a long passage describing the dangers of wet nurses, who, in a predictable transference, are the transmitters of sexual and other contagious diseases.[33] Even in the ubiquitous cigarette ads we find a picture of domestic comfort as an elaborately dressed housewife (clothed in the same style as the woman in the cover portrait cited earlier) offers a tin of Golden Dragon Cigarettes to her traditionally clothed husband sitting on a modern sofa. The four lines of Chinese words set into a square form an awkward but blatantly exploitative message: "Beauty is lovely; cigarettes are also lovely. The cigarette that is a national product is even more lovely."

Perhaps the most revealing is a set of three ads for Quaker Oats which give us three variations of the same story: in the first one a wife wearing an apron offers a bowl of Quaker Oats to her seated husband, who is reading a newspaper (the heading reads, "Ideal Breakfast"); in the second a mother holding her beloved baby feeds him a spoonful of Quaker Oats; in the third there is no direct representation of the cereal, only a picture of two youngsters, a boy and a girl, carrying their satchels as they run off to school. The message reads, "Give the energy, Nourish the soul: Youngsters in school consume a lot of energy, and the development of their bodies and hearts consumes even more. For nourishment, this is proper food." From the three ads we can easily piece together a Quaker Oats "story": the healthy living of a couple leads to a healthy family, which in turn strengthens the children's body and soul. This American product therefore contributes its share to the education of a healthy people. This crude bildungsroman is given a shot of nationalism in the two lines of another Momilk ad: "To strengthen the nation, one must first strengthen the people; to strengthen the people, one must first strengthen the children."[34]

The emphasis on children is further evidenced by the many photos of naked babies. In late 1926 *Liangyou huabao*, together with Momilk, sponsored a healthy baby contest, with an award of four hundred yuan for the top thirty. Hundreds of photos of eager entrants appeared in subsequent issues. The whole enterprise is but a "healthy" echo of the American-style beauty contest, a competition the journal also featured in its twentieth issue. The Chinese headings for the beauty contest use three terms: *meiren* (beautiful person), *meinü* (beautiful woman), and *renti mei* (beauty of the human body). The last also became the recurrent theme of a series of photographs displaying women's bodies with an increasing degree of nudity. The 1926 issues featured Western sculptures and paintings of nudes and photos of Japanese women in bathing suits, accompanied by drawings by contemporary Chinese artists (for instance, issue 15 featured the works of Wan Laiming). In issue 30 (1928), a number of "nude poses" appeared together with an ad for a book of Wan Laiming's paintings. When four photos of a nude Chinese model appeared for the first time, they showed only the contours of her back. In issue 40 (1929), a "photographic study" by Chang Chien Wen showed a full-page nude facing a mirror; the explanatory remarks laud the naturalness of her body ("a healthy body is the first principle of beauty"). In issue 50 (1930), a photo of a frontal nude takes up a whole page, with the English caption "Under the shade of a willow tree (a photo by P. C. Chen)"; the Chinese caption again lauds "a healthy and beautiful body."

It would take a lengthy treatise to put the public display, artistic or otherwise, of the female body in a modern Chinese cultural context. (It would be relatively easy to see it as an invasion of Western culture and aesthetics inscribing the long Western history of the human body on the Chinese mind.) As Mark Elvin has shown, the discourse of the body in traditional Chinese culture is full of complexities. The Chinese word for body, *shen*, is translated by Elvin as "body-person," as it is often connected with extra-physical attributes of person, self, life, or lifetime.[35] There was, of course, a considerable obsession with the physical side of the human body in both Confucianism and Daoism. But, according to Elvin, the purpose was above all to preserve longevity: "Late-traditional Chinese were hypochondriacs, obsessed with diets, medicine, and health generally"—all presumably for such a purpose.[36] (One should add, too, that these hypochondriacs were mostly men.) Elvin notes that

> the body-person is also the heart-mind's most important single resource. It is (obviously) the carrier of physical beauty, both female and male. It is the repository of "face," both in the all-or-nothing sense of social credit-worthiness and in the incremental-decremental sense of prestige. Even its wealth seems to stick to it like a physical characteristic, and affects how it is perceived by others. The expected dowries and inheritances of the sons and daughters of the rich are discussed in the same breath as their appearance and their behavior. Female bodies have a precise market value. It goes without saying that this is so for the young ladies—far from the most unfortunate in this society—who are purchased as investments when young by the madames who run the houses of pleasure, and sell them off later as secondary wives to rich businessmen in whom a besotted lust has been artfully introduced.[37]

The relevance of this observation for our purposes is that this last instance may well have been preserved in the cultural memory of readers of *Liangyou huabao*. As I argued earlier, the journal's effort to maintain a healthy respectability and friendliness may have stemmed from an awareness of the popularity of countless journals and a mosquito press devoted to the "pleasure quarters." Catherine Yeh has demonstrated that in the late Qing period, the courtesan journals also held beauty competitions; each "famous flower" had her own literati following.[38] Yeh surmises that the vogue faded from the publishing scene after such journals were replaced by movie magazines. But courtesan literature, in fact, did not fade from modern Chinese publishing; only its public image was displaced by photographs and paintings of modern, and more respectable, women. Thus the display of the female body either as a work of art (Western) or as an embodiment of physical health marked the beginnings of a new discourse which was made problematic precisely because it was derived from the courtesan journals, in which female bodies indeed carried a market value. Insofar as it portrayed young ladies, a new pictorial such as *Liangyou huabao* had to reinvest the female body with an entirely new meaning and ethical value. The new women portrayed or photographed were not poor, or at least not from poor families. And when they were placed in an interior setting of the modern family, they were made to embody a totally different style of life from that of the courtesans. Their bodies, therefore, were placed in new "persons": that is, to follow Elvin, their new house would be where they could *an-shen* (settle down in life), just as their *chu-shen* (upbringing) and *shen-fen* (personal status) were purposefully given a "dressing-up" of bourgeois wealth and respectability. Thus, fashion—styles of dressing up—became a modern element in a culture which had no such tradition, except in a trivial form (according to Elvin, "chiefly hairdo and makeup, it seems").[39]

To move from the portrait of a fashionable woman to that of a female nude generated a further anxiety for readers living in that still transitional age, because drawings of naked female bodies in traditional Chinese culture were found largely in pornographic books. The invention of photography and its adoption by the modern newspaper and magazine added a mimetic dimension: the nude figure now looked like a real person. This "shock of recognition" could incur all kinds of misinterpretations by the average readers of the time—most of all those derived from the male gaze and lust, hence leading to objectification and commodification of the female body, a familiar view among current feminist and postcolonial theorists. But what if some (even large numbers) of the readers were women? And what if pages of nudes were placed in the journal together with pictures of Chinese and world leaders, athletes, and Hollywood movie stars? Such issues were not confined to the female body alone; I would argue that the display of the female body had become part of a new public discourse related to modernity in everyday life.

Advertising Modernity

The problematic of everyday life has received considerable theoretical attention in the field of cultural studies because, among other reasons, it addresses directly the problematic of the (Western) culture of modernity and postmodernity.[40] As I mentioned before, in the Chinese context of the early twentieth century, the theme had gradually become an "imagined reality" as created by print media. The everyday life depicted therein was modern and urban, no longer seen as traditional and unchanging. When we look into the basic content of such a new form of everyday life, we realize that it is very much structured and governed by a semiotics of *material* culture. The contours of such a material world can be detected, again, in the advertisements in the magazines. I have already mentioned Quaker Oats, Momilk, Colgate Dental Cream, and Fab detergent. These products fulfilled, functionally, the needs of the family's morning ritual: they clean their teeth with dental cream and breakfast on oatmeal and milk; yesterday's laundry can be washed with detergent. From these and other ads we can easily reconstruct a list of daily necessities and luxuries for the modern urban household: electric cooking pots (*zhufan dianlu*) sold by the Oriental Trading Company, Ltd.; automatic pots or gas burners (*zilai huolu*) from the Shanghai Gas Company (the ad notes that "recently Chinese people have largely replaced coal burners with gas burners" and that gas is especially suitable for Chinese houses in winter for purposes of "hygiene for the whole family"); cameras, Agfa and Kodak film (the journal took great pride in its photography); Ever-ready batteries; gramophones and records (Pathé and RCA)—though not yet the telephone—and fountain pens. An ad in issue 7 for the Hong Kong branch of the Wing On department store presents a neat mosaic of these items: a Conklin fountain pen (and a Western-clothed man using it), various kinds of cotton cloth, Swan brand silk stockings and cotton socks, Pilsner Art Export Beer, and a copy of *Liangyou huabao*. The materials of daily comfort for an urban household, both inside and outside, seem complete.

By the early 1930s, an entire imaginary of urban modernity was being constructed in the pages of *Liangyou huabao*. More and more photos appeared showcasing the various attractions of the city itself. Issue 87 in 1934 includes a two-page photographic extraganza billed, in English, an "Outline of Shanghai"; its Chinese title is even more revealing: "So This Is Shanghai: Sound, Light, and Electricity." Other photos show Shang-hai's famed department stores, hotels, ballrooms, cinemas (together with movie stars), and women. A 1934 issue presents a photographic collage with headings in both Chinese and English—"Intoxicated Shanghai," or "Duhui de ciji" (excitements of the metropolis)—with photos of a jazz band, a new twenty-two-story skyscraper, scenes of horse and dog rac-ing, a movie poster for *King Kong*, and two parallel scenes showing a row of women baring their legs in athletics and cabaret dancing.[41] At the center is a young Chinese woman wearing a fashionable *qipao* with high slits who is seated in an alluring pose. Lest it be considered too seductive, the journal, in an apparent act of self-criticism, printed in a subsequent issue another series of pictures titled "On the Sidewalks of Shanghai" that showed other aspects of the city: used book and magazine stands, profes-sional scribes whose business was to read and write letters for the illiter-ate at a modest price, four men gawking at pictures of women on a wall, a newsstand, a bucket of cheap fountain pens, two men and a boy reading old pictorial storybooks, and beggars with their open letter to the public unfolded on the ground.[42] These photographs combine to reveal an intriguing self-reflexivity: the city to which the journal owed its very existence is first glamorized and then critiqued, as if to show that the imaginary modernity embodied in its photographs was but a fantasy pieced together by a clever arrangement in print; at the same time, however, the mimetic intent of the photograghs seems also to imply that this fantasy was based on reality. No matter how hard the journal's editors sought to present the other side of Shanghai, it was this modern fantasy that took hold of the popular imagination of its readers. What makes the story of *Liangyou huabao* worth telling is precisely its conscious effort to advertise modernity, thereby helping to construct it in Shanghai's urban culture. As such the magazine marked not only a significant chapter in the history of modern Chinese journalism but also a historical step in representing the progress of Chinese modernity itself.

Calendar Posters

It remains for me to discuss one last specimen in this series of commercial advertisements for modernity, perhaps the most significant one as it signifies the crucial temporal scheme of everyday activity: the commercial calendar poster.

The calendar poster began as an advertising gimmick introduced by Western capitalism—principally the British and American tobacco, medicine, cosmetic, textile, and oil companies. As early as the 1910s, the American Tobacco Company (Yingmei yancao gongsi) had introduced offset lithograph printing, formed its own advertising department, and set up an art school for the sole purpose of training commercial artists. But its dominance was soon challenged by native Chinese entrepreneurs, in particular Huang Chujiu, the owner of the Great Eastern Dispensary and the "Great World" amusement building, who spotted the artistic talent of a Hangzhou painter, Zheng Mantuo, and promoted him.[43] Thus calendar posters painted by Zheng and his disciplines became highly sought-after items, thereby establishing a new tradition of commercial art that combined traditional Chinese painting techniques with modern design (they were sometimes framed with Art Deco patterns) and utility. In the 1920s and early 1930s, the calendar poster reached a peak of popularity.

The basic composition of the calendar poster is invariable: an oblong square frame, as in a traditional Chinese painting, with the portrait of a woman occupying about two-thirds of the frame, and at the bottom a calendar; above either the large frame or the calendar is printed the name of the company which is advertising its commodity, mostly cigarettes and medicine. In some ways this makes for a perfect summation of some of the central elements I have discussed in this chapter, including not only the veneer of modernity as seen through advertisements, but also the paraphernalia associated with the women in the picture. In fact, the cover girls in *Liangyou huabao* and the women in the calendars bear some striking similarities in terms of fashion, posture, and facial and background features. They also betray a painting technique which, while clearly linked to traditional brush styles and popular roots (such as the *nianhua*, or New Year pictures in rural households), nevertheless added some innovative touches. This new vogue was popularized by Zheng Mantuo and his friends and disciples. A special technique of Zheng's was to begin drawing the woman's face with charcoal powder and then touch up with colored hues, thus creating a tender, subdued look. This kind of "portrait of a lady in modern dress" (*shizuang shinü tu*) became a representative fixture of the calendar, and the discerning viewer or collector supposedly could even see "her eyes following people."[44]

Allow me to "read" one such woman in a calendar which I own.[45] It is one of the more traditional versions of the calendar, which advertises Hatamen brand cigarettes. It is painted with a special 1930s technique of light-colored brushwork (*caibi dancai hua*) first used by Zheng Mantuo in the late Qing period.[46] In this particular case, the body of the woman is not elongated, as was sometimes necessitated by the oblong shape of the frame. She sits sideways by a patch of water, where a pair of swans swim together; on the upper- and lower-right corners branches and grass are painted in the traditional style. The whole ambiance seems to transport us away from modern reality. In my view the painting evokes the fictional world of the Mandarin Ducks and Butterflies school; the pair of swans, in particular, is a visual reference, metonymically, to mandarin ducks. This allusion to a common traditional style may serve to "tone down" the blatantly foreign (English) origin of the cigarettes. In order to spotlight the commodity, however, the cigarette pack is red.

As we gaze at the picture of the woman, we find that although her clothing is traditional—she wears a simple and tastefully light-colored *qipao*—there are some very modern touches which distinguish her from the myriad traditional women who graced magazine covers. For one thing, the large flower she wears on her shoulder is a striking pink, which contrasts with the pale green of her gown (with slim pink stripes to match), thereby both bringing out and yet muting the familiar aesthetic association of the primary colors red and green. The central position of the flower, of course, also serves to point to the woman herself, thus suggesting the familiar poetic metaphor for woman, *yizhi hua*, a solitary flower of faded splendor, which conveys a vague sense of passion soured by pity and sorrow. What kind of flower is she wearing? A rose, a peony, or even a pear blossom, as in the evocative poetic line, "A pear blossom, bringing spring and rain" (Yizhi lihua chun dai yu)? I may be intentionally overreading such flower associations because I find her face reminiscent of the movie actress Ruan Lingyu, who rose to great fame around 1930—a great icon and a legendary woman of passion who later committed suicide for love. In fact, movie actresses often served as models for these commercial calendars. (Another famous example is the actress Li Lihua, who posed for a poster advertising *yindanshilin bu*, a blue fabric commonly used for women's clothes.)[47] As on movie screens, they are displayed objects who nevertheless make a subjective visual impact on individual viewers. What distinguishes a good calendar from a mediocre one lies precisely in this particular combination of the striking and the stereotypical, the real and the fantastic. The woman in the calendar, I suspect, became a key factor in the buyer's choice (if the calendar was not simply given out by the company as a New Year's gift, the custom then as now), and the tobacco company's "legendary" reputation may have had something to do with its posted, hence fetishized, women. Thus the figure of the woman, like the cigarette, became a commodity.[48]

But the real function of this poster, hence the real content of this "text," is the calendar itself, which is limited to the lower half but framed with a striking Art Deco design. What makes it immediately relevant to our purposes is that the calendar uses two sets of modern year indicators: 1930 of the Western calendar on the left and the nineteenth year of the Republic of China on the right. The rest of the calendar is divided by months, which are further divided into weeks, at which point the traditional lunar dates enter in. I have no idea when this dual arrangement became standard, but the cultural significance cannot be overemphasized. Not only does the calendar bring two clear time markers together (Chinese and Western, both decidedly modern), but also the two combine to inscribe a modern organizational time scheme onto the traditional one. The division into month, week, day is manifestly Western and modern, a concept that now governed the everyday lives of Chinese urbanites; a few seasonal dates from the lunar calendar appear at the top of the month column, perhaps as a reminder of the important rituals people still needed to perform or, as is still practiced now, as a form of "fortune-telling," helping the modern city dwellers equate their modern date keeping with a tabulation of divine fortune and determine which day might be auspicious for a particular ritual. All of these features have become common in the Chinese calendars used today. But their invention must be duly credited, for I believe that time—and the system of calendrical dating—is the foundation on which modernity is constructed. This is also the underlying thesis of Benedict Anderson's book, that nationalism could be imagined only as a result of a fundamental change in the conception of time: the "imagined community" of the nation springs from an idea of "homogeneous, empty time, in which simultaneity is, as it were, transverse, cross-time, marked not by prefiguring and fulfillment, but by temporal coincidence, and measured by clock and calendar."[49] To bring Anderson's abstraction to the level of urban Shanghai, we could almost say that the daily life of the kind of "imagined modernity" I have described was also measured by the clock (like the big one atop the Shanghai Customs House) and the calendar.

Throughout this chapter I have used the term "imaginary" in the sense of a cluster of linked images which collectively represent an ideal (in this case, an image of Chinese modernity). I have also emphasized the process of construction rather than reception for reasons that should by now be clear. For I believe that this imaginary of modernity was still in the making in the early Republican period, chiefly in the urban culture of Shanghai. I have further suggested that, following Anderson, it was also related to the formation of the modern Chinese nation, first as an "imagined community." Proof that this imagined community had become a reality can be found in *Liangyou*'s weighty pictorial album *Zhonghua jingxiang* (China as she is: a comprehensive album), published in 1934.[50] Further research is needed to establish the relationship between this cultural enterprise and state policy and institutions, particularly in education (for instance, which textbooks published by Commercial Press were adopted and how many copies were printed). But it is beyond the scope of the present book.

Of more crucial significance would be the connection and interplay between editors and readers, producers and consumers. What was the composition of the urban (and rural) readership? How diverse was it? Would different kinds of readers respond to different journals? So far my evidence is merely textual, as I try to gauge the range and number of readers from the printed advertisements in the journals themselves, a system that incurs the danger of self-serving exaggeration. I am not sure that research in this area could ever be complete—and completely convincing. My purpose, however, is not to demonstrate the final result in empirical research but to explore the possibilities of a new approach, that of cultural history. I hope that I have at least blazed a small trail by shifting scholarly attention from the elite domain of lofty ideas and grand narratives to a more popular realm of urban print culture. As the next chapter will show, the popularity of this print culture had a direct impact on another, even more popular medium: modern Chinese cinema.

THE URBAN MILIEU OF

SHANGHAI CINEMA

In the last chapter I tried to deal with two significant aspects of Shanghai's emerging print captalism: the ambitious project of enlightenment undertaken by the Commercial Press through the publication of new textooks and massive compendia, and the construction of a modern lifestyle through commodity advertisement. My emphasis on these artificial aspects of urban culture stems not only from a cultural historian's disciplinary concern with everyday life but also from a belief that these aspects of urban modernity provided the cultural matrix in which a special set of literary and artistic sensibilities was nurtured. Cinema was both a popular institution and a new visual medium which, together with journals, books, and other kinds of print culture, constituted this special cultural matrix in Shanghai. It was also the key source of inspiration for some of the fictional texts I will discuss in the second part of this book. As such it deserves a full treatment. In what follows I try to perform two necessary tasks: to delineate the urban milieu of the cinema and to present an argument about Chinese film spectatorship and its relationship to print culture. In so doing I take issue with some standard interpretations of the development of modern Chinese cinema.

Movie Theaters

One of the best sources of information about the cinema industry in China can be found in the official reports to the U.S. Department of Commerce by the chief of the Motion Picture Section of the Specialties Division, based on reports from "the overseas representatives of the Departments of State and Commerce." One such report issued in 1927 gives valuable information about the film milieu in China that is worth citing in some detail: "There are in China at present about 106 motion-picture theaters with a total seating capacity of about 68,000. These are divided between 18 large cities," chiefly treaty ports; and of the 106 movie theaters, 26 were in Shanghai.[1] According to the report, the most lavish of the movie theaters at the time was the Odeon, with a seating capacity of 1,420: "The seats on the lower floor are of modern theater design, and those in the balcony heavily upholstered. (In Shanghai the best seats are always in the balcony and the cheaper seats on the ground floor.)"[2] Another report issued in 1930 quotes the price of admission to the deluxe movie theaters as ranging from "20 cents to $3 local currency (U.S. $0.07 to $1)." The same report also notes that "all the larger motion-picture producers in the United States and Europe have agents or distributors in Shanghai," and thus "the best pictures produced anywhere are released in Shanghai almost as soon as they are in the country of production." To attract audiences in Shangai, "almost every known form of advertising is used by the motion-picture theaters, especially the first-run theaters. The principal mediums of advertising are the daily papers, both Chinese and foreign; posters and billboards in various parts of the city and on trams and buses; neon and other electric signs and displays; and mailed notices of new pictures," as well as a number of movie magazines sold in theaters.[3]

These official reports give us a fascinating glimpse into Shanghai's thriving cinema business. In fact, a series of renovations of old movie theaters and the construction of new ones had been underway since the late 1920s. An advertisement in English for the Odeon Theater published in several issues of *Liangyou huabao* describes the theater as "the largest and most sumptuous Cinema Palace in the Orient. Perfect in construction and design. Careful attention has been given to arrangement for the comfort and health of their patrons. With other picture [sic] of the highest merit Odeon Theatre presents for the first time in China." The Odeon was but one of a dozen "cinema palaces" bearing such colonial-sounding names as Carlton, Empire, Embassy (formerly Olympic), Palace, Victoria, Paris, Isis, and Majestic, with which the eight major Hollywood studios had exclusive contractual rights to show their first-run movies. The Odeon's deluxe glamour was soon superseded by the opening of the newly renovated air-conditioned Grand Theater (Daguangming) in 1933, designed by the Czech architect Ladislaus Hudec, complete with two thousand sofa-style seats (all equipped in 1939 with earphones—*yiyifon*, or what a local English newspaper called "Sino-phone"[4]—for simultaneous translation), a spacious Art Deco lobby, three fountains, a huge neon-lit marquee, and restrooms painted light green.[5] Although these newly renovated movie palaces dominated the foreign film market, the situation did not hinder the rapid growth of China's native film industry. Indeed, the movie theaters created both the material conditions and a cultural climate for moviegoing as a new habit of urban life, without which the development of the native Chinese cinema would have been impossible.

The early history of Chinese cinema has been fully documented. Suffice it to mention here that despite its primitive conditions, it managed to keep pace with the development of Western cinema. One of the early patrons of movie production was in fact the Commercial Press.[6] By the 1920s, Chinese silent films based on subjects drawn from popular fiction and opera already commanded a sizable audience. In 1927, one year after the world's first "talkie" premiered in Hollywood, Shanghai's first-run movie theaters also began to show sound films, and in 1931 the first Chinese sound film was produced.[7] Chinese audiences thronged into the cinemas with the same zest with which they greeted the opening up of the foreign concession parks.[8] By the end of the decade, there were between thirty-two and thirty-six movie theaters in Shanghai. One movie pictorial (*Diantong huabao*) mounted photographs of all these theaters on a map of Shanghai with the splashy announcement: "The houses which devour a million people every day!"[9] The thriving business of the new movie houses may have led to the decline of the amusement halls after 1931.[10]

Unlike the deluxe movie houses which showed first-run Hollywood movies, those showing Chinese films were often second-run houses of lesser grandeur. The situation was somewhat ameliorated when some enterprising Chinese film companies purchased old first-run theaters or formed a chain of theaters to show their own films—a move in direct imitation of the Hollywood distribution system.[11] A campaign was launched in the early 1930s to make more serious, high-quality Chinese films in order to counter the Hollywood products. Lianhua took the lead in this direction, followed by Mingxing and other companies. After the January 28 bombing of Shanghai by Japanese warplanes in 1932, the film columns of some journals and newspapers also began to promote native Chinese films (*guochan dianying*), which coincided with the movement toward promoting native goods (*guohuo*). The annual rates of Chinese film production increased.[12] Thus it was not until the 1930s that a notable Chinese film industry (*yingtan*) was established.

Movie Magazines and Movie Guides

The popularity of movies went hand in hand with the popularity of movie magazines and special columns and issues about movies in the general interest magazines. According to recent research, the appearance of movie magazines can be traced to 1921, when the Shanghai newspaper *Shenbao* published its *Yingxi congbao;* around the same time, the first independent film magazine, *Yingxi zazhi* (note the use of the compound *yingxi*, or "shadow play"), was published. A list of film magazines published in the period 1921–1949 contains a total of 206 titles, including film monthlies, weeklies, and special issues.[13] Some were published by the film companies: the *Dianying yuebao* (Film monthly) was a prime example of a trade journal of the six Chinese film companies.[14] Other companies also promoted the publication of film magazines. One of the largest and most enterprising was the Liangyou Publishing Company, which in addition to featuring photographs of famous movie stars in its best-selling magazine *Liangyou huabao* also published a special film issue in 1934 and inaugurated another magazine devoted entirely to the movies, *Yinxing* (Silver star), edited by Lu Mengshu. A book of essays on film and literature edited by Lu included contributions by such famous writers as Tian Han, Zhang Ruogu, and Fu Yanchang. The journal *Yinxing* was later combined with *Tiyu shijie* (Athletic world) into a monthly which received equal billing with the company's two other journals, *Zhongguo xuesheng* (Chinese student) and *Jindai funü* (Modern woman). It became an increasingly common practice to feature news and photos of movies and movie stars in the mushrooming journals for women. In the newly constructed "modern woman" image and lifestyle, an interest in the movies was definitely de rigueur. The trend was promoted in many other women's magazines and pictorial journals, which also tried to boost sales by providing gift photos of Chinese and Western movie stars to their subscribers.

To take one popular and by no means atypical example, I have located a women's weekly in a mini-format, *Linglong funü tuhua zazhi* (a magazine with its own English title, *Lin Loon Lady's Magazine*, or literally, "Petite: a pictorial magazine for women"), edited by a woman, Chen Zhenling, and featuring numerous photos of young women. But the most inventive feature is that its back pages were a movie supplement, with the English title "Movies"; its Shanghai-accented Chinese translation, *mu-vie* (*muwei* in Mandarin, literally, "screen flavor"), conveys the obvious pun on a "taste" (*wei*) for movies. It is billed as "the only movie weekly in the nation." In addition to displaying glamorous photos of Hollywood stars, each issue included ratings of current films being shown in Shanghai, taken from another newspaper, *Funü ribao* (Women's daily). For instance, the December 6, 1933, issue of *Linglong* features on its back cover (the cover for the "Movies" supplement) the famous star Ruan Lingyu (who committed suicide two years later) in a chic long gown, or *qipao*. Amidst advertisements for Cutex, the Canidrome (a dog-racing track), and "Koda Verichrome Film Pack," as well as tidbits about Greta Garbo and Al Jolson, and mention of Hitler's recalling all German stars from abroad, is this list of "Ratings of Chinese and Western new films in the past two weeks" (2425):

1.	*One Sunday Afternoon*	B—
2.	*The Great Decision*	C+
3.	*Golden Harvest*	B
4.	*42nd Street*	B
5.	*Sweepings*	B—
6.	*Torch Singer*	B
7.	*Xiangcao meiren* (Flowers and beauty)	B—
8.	*Modern Womanhood*	B
9.	*Beauty for Sale*	B
10.	*Her Highness Commands*	B

There is only one Chinese film in this group of ten films, *Xiangcao meiren*, which receives a relatively low rating. Yet seldom did any Hollywood film receive an A rating, which was given to only two films in the entire year: *My Weakness* (a film chosen for the premiere of the newly opened Grand Theater) and *Don Quixote*. Later issues include only a listing of "average or above average" films, without ratings—perhaps an indication of the Chinese attitude toward the general quality of mass-produced movies from the big Hollywood studios.

At the same time, however, considerable space in each issue is devoted to female movie stars. The January 31, 1934, issue is a special number devoted entirely to Hollywood movie stars, with both front and back covers plus eleven pages devoted to photos of Katharine Hepburn, Marlene Dietrich, Helen Hayes, Janet Gaynor, Claudette Colbert, Kay

Francis, Myrna Loy, Dolores Del Rio, and the ubiquitous Greta Garbo. This massive influx of glamorous pictures of Hollywood stars may have been the result of publicity efforts by the Shanghai branch offices of Hollywood's "big eight." But more likely they were reproduced from the many American movie magazines. In addition to rating films, *Linglong* also quoted ratings by American reviewers for journals such as *Film Classics* and *Film Mirror.* As in the case of the Chinese reception of Western literature (see Chapter 4), the major source of information was American popular journals, to which there was easy access through Western book-stores— (particularly Kelly & Walsh) and libraries (including the foreign books library of the Commercial Press) and even through direct sub-scription.

In what ways did the two popular genres of print and film culture combine to shape the viewing habits of Chinese film spectators? How do we gauge such viewing habits? What kinds of social and cultural meaning could be derived from going to the movies? A vivid testimony of the moviegoing experience can be found in a popular Chinese guidebook, *Shanghai menjing* (Keys to Shanghai), published in 1932. The section on cinema begins:

> Cinema originally was a foreign medium. After it was imported into China, it not only was taken as entertainment but also was found to have true artistic worth, and it could be an effective instrument to aid social education. So the intellectuals were among the first to welcome it. . . . Now, the average man and woman have considerable knowledge about cinema, and "going to the movies" has become a modern slogan. Young boys and girls in schools do it; even old people are patronizing movie theaters. Although the native film industry has not prospered in recent years, movie theaters are still in demand among the gen-eral public. More than twenty movie theaters have been built. [Cinema] is in a thriving state and threatens to wipe out the stage and the amusement hall.[15]

The author, Wang Dingjiu, admits from the outset that "going to the cinema does not mean catering to the foreign, but Chinese movies are really not as good as foreign movies. This is undeniable in industrially backward China . . . If a Chinese film costs two or three hundred thousand yuan, it is called a big production. But in America's Hollywood, the headquarters of world filmmaking, frequently a film would cost tens of thousands and even millions of dollars. With such a discrepancy in capital, the distance in achievement is likewise large."[16] The author lists a total of eighteen "modern cinemas" and gives brief evaluations of each of them, singling out such theaters as the Carlton, Grand, Nanking, and Odeon for special praise. But ticket prices in these cinemas were costly, ranging from one to two yuan, almost ten times the matinee price at the cheapest second- or third-run theaters. Thus the author cautions moviegoers to choose good films well in advance by obtaining information about the fame and talent of their stars and the past record of their directors and screenwriters. He also gives tips such as buying snacks outside the theater (to avoid the high price inside), bringing a newspaper or book to read before the show, and sitting upstairs if one brings a date. Above all, he urges patrons to keep the bilingual plot sheets (*shuoming shu*) and read them in the English original (for those who can), because meaning is often lost in the translations. In addition, he advises, "if you keep all the sheets of all the movies you have seen, together they become a marvelous collection of fiction."[17]

This source offers an intriguing glimpse into one crucial facet of the kaleidoscopic world of leisure and entertainment in Shanghai. (The guidebook also contains sections on food, clothing, lodging, shopping, and entertainment, with guides to restaurants, amusement halls, opera theaters, department stores, hotels, even houses of prostitution.) The nature of the guidebook tells us that the author, whatever his background (Wang may have been a journalist from one of Shanghai's *xiaobao* or mosquito newspapers), must have been an insider whose familiarity with the details of Shanghai life lent both authority and authenticity to his work. He is clearly enamored of the Hollywood movies shown in first-

run theaters, to which Chinese movies were in his opinion clearly inferior. His advice on how to behave in movie theaters provides a clue to a
new form of social etiquette. His point about keeping the bilingual plot
sheets as a "collection of fiction" is especially revealing because it points
to a possible link between film and popular fiction—film plots read as
written stories. Interestingly, the few samples I was able to obtain show
that the language of these plot sheets was not the modern vernacular
(baihua) but simple classical Chinese.[18] It seems to indicate that the kind
of "semi-traditional" style and aesthetic which informs Butterfly fiction
also had an impact on the language of the plot sheets and translated titles
of Hollywood movies.[19]

A large majority of translated film titles were rendered in a classical
vein, often with four Chinese characters suggesting obvious references
to traditional Chinese poetry and fiction: for instance, *Liangyuan chiaohe*
(Good romance and happy coincidence) for *One Sunday Afternoon; Jinyuan
chunnong* (Ripe spring in the imperial garden) for *Her Highness Commands;*
and, interestingly, a most appropriate title for the Busby Berkeley musical
Gold Diggers of 1933, Gewu shengping (Singing and dancing for peace and
prosperity). The novelty of a foreign film was thus familiarized by virtue
of a pseudo-literary inscription in Chinese. In the case of Hollywood
movies based on works of Western fiction which had already been translated into Chinese by the likes of Lin Shu (1852–1924) or Zhou Shoujuan, this fortuitous connection would have been even more
welcome—for example, for the Sherlock Holmes stories or romantic
novels such as *La Dame aux camélias* by Alexandre Dumas fils, which had
achieved a status of immortality by virtue of the elegant translation by
Lin Shu; the heroine was known to all Chinese readers as Chahuanü,
"Lady of the camelias."[20] Thus for a native filmgoer of the time, spending
a few hours watching a Hollywood movie provided a double pleasure: a
chance to lose oneself in an exotic world of fantasy while having one's
reading habits, as nourished by the countless popular novels of romance
and chivalry (including those translated into classical Chinese), further
enriched by this new visual medium.

Writing about Cinema

Of course, the close relationship between film and print culture was not confined only to readers of a more traditional sensibility. Moviegoing was the predominant leisure habit for many writers of New Literature in general and Shanghai writers in particular—from Lu Xun, who favored Soviet films, to Shi Zhecun, Xu Chi, Liu Na'ou, Mu Shiying, Zhang Ruogu, and Ye Lingfeng, in addition to leftists such as Tian Han, Hong Shen, and Xia Yan. The poet Xu Chi told me that he saw practically every Western film shown in Shanghai.[21] Shi Zhecun wrote an erotic story with the Paris Cinema as its setting, but both writers also frequented such deluxe cinema houses as the Grand Theater, the Metropole (Da Shanghai), Cathay (Guotai), Majestic (Meiqi), and Carlton (Ka'erdeng), the last being also a theater for stage plays. Their favorite pastimes consisted of going to three kinds of places: the cinema, bookstores, and coffeehouses. For Liu Na'ou and Mu Shiying, however, the cinema and the dance hall were almost interchangeable as a favorite hangout in both fiction and real life. Liu Na'ou became a film devotee and wrote a large number of film reviews and articles on film aesthetics in journals such as *Furen huabao* (Women's pictorial) and *Xiandai dianying* (Modern cinema), on topics ranging from film writing, film rhythm, and camera angles to an appreciation of Greta Garbo's and Joan Crawford's beauty.[22] He also became actively involved in filmmaking during the late 1930s before he was killed in 1939.

Liu's writings on film show a surprisingly modern sensibility, though he has received a negative press among leftist Chinese film historians owing to his presumed advocacy of "soft-core cinema" (*ruanxing dianying*).[23] The charge is ideologically tinged, since all Chinese leftists, writers and filmmakers alike, became deeply convinced that a work of art must reflect social reality. Liu Na'ou, by contrast, was one of the very few who became excited by the aesthetics of form—as opposed to social content—in this new medium. In a revealing essay bearing an original French title, "Escranesque," Liu defined cinema as "a motion art that combines the feeling of art and the rationality of science. As architecture embodies the purest form of rationality of the mechanical civilization [*jiqi wenming*], so the art form that most characteristically depicts the social environment of this mechanical civilization is the cinema."[24] The basic source of this new civilization for Liu lies in motion: "The changes of speed, direction, and energy thus generate its rhythm." Liu's ecstatic panegyric to the cinema had a lot to do with his obsession with this hallmark of Western modernity—time and speed—which he considered to be the true essence of modern life. This in turn led him to an aesthetic position which is at the heart of his brand of "neo-sensationalism," the belief that modern art and literature aim to capture and describe the tumultuous effect on the human senses and feelings caused by speed—the *jouissance* (Liu's term is *kuai gan*) that one experiences while driving a "roadster" or watching a movie. In film, as in all the arts, "it's the Form that counts" (Liu wrote the sentence in English). "A work of art becomes a work of art because of form. Content is but an appearance of form; artistic content exists only within artistic form."[25]

As I will demonstrate in Chapter 6, several of Liu's stories, as well as those by Mu Shiying, are clearly indebted for their language and form to the foreign movies the authors watched. Thus, not only did written literature and print culture—particularly popular journalism and fiction—lend a helping hand to support the new visual medium of film, but also together they became the main instruments for the creation of a new popular cultural imaginary of urban modernity. I dealt with the role of print culture in the construction of a Chinese modernity in Chapter 2. Moviegoing easily fit into this new lifestyle, just as movie theaters became a visible institution—together with coffeehouses, dance halls, and department stores—in the new urban space of leisure and consumption. What remains to be explored is the complex problem of *how* this new urban film spectatorship figured in the construction of such a modern imaginary and in the making of native Chinese cinema and fiction. Because the subject is closely related to the impact of Hollywood movies in Chinese urban culture (75 percent of all foreign films shown in China were American in origin),[26] some discussion of the theoretical underpinnings of American cinema is in order.

Popular Tastes: Film and Spectatorship

In recent American film studies there have been some notable works which have attempted to theorize about film spectatorship. In her analysis of American spectators during the era of the silent film, Miriam Hansen has argued that cinema "offered the possibility of a new, different kind of public sphere, a chance to close the gap . . . between a genteel literary culture and the encroachment of commercialism."[27] In creating such a public sphere, the Hollywood film industry catered specially to the female consumer by way of a "discursive apparatus surrounding the film rather than the text itself, as for instance fan magazines devoted to the purportedly female obsession with stars, glamour, gossip and fashionability."[28] In my own research on urban popular journalism, discussed in the last chapter, I have found a similar orientation toward female consumers, for whom a wide range of goods for domestic use were advertised. In this new world of modern women, clothes and fashion occupied a central place, and Chinese female film stars appeared as their very embodiment.

At the same time, however, we must be aware that the emergent world of consumerism and commodification in Shanghai, in which film played a part, did not entirely replicate the American culture of high capitalism. One significant sign of difference is that the "fashionable femininity" exhibited in the Chinese movie magazines does not convey the same strident sexuality of the Hollywood stars. In my samples drawn from *Linglong* magazine, the glossy photos of Hollywood stars invariably convey a rampant body fetishism—the face glamorously made up, a half-revealed torso, and most frequently a pair of exposed legs. By contrast, photos of famous Chinese stars such as Hu Die and Ruan Lingyu show them wearing long Chinese gowns which cover the entire body except for their bare arms. This elementary difference betrays a different aesthetic of the feminine—an aesthetic derived from the women's portraits and photos on magazine covers from the turn of the century on, perpetuated in the numerous calendar posters, to which these star photos bear a striking intergeneric resemblance.[29]

Instead of—or in addition to—serving as objects of the male gaze in a patriarchal society, these cover photos also helped to project a new persona for Chinese women, that of the "modern" woman in possession of certain new qualities, who is not ashamed to display her personality in public. As a revealing article in *Linglong* comments, such a modern woman should not be known merely by her chic appearance: "a permanent wave hairdo or a powdered face" is not enough; the true modern woman must also possess such qualities as "rich knowledge, lofty thinking, and strong will," all derived from reading and studying.[30] In other words, behind their bodies there was instilled a certain spiritual essence which made these women virtuous. One could, of course, consider all this written rationale as the purposeful imposition of a "false consciousness" by the producers of this new commercial culture. But a reading of the visual evidence tells a similar story. When we peruse the various photos of Ruan Lingyu, for instance, we find a traditional-looking woman touched with sadness: this is not merely due to her traditional dress (the *qipao* could be "sexy" too) or to our knowledge that she committed suicide in 1935. Rather, a more plausible reason may be that the public image of Ruan Lingyu was closely connected, in the audience's mind, with the roles she played, of which the most famous was that of a virtuous prostitute in *Shennü* (Goddess, 1934). In fact, I find close similarities of dress and appearance between photos of Chinese movie stars in magazines and portraits of women in commercial calendars (as described in the previous chapter). This is but another link between print culture and film which provides a precondition for the tastes and viewing habits of the popular audience.

The eminent film historian Jay Leyda has remarked on "the Chinese spectator's love of tradition, with all the security and serenity that tradition represents."[31] By this he meant the old popular sources of "Peking opera, fairy tales, myths, and folklore" on which Chinese films of the 1920s drew for their adaptive material. Leyda acknowledges that "these 'old subjects' were so extremely popular with film audiences then that we are forced to look beneath the 'escapist' surface and beyond the ticket-buyer's wish to forget for a couple of hours the huge political issues and the prospect of disturbing change that were coming down upon Shanghai."[32] Perhaps the ticket buyer's wish was for more than mere escapism. The question nevertheless remains: why were audiences drawn to such formulaic plots? A Chinese film scholar has argued that this is precisely a "national characteristic" traceable to the traditional aesthetic taste in narrative art. Such a narrative mode emphasizes the "story quality" (gushixing) and tends to impart a "romantic" or legendary (chuangqi) spell—to use a term that harks back to Ming drama, if not to Tang fiction, and that is further defined as a pronounced formal feature of traditional Chinese fiction and drama, which "excels by the richness, novelty, and copious twists and turns of plot."[33] Such plot structures easily incorporate coincidences and chance encounters in which certain "contradictions" are unfolded or uncovered. One could venture even further by speculating on the popularity of certain foreign films over others on account of their narrative affinities to such formulaic plot twists from traditional fiction. The story of a virtuous hero or heroine of feeling who is made to suffer through hardships or to struggle against forces beyond his or her control was a recurring feature in late Qing fiction and translations (for instance, Wu Wuoyao's Henhai, or The Sea of Regret, and Lin Shu's translation of Uncle Tom's Cabin, from which a play was adaped focusing on only a few scenes of the heroine's escape.) Such narrative affinities would appeal to a native audience, especially in the case of silent films, because the plot is necessarily "written out" on the screen, thus simulating the experience of reading popular fiction. Some evidence indicates that such linkages between film and print may have been made consciously through the plot summary sheets distributed to the audience as they entered the theater. In a few cases the plot summary was even shown on the screen. An article in a Butterfly school magazine,

Banyue (Half-moon), edited by Zhou Shoujuan, complains that the theater showing a Hollywood film, *Hongfen kulou* (literally, Skull of a beauty), projects on screen a plot summary at the very beginning, thus ruining the audience's pleasure in all the unexpected twists and turns of the plot.[34]

Chinese Film Narrative: Hollywood Influences versus Native Aesthetics

What I have tried to suggest is that the Chinese audience's tastes and viewing habits may have been to a large extent shaped by print culture, particularly popular fiction. To this factor of native cultural predisposition must be added the enormous popularity of Hollywood movies, which exerted a poweful impact on both the Chinese film audience and the filmmakers. In this connection the problems—both technical and ideological—become even more complex, so we must first understand the basic features of the Hollywood film before we can address its possible influence. Again, the official trade report cited earlier serves as a good point of departure. "The American motion picture enjoys far greater popularity among the Chinese than do the films of any other country outside of China. Aside from the greater lavishness of American pictures and their superior direction and technique, the Chinese also prefer the 'lived happily ever after' and 'triumph of right over wrong' ending which concludes most of our films, as compared with the more tragic finales of many European pictures."[35] In the section on "Chinese tastes in motion pictures," the report becomes even more detailed:

> At one time it seemed to be the policy of certain American exporters to send to China pictures of a particularly lurid nature which would never receive first-run showings in the United States . . . As examples of these may be cited the earlier and more sensational type of "wild west" picture, which immediately achieved startling popularity among Chinese theatergoers . . . Later on came the social picture—really of the same general nature as the "wild west" film—and this created even greater

excitement among Chinese audiences. It is reported that the police had to be called in at the showing of one episode in a Peking theater in order to save the villain—and the screen—from damage . . . Of the modern type of feature picture those featuring social problems—"the eternal triangle"—do not take well with the Chinese and tend to lower the prestige of the foreigner. Stories of the "jazz" age have a like effect, particularly if it [sic] involves a clash between parents and children, for the Chinese, being an ancestor-worshipping people, have profound veneration for their elders and can understand no other attitude. Historical pictures, on the other hand, always draw good crowds; and love stories, particularly of an idyllic nature, always take. When all is said and done, however, it is the comedy and in a lesser degree the picture featuring children which takes in China.[36]

These comments, made by an American government trade official based on "field reports," are nevertheless quite revealing. Aside from its self-serving attitude, the report does confirm in a rather rudimentary fashion certain affinities between the Hollywood narrative tradition and some prevalent formulaic devices in traditional Chinese popular fiction, for example, the *da tuanyuan* (great reunion) ending and the melodramatic necessity of the "triumph" of right over wrong. The report uses generic types in its comments on classic Hollywood cinema. The lurid "wild west" and "social picture" labels refer to the early silent serials, whereas the "eternal triangle" type of social satire and comedy became a subgenre of the "talkies" after 1930. The popularity of the so-called historical pictures is easily explainable, as it can be related to the Chinese audience's interest in traditional folktales and historical romances, to which Leyda has alluded. But the report's author seems unaware that although the modern formula of the "eternal triangle" in Hollywood comedies usually revolves around one woman and two men—that is, a heroine pursued by two male suitors—in traditional Chinese fiction and drama the eternal triangle is often the reverse, as one man, often a talented scholar, becomes entwined with two women. The classic model was of course *Dream of the Red Chamber*. The modern triangle, however, also found its way into contemporary Chinese fiction, as in a famous story by Lao She, "Black Li and White Li," and the more sophisticated Hollywood product known as screwball comedy had a direct impact on more sophisticated writers in the 1940s such as Eileen Chang, who later adapted the Broadway play *The Tender Trap* into a Chinese screenplay which was made into a film in Hong Kong.[37]

All this brings us to a rexamination of the aesthetic tradition of Hollywood cinema itself. Miriam Hansen argues that there was a paradigmatic shift from early to classical American cinema during the decade 1907–1917, which was "defined by the elaboration of a mode of narration that makes it possible to anticipate a viewer through particular textual strategies, and thus to standardize empirically diverse and to some extent unpredictable acts of reception."[38] Hansen stops short of saying whether such "empirically diverse acts of reception" can be extended to other cultures and countries. But she does define this dominant Hollywood mode of narration as based on a new "American hieroglyphics," which was "troped in the ambiguous celebration of film as a new universal language."[39] What are the rules of this "new universal language" which presumably would apply to the viewing habits of empirically diverse audiences everywhere? To begin with, Hansen notes "the industry's increasing focus on the dynamic of character, individual psychology, and the personality of the star," since "the star system had been flourishing since 1910, and by 1916 the cultivation of stars was more than an established publicity device."[40] From this focus was developed a mode of narration that became the hallmark of classical Hollywood cinema: "the interweaving of multiple strands of action moving toward resolution and closure, a web of thorough motivation centering on the psychology of individual characters, and the concomitant effect of an autonomous fictional world offered to the spectator from an ideal vantage point."[41]

In what ways did this narrative mode exert either a direct or an indirect impact on classical Chinese cinema (by which I mean films produced in the 1930s and 1940s, both silent and sound)? On the one hand, as Paul Pickowicz has shown, "films by such recognized masters as D. W. Griffith and Charlie Chaplin were well known in China by the early twenties,"[42] and presumably Chinese filmmakers learned much from watching them and other Hollywood films. On the other hand, we must be aware that the same Chinese practitioners also came from a *Chinese* background. Recent film scholars from Hong Kong have separated these background influences into two categories of films: *wenren dianying*, or films made by those with a background in May Fourth literature, such as Tian Han, Xia Yan, Hong Shen, and other leftist writers who penetrated the film world in the 1930s; and *xiren dianying*, or films made by those craftsman-directors whose aesthetics were derived from the conventions of traditional Chinese theater, particularly the *wenming xi*, or "civilized plays," a hybrid form of popular drama with some modern content.[43] The established view among Chinese communist film historians is that the former began to dominate the film scene beginning in the early 1930s, thereby effecting a total transformation of the latter, changing the quality of Chinese cinema from frivolous entertainment into a serious art of social criticism that served to advance the cause of revolution.[44]

To some extent, and from the party's own point of view, this thesis sounds plausible. In reading a number of popular magazines from this period, I have found that increasing attention was paid to native Chinese cinema. For example, a journal called *Xin Shanghai* (New Shanghai) featured a column on cinema in its inaugural issue in 1933, in which the editor proclaimed that the column would be devoted only to Chinese cinema, which had survived the onslaught of Hollywood films chiefly through the efforts of a couple of native film companies (presumably Lianhua and Mingxing).[45] One article lauded the entry into the film world of such central literary figures as Tian Han, Lu Xun, and Mao Dun (a partial error, since the latter two did not become personally involved) for "injecting a shot of morphine" (meaning a new stimulus): "I can state emphatically that the success of Lianhua films is due not so much to directors . . . , cameramen and actors but to the contribution of members from the literary circles who entered into the film world. They [directors and so on] merely helped a bit with their specialized film knowledge."[46] The director Cheng Bugao was singled out as the most promising and progressive director of the Mingxing company, and one who had connections with literary circles. Another article praised Lianhua for introducing the new subject of the "suffering masses of laborers" in films by directors such as Fei Mu (1906–1951), Bu Wancang, and Cai Chusheng (though neither Fei nor Bu was a leftist). It also praised Mingxing not for its enlightened ideology but for its clever marketing strategy of postponing the premiere of its prized films such as *Xiangcao meiren* (which eventually received a B- rating from the journal *Linglong*) and *Chuncan* ("Spring silkworms," based on Mao Dun's famous story) in the non–air-conditioned Zhongyang Theater until the weather turned cooler in the fall.[47]

Pickowicz has questioned this leftist thesis: he charges that most mainland Chinese film historians have failed "to acknowledge the close connection between the 'May Fourth' films of the thirties and the popular melodramas of the twenties."[48] In fact, he redefines the nature of leftist filmmaking as a "marriage between classic melodrama and elementary Marxism,"[49] by which he means the new subject of the laboring masses and the focused sympathy for it. But the emotional force comes from classic melodrama, which the film theorist Nick Browne considers "the most complex and compelling popular form that embodies the negotiation between the traditional ethical system and the new state ideology, one that articulates the range and force of the emotional contradictions between them."[50] Browne defines melodrama as, among other things, a "theater of social misfortune in which personal virtue is contested, hidden, misrecognized, or subverted, a form of theater that seeks within the confining and largely recalcitrant parameters of the old society to restore and recenter the ethical imperatives required of the bourgeois age."[51] Following Browne, Pickowicz finds in modern Chinese cinema a tradition of melodramatic representation characterized by "rhetorical excess, extravagant representation, and intensity of moral claim"; its purpose "is not to deal with the monotony of everyday life. Rather, it seeks to put an insecure and troubled mass audience in touch with the essential conflict between good and evil that is being played out just below the surface of daily life." Hence, "melodramatic representation was appealing to low-brow, non-intellectual consumers of urban popular culture in the troubled early Republican period because it provided clear answers to nagging questions."[52] This is indeed a much-needed corrective of a long-standing ideological interpretation.

My own argument is obviously closer to Pickowicz's, though I hesitate to use the term "melodrama" to characterize the kinds of materials I have been discussing. In my opinion, while Chinese cinema had indeed improved in quality in the 1930s, thus establishing a firmer foothold among the urban audiences and becoming more competitive with Western films, it certainly did not owe its popularity entirely to the influence of the leftist literary movement. From Xia Yan's memoirs we learn that he was in fact *invited* by the manager of the Mingxing film company to be a "script adviser through a mutual friend.[53] The manager and the veteran film directors at Mingxing—Zhang Shichuan and Zheng Zhengqiu—realized that Japanese aggression in Manchuria and the bombing of Shanghai had created a changed mood among Shanghai audiences, whose newly aroused patriotism lessened their interest in the usual sword flicks and ethical-sentimental films. This patriotic feeling made it possible for the leftist intellectuals to gain a foothold in the film world. But they made their inroads initially through journalism—that is to say, by publishing a massive amount of film criticism in the film supplement pages of all the leading newspapers—before their own written scripts began to make any headway. In other words, they were able to manipulate consciously the existing structure of the urban "print public sphere" in the same way that other journalists and publicists had done to help promote and shape audience interest. This linkage of the two media—print and film—worked to their advantage, because the major figures—Xia Yan, Tian Han, Yang Hansheng—were all writers and dramatists from a *huaju* (spoken drama) background. Their initial advisory role was, in fact, to "write up" the rather rudimentary scenarios (*mubiao*) used by directors into more elaborate scene-by-scene film scripts.[54]

Furthermore, according to Xia Yan's memoirs, the leftist screenwriters *refrained from* imposing their own ideological opinion on the directors they worked with. Instead they were quite respectful of the director's intentions when they wrote their scripts, and eventually developed friendships while working together. This is how the director Cheng Bugao gradually became more "progressive" in his thinking. The directors in turn were delighted by the "higher quality" of the stories, in which some leftist ideas—"elementary Marxism" in Pickowicz's words—managed to "seep in" without their notice.[55] Thus it can be said that the leftist scriptwriters managed to tap into the anxieties of the Chinese audience not by injecting any blatant political ideology into their screenplays (censorship made this impossible) but by employing a new narrative mode: the depiction of petty city dwellers living in limited urban space as a mirror of social hierarchy and the thematic trope of city and country as contrasting worlds of evil and good. In this new narrative structure, the city—a projection of Shanghai—took on increasingly darkened colors and negative tones, whereas the countryside became the idealized "other" to this urban mode of cinematic self-reflexivity. In short, film stories began to incorporate and foreground the experiences of the ordinary men and women of rural origin or character who were increasingly victimized in the urban environment.

As we read the published film scripts, some of them read like short stories: the literary quality seems obvious. I have argued elsewhere that the descriptive verbiage of these scripts is "rich in plot and characterization but rather sparing in what might be construed as montage sequences."[56] While the script provides a film's content, it is the montage sequences and other formal qualities that constitute the *visual* style of the film itself. Here I would argue that regardless of their ideological background, most Chinese film directors, with a few notable exceptions, came to share a basic technical "language" of Chinese filmmaking that had evolved through both imitation and innovation. What, then, constitutes this basic cinematic language, and what is its relationship to the viewing habits of the film audience? Once we enter into such a discourse, the issues become complicated indeed. The remarks that follow are made in the spirit of a preliminary exploration.

One film theorist from Hong Kong, the late Lin Niantong, has characterized this native film language as a combination of two separate principles of film aesthetics—the "montage" and the "long take"—the former derived from Soviet, the latter from French and American traditions of filmmaking. According to Lin, the principle of the long take tends to emphasize continuous sequentiality of time and contiguity of space, whereas the montage principle of composition is built on discontinuous and noncontiguous shots, thus emphasizing conflict and tension. The technique of "long take, deep focus" is often composed of medium and long shots which encompass greater space and longer temporal duration, so that, on the one hand, it can put human beings in a larger environment and create a unity among them while, on the other hand, manifesting their contradictions in the same time and space.[57] I have described this cinematic technique as used in Chinese filmmaking as "a direct transposition from the convention of spoken drama" in order to "serve as its cinematic equivalent."[58] I now realize that this assertion needs some further "renegotiation" in light of Lin's theoretical ideas.

In her book *Babel and Babylon*, Miriam Hansen argues that classical Hollywood "offered its viewer an ideal vantage point from which to witness a scene, unseen by anyone belonging to the fictional world of the film, the diegesis."[59] In spite of its claim to reflect "reality," the Hollywood feature film creates a self-contained world, an *illusion* of reality, which exerts a spell on the audience over the duration of its screening. Toward that goal, "the resources of cinematic discourse, of framing, editing, and mise-en-scène, were increasingly integrated with the task of narration."[60] This "diegetic" process is intended to achieve the desired effect of naturalness: "The camera must be made to see, as with the eyes of the spectators . . . all that takes place, but that which the camera sees and records should appear truthful and natural and should not bear on its face the stamp of counterfeit."[61] It seems that this was precisely the "realistic" effect that Chinese film writers and directors, particularly leftists, wished to achieve. At the same time, however, compared to Hollywood products since Griffith, Chinese films fell far short of achieving a total diegetic effect, for obvious institutional reasons. For one thing, classic Hollywood cinema cannot be said to stem from the "long take" tradition alone.[62] The film scholar Noël Burch has remarked that its diegetic effect centers on the basic principle of "shot-counter-shot: the absence/presence of the spectator at the very centre of the diegetic process," whereby "the spectator becomes the invisible mediator between two gazes, two discourses which envelop him/her, positioned thus as the ideal, invisible voyeur."[63] The basic shot-counter-shot unit depends on a large number of camera shots—long and medium shots and close-ups—in order to manipulate audience reaction. Owing to their limited budgets, Chinese filmmakers simply could not afford to produce such elaborate film footage. Still, when we look at Chinese films made in the 1930s, it is difficult *not* to see ample traces of Hollywood influence, since Hollywood films dominated the film market in Shanghai, and Chinese filmmakers (especially from the *xiren* background) had nowhere else to go for inspiration. They simply imitated the acting styles and lighting design as well as the camera movements of Hollywood pictures. Even some of their film plots were adaptations of foreign films.

At the same time, however, some Chinese film scholars, following Lin Niantong, have taken great pains to establish the theoretical claim that Chinese filmmakers developed their own tradition beyond or despite Hollywood influence. In a learned essay the Hong Kong film scholar Huang Ailing has argued forcefully that the Hollywood-style diegetic effect—in which, by putting the audience's gaze "at the ideal vantage point within narrative space," the camera in fact becomes concealed—was *not* what Chinese filmmakers wanted to achieve. In her opinion, the Chinese directors' penchant for the "long take, deep focus" shots derives essentially from the traditional Chinese aesthetic principle (for instance, in classical painting) which does not place the viewer in any ideal vantage point but rather gives a prominent role to space itself. Hence, "Chinese filmmakers have a strong desire to maintain the distance between the audience and the drama [inside the film], and to destroy the illusion of reality represented on the screen."[64] Following Lin Niantong, she further points out that Chinese filmmakers were quite aware of the Soviet theory of montage; in fact, Tian Han had premiered Eisenstein's film *Battleship Potemkin* in 1926, and Xia Yan and Zheng Boqi had translated essays by V. I. Pudovkin (1893–1953). They considered this theory progressive, but still they preferred to use long takes to maintain a sense of spatial and temporal continuity. Thus, they tried to achieve their montage effect through other means within a general frame of contiguity.[65]

This is indeed a powerful nationalistic thesis. In my view, however, Huang seems to have given too much credit to the ingenuity and originality of Chinese film directors, as if they knew exactly what their choices were aesthetically and technically. She does not seek to explain why montage sequences are used so sparingly in the slow, even leisurely rhythm of the film's narrative passages. Nor does she say anything about film acting, perhaps because it is not crucial to any consideration of film aesthetics. In my view, the narrative weight of Chinese films is carrried, to a large extent, by acting and other aspects which film theorists tend to dismiss as irrelevant to the formal quality of film.

By far the most insightful study of leftist filmmaking is by the mainland film scholar Ma Ning, whose article 'The Textual and Critical Difference of Being Radical: Reconstructing Chinese Leftist Films of the 1930s" itself makes a "radical" argument against previous interpretations. Through a close reading of the film *Malu tianshi* (Street Angel, 1937), Ma argues that the leftist mode of filmmaking is influenced by Hollywood melodrama but goes beyond it, as it contains "extra-diegetic instrusions and explicit social references."[66] Moreover, it incorporates two different discourses—what Ma calls the "journalistic" and the "popular":

The journalistic discourse in these films in the form of news items such as newspaper headlines and historical footage, because of its quasi-objective nature and its emphasis on individual rights and the supremacy of law, can be identified as that of the Chinese bourgeoisie. On the other hand, popular discourse manifests itself in such cultural forms as folk songs, shadow plays, word-plays and magic shows that can be seen as proletarian because of its collective nature and its appeal to radical actions.[67]

It is these native, extrinsic elements that, in Ma's view, transform the Hollywood conventions and help provide "a larger system of intelligibility that gives the text its allegorical structure." In one sense, one could draw a class distinction between "bourgeois" and "proletarian" tastes. But these native tastes were often mixed up in the lifestyle of the urban spectators of the period. In my view, Ma's argument could be seen as confirming the linkage between the genres of written, oral, and film culture, which combined to condition popular tastes. In particular, the insertion of newspaper headlines into the film narrative, as in *Street Angel*, further betrays the leftist filmmaker's background in print culture. (Lu Xun plays a similar game of distrust of news reporting in his many miscellaneous essays, or *zawen*, written at the time.) It must also be noted, however, that for all the brilliance of their cinematic technique, Chinese films of the 1930s—leftist or not—continued to emphasize the development of plot, a feature they share in common with popular fiction of the time. What Ma calls the "proletarian" elements of folksinging and the like further reinforce the impression that certain scenes are "staged"—hence the foregrounding of acting.

Three Case Studies

The primary "text" for Ma's argument is *Street Angel*, directed by Yuan Muzhi, which was based on an American film of the same name (1928).[68] Jay Leyda also gives high praise to this film classic: "Regardless of its source, Yuan made the film in his own style, with sharply incised characters, spare dialogue, an always alert use of sound, and story points indicated in gesture or camera movement; the film opens with a long camera movement, from the highest roofs of Shanghai to the cluttered surfaces of a canal."[69] The film, in fact, begins with a very fast-paced montage sequence of the city with shots of the Shanghai skyscrapers from extreme angles, streets crowded with automobiles and streetcars, and flashes of the neon signs of the entertainment quarters, especially the cafés and dance halls. Moreover, in this brilliant sequence Ma counts a total of fifty-two shots, of which thirty-six, however, contain onlookers who are seen as passive, a reminder of Lu Xun's famous critique of the Chinese crowd. By contrast, the central characters, in Ma's view, are given privileged visions which entitle the spectator to embrace this sequence of the urban spectacle as "a metaphorically forced coupling of Chinese feudalism and foreign powers."[70] Still, however brilliant these establishing shots may be, when the main story unfolds, the film shifts to a different, more "realistic" mode, consisting of a series of largely interior sequences in which comic and sentimental encounters followed by episodes of hardship, victimization, and suffering are played out, leading to the final denouement. Interestingly, the narrative tempo slows down considerably, dragging the sentimental plot to a close.

Of course, as latter-day spectators used to speedier rhythms, we cannot fully replicate the viewing habits of contemporary audiences, who may well have been drawn to the story's sentimental plot precisely by its slow tempo. It would be intriguing to compare the narrative devices and rhythms of *Street Angel* with the original Hollywod version on which it was based. Does the Hollywood version likewise contain singing? Whereas singing, dancing, and comedy had become integral components of the Hollywood musical (as in Busby Berkeley spectaculars and the early films starring Fred Astaire), Chinese films of that period featured hardly any dance sequences. Singing, however, had become quite popular not only in Shanghai nightclubs but also on the burgeoning radio programs. Thus it had become not so much a "proletarian" form, such as native folk song, as a modern form of urban entertainment.

The Chinese sound film therefore incorporated this popular practice and created the singing actresses Zhou Xuan and Bai Guang as well as the convention of film songs. In *Street Angel,* the plot progression literally stops when Zhou Xuan is singing, a practice also found in countless Hollywood musicals; but generically this film is not a musical or a comedy but a social-ethical drama with comic touches, provided mainly by Zhao Dan and the ensemble acting of other performers. Thus, the Chinese film does not strictly follow the established conventions of the Hollywood genre film (e.g., the musical, the slapstick comedy, the western, film noir, and so on) but rather uses some of its generic devices for its own purposes. We can conclude therefore that contemporary Chinese audiences may not have expected from the Chinese films the same kind of smooth, natural rhythm of diegesis characteristic of Hollywood movies. The narrative tempo fluctuates precisely because the Chinese film is made to contain diverse elements from different film and cultural genres.

The slow tempo also marks the speech pattern of the actors and actresses, some of whom enunciate their words in imperfect Mandarin. By present-day standards their acting style seems overdone, with exaggerated facial expressions and gestures reminiscent of Hollywood stars of the silent film era. I would maintain, nonetheless, that such an acting style shows traces of spoken drama. But another source of inspiration may have been foreign silent films, including works of German expressionism such as Fritz Lang's *Metropolis,* which were shown in Shanghai. One clear debt to German expressionism can be found in the close-ups of faces lit from below, often to punctuate a character or an act of villainy.

When we look at another film, *Taoli jie* (Plunder of peach and plum, 1934), in which Yuan Muzhi, who wrote the screenplay, collaborated with director Ying Yunwei, another former actor, the acting almost seems to carry the weight of the entire film. This may not be the best film produced in the 1930s, but it is representative in many ways in terms of its thematic content (the story of a well-educated intellectual couple forced by the urban environment into poverty and theft). Interestingly, we find a contemporary evaluation of Ying Yunwei's directorial style by a pair of Western critics, W. H. Auden and Christopher Isherwood, who traveled to Hankow in 1938 and saw the rushes of a war film directed by Ying. "The producer [Ying Yunwei] had an astonishingly subtle feeling for grouping; his weakness lay in the direction of the actors themselves—he had indulged too often the Chinese talent for making faces. All these grimaces of passion, anger, or sorrow, seemed a mere mimicry of the West. One day a director of genius will evolve a style of acting which is more truly national—a style based upon the beauty and dignity of the Chinese face in repose."[71] It is a pity that Auden and Isherwood never saw the work of Fei Mu, particularly his masterpiece, *Xiaocheng zhichun* (Spring in a small town).[72] Still, their comment on acting is relevant, for Ying Yunwei's directorial style is by no means idiosyncratic but is quite characteristic of other directors as well. Whether or not directly influenced by spoken drama, Chinese cinema always foregrounds acting, especially performances by big-name stars with acting talent such as Ruan Lingyu, Zhao Dan, Shi Hui, and others. (Since the 1930s Mingxing and other big companies of the Chinese film industry had gladly adopted the Hollywood star system.)[73]

Approaching the film from a technical angle, Huang Ailing argues that the "tragic power" of *Plunder of Peach and Plum* is derived from "camera movement and the long-take shots in which [the camera] steadily stares at the actors."[74] Why does the camera "stare at" the actors all the time? Huang's theory gives exclusive attention to the role of the camera in its "relentless siege of the downtrodden characters." At the beginning of the film, the camera in a "marvelous long take" introduces the protagonist as it follows the school principal and the three prison guards to locate him in a corner of his cell, his back to the camera. Thus begins the story, told in flashback. Huang also discusses a crucial scene in which the protagonist's wife, physically weak after childbirth, carrying a bucket of water up the stairs. She mounts toward the camera, her face distorted as she comes near, and tension builds until suddenly she falls down the stairs and faints. Throughout the whole sequence, the camera remains immobile.[75] In her discussion Huang does not comment at all on the acting of Yuan

Muzhi, who plays the intellectual protagonist, and Chen Bo'er, who plays his wife. When seen in isolation—that is, without following the story—the acting, though expressive, confirms Auden and Isherwood's impression, but it takes on an emotional force precisely because, especially in the stairway episode, it is one of the high points of the story, and the lowest point in the life of this couple. In narrative terms, therefore, it seems that Ying Yunwei wants to play up moments of suffering with cinematic flourish in order to accentuate these key points in the film's plot and to heighten their emotional impact on the viewer. Interestingly, because of the emphasis on this melodramatic moment, the film's portrayal of the two protagonists may have departed from the original intention of the script. At least according to one contemporary reviewer, the honest male protagonist, who should have been the central focus of the film but who is not effectively delineated in it, becomes displaced by the suffering wife, whose death is seen by "the innocent audience" as a sacrifice to the stubborn self-righteousness of her husband.[76]

The Role of the Audience

In the 1930s writings about Chinese cinema we find constant references to the audience and its important role in governing the choices—and sometimes the compromises—of the filmmakers. I would like to give two samples from an extensive collection of archival material. First, a confession by Cai Chusheng, director of *Yuguangqu* (Fisherman's song, 1934, now generally acknowledged to be a masterpiece) shortly after the film's first showing:

> Having seen a few films which did not achieve their desired good results, I believe even more firmly that the most fundamental condition of a good film is to make the audience interested. Why is it that some films produced did not achieve perfect results despite the correctness of their ideological tendency? Because they are too boring to draw the audience's interest. Accordingly, in order to make the audience accept the intentions of the author

more easily, we cannot but put a sugar coating on correct ideology . . . Regrettably, few workers and peasants at present have
the opportunity to go to the movies, and the vast majority of the
audience consist of urban residents of the cities.

He apologizes for his film's happily coincidental ending, which compromises his concern for "dramatic quality," but blames it on the fact that
"the general audience love more plot [twists]."[77]

Second, Song Zhidi, another famous leftist script writer, wrote an
article, "Film Appreciation and Audience Psychology," in 1935 in which
he argued, from an audience's point of view, that before making a film, a
director must give careful thought to both the choice of subject matter
and the method of expression:

> The eyes of an average member of the audience are rather
> opaque. We can see only the general contour of an event, and a
> contour is not very exciting and can hardly get our response.
> Therefore, what a film shows to us should and must be those
> parts with the most sharpness hidden within the core of a phe-
> nomenon. The director considers, analyzes, organizes, and then
> uses them in order to stimulate and move us. We are not wooden
> puppets. A direct application of subject matter would be a waste.
> The organization of shots and the editing of "cuts" should be
> simple, clear, and lively [to set] an emotional rhythm that links
> up the whole drama and that controls the pulse of the drama.
> Paying attention only to the emotional linkage between con-
> tiguous shots would still be considered a waste. What is neces-
> sary is not only to sustain the dramatic emotion of the entire film
> but to make it pour out like the torrent of a big river.[78]

What does Song mean by "those parts with the most sharpness"?
And what does he mean by a sustained "emotional rhythm" that pours
out like a river's torrent? The awkwardness of his wording certainly does
not make it any easier to translate his meaning into the language of

present-day film theory. He could be talking about the necessity of montage, a technique that is supposed to sharpen a film's emotional impact; more likely, however, he was talking about a Hollywood type of diegesis—a dramatic rhythm achieved by a judicious application of film "craftsmanship" (jiqiao), which he carefully differentiates from "technique" (jishu), or mechanical condition. When we read Song's statement together with Cai Chusheng's apologia about the necessity of "dramatic quality" but the audience's love of "more plot," it becomes clear that for both directors, film technique (in the nonmechanical sense of the term) is made to serve the dramatic, even melodramatic twists of plot. To the extent that narrativity—the need to tell a story—is still foregrounded in modern Chinese cinema, I would argue that the slow rhythm is maintained precisely to highlight the dramatic moment and to accommodate the audience's demand for "more plot"—to create, in other words, a Chinese-style diegetic effect. It is perhaps in this sense that we can agree with Lin Niantong that Chinese films combine both the montage and long take traditions. But does this mean that they represent a case of pure native originality? Instead of originality, I would opt for a position of stylistic "hybridity" for the following reasons.

First, we must consider the physical conditions of filmmaking in the 1930s. There is moving testimony about the crude conditions of filmmaking from Shen Xiling, director of Shizi jietou (Crossroads, 1937):

> In Chinese cinema there is neither adequate equipment nor sufficient capital, and the entire condition of filmmaking has reached a state of utmost poverty. [Background] music and dialogue cannot be synchronized with each other; to record the sound of a shot you cannot but use several cotton quilts [to muffle the sound of the recording machine]. To make movies under such difficult conditions, we cannot but admit that we really have suffered enough hardship. But even more painful than this is the creative freedom which is denied us. In this treaty port, we cannot utter a single word about recovering the lost

territory; we cannot hang up a map of the Northeast . . . We . . .
I cannot go on; we can only swallow our tears.[79]

Contemporary and latter-day viewers of *Crossroads* may well marvel
at the clever way in which the social and patriotic messages are "sneaked"
into the film via the use of print culture, namely, shots of newspapers
headlines. At the same time, the film tells a story with a romantic plot
twist about how two poor urbanites living in a single rented room separated by a thin wall finally meet each other and fall in love.[80] At the beginning of the film, the credits are superimposed on a montage sequence of
slanting Shanghai skyscrapers shot from extreme low angles and linked
by "wipes." This sequence is subdued in comparison with the beginning of
Street Angel, which is a more surrealistic evocation of the speed, energy, and
decadence of this foreign-flavored metropolitan city.[81] (The city is
evoked in a similar fashion at the beginning of many films of this period.)
Then follow a few stunning exterior shots and close-ups of a man about to
jump into the river—as if lifted from a silent film by Eisenstein. But then
the story settles down to a typical slow narrative rhythm, compounded by
technical problems which fully confirm the director's complaint about
non-synchronicity of dialogue and background music (consisting mostly
of arbitrary chunks of symphonies by Sibelius, Tchaikovsky, and Berlioz,
followed by some badly played cello music). These crudities are compensated for, however, by the inventive use of lighting. Still, the film's dream
sequences of a girl on a swing are clearly borrowed from Hollywood musicals. Needless to say, the acting is in the usual exaggerated style.

As for formal invention, the evidence must be sought in films by
mostly non-leftist directors, some of whom in fact reached unexpected
artistic heights. For instance, Wu Yonggang's silent film, *Shennü* (Goddess) is truly a masterpiece,[82] not only because of Ran Lingyu's remarkable performance but also as a result of the director's creation of a
sustained lyrical mood which reminds this viewer of the works of the
French master Robert Bresson. Even more unusual is Wu's sound film, the
first produced by Lianhua, *Langtaosha* (The desert island, 1936), which

succeeds in conjuring up within its humanistic plot about a criminal and a policeman an almost existential plight when, near the end of the film, both men are stranded on a deserted island. (We must remind ourselves again that Wu Yonggang came from a *xiren* background.) The artistic worth of his work has only recently been given its due by film scholars outside China, in particular Chen Huiyang, who views the film's beginning sequence—a virtuoso display of "framed montage" composed of a series of "scroll shots"—as a kind of formal metaphysics based on traditional Chinese aesthetics and philosophy.[83]

Another exceptional example is Ma Xu Weibang's *Yeban gesheng* (Singing at Midnight, 1937), now acknowledged as "the first Chinese film which was overtly influenced by expressionism."[84] Its first half-hour and the ending, which enclose a plot derived from the Hollywood film *The Phantom of the Opera*, is a masterly adaptation of German expressionist cinema. We can be sure that the film's success at the box office lay not in its implausible and forced political message of patriotism and revolution (in some ways an addition by Tian Han) but rather in the director's unique cinematic vision and craftsmanship as the first "master of the horror film."[85]

These unusual specimens from the burgeoning film industry of the 1930s have given a dimension of stylistic variety to the legacy of Chinese cinema as they enrich its subject matter and content. Still, they have not received all the critical attention they deserve. Neither Wu Yonggang nor Ma Xu Weibang is included in Leyda's list of "Contributors to the Art and History of Chinese Films" appended to his book *Dianying: An Account of Films and the Film Audience in China*. Predictably, both men receive scathing ideological criticism in Cheng Jihua's *Zhongguo dianying fazhan shi* (The development of modern Chinese cinema).[86]

Cinema and the City

In this chapter I have argued that Chinese cinema was a popular hybrid genre consisting of diverse cultural elements—both old and new, drawn from both visual and print sources—which seemed to reflect, or appeal to, the equally mixed composition of its audience in terms of both gender and class. A detailed empirical study of such a sizable filmgoing audience remains to be done and cannot be attempted here. Nevertheless, I would still like to offer a few concluding reflections on the relationship between film spectatorship and the culture of modernity in 1930s Shanghai.

Extending Benjamin's depiction of the *flâneur*, the film scholar Giuliana Bruno has observed that "grounded in seeing, the idler's way of loitering reminds us of the film spectator's"; in fact this "wandering urban spectator, historically eclipsed by the life of the big modern city, is transformed, reinvented, and reinscribed in the figure of the film spectator. The modern *flâneur* is the film spectator. The perfect *flâneur* is the passionate film spectator."[87] She also argues that since "the figure of the *flâneur* is traditionally male, going to the cinema thus "triggered a liberation of the woman's gaze"; and, given the analogy between film viewing and window-shopping, the cinema, like the department store, "provided a form of access to public space, an occasion to socialize and get out of the house," thus "enabling [a woman] to renegotiate, on a new terrain of intersubjectivity, the configuration of private/public."[88] These insights are quite relevant to the Chinese case in Shanghai, just as Naples in the period 1900–1930, the subject of her study, serves as an interesting site for comparison.

In Naples, the central public place that first attracted filmgoers was the city's main arcade, the Galleria Umberto I. The Neapolitans flocked daily to its movie theater, the Salone Margherita, and at the arcade's entrance there were also open-air film screenings.[89] In Shanghai there was no central arcade, and the earliest film screenings at the turn of the century took place in teahouses and amusement parks—even in a skating rink and a restaurant.[90] It would seem that in the beginning this new visual medium shared space with the old forms of popular entertainment. Later on, film began to compete with the traditional stage for popular attention. In his book Leyda quotes an advertisement in *Shenbao* (July 29, 1921) for the opening of the film *Yan Ruisheng* at the Olympic Cinema:

> This *Yan Ruisheng* play, who would not enjoy seeing it?
>
> This thing called shadow play, who would not welcome it?
>
> Whenever the play *Yan Ruisheng* is done on any stage, it always takes a great deal of your time. And you must continue to watch it for two or three nights before you reach the end of it. Each spectator's backside becomes sore and his legs go to sleep painfully even before getting halfway through it. But we now employ the most economical method of presenting this play: with one visit you can see it all. Furthermore, the seats are comfortable, and we are positive that the spectator will sing the praises of all these matters . . .
>
> Our play has ten reels. We invested six months of effort and tens of thousands of yuan. It represented the crystallization of more than a hundred people's hard work, and the acting stars are youths who enjoyed an advanced education . . .
>
> All settings . . . were real and filmed in their real places, and cannot be compared with painted backdrops.[91]

This is a most revealing advertisement. The design around the edge contains the term *yingxi*—literally, "shadow play," the earliest Chinese term for movies—which clearly shows the generic connection of film with the traditional *piyingxi*, or shadow puppet plays. We know from other sources that this particular film was based on a "civilized play" (*wenming xi*), which was itself based on a scandal involving a comprador named Yan Ruisheng who killed a prostitute for her money. The film was made in 1920 by the China Film Study Society (Zhongguo yingxi yanjiu she) on a rented lot owned by the Commercial Press and shown at a rented theater, Olympic Cinema, owned by a Spanish businessman, Antonio Ramos, whose company controlled half of Shanghai's cinemas.[92] As the advertisement indicates, what made a real difference between film and stage play was precisely the theater in which it was shown, the former affording more comfort for the spectators. The ad makes no specific reference to the film medium itself except to claim that it is the most "economical" (it saves the spectator's time) and that "all settings were real and filmed in their real places." It then proceeds to name several real public places such as Baihuali (Hundred flowers house) and Fuyuli (Wealth and fortune house)—most likely courtesan houses—the Wang Dechang teashop, the racecourse, the Yipingxiang restaurant, the Xuzhou Railway Station, and the Longhua garrison quarters. The appeal behind all these real sites, it would seem, lies not only in the film's ability to capture them in celluloid, like photography, but also in its linkage between the private and the public, the ability to bring the outside world onto the theater's screen or to transport the individual viewer from inside the theater to outside. In either case the film's diegetic effect is not emphasized, nor is there any mention of the more private psychological relationship between the film and the film viewer, as some Western theoritsts would lead us to believe. The early movie theater in Shanghai was itself a communal setting in which the spectators celebrated the wonders of their shared public space, the city, and most likely their viewing habits were not so different from the act of watching a local opera; a truly *private* experience of watching a film in the dark was not yet possible in these early years.

Later on, it was the architecture of Shanghai's newly built movie palaces, together with their marble-floored lobbies and Art Deco design, not to mention the comforable seats, that became the "spectacle," dazzling the eyes and senses of the spectators, a world unlike anything they had experienced before, either in public or in private. This novel public setting added immeasurably to the enjoyment of the films themselves. Moviegoing in Shanghai, therefore, had become a new social ritual of *going* to the movie house—for both male and female Shanghai residents. As I mentioned earlier, the movie palaces for first-run foreign films were all located in the Western concessions; the second-run movie theaters and theaters showing Chinese films were often situated in the Japanese "concession" in the north. Whereas foreigners seldom set foot in the second-run theaters, Chinese moviegoers thronged *all* the theaters.[93] Thus, despite the conspicuous hierarchy of the theaters' standing, the increasing popularity of moviegoing for Chinese audiences in the 1930s can be seen as both a case of boundary-crossing and an illustration of the native appropriation of the urban public space that was initially demarcated along colonial lines between the foreign concessions and the native city.[94]

"As a tactile appropriation of space, in a public building," Bruno argues, "film reception is related once more to the perception and reception of arcades and their cafés, to railway terminals and their arriving trains."[95] To these urban public sites of modernity can also be added the department store, in the sense that film spectatorship can be likened to a form of window-shopping.[96] In other words, moviegoing had become part and parcel of the modern way of life in the metropolis. Can we then infer that the Chinese audience in Shanghai's movie theaters would have reacted to what was shown on the screen in the same way as audiences in Naples, Paris, or New York? I have argued that Chinese audience responses may have been mediated by the kinds of reading habits nurtured by print culture. So too could we find certain similarities in Bruno's portrait of audience reception of early Italian films, particularly those by the woman director Elvira Notari. In both cases the early films tended to draw on popular journalistic sources. The differences may lie in the process of accommodation and appropriation, in the ways in which native spectators negotiated the distance between their own viewing positions and the "foreignness" of the experience itself—the product, the theater, and the location—since most foreign films were shown in the foreign concessions. (The comparable case in Naples, clearly absent, would have been watching American films in a theater located in an exclusively American "concession.")

It is all the more remarkable that Chinese audiences in Shanghai were able to overcome this triple barrier and appropriated film and filmgoing as a new habit and hobby of their own. This process of appropriation, as evidenced in the Chinese filmmakers' unabashed borrowing from Hollywood films, did not produce the effect of colonial mimicry but rather resulted in varying degrees of "Sinicization"—from "misreadings" of narrative affinities (as in melodramatic formulas) to print-mediated "rewritings" in the form of plot sheets and fan magazine articles that reinscribed a Chinese set of values onto the foreign films themselves. Without such a background, native Chinese cinema could never have been established. If print culture served as a crucial aid in this process of appropriating visuality, the popularity of this visual medium soon triggered a reverse process—of the visual entering into the written and of film providing the key source for fictional technique. Needless to add, the writers who specialized in such new cinematic modes of fiction writing—Liu Na'ou and Mu Shiying in particular—were themselves avid film spectators.

TEXTUAL TRANSACTIONS:

DISCOVERING LITERARY MODERNISM

THROUGH BOOKS AND JOURNALS

For Shanghai writers the most important pastime, aside from going to the movies, was going to the bookstores. Here Shanghai's urban space offered a unique opportunity: more than 80 percent of the Chinese bookstores were concentrated in one area, the two or three blocks north and south of Fuzhou (Foochow) Road, also known as Simalu (Fourth Avenue), which had long been called *wenhua jie*—street of culture. By January 28, 1932, when the Japanese suddenly bombed Shanghai, there were more than three hundred bookstores selling new and used books.[1] The two largest were the Commercial Press and the Zhonghua Bookstore, whose office buildings faced each other at the intersection of Fuzhou and Henan roads; the stores were locked in fierce competition,[2] very much like the Sincere and Wing On department stores on Nanking Road. Nearby were many smaller bookstores, some that enjoyed great fame by their association with New Literature journals and writers: Qunyi, which first published *New Youth*, edited by Chen Duxiu; Beixin, publisher of Lu Xun's works; Kaiming, noted for its textbooks for young readers; Shenghuo, known for its progressive journal of the same name edited by Zou Daofen; and Xiandai, which sponsored Shi Zhecun's *Xiandai zazhi,* or *Les contemporains,* and Ye Lingfeng's *Xiandai xiaoshuo* (Modern fiction). The list of bookstore-sponsored journals is even longer if we include the well-known *Dongfang zazhi* (Eastern miscellany) and *Xiaoshuo yuebao* (Short story monthly) published by the Commercial Press; *Liangyou huabao* (The young companion), published by the Liangyou Book Company; *Xinyue* (Crescent moon), published by Xinyue shudian; *Yusi* (Thread of talk) from Beixin; and Shao Xunmei's fanciful Jinwu shuwu (La Maison d'or), which published his *Jinwu yuekan* (House of gold monthly), itself modeled after the *Yellow Book* of the Bloomsbury group in England; not to mention an amazing number of pictorials, women's journals, and movie magazines. One bookstore, Shanghai shudian, boasted in the mid-1930s some thirty journals, publishing an average of one journal per day!

In the same area around Fuzhou Road were also located some of the established traditional stationery stores, old restaurants and teahouses, hotels, and brothels. Extending southward to the Old City area, this was the "life-world" of the litterateur-journalists of the so-called Mandarin Ducks and Butterflies school—men such as Bao Tianxiao, Di Chuqing, Chen Dieyi, and Zhou Shoujuan—whose leisure activities revolved around bookstores, teahouses, and brothels. The sight of horse-drawn carriages carrying famed courtesans on their way to meet clients for dinner at restaurants was a fixture of this old world landscape until the 1920s, when motor cars and movie stars began to steal the spotlight. Although the shift of commercial prosperity from Fourth to First Avenue became inevitable, this apparently did not eclipse the reputation of Fuzhou Road as one of the areas most frequented by the new-style writers and modernists. The poet Xu Chi recalled with fondness how as a novice writer he was taken by Shi Zhecun to make the rounds of bookstores, first to the Zhonghua Bookstore and the Commercial Press (with its own library of foreign books) and then to Kelly & Walsh and the Sino-American Bookstore on Nanking Road, followed by afternoon tea.[3] It was an almost daily routine for many other writers as well. In the

Chinese bookstores they were able to locate not only most of the recently published works and translations by their fellow writers, but also recent issues of journals published by the bookstores themselves. In the Western bookstores on nearby Nanking Road, they could purchase foreign language books or order them c.o.d. Moreover, as Shi Zhecun told me during several interviews, copies of Western-language books, mostly fiction, were also readily available at a number of used bookstores and bookstalls: some of these were the shipboard reading material of foreign tourists who dumped them as they came ashore in Shanghai. In one such bookstore Shi was lucky enough to obtain a complete edition of Baudelaire's poetry.[4]

It was in this bookish milieu that Western literature—the texts of Western modernism in all their "materiality"—was assimilated and reproduced in Shanghai's literary scene. Scholars doing "influence studies" of Western authors or works on modern Chinese literature normally choose to ignore this material context of how works by Western authors, whether in book form or included in journals, were actually located, read, translated or rendered into Chinese in some fashion, and consequently assimilated by the Chinese writers into *their* writing. This complex process of textual transaction unveils another facet of Shanghai's emerging modern culture; in a way, it also helped to produce that new culture.

Entering a "Brave New World" through Books and Journals

Xu Chi's memoirs offer a most vivid testimony to the power and allure of this urban world of books and journals. As a student at Yenching University, he befriended the chairwoman of the English Department, who gave him four issues (1932–33) of the American literary quarterly *Hound and Horn*, which truly opened his eyes:

> It unfolded a brave new world of world literature and a brand-new spirit—I came directly into contact with the original texts of the modernist school of literature and art of the 1930s. In one

issue there were a number of sketches . . . I can't remember by which masters of art, possibly Matisse or Henry Moore. Their lines were gorgeous—such big legs and big hips, the distorted beauty of the human body. They left me, this latter-day youth who came to the capital from a small town in Jiangnan, dumbfounded . . . The expressive form was so novel that I had never seen or heard of it before. That the world should have produced such daring, but never obscene, sketches of nudity, such a beautiful and sexy trend of art!

In another issue of *Hound and Horn* (Spring 1932) he found Gertrude Stein's "Scenery and George Washington." Although he translated it, he still found it incomprehensible, but "it gave me a sense of beauty, of appreciation, and a kind of enjoyment."[5] This singular journal had become Xu's primer on modernism.

Xu never finished his studies at Yenching, although he seems to have taken full advantage of its excellent faculty in English literature and listened to lectures by George K. C. Yeh (later a well-known diplomat) on T. S. Eliot's long poem *The Wasteland*. After he returned south to find a teaching job near Shanghai, he used his first month's salary (15 yuan) to order c.o.d. from the Sino-American Bookstore a copy of Eliot's essays, which cost 12 shillings and 6 pence (1 pound sterling was equivalent to 18 yuan, or U.S. $5.00; thus U.S. $1 was about 3.6 yuan).[6] The first essay he read in the book was Eliot's "Tradition and Individual Talent." In addition, Xu also patronized the British publisher Kelly & Walsh, which had five branch offices in Asia (in Shanghai, Hong Kong, Hankow, Singapore, and Yokohama), the foreign books section of the Commercial Press, as well as the library at Soochow University, where he taught, and private collections of his friends. When the poet Dai Wangshu, one of his esteemed friends, returned from France in 1935, he apparently brought back thousands of books in French and Spanish. Another friend, the rich dandy Shao Xunmei, also had a private collection of Western-language books which he freely shared with his coterie of writers and artists. It is of course impossible now to trace the titles in their collections, but a fortuitous encounter with a bookseller in Shanghai in 1994 allowed me to buy a small number (about thirty) of Shi Zhecun's large collection of Western-language books which he had accumulated over the years. They not only gave me a solid grasp of the circumstances of Shi's book-buying ventures but also helped me establish a direct, albeit partial and limited, connection between the accessibility and the "reproduction" of Western literary materials: that is to say, on the basis of an examination of these books in Shi's possession, I am prepared to argue not only that Shi's literary imagination was fired by the books he bought and read, but also that he liberally quoted them in his own creative writings. Shi's case in turn may throw some new light on the textual connections between Chinese and Western modernisms.

Most of Shi's Western books are in English and French, published in London, New York, and Paris. Some of them were used books when Shi first purchased them at bookstores such as the Great China Second-Hand Bookstore, 429 Kiukiang Road, no. 116–117 (the address is stamped on the back cover). Some of them were gifts from one foreigner to another, as evidenced in the inscriptions by the original donor: for instance, "To My Dear Cousin, Ezra, from Tom, 3/13/23," on the cover page of *Afternoon* by Émile Verhaeren, as translated by Charles R. Murphy (1917). Many of Shi's new books were from the Modern Library editions published by Macmillan in New York. Shi told me that they provided him with a key source of modern classics at prices he could afford. An advertisement on the back of the dust jacket of one such book announces: "The Modern Library series consists today of 245 books. It includes at least one representative work by almost every modern author of first rank. It is prominently displayed by every bookstore in the United States and Canada, and has authorized agents in every corner of the world where English books are read."[7] Two such agents were surely the Sino-American Bookstore and Kelly & Walsh in Shanghai. But Shi also bought other valuable books, new or used, as published by prestigious presses such as Faber and Faber in London and Gallimard of Paris:

for instance, *Poems, 1909–1925* by T. S. Eliot; *Selected Poems* by W. H. Auden (1938); *Les Poèmes d'Edgar Poe*, translated by Stéphane Mallarmé (1928); and *L'Amour la poésie* by Paul Éluard (1929). Shi's great interest in Havelock Ellis may have originated with a book of his *Selected Essays* (Everyman's Library, 1936). By another of Shi's favorite authors, Arthur Schnitzler, I found two works in German—*Fräulein Else* (Miss Elsa, 1926) and *Leutnant Gustl* (Lieutenant Gustl, 1919)—and one in English translation, *Daybreak* (1927). Shi must have possessed other books by this Austrian author, some of which he translated into Chinese.

These examples are meant to suggest that, given Shanghai's resources, it was possible not only to find up-to-date editions of Western literary works in their original languages and/or in English translation but also for a literary editor such as Shi Zhecun to build up his personal collection of selected titles. Shi adopted the traditional Chinese custom of affixing his own name seal on the front pages of his foreign books and later designed his own bookplates in Chinese and Latin: "Ex Libris C. Z. Sze." One can well imagine how, with the aid of Chinese-English or Chinese-French dictionaries, he struggled to make some sense of the originals from which he gradually developed his own taste in Western modernist literature. When I asked how he learned to read in French and English, Shi regaled me with an interesting anecdote about how, as students at the Catholic Aurora University in Shanghai's French Concession, he and Dai Wangshu were taught French by the priests from the "morally uplifting" works of Hugo and Balzac, while they secretly devoured the "immoral" and decadent works of Baudelaire, Verlaine, and Rimbaud—and thus they learned to love French symbolist poetry. Of course they first had to master a few grammar books: the most popular in English was the *English Grammar Series for Chinese Readers* by J. C. Nesfield, a common text adapted from British colonial textbooks in India and published by Macmillan in London (with branch offices in Bombay, Calcutta, and Madras).[8] A comparable French grammar book, *Grammaire française élémentaire à usage des élèves chinois*, by Le P. L. Tsang, S. J., was printed in 1924 (the seventh edition) by the "imprimerie de la mission catholique à l'orphelinat de T'ou Se-We," a Catholic mission in Shanghai's Xujiahui district.[9] In this bilingual grammar book, the Chinese sentences and explanations are written in the classical (*wenyan*) style.

A more significant source of information about Western literature was the literary journals. Both Shi Zhecun and Xu Chi told me in interviews that they had read or gained access to journals such as *Vanity Fair, Esquire,* the *New Yorker, Harper's, Saturday Review, Saturday Evening Post,* (all American), *Living Age, The Dial, The Criterion* (British), and *The Bookman* (both British and American); newspapers such as the *New York Times, The Times of London, Le Monde, L'Humanité,* and *Lettre française* (a weekly)—not to mention Shanghai's own English-language newspapers such as the *North China Herald,* the *North China Daily News,* and the *Shanghai Evening Post and Mercury.* While readers in America might treat a copy of *Vanity Fair* or the *New Yorker* as casual reading matter, Chinese readers in Shanghai in the 1930s did not take them so lightly, because these journals provided for them a window on Western literature, art design, and a sophisticated urban lifestyle. The more highbrow journals—*The Criterion, The Bookman, The Dial*—carried articles, poetry, and reviews of high literary quality. After all, Eliot's *Wasteland* first appeared in the inaugural issue (October 1922) of *The Criterion,* a journal he edited for seventeen years. The managing editor of *The Dial* was the poet Marianne Moore, and included in its contents were copious book reviews and poetry by notables such as Ezra Pound, D. H. Lawrence, Paul Valéry, Kenneth Burke, and Yvor Winters (a sampling just for the year 1929). Aside from the modern art of Matisse and Henry Moore which so excited Xu Chi, it also published the poetry of Eliot and e. e. cummings, among many others.

There were two different journals called *The Bookman* (published in England and America, with the American one more intellectually highbrow than the British); most likely both were available in Shanghai. If Shi had indeed glanced through their contents for 1929–30, he would have found an article by G. K. Chesterton, "Magic and Fantasy in Fiction," in the March 1930 issue of the American journal and Edgar Wallace's "Magic, Ghosts, Detectives, and the Mysterious in Literature" in the

1929 Christmas number of the British journal. These may have inspired him to experiment with magic and mystery in his own fiction (see Chapter 5). And to trace a further literary connection, one of the favorite authors of the Chinese neo-sensationalists, the French writer Paul Morand, whom Liu Na'ou first introduced from Japan, was also a regular contributor to *Vanity Fair*—surely the most glamorous of the glossy journals and Shi's personal favorite.[10] That Morand's exotic travel notes and stories (including one set in "mysterious China") found their way into the pages of *Vanity Fair* only added to the special appeal of this New York–based magazine for its Chinese readers in Shanghai. *Vanity Fair* devoted a good deal of space to commentary on literature, theater, and cinema, and the magazine's Art Deco design conjured up the sophisticated lifestyle of the "smart set" of New York urbanites with its goal of portraying "the brighter side of life" following the gloom of the Great Depression in 1931. Its many advertisements for clothing, perfume, jewelry, hotels, and automobiles displayed precisely those fabled goods which constituted the *modeng* image which wealthy urbanites in Shanghai sought to emulate.

It was probably from these periodicals, plus whatever books he could afford to buy, that Xu Chi was able to gain access to works such as Hemingway's *A Farewell to Arms*, which he translated (at a time when Hemingway was known to only a few writers in China, such as Xu and Ye Lingfeng), and to authors such as Ezra Pound, Amy Lowell, H.D. (Hilda Doolittle, whom Shi translated), and many others.[11] In *The Bookman*, Xu found an article about the Turkish poet Nazim Hikmet and wrote his own article based on it, which was half translation and half rewriting—a common practice among Shanghai writers—and contributed it to the special issue (June 1934, "Literature of Weak and Oppressed Peoples") of the journal *Maodun* (Contradiction).[12] During my interviews with him, he gave an impressive list of writers and artists he had known about and liked as a "young man of twenty" (the title of his first collection of poetry), including James Joyce (*Dubliners*, *Portrait of the Artist as a Young Man*), William Saroyan, John Dos Passos, Waldo Frank, Edgar Lee Masters, e. e. cummings, A. E. Houseman, Louis Aragon, Paul Éluard, Pablo Neruda, Rainer Maria Rilke, Sigmund Freud, and Havelock Ellis.

For Xu's mentor Shi Zhecun, the list is even longer, as gathered from my interviews and from the books in his possession. Shi showed a particular penchant for authors and works with a surrealistic and supernatural imprint—what he called the grotesque, the erotic, *magie noir* (black magic): Edgar Allan Poe, Barbey d'Aurevilly, W. B. Yeats, Fiona McLeod, J. Sheridan LeFanu, James Frazer, Arthur Schnitzler (Shi translated his *Frau Beatrice und ihr Sohn* (Mrs. Beatrice and her son), *Fräulein Else,* and *Bertha Galan* from English—as he knew no German—into a trilogy about women, plus two other works, *Leutnant Gustl* and *Theresa*), Thomas De Quincey ("Confessions of an English Opium Eater"), and the marquis de Sade (under whose spell Shi rewrote a chapter of the classical novel *Shuihu zhuan,* or *Men of the Marshes,* into a sadistic story of misogyny). Shi and his former classmate Dai Wangshu, who spent some time in Europe and knew both French and Spanish fairly well, translated a sizable number of modern poets from the two countries: Victor Hugo, Paul Verlaine, Rémy de Gourmont, Paul Fort, Francis Jammes, Pierre Reverdy, Jules Supervielle, Paul Valéry, Guillaume Apollinaire, Paul Éluard, and Charles Baudelaire (selections from *Les Fleurs du mal*) from France; and Pedro Salinas, Gerard Diego, Rafael Alberti, Manuel Altolaguirre, Vicente Aleixandre, and Federico Garcia Lorca, as well as some folk songs from the Spanish civil war.[13] If we check into the personal library of Shao Xunmei, who came from a wealthy family background, the hoard of Western books and authors is even more impressive, including Sappho, Baudelaire (he translated parts of *Les Fleurs du mal,* which in turn served as a model for one of his own poetry collections), Swinburne, Beardsley, and the entire Bloomsbury group.

The listings of names and titles, of course, do not tell the full story. Did the Shanghai writers read all of them, or did they merely use them to boast of their knowledge? How accurate were their translations—or did they revise, condense, and rewrite in the name of translation? In the literary scene of the 1930s, debates over errors of translation were heated and legion among such self-styled authorities as Zhao Jingshen, Shao Xunmei, Ye Lingfeng, and Zhang Ruogu, not to mention the members of the combative Creation Society—Guo Moruo, Yu Dafu, Qian Xing-cun—and the leftist camps of Lu Xun and his protégés and enemies, who retranslated Soviet revolutionary theory via Japanese translations. Shi Zhecun divided Shanghai's new writers into three main groups in accordance with their educational background: the English-language group (those educated in England, America, or the prestigous missionary universities of Yenching, Tsinghua, or St. John's); the French-German language group (those, like Shi himself, educated at Catholic universities such as Aurora in Shanghai—more French than German—or those who, like Dai Wangshu, had studied or wandered around in Europe); and the Japanese-language group (mainly leftists such as Lu Xun, Feng Xuefeng, and many others who had studied in Japan).[14] Thus the debates among them were as much a feud over their command of Western languages as a peer clash between different sources of "cultural capital." Still, for our purposes, the constant nitpicking about a name or term (e.g., over whether Manon's brother should be called Lescaut) reveals a genuine fascination with a large corpus of foreign literature to which they all wished to gain direct access and for which they served as China's leading spokesmen. Those who were capable or lucky might correspond with their favorite foreign writers and show off their own translations of their idol's letters. Others met foreign writers in person, as the foreigners traveled as tourists to Shanghai: Lu Xun's grudging portrait of G. B. Shaw is a classic example, but Shaw also met Lin Yutang, Shao Xunmei, and several other writers and celebrities, including Song Qingling (Madam Sun Yat-sen) and Cai Yuanpei. In fact, there was a steady stream of foreign writer-tourists to Shanghai in the 1930s, such as Eugene O'Neill, Noël Coward (who came down with the flu and wrote a play in the famous Cathay Hotel), W. H. Auden, Christopher Isherwood, Paul Mo-rand, and Boris Pilnyak, as well as the movie stars Charlie Chaplin and Mary Pickford,[15] not to mention a large number of writers from nearby Japan (Yokomitsu Reichi, Sato Haruo, and others). The traffic of literary tourism remains to be fully studied, for its impact on Shanghai's literary scene was by no means negligible.

With this background of a thriving urban book trade and easy access to foreign books and journals, it is only natural that most Chinese writers, Shi Zhecun and his friends included, wanted to try their own hand at "doing" literature. They began by submitting a few pieces of writing or translation to an established journal, such as the *Short Story Monthly*; once published, they became emboldened to publish journals of their own. In some cases, they preferred to found their own journals first, in order to showcase their own literary talent and/or their newly gained knowledge of foreign literatures. One story about the publishing ventures of a small circle of friends who, upon graduation from Shanghai's Aurora University, immediately set out to establish their own bookstores and journals that finally led to their literary fame in the journal *Xiandai zazhi* is now, after half a century of neglect, celebrated as marking the beginning of Chinese literary modernism. It deserves retelling for our purposes because most of the texts and writers (with the exception of Eileen Chang) treated in this book were published in this important journal. The following account is based largely on Shi Zhecun's published reminiscences and my interviews with him.

Les Contemporains

After the Japanese bombardment in January 1932, which badly damaged the printing facilities of the Commercial Press and demolished its valuable library of Chinese and Western books, the hegemonic reign of the Commercial Press seemed temporarily in jeopardy. Zhang Jinglu, an enterprising publishing genius and owner of the much smaller Xiandai (Contemporary) Book Company, decided to seize the day and publish a general literary journal to challenge, if not replace, the domination of the popular *Short Story Monthly* of the Commercial Press. In view of the polemics unleashed by the leftists from the Creation Society and its associated groups, which aroused the suspicions of the Nationalist government, Zhang wanted to find an editor for his journal who had no pronounced ideological sympathies. He finally decided on Shi Zhecun.[16] The two men agreed that Shi would assume full responsibility for editing the new journal, which was called *Xiandai zazhi* (which Shi rendered in French as *Les Contemporains*). Another literary figure, Ye Lingfeng, who soon became editor of the company's other magazine, *Xiandai xiaoshuo* (Modern fiction), would be in charge of the company's publication of literary books under Zhang's overall supervision.

The editorial office was located in a small alley, a typical *nongtang* off Gordon Road in the International Settlement. As editor, Shi was paid 100 yuan a month (about U.S. $37), plus another 100 yuan for his articles and translations published in the journal (at a regular rate of 4 to 5 yuan per thousand characters). His 200 yuan monthly income enabled him to pay his rent (16 yuan a month, later 50 yuan when he and his family moved to the third floor of a Western-style building on Yu Yuan Road in 1938, where he still lives). For pastimes he would often go to the movies at first-run theaters (about 1 yuan per ticket) or eat and drink at his favorite cafés and restaurants. (Coffee at D.D.'s or Sullivan's Chocolate Shop cost more than 1 yuan for two cups, and cakes were even more expensive, at about 5 yuan; but for 3 yuan he could have a regular Chinese meal of two dishes and soup at one of his favorite Chinese restaurants.) His greatest passion, of course, was reserved for books: he loved to frequent bookstores and developed a habit of book buying (used foreign-language books cost about 1 yuan per book, new ones about 7 or 8 yuan). He did not like dancing, but told me that at the dance halls in the Japanese section such as the Blue Bird, 1 yuan could buy three dance tickets, plus a cup of tea. Occassionally he would go with friends to a jai alai game or to the horse races. The Western clothing he bought was rather expensive: 40 yuan for a suit, 7 to 8 yuan for a pair of pants, 8 yuan for a hat, and 5 or 6 yuan for a pair of leather shoes.[17] In many ways Shi seemed to lead the life of a typical Shanghai writer, but he had gained more cultural capital than most by assuming the editorship of *Les Contem-*

porains, which catapulted him to instant fame on Shanghai's literary scene.

Shi came to this prestigious position not without some previous experience in publishing. In 1925, while still a student at Aurora University, he had started a journal, *Yingluo*, which lasted four issues. In 1928 he had started another journal with his friends Dai Wangshu, Du Heng, and Feng Xuefeng called *Wenxue gongchang* (Literary atelier), which folded after only two issues, presumably because the small company which published the journal was frightened by its leftist content.[18] Then one of his classmates at Aurora, Liu Na'ou (who was born in Taiwan and grew up in Japan, where he studied literature before returning to Shanghai to study French at Aurora), asked Shi and Dai to join him in some publishing ventures. Liu founded the Diyixian (Frontline) Bookstore in 1928, and published another journal, *Wugui lieche* (Trackless train), which was soon banned after six issues for its promotion of "Red" ideology. Liu followed the next year with the Shuimo (Froth) Bookstore and launched *Xin Wenyi* (original French title *La Nouvelle Littérature*), which lasted for eight issues (September 1929–April 1930). With these short-lived journals this group of novice writers gained their first experience as authors and translators.[19]

Reading through the latter two journals, we find an array of works and translations that stamped a distinct imprint of both political and artistic radicalism. The early issues of *Trackless Train* (the title is an urban "mechanical" signifier) contain poems by Paul Valéry and Paul Fort translated by Dai Wangshu and Xu Xiacun, some stories by the Japanese neo-sensationalists (Shin kangaku ka) translated by Liu Na'ou and Guo Jianying, articles on John Reed, and Henri Barbusse's interview with Maxim Gorki. But the key figure was Paul Morand, who was featured in a long article plus translations of two of his stories.[20] The mastermind behind it was certainly Liu Na'ou, who was said to adulate this French diplomat and writer, whose stories about encounters with prostitutes in exotic places must have appealed to Liu's own fascination with the image of the femme fatale (see Chapter 6). We also find a bizarre story by Shi

Zhecun titled "Pursuit" (Zhui), which is a blatant imitation of a Soviet revolutionary story,[21] some original poems by Dai, and a serialized random essay on cinema by Ge Muomei (possibly a peudonym of Liu Na'ou). There is also an essay titled "Revolution and Intelligentsia" by Feng Xuefeng, who was by then already a dedicated communist and reportedly supervised some translations of Marxist literary theory to be published by the Shuimo Bookstore.[22]

This extraordinary combination—of French symbolist poetry, Japanese fiction, and revolutionary articles inspired by Soviet Russia—betrays the intellectual and aesthetic preferences of the contributors: Liu was attracted to the decadent sensibilities of Paul Morand and Japanese neo-sensationalist fiction, whereas Dai Wangshu was drawn to French poetry. From his meager contributions, Shi Zhecun's own interests were not yet clear. If his imitation revolutionary story is a failure, his other fictional work, "Ninong," which allegedly imitates the prose of Edgar Allan Poe, is a fascinating experiment in first-person monologue.[23] Shi's creative talent is more in evidence in the ensuing journal Xin wenyi. The first item in its inaugural issue is Shi's story "Jiumuoluoshi" or "Kumarajiwa," a work of prodigious imagination about the temptations of the famous Buddhist monk Kumarajiwa, which may have been inspired by Anatole France's novel of a similar theme, Thaïs.[24] The story is the first of a series of unconventional historical fantasies that established Shi's reputation as a fiction writer. Another story, "Fengyang nü" (The girl from Fengyang), ushers in another experimental mode of what might be called gothic fiction, a unique hallmark of Shi's later creative output (see Chapter 5). Shi also contributed a long translated article on modern French poets and a few essays. The majority of the contributions belonged, however, to Shi's friends: several stories by Liu Na'ou and Xu Xiacun and a debut fictional piece by Mu Shiying, "Our World" (Zanmen de shijie), written in a pseudo-proletarian mode. We also find three short essays by the famous leftist novelist Mao Dun. But the journal's "special attractions" are reserved for foreign literature—not only more translations but also more news about an impressive range of authors and works, with the main focus on French poetry (Stéphane Mallarmé, Francis Jammes, Paul Fort) and fiction (a serialized work by Colette). The journal also introduced a special information column on the international literary scene. Appearing in the first four issues, it contained news fragments about such diverse subjects as Goethe's house, Colette's activities, Pirandello's interest in the sound film, Thomas Mann's winning the Nobel Prize, the sudden demise of the American highbrow journal *The Dial*, and the Chinese translation of the novel *All Quiet on the Western Front* by Erich Maria Remarque.

These two journals obviously paved the way for *Les Contemporains*, not just in their shared roster of contributors but in the continuation of an avid interest in modern European literature as well. It is noteworthy that the two early journals also contained a sharper edge of artistic and political radicalism—a certain reflection of the radical temper of Chinese writers in the late 1920s, when slogans and outcries for "revolutionary literature" were being voiced by young members of the Creation and Sun societies. But the Liu-Dai-Shi circle differed from other Chinese leftist groups by its members' refusal to form a power clique and by an intense artistic temperament nurtured by their educational background and linguistic expertise. Whereas most leftist writers of the time became influenced by Japanese proletarian movements and borrowed entirely from Japanese sources, Shi and his friends were more cosmopolitan and avant-gardist. According to Shi, the term *qianwei* (avant-garde) was first introduced to China around 1926–1928 from Japanese sources on Soviet literature. Shi and his friends were initially attracted to this radical revolutionary metaphor because they believed that all the best Soviet writers active in the 1920s—Mayakovsky, Babel, and others—were avant-gardists, which they equated with the "modern" trend in art and literature in Europe as well.[25] In other words, they saw themselves as both revolutionary and aesthetic rebels on an international "frontline." This pose was apparently continued in *Les Contemporains* without any flaunting of a self-styled radical stance partly because Shi wished to remain politically neutral and partly because the term "avant-garde" proved to be short-lived in China. It was fashionable among Chinese leftist circles for only a brief period—in the late 1920s and early 1930s. The newly formed League of Left-Wing Writers soon renounced it in favor of socialist realism—certainly a regression in artistic terms and not to Shi's liking.

When Shi moved from the sidelines of two small avant-gardist journals to become editor of a major mainstream literary magazine, he found himself suddenly thrust to the forefront of Shanghai's polemic-ridden literary scene. There were scores of serious literary journals at the time[26]—not to mention hundreds of popular magazines and news-papers—with which he had to compete for readership. Thus he had to proceed with caution without losing his earlier literary flair. The ap-pearance of the first issue of his large-format journal in May 1932 created quite a stir. It comprised 198 pages and cost 30 cents. The first printing of 3,000 copies quickly sold out in five days; a second printing of 2,000 more copies was added. The record was reached with volume 2, number 1, at 10,000 copies.[27] The magazine's cover, printed in black and red, with the Chinese and French titles of the journal set side by side on the upper half, punctuated by a red star (one star for the first issue, two for the second, and so on), clearly conveys a modernistic impression. A red and white design below the Chinese title is an art-work which resembles a mixture of French surrealism and Russian fu-turism. In subsequent issues the cover artwork became increasingly stylish. On the back of the journal's front page is printed a short manifesto which was written hastily by Shi just before the first issue was to be set in print. In an informal but forceful tone, Shi announces that this journal is "a general literary magazine and not a partisan journal"; it is not intended to promote any literary trend, doctrine, or faction, and the editor wishes to obtain "the support of all Chinese writers so as to make a contribution to the community of lovers of literature." Then Shi adds an emphatic note of his own: "Articles will be chosen for publication in accordance only with the subjective criterion of the editor himself. This criterion, of course, refers to the inherent quality of the literary work itself."[28]

Shi's emphasis on nonpartisanship was meant to distinguish his editorial policy from prevailing practice: most literary journals were in fact run by small "cliques"—groups of several like-minded friends who belonged to a literary society and advocated the same literary and ideological position. Even the largest literary journal, *Short Story Monthly*, was apparently the organ of the Association for Literary Studies and was edited by one of its founding members, Mao Dun. Given the increasingly politicized atmosphere on Shanghai's literary front, however, it was all but impossible to maintain a neutral stance. The journal soon became involved in a debate on the so-called "Third Category" of writers started by Shi's friend and later co-editor Du Heng (using the pseudonym Su Wen), who presumably wished to plead for the creative freedom of the politically unaffiliated writer between the CCP-dominated left and the Guomindang-directed right against ideological control of any kind. But this position aroused both suspicion and calumny from members of the League of Left-Wing Writers. With heated criticism coming from Lu Xun and Shi's former friend Feng Xuefeng, Shi seemed to have no choice but to lend tacit support to Du Heng by arguing that even progressive writers "do not necessarily have to establish a direct relationship with politics," by which he really meant that writers need not become members of the CCP. Shi also defended the independence of the writer by saying that "every person should at least have some egotism." The use of the word "egotism" may not have been appropriate, Shi later admitted in his memoirs, but it really referred to the writer's sense of "individual freedom."[29]

This admission of egotism could be better applied to Shi's own temperament as editor of a major literary journal. The journal's French title, *Les Contemporains*, while conveying an exotic foreign flavor, made a pointedly elitist and vaguely avant-gardist reference: it inscribes a collective self-image of Shi's group as people who saw themselves as "moderns" (as the Chinese title *xiandai* so clearly indicates) and who also claimed to be "contemporaries" of world literature—men who were abreast of the most recent, hence fashionable, literary movements everywhere. In this endeavor Shi and Dai Wangshu were undisputed leaders, with their old and new friends as followers. While Dai soon traveled to France and Spain and experienced European modernism at first hand, Shi stayed in Shanghai and tried to gain some knowledge, in part through correspondence with Dai, but mainly by reading British and American literary journals and foreign books he could obtain from Shanghai's bookstores. During our interviews I was continually surprised by the breadth of Shi's knowledge of what was going on in world literature at the time. He told me that in addition to *Vanity Fair* and other journals, he and his friends had also read the *New York Times* and the *Times Literary Supplement* of London. He learned about the paintings of Picasso and the works of the art historian Herbert Read. He first read about the lifting of a ban on Joyce's *Ulysses* in America, which was later publicized by his friend Ye Lingfeng in *Xiandai xiaoshuo*. Thus, in spite of his avowed refusal to promote any literary trend or doctrine, the works on foreign literature published in the journal clearly mirrored his own literary preferences for European modernism, although he was not conscious of a modernist movement as such.

Toward a "Modern" Literature

Shi's editorial policy about introducing foreign literature in his journal was very much shaped by his readings and by a cosmopolitan sensibility toward world literary trends. The table of contents in the first three years of *Les Contemporains* (1932–1934) when Shi was in sole charge showed a broader international range than most other literary journals of the time. In addition to translations, Shi established a special column, "Yiwen qingbao" (Art and literature information), to keep readers abreast of notable figures and events on the world literary scene. In an editor's afterword in the August 1932 issue he announced that he intended to form a network of literary correspondents in six countries: England, France, Germany, America, the Soviet Union, and Japan. The subsequent issues did in fact feature articles—not reports by his own correspondents but translations from eminent European writers and critics—on the recent state of literature in Italy (by Mario Praz and Luigi Pirandello), Soviet Russia (Richard Lewinsohn), Spain (V. S. Pritchett), and England (Hugh Walpole) as well as articles on postwar French literature, on the recent Nobel Prize winner John Galsworthy, and on trends such as neoromanticism, dadaism, surrealism, futurism, and American imagism.

The task of translation was initially divided between Shi and Dai Wangshu, but soon Zhao Jiabi, Zhao Jingsheng, and several other friends joined the ranks. While Dai continued to translate from French and Spanish works and reported on his European travels (including meetings with the Italian futurist Marinetti, who openly defended his sympathies with Mussolini), Shi translated works by Aldous Huxley and Julian Green and became drawn to modern American poetry. In the July 1932 issue Shi translated seven imagist poems by three American women poets (he called them by the late Qing term *nüshi*, or "woman scholar"), Hilda Doolittle (H.D.), Evelyn Scott, and Amy Lowell. In the May 1933 issue he translated, together with Xu Xiacun, eight poems by Carl Sandburg. In December 1933 Vachel Lindsay's poem "Santa Fe Trail" appeared, as translated by the young poet Xu Chi.

These efforts culminated in the special enlarged issue devoted to American literature (October 1934), which provided a showcase for Shi's ambitious editorial vision. This special issue contained four long survey articles on the state of American literature under the categories of fiction, poetry, drama, and criticism together with individual articles on eleven American authors: Jack London, Upton Sinclair, Theodore Dreiser, Willa Cather, Sinclair Lewis, Eugene O'Neill, Maxwell Anderson, Ezra Pound, Ernest Hemingway, John Dos Passos, and William Faulkner. In addition, there were translations of sixteen short stories (mostly by the same authors, but also by O. Henry, Edith Wharton, Conrad Aiken, Kay Boyle, and others), one play (*The Rope* by Eugene O'Neill), and thirty poems (by Robert Frost, Amy Lowell, Conrad Aiken, Carl Sandburg, Ezra Pound, H.D., and others) translated by Shi himself. It also contained five essays, a list of postwar American literary journals, a long biographical article about American authors, twelve short entries (including one on Gertrude Stein), and four pages of thirty-six photos. In the editor's afterword, Shi added that T. S. Eliot would have joined the list if he had not adopted English citizenship, and that he had included a special article on Irving Babbitt by his Chinese disciple Liang Shiqiu, in defiance of criticism from Chinese leftists. The main reason for Shi's decision to publish a special issue on American literature was that "aside from Soviet Russia, only the United States can fully be called 'modern,' whereas other nations are all trapped by their own traditions." Consequently, "the spirit of American literature is creative and free. The America of today offers the possibility of an independent national literature for the twentieth century; and this example should also be a powerful encouragement for our new literature which is being created independently, having cut itself off from all past traditions."[30]

Among the survey articles, particularly noteworthy is the survey of American poetry by Shao Xunmei, which cites the works of e. e. cummings, Robert Graves, Ezra Pound, Gertrude Stein, and T. S. Eliot. Shao gives a perceptive analysis of *The Wasteland*, which he considered the greatest work of "literary internationalism."[31] In his survey of American fiction based on a battery of American journalistic sources (including the *American Bookman*), Zhao Jiabi points out the innovations of language and style that distinguished American fiction from its English literary origins. At the end of the article he grudgingly compliments the art of both Hemingway and Faulkner, though he sees them as "new pessimists" whose fame is being challenged by a "shining new star of social realism," John Dos Passos.[32] In the article on Hemingway, however, Ye Lingfeng, his self-styled Chinese follower, gives a positive review of Hemingway's fiction, whose focus on character and action Ye regarded as a refreshing reaction against the "obscure psychologism" of Joyce's *Ulysses*. Most revealing is the article on Faulkner by Ling Changyan. This Chinese critic saw Faulkner's fiction, despite its novel technique, as the product of an "unhealthy age": "What Faulkner can offer is not the expression of a normal society and life; he gives only thrills, abnormal sensory thrills, and what modern man demands . . . are precisely these momentary thrills." For this reason, Faulkner's art, Ling implies, may not last long.[33]

These reactions to Hemingway and Faulkner indicate a perceptible degree of ambivalence among Chinese commentators toward the writers of American modernism: while they were attracted to the novelty of the Americans' art, they were generally repelled by the pessimism of their outlook.[34] The negative attitude was shared especially by Chinese leftists who were about to make an ideological return (Shi would consider it a regression) to socialist realism. For instance, Mu Mutian, a veteran member of the Creation Society, had warned readers in an earlier issue (volume 4, number 6) against such recent Western trends as impressionism, psychologism, and mysticism, which he deemed basically decadent and escapist, and thus unsuitable to the social and realistic demands of the age.[35] At the same time, however, other writers were more struck by American modernism as marking a rupture—the sharp break of the twentieth century from the nineteenth—and were baffled by the great contradictions of the era they lived in. In his article on Faulkner, Ling Changyan expressed his own perplexity as he faced this American artist of the "modern spirit" (xiandai xin):

> Civilization is something inconceivable. Sometimes it leads people to progress forward; sometimes it brings mankind back to the barbarism of the primitive age—but no, even in primitive ages there was not so much irrationality as we see in the present era. Civilization on the one hand prohibits evil by such things as morality and religion, yet at the same time, precisely because of the development of civilization, morality and religion have lost their restraining power. The wild passions of mankind, like wild animals breaking loose from their cage, are running rampant with redoubled force. And the world created by so many uncaged animals has become chaos—a maddening chaos.

The twentieth century is an age in which civilization has
reached its peak and at the same time it is an age of madness!
The United States of America,
The center of modern civilization
A country of madness![36]

This could be read as typical hyperbole from a Chinese writer, who
probably had found similar hyperbolic expressions in the American
sources he was given to read (by his friend Zhao Jingshen). Still, such
apparent clichés disclose a sense of shock—at a new world too unfamiliar for his sensibilities, but that nevertheless could be profoundly exciting (the word compound *ciji* can mean both sensory thrills and
intellectual excitement). What Ling found particularly maddening in
modern American culture was jazz music, in which "the noise of the
saxophone, whining like a stupid donkey," has replaced the "frail melody
of the mandolin"; yet precisely the same jazz music was deemed most
exciting by Mu Shiying, whose stories—in particular "Five Characters in
a Night Club" (see Chapter 6)—evoke the intoxicating atmosphere produced by jazz in an urban nocturnal landscape that was Mu's "normal"
world in both fiction and real life. In Ling's essay, however, the author's
hidden sympathies are not with the city but with the countryside. Thus,
Ling finds Faulkner's stories puzzling because they are set in the countryside of the American South: "One feels strange that this typical writer of
modern life turns out not to be a city writer but a country writer." But
then he proceeds to rationalize his way through Faulkner's work by
arguing that its "depiction of violence, evil, and primitive sexuality makes
him naturally beloved by the city readers who seek the same thrills, and
there cannot be a more suitable background for evil and violence than
the primitive wildness of a remote region."[37]

It is revealing to see how Shi Zhecun himself, a man who also had
family roots in the Jiangnan (lower Yangtze) countryside, reacted to this
shock of the modern. In an editorial comment in the November 1933
issue, he responded again to a reader's complaint that the poetry con-

tained in the journal was difficult and incomprehensible.[38] Shi's comments should be read in the same contemporary context, though he reveals himself to be a true urbanite:

> The poems published in *The Contemporary* are poetry, pure modern poetry. They express the sentiments felt by modern people amidst the experiences of their modern lives who use modern phrases and idioms to construct a modern poetic form.
>
> The so-called modern life contains all kinds of special sites and situations: the harbor where large ships are anchored, the factories roaring with noise, the mines deep underground, the dance halls with jazz music, the skyscraper department stores, the airplanes in combat in the sky, the spacious horse racing course . . . Even natural scenery is different from before. What this kind of life gives to our poets—can their feelings be the same as what poets of previous ages felt in their lives?[39]

It is obvious that the sites of "modern life" Shi describes are none other than those of his own city of Shanghai—including the reference to Japanese air bombardment the year before. His prose conjures up an urban spectacle full of excitement, which directly shapes the feelings and sensibilities of his contemporaries. Shi's modernism is, therefore, indisputably urban, and he contrasts the "pure modern poetry" in his journal with classical Chinese poetry of previous ages, in which the sensibility is decidedly pastoral. In this regard, it is no surprise that he was drawn to Carl Sandburg's poetic eulogies to the city and modern technology in poems such as "Chicago," "Prayer to Steel"—and to the Special Express trains that swept across the American prairie. In his introduction to Sandburg, Shi sings his own eulogy to Chicago, "this metropolitan city where capitalist development has reached its utmost" with its "skyscrapers towering into the clouds, where people ride electric elevators going up and down, where there are big banks and big money, and stocks flow rampant, where the flat, endless highways crisscross one another."[40] This effusive urbanism which Shi promoted was echoed in some of the poems written by his younger protégés Xu Chi and Luyishi (though not by his old friend Dai Wangshu). Here is a poem, "Full Moon in the City," by Xu Chi published in the May 1934 issue:

Written in Roman numerals
The twelve stars signaled by I II III IV V VI VII VIII IX X
    XI XII
Circle around a spiked wheel

Full moon every night, machine tools in plane and geometric
    shapes
Full moon, pasted on the tower of the skyscraper
Under the gaze of another skyscraper, full moon in the city

A person, like a clock's short hand
A shadow, like its long hand
Casts an occasional stare at the full moon's surface

Knows the philosophy as carried afloat by the city's full moon
Knows the difference between the hour and the minute
The combination of moon, lamp, and clock

A naive work from a twenty-year-old novice, perhaps, the poem attempts to capture the urban mood by juxtaposing two objects: the full moon, certainly a poetic symbol prevalent in both Chinese and Western poetry, and the clock atop a skyscraper, a most fitting signifier of modern temporality. It should not be surprising that Xu's real-life model for the Western-style clock was none other than the clock on top of the Shanghai Race Club.[41] Like Shi Zhecun, Xu was hopelessly enamored of the city of Shanghai for the simple reason that, as he told me, there was no other city like it in China. In our interviews he recounted with visible excitement—some half a century later—how as a schoolteacher in nearby Soochow he would take the train to the city on weekends, catch a movie and go to a concert by the famed Shanghai Municipal Orchestra conducted by Mario Paci, an Italian, or a band concert on Sunday afternoon in one of the parks, before he eventually settled in Shanghai.[42]

Chinese Receptions: Translation as Cultural Mediation

I hope the foregoing details have provided sufficient proof that, more than any other literary journal, *Les Contemporains* was a product of Shanghai's evolving urban culture; without the city's physical environment and facilities it would have been impossible for Shi and his Shanghai "contemporaries" to create—or even imagine—a modern literature of their own. At the same time, however, for all its superficial resemblances to European modernism, this urban cultural production of a Chinese modernity was also shaped by its *Chinese* characteristics, in terms of both time and space. The foreign concessions in which Shi and his friends lived and worked, as we have seen in the previous chapters, were inhabited largely by Chinese; and most Chinese writers, with few exceptions (Shao Xunmei being one), had little contact with the foreigners in the city. Rather, Shanghai's treaty port setting enabled them to conjure up a set of images and styles on a literary plane that served to construct what may be called a cultural imaginary of modernism. While the sources drawn upon were largely Western, the activities of cultural construction were conducted in written Chinese. The crucial task therefore was translation, not only as a technical act of rendering a Western-language text into Chinese, but also, and more important, as a process of cultural mediation.

In approaching this problem from the angle of cultural history, we are reminded of Walter Benjamin's famous dictum that "a translation issues from the original—not so much from its life but from its afterlife," that is, from the posthumous fame the original work enjoys in succeeding generations.[43] Yet we must also qualify Benjamin's concept of the "afterlife" by further divesting it of the aura of the original work, on which Benjamin continues (albeit implicitly) to rely, when we seek to understand the mediational role of translation on the part of a Chinese literary journal. If, according to Benjamin, such an "afterlife" is perpetuated by the translator, what happens when the translator comes from a cultural and linguistic context totally different from Western traditions? The original must then undergo great transformations. For all his knowledge of Western literature, Shi and his contemporaries were by no means on familiar ground when discussing the West's "history of great works of art," especially when such a history was conceived to be ruptured by modernity. Besides, for the average Chinese reader, who had no sense whatsoever of the originals, what was the "afterlife" of a Western work in Chinese anyway? Rather, it was given an entirely new life by the translator—and a range of cultural meanings embedded in the reception culture. In other words, the "afterlife" was conferred on the original by the translator, whose own fame was sufficient to make the reader accept on faith the original work's artistic value; but in fact the value was *created* and may have had little to do with the original.

In the case of Shi's journal, the task of translation was to some extent facilitated by material access to Western books and journals available in Shanghai. The horizon of the translators' knowledge, therefore, was shaped by this cross-cultural traffic, which represents an expanding sphere of production and consumption in print culture. Some would consider it a form of Western cultural colonialism. The crucial question becomes, however, how the culturally "colonized" received or reacted to it—or whether the reception can be considered, in Homi Bhabha's words, an act of "mimicry" without adopting the colonial language. The Chinese case is further complicated by the fact that, in the period under study, Western literary modernism, like Hollywood movies, was received as a "popular" product and not in any way as an elitist educational curriculum in the classroom. (The English curriculum at the new missionary universities such as Yenching and Tsing-hua in Beijing or St. John's in Shanghai was still modeled after Harvard's "classic" curriculum, in which modernist literature did *not* form an integral part.) In other words, modern Western literature was not received in terms of an established canonical history of great works. Consequently, for Shi and his friends, translation was indeed a creative act involving little concern for the possible "betrayal" of the meaning and worth of the original in order to set a new literary fashion with which to defy established conventions in Chinese literature, both past and present.

We see this in Shi's defense of the poetry published in his own journal. He was proud that the new poetic works are "largely rhymeless, and their lines are not neatly metrical, but they all possess rather fine texture, they represent the form of modern poetry, they are poetry."[44] What Shi had in mind in this statement was the free verse form (vers libre) to which he had become attracted through his translations of Yeats, Amy Lowell, and other imagist poets. It was a form in reaction against the "new poetry" of the early May Fourth period which to some degree still exhibited the rhyming patterns of classical Chinese poetry. In short, Shi's notion of poetic "texture" can refer only to poetic language itself, as opposed to the external concerns of social reality or the poet's own sentimentality which he found in May Fourth poetry.

In what ways did Shi's "modernism" resemble or differ from what we know about European modernisms of the 1920s and 1930s? In one sense, as I demonstrated earlier, the Chinese modernists were quite well informed about writers and trends on the world literary scene. But their eager reception did not mean that they wished to replicate exactly what they knew about the West. According to Matei Calinescu's well-known study, modernity as conceived in the European context had broken into two separate and diametrically opposed strains: sometime during the first half of the nineteenth century "an irreversible split occurred between modernity as a stage in the history of Western civilization—a product of scientific and technological progress, of the industrial revolution, of the sweeping economic and social changes brought by capitalism—and modernity as an aesthetic concept." This other modernity, "the one that was to bring into being the avant-gardes, was from its romantic beginnings inclined toward radical anti-bourgeois attitudes. It was disgusted with the middle-class scale and values . . . [W]hat defines cultural modernity is its outright rejection of bourgeois modernity, its consuming negative passion" as a result of a profound disillusionment with the philistinism of bourgeois society.[45] As we look at the Chinese literary scene of the 1920s and early 1930s, at a time when variants of this aesthetic modernism had reached a height in Europe, it is obvious that no such attitude of aesthetic hostility, as summed up in the famous metaphor *épater le bourgeois*, can be found. In their pursuit of a modern mode of consciousness and modern forms of literature, Chinese writers did not choose—nor did they feel the need—to separate the two domains of historical and aesthetic modernity. There were no tangible masses of the bourgeoisie to shock: in fact, the concept of the "bourgeois" (translated phonetically as *bu'erqiaoya*) itself was just being introduced by the Chinese "revolutionary" writers on the left in a vulgar Marxist framework. Unlike European modernists, they were yet to comprehend the full impact of the industrial revolution—and for that matter a full-fledged "high capitalism"—even in Shanghai. In other words, modernity may have become a literary fashion, an ideal, but it was not a fully verifiable objective reality. In their eagerness to catch up with the West, Chinese intellectuals and creative writers did not have the luxury of hindsight to adopt a totally hostile stance toward modernity. As we saw earlier, their attitudes toward Western literary modernism were quite complex, full of anxiety and ambivalence but also with a sense of shock and excitement.

On a more artistic level, it may be noted that one of the central intellectual fountainheads of Western modernism—a theory that radically altered the way in which Western artists and writers reenvisioned reality—did not have the same effect in China. The theories of Freud, despite their introduction in China as early as 1913, failed to make profound inroads into Chinese literary thinking and practice.[46] There was no special issue—nor any translation—devoted to Freud in *Xiandai*. Instead, Shi Zhecun translated the stories of Schnitzler, who was Freud's contemporary in Vienna and whom Freud considered a kindred spirit (though Schnitzler knew nothing of his theory). Besides Shi, most other Chinese writers were not ready to embrace the Freudian concept of the

unconscious as some had embraced, quite fervently, the Marxist concepts of social class and historical materialism as "scientific" laws governing "objective" reality. In fact, Freud's theory of dreams was also first
received as a science. Consequently, the most notable tendency of Western modernist literature—the incessant probing of the inner fragmented
psyche through a comparably fragmented language, as manifested in
Joyce and Faulkner—had an ambivalent reception in China. Again, as I
will analyze in a later chapter, Shi Zhecun was an exception: his fictional
experiments in pursuit of what he called the erotic and the grotesque
provide a valuable test case for his daring application of the theories of
sexuality drawn from Freud, Havelock Ellis, the marquis de Sade, and a
large number of Western works on abnormal psychology, mysticism, and
mythology. But it was also his fictional experimentation that proved his
undoing in the increasingly politicized Shanghai literary scene of the
1930s.

A Political Postscript

Shi Zhecun's relations with the Chinese leftists were quite delicate. On
the one hand, in spite of his journal's surface neutrality, Shi did not wish
to offend the leftists. Thus he was able to publish some of the best works
by major writers, both leftists and non-leftists (but not those of the
Guomindang)—Lu Xun, Mao Dun, Lao She, Zhang Tianyi, Ba Jin, Shen
Congwen—together with works by his own friends and protégés, such
as the journal's rising star, Mu Shiying. On the other hand, Shi seems to
have been deeply wounded by the adverse criticism from the left, which
caused him eventually to abandon his fictional experiments with the
Freudian unconscious. The reason behind Shi's ideological debacle was
that both the Nationalist government and the CCP-dominated League
of Left-Wing Writers had begun to tighten the reins of control in the
mid-1930s, the former through censorship and random arrest, the latter
through increased polemics in order to establish its hegemony over
Shanghai's literary scene. By the end of 1934, Shi was also under pressure

from his own publishers: presumably financial problems at the Xiandai Bookstore caused Zhang Jinglu to leave. The journal's issue on American literature turned out to be a kind of farewell extravaganza, though it was originally designed to pave the way for another special issue on Soviet literature. Tensions created by Du Heng as a result of the "Third Category" debate finally led to the resignation of both Shi and Du after the November 1934 issue. Beginning in March 1935, the editorial board changed hands, and two other writers, presumably designated by the Guomindang, took over but managed to publish only two more issues. The journal formally folded in April.

It could be said that Shi's intellectual leftism conformed to the general ideological temper on the literary scene at the time—a leftism reinforced by the rising sentiment against Japanese aggression among writers in China and against fascism among European writers as a result of the Spanish civil war. Thus, a kind of informal international brotherhood was forged. The French writer Henri Barbusse, who took a leading role in this movement, was however unable to visit China; another French writer, Vaillant Couturier, an editor of the leftist French newspaper L'Humanité, came instead. Shi and Du visited him at his hotel and published his article written especially for Chinese readers, "To the Chinese Intelligentsia," in the November 1933 issue. In the same issue we also find an article titled "Socialist Realism and Revolutionary Romanticism" by Zhou Yang, one of the rising theoreticians of the leftist camp, who would soon be a leading commissar of art and literature in the CCP. Zhou had contributed a long article to the journal a few months earlier (May 1933), "Realism in Literature" (Wenxue de zhenshixing). Interestingly, Zhou's articles published in Xiandai did not take a dictatorial stance. In reporting about the new tenet of socialist realism adopted by the newly formed All-Soviet Union of Writers in late 1932, he quoted the views of the Soviet theoreticians V. Kirpotin and J. M. Gronski that it was neither "a general panacea applicable to all" nor a "consolidated canon and inflexible rule out of the blue" but rather a reflection of the concrete realities facing Soviet writers.[47] Thus, Zhou continued to de-

fend the need for literary realism, from which socialist realism represented a progressive step forward, and under which revolutionary romanticism could also be embraced. It turned out that Zhou's political
fortunes soon overtook Shi's.

The delicate balancing act Shi was able to maintain for about three
years on the literary-ideological front proved all but impossible by 1936,
as the leftists took upon themselves the ideological task of arousing the
patriotic emotions of the Chinese people against the aggression of Japan.
A more narrowly focused nationalism directed against the imperialist
enemy soon displaced Shi's brand of urban internationalism. As the
gathering storm of impending war finally broke in 1937, the entire
modernist establishment in Shanghai was wiped out. Shi retreated into
the hinterlands, and his wartime writings were cast in an entirely different mode, rarely harking back to an era that, for him and his generation,
was gone forever. After 1949 he plunged into research and teaching of
traditional Chinese literature at Shanghai's East China Normal University, and, in spite of years of suffering during the Cultural Revolution, he
became a leading authority on classical Chinese poetry. It was not until
the early 1980s that he was "rediscovered" and acclaimed by a new
generation of young writers and scholars as a founding father of Chinese
modernism.

"Intoxicated Shanghai." Photographic collage from the popular pictorial magazine *Liangyou* (The young companion, no. 85, February 1934). The Chinese heading reads, "Metropolitan excitements." The dominant figure of a young woman wearing a fashionable *qipao* is surrounded by clips of (clockwise) a jazz band, a new 22-story skyscraper, racetrack and viewing stand, and a movie poster for *King Kong*.

"Intoxicated Shanghai—Dance troupe performance: licentious singing, lurid dancing."
The Chinese commentary that accompanies these alluring pictures adopts a consciously
moral tone: it decries such "metropolitan excitements that displace the fervor for normal
endeavors" and blames the evil effects on "capitalist civilization." The last sentence states,
"In saying that there is a second Paris in China, we really don't know whether to rejoice
or to lament" (*Liangyou*, no. 85, February 1934).

"Such Is Shanghai." Stylized Chinese characters above a slanting memorial monument refer to "a finger against the sky," but the phallic symbolism is inescapable. At the upper left corner, the close-up of a woman's legs and high-heeled shoes carries a succinct comment in English: "Symbol of Household Authority." A 14-story skyscraper "lifts its back straight and looks down upon its neighbors with a domineering gaze." One such dwarfed neighbor is the Lyceum Theater, famous for its theatrical productions. The double-decker bus carries the omnipresent advertisement for "Dr. Williams' Pink Pills," while the English caption for a cigarette ad reads, "When you read the time, you read the Ruby Queen" (*Liangyou*, no. 88, May 1934).

Shanghai's cosmopolitan attractions. The English captions under these photographs read (clockwise from upper left): "Mansion—Jewish" (the Sassoon Mansion, now Peace Hotel), "Restaurant—German," "Hai Alai—Spanish," "Bank—British," "Dancing Girls—Russian," "Steamship—Italy," and "Shoe-maker—Czechoslovakia" (*Liangyou*, no. 89, June 1934).

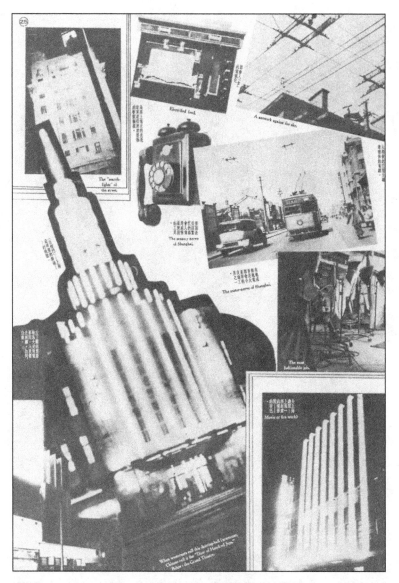

Shanghai's modern conveniences (from top to bottom): web of electric wires for trackless streetcars ("the motor-nerve of Shanghai," upper right), the "searchlights" of the street (upper left), telephone, photographic equipment, the Paramount lit at night ("When Westerners call this dancing-hall Paramount, the Chinese call it the 'Door of Hundred Joys'"), and the Da Shanghai (Great Shanghai, lower right): "Movie or fire work?" (*Liangyou*, no. 87, April 1934).

The Young Companion, drawing of a semi-traditional cover girl for a *Liangyou* pictorial (no. 27, June 1928), shown with a traditional hairdo but a modern fur scarf. Her high-heeled shoes are the fashion of the time. The background landscape is drawn in the traditional style.

Miss Yang Aili on the cover of *Liangyou* (no. 4, May 1926). Note the Western-style floral border around her photo. The magazine went through several different cover designs in its long history (1926–1945).

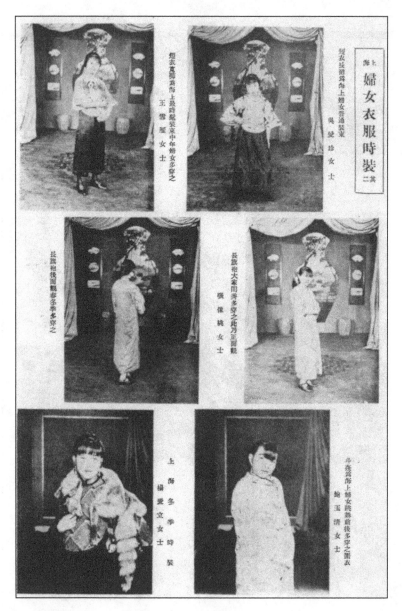

上海

婦女衣服時裝

其二

短衣長裙露胸為海上摩登女普通裝束

吳愛玲女士

短衣寬褲為海上最時髦裝束中年婦女多穿之

玉雪屏女士

長旗袍淺圓鬚春冬季多穿之

長旗袍大家閨秀多穿之此乃正面觀

張像娥女士

斗篷露海上婦女跳舞前後多穿之圍表

鮑玉清女士

上海多季時裝

楊愛立女士

Yang Aili (lower left) models winter fashions along with five other young women. The top two photos show casual wear, blouses and trousers; the middle two, *qipao*, or Manchu-style long gowns. The woman at the lower right wears a cape, which "Shanghai women often wear before and after they go dancing." These named ladies are not professional models but possibly society women (*Liangyou*, no. 4, May 1926).

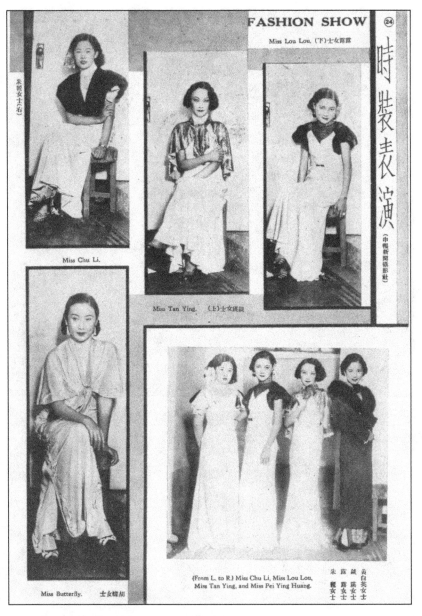

FASHION SHOW ㉔

Miss Lou Lou. (下)士女露露

朱鵬女士(右)

Miss Chu Li.

Miss Tan Ying. (上)士女鶯談

時裝衣演（申報新聞攝影社）

Miss Butterfly. 士女蝶胡

(From L. to R.) Miss Chu Li, Miss Lou Lou, Miss Tan Ying, and Miss Pei Ying Huang.

黃白英女士
談露鶯女士
朱鵬女士
宋露女士

"Fashion Show." The models are mostly movie stars (the most famous being Tan Yin and Hu Die, or Miss Butterfly); their clothes are more modern than those in the previous illustration, only seven years earlier (*Liangyou*, no. 82, November 1933).

Fashion, modern Chinese style: long gowns and everyday wear (*Liangyou*, no. 107, July 1935).

Fashion, foreign style: daytime dresses and evening gowns (*Liangyou*, no. 107, July 1935).

One of the most striking cover designs of the *Liangyou* pictorial (no. 84, January 1934). The woman, dressed Western-style in a dancer's pose, stands against a "futuristic" background with the year 1934 and a gigantic clock—a clear invocation of modernity. The English title boasts, "The most attractive and popular magazine in China."

"A Typical Modern Home" (reprinted from *Shenbao*), showing Western-style modern furniture. The parlor (lower right) has a fireplace, sofas, and a carpet on the floor. (*Liangyou*, no. 50, September–October 1930).

Advertisement for Golden Dragon cigarettes. The four lines of Chinese read: "Beauty is lovely; cigarettes are also lovely. The cigarette that is a national product is even more lovely" (*Liangyou*, no. 1, February 1926).

Advertisement for Momilk. Below the illustration are four Chinese characters indicating that the product is "made in the United States," but the two lines beside it appeal to the prevailing national sentiment: "To strengthen the nation, one must first strengthen the people; to strengthen the people, one must first strengthen the children" (*Liangyou*, no. 14, April 1927).

Calendar poster from Hatamen cigarettes. The woman resembles the famous movie star Ruan Lingyu. The lyrical mood of the traditional-style painting is framed, however, by Art Deco ornamentation. The two packs of Hatamen cigarettes are in red. The calendar is marked "the year 1930 of the Western calendar" (left) and "the nineteenth year of the Republic of China" (right).

Movie theaters in Shanghai. The Strand (top, center) has a poster of Harold Lloyd, a popular Hollywood comedian of the silent era; the Grand Theater (center oval) showcases "Sound & Talking Pictures"; the Paris Theater (center square) is the setting of one of Shi Zhecun's short stories (*Liangyou*, no. 62, October 1931).

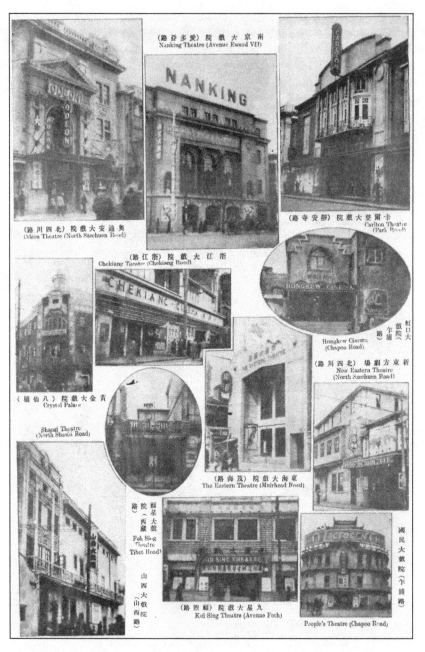

Nanking Theatre (Avenue Eward VII)

Odeon Theatre (North Szechuen Road)

Carlton Theatre (Park Road)

Chekiang Theatre (Chekiang Road)

Hongkew Cinema (Chapoo Road)

New Eastern Theatre (North Szechuen Road)

Crystal Palace

Shansi Theatre (North Shansi Road)

The Eastern Theatre (Muirhead Road)

Foh Sing Theatre (Tibet Road)

Kui Sing Theatre (Avenue Foch)

People's Theatre (Chapoo Road)

More movie theaters in Shanghai. The Carlton (upper right) was famous for both movies and stage shows. The Odeon (upper left) boasted sumptuous comfort (*Liangyou,* no. 62, October 1931).

Dai Wangshu's wedding, circa 1930. The best man is the poet Xu Chi.

Shi Zhecun.

Liu Na'ou.

Mu Shiying.

Portrait of Shao Xunmei by the famous artist Xu Beihong.

Ye Lingfeng in his later years.

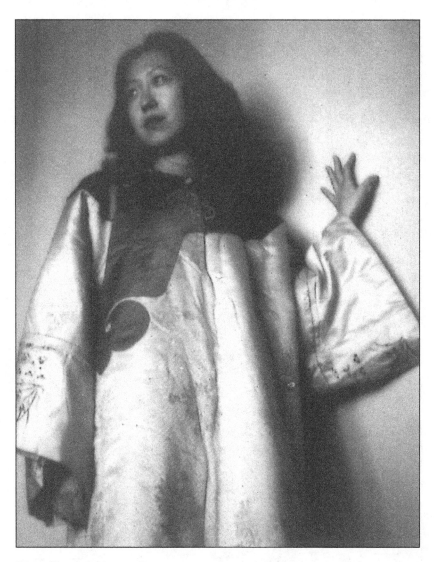

Eileen Chang in a theatrical pose.

The cover design of Eileen Chang's story collection, *Chuanqi* (Romances).

THE MODERN LITERARY IMAGINATION: WRITERS AND TEXTS

THE EROTIC, THE FANTASTIC,

AND THE UNCANNY:

SHI ZHECUN'S EXPERIMENTAL STORIES

Having laid out the cultural context of urban Shanghai in the first part of this book, I would now like to focus on some literary texts and their authors. The privileging of certain texts for study over others is always a thorny issue which has never been adequately solved by literary theory. In this section I take a more conventional route by focusing on what I consider to be significant texts by writers who are generally known as urban modernists, most of whom have already been mentioned in the previous chapters. I have chosen to discuss the works of Shi Zhecun, Liu Na'ou, Mu Shiying, Ye Lingfeng, Shao Xunmei, and Eileen Chang (Zhang Ailing). The obvious criterion for their inclusion is that as modernists they were all preoccupied with the city of Shang-hai. This urban sensibility, which is taken for granted by Western scholars of modernism, is nevertheless a novel one in the study of modern Chinese literature, for reasons that will become clear by the end of this book.

Beyond Reality

As we saw in the previous chapter, Shi Zhecun (b. 1905) became an important man of letters when he assumed the editorship of the influential journal *Xiandai zazhi*. As a creative writer he was a pioneer and a trailblazer who dared to break into the new inner terrain of the human psyche and cast a daring glance into the forces of the irrational. He may well have been the first modern Chinese writer to have consciously used Freudian theory in order to bring out an undercurrent of sexual obsession in his fictional landscape, a landscape both realistic and surrealistic. Most of his experimental stories were not simply inspired by but literally constructed on the Western works he had read. His short stories therefore offer an interesting case study of a different kind of intertextual transaction. In this chapter I am concerned not with Western influences on Shi's fiction but rather with Shi's imaginative use of the Western literary materials at his disposal. In this approach, the author as well as the cultural background are very much present in the text, albeit in unexpected configurations.

Shi Zhecun began writing while still in high school, where he was reportedly steeped in classical Chinese poetry. (He is a renowned scholar of Tang poetry.) In 1921, at age sixteen, he began to submit his writings to the magazines of the Butterfly school and had his first story published in its leading journal, *Libailiu* (Saturday), in 1922. By age eighteen he had published his first story collection with his own money.[1] In 1926 he contributed two stories to a journal he had started with his classmates, *Yingluo* (Necklace), which received hardly any notice. In 1928, with the publication of another story in the prestigious *Short Story Monthly*, he finally emerged on the May Fourth literary scene at age twenty-three as a recognized writer of New Literature. Except for his literary precocity, this profile of his early creative career shows nothing extraordinary: it is typical of many other May Fourth writers as well. What distinguishes him as a fiction writer lies entirely in the experimental technique with which he has come to be known as China's pioneer modernist. Thus, departing from the standard Chinese scholarly view of Shi's fiction, which places a higher premium on the realism of his early stories set in a traditional countryside,[2] I would like to concentrate on his more experimental fiction in an urban setting, which was produced around the same time that he was editing three literary magazines—*Trackless Train*, *La Nouvelle Littérature*, and *Les Contemporains*—from 1928 to 1935. They obviously were products of an artistic sensibility nurtured by his abiding interest in modern Western literature.

Shi's early stories written before 1928 were set largely in the rural countryside, a pastoral landscape reminiscent of his own childhood milieu in Songjiang near Shanghai. They are full of lyrical evocations of the scenery and languid atmosphere of the lower Yangtze region, in which remembrances of a romance long past are recalled with a sense of melancholic nostalgia.[3] In most of these stories, which show the influence of Lu Xun and Yu Dafu, the evocation of the past is often traumatic, intended as a contrast to a changed present. Yet for all their considerable lyricism there is nothing striking in such evocations, except for an occasional depiction of a repressed passion, as in the story "Zhou furen" (Mrs. Zhou). To depict the melancholic mood, Shi frequently resorts to quotations from classical Chinese poetry—a natural resource from his childhood education. But these early stories can be read only as compositional exercises in a rural mode in which Shi had yet to find his own fictional métier. He was groping toward something not usually found in the typical works of rural realism of the time—an abnormal psychology, a bizarre happening, a strange encounter with a mysterious figure, through which he could lead his reader into an "extra-ordinary" world. He clearly wanted to go beyond the world of realism.

An inkling of such unusual attempts can be found in the story "Fengyang nü" (The girl from Fengyang), which depicts a man's obsessive desire for a flirtatious circus performer, a youthful femme fatale (*youwu*), a word used here for the first time in Shi's fiction. Although Shi strives for verisimilitude by invoking real Chinese place-names, his indebtedness to foreign literature seems obvious: the trope of a central character trapped by his object of desire—a Gypsy woman in a circus or a chanteuse in a cabaret—is a familiar one in European fiction. The imposition of a Western theme of psychological obsession onto the pastoral landscape of the lower Yangtze region—with its rivers and bridges and country taverns—gives rise to a certain incongruity of mood and tone. What sustains the interest of the story's implausible plot is a narrative device that frames the plot within a series of eight letters written by the protagonist, who finally disappears (and joins the circus performers, as it turns out in the final letter). The device recalls Lu Xun's famous story "Diary of a Madman" (1918), but without its probing and highly original intellectual insights. Rather, Shi's story is set up as a mystery that gradually unfolds the protagonist's growing erotic obsession. But the story fails in this mission because, having invoked the femme fatale, Shi does not know how to characterize her power of allure. At the story's close, the implied author-as-narrator has to explain away the protagonist's obsession by telling the reader that his friend has always had a strange temperament after all. It is as if Shi were unsure of his characters' plausibility as "real people" as he attempts to endow them with unrealistic qualities. It is precisely this hesitancy—an unwillingness to go all the way beyond the demands of realism—that prevents Shi's ingenious ideas from being realized. It required more experimentation for him to realize that the power of eros must be embodied in a protagonist whose behavior is beyond his own control and defies any commonsensical explanation.

Historical Tales

It was not until Shi tried his hand at writing historical tales, four of which were later collected in a volume titled *Jiangjun de tou* (The general's head) that he finally found his artistic métier. The collection deserves our attention because in it Shi invented a fictional subgenre in which he could pursue the theme of eroticism without the need for verisimilitude or fear of moral censure. His figures are all drawn from the remote past, and most of them, such as the famous Indian monk Kumarajiva, are ethnically not even Chinese. In his preface to the collection, Shi states that he intends to depict the conflicts of love and religion in the story "Kumarajiva," love and race in "The General's Head," and a special kind of sexual desire (sadism) in "Shixiu," which is a rewriting of a chapter from the classical novel *Shuihu zhuan* (Outlaws of the marsh).[4] These are grand themes for any short story writer. Other May Fourth writers have of course dealt with historical subjects: Lu Xun published an entire collection, *Gushi xinbian* (Old stories retold); Guo Moruo and Tian Han wrote several historical plays. But none has so extensively used Freudian theory to probe the depths of abnormal psychology. Since Shi set out to write his historical tales in the grand manner, the use of Freud represents a daunting challenge: how to depict the conflict between love, religion, and race in a cultural tradition in which such conflicts have not been particularly foregrounded in the canonical texts? Although Shi had not read Freud's seminal work *Civilization and Its Discontents*, his ambition can be compared to Freud's: that is, to uncover the libidinous forces suppressed by the civilizational superego.

The religion in "Kumarajiva" is obviously Buddhism, an alien (Indian) religion introduced into China in the Six Dynasties period, which gradually became Sinicized into one of the strands of Chinese popular religion. But Shi is not at all interested in tracing the Buddhist influence; rather, he uses one of its most famous proselytizers, the Indian monk Kumarajiva, as a fictional figure to embody the conflict between eros and religion. Shi may have read Anatole France's *Thaïs*, another work depicting the conflict between love and religion, but Shi's resolution to the conflict is entirely different. He takes advantage of the historical fact that the Tang dynasty was among the most cosmopolitan of all Chinese dynasties. Although the influence of Confucianism was already strong, it had yet to gain the "superego" status of imperial ideology. Thus, Shi was able to infuse his imagined Tang landscape with an outlandish "Orientalized" splendor. But questions of cultural identity also become equally confused: in the land where Kumarajiva goes through his trials of erotic temptation, which culture—Chinese or Indian-Buddhist—represents "self" and which "other"?

In this story, Shi has chosen to place the issue of cultural and racial identity (which becomes a central issue in a later story, "The General's Head") in terms of Kumarajiva's own sexuality. As a monk, he struggles for the ideal of celibacy but finds himself succumbing first to the love of his wife, who in the first part of the story sacrifices her own life on her way to the Tang capital in order to ensure his redemption. The episode is depicted in language full of exotic imagery. But the monk's real trial begins after he reaches Tang China: as he feels more and more at home in the Tang court, one day at a public lecture he finds himself tempted by the beauty of a Thaïs-like courtesan, an easy transference of the image of his dead wife. Consequently the monk succumbs again to the power of eros and spends his nights with various court ladies the Tang emperor has procured for him. In the end, Kumarajiva does not attain nirvana; his body rots like a mortal man's. Only his tongue, which his wife kissed before dying, does not: "it has replaced what the Master has left to his true believers," as the story's last sentence tells us. With eros winning out, the story provides little conflict with religion—certainly not the kind of Catholic faith in Anatole France's *Thaïs*, which is pitted against eros in an eternal struggle in the soul of the priest. Without the oppressive burden of the superego, the id is given free rein in Shi's fiction. He thus turns the Freudian "discontent" into "civilization" itself, a reversal that represents, in a way, his own response to the May Fourth call for sexual emancipation. But he goes a step further: experimental fiction, like eros, has liberated his talent from the Chinese literary tradition and provided him with an appropriate space in which he is free *not* to concern himself with contemporary social reality but instead to indulge in his wildest imaginings.

Shi's famous story "The General's Head" marks another breakthrough in his art with the depiction of repressed desire as racial conflict. The protagonist, a Tang general, is a racial hybrid of Han Chinese and Tibetan blood. He is caught in a conflict of loyalties when he is ordered to lead a platoon of Han troops to fight the "barbarian" Tibetans in the border territory of Szechuan. He is ashamed of his pillaging soldiers, whom he sees as the embodiment of the "corrupt and unrighteous" nature of the Han Chinese (Shi must have been one of very few writers of that period to denounce Han nationalism). Then in a chance encounter he finds himself hopelessly attracted to a young Han village woman—a seduction trope reminiscent of his early story "The Girl from Fengyang." But the general's pursuit of carnal desire leads to a more violent end. Haunted by the girl's image in combat, he suddenly sees a Tibetan general he once knew (an alter ego) come from behind and cut off his head. The headless general, now only an erect torso, still manages to cuts off the Tibetan's head and ride back to the village. He finds the young Han woman, the object of his desire, washing dishes by the stream. When the general steps down from his horse and stoops to the stream to wash himself, he cannot find his own reflection in the muddy water. The girl jeers at him: "Defeated, eh? Your head is chopped off, why bother washing? Why don't you just drop dead quickly, and what else do you want to do anyway? A headless ghost still wants to be a human being? Bah!" The general feels a sudden emptiness and falls down. "At that moment, the head of the Tibetan that the general holds in his hand begins to smile. At the same time, far away in the distance, the general's head in the Tibetan's hand begins to weep."[5]

In this "magical-realistic" ending, Shi has neatly put together the story's central themes: sexuality, identity, eros, and death. Each action takes on symbolic significance. The story has a conspicuous sexual connotation. By letting his Tibetan alter ego cut off his head, which is a form of self-punishment inflicted upon himself, the general is left only with a body. His erect torso, an emblem of his physical desire sustained by sexual energy alone, thus takes on the surrealistic shape of an erect penis riding recklessly in search of its object. There cannot be a more physically concrete depiction of the male libido. The cutting off of the general's head can also be read as castration, and the Freudian connotations extend even further. As Jingyuan Zhang has argued, the story

> carries a philosophical message about the separation of the body
> from the mind. Although the mind-body problem is an age-old

philosophical inquiry, the presentation of the issue here is specifically modernist because psychoanalysis teaches that the body has a life of its own but is unable to express itself well through the tropes and rules of language. Here, in an uncanny moment, the dead returns, a mere body which has literally lost its head . . . As a Freudian allegory, the story dramatizes the sometimes alarming independence of the body from the mind's conscious control.[6]

Along similar lines, the story can also be read as the unfolding of a "death instinct," which is insinuated earlier in the story when the general ponders the execution of a soldier who is charged with raping a woman and wonders if he did so for reasons of love. Death, therefore, becomes both a culmination and a consequence of eros—and the "logical" end of the general's human identity. Thus, a touch of his deflated narcissism (no reflection in the water) presages his final loss of identity and his physical defeat; the sneering words of the young woman serve merely as the final coup de grâce in the delayed death of the general's body. It is an uncanny ending rich with challenging implications when read in a Chinese cultural context.

It seems from these examples that Shi has a particular penchant for the sexual body. He has succeeded in boldly distorting and fetishizing parts of the human body—the tongue in "Kumarajiva" and the head and torso in "The General's Head"—in a cultural tradition in which the body (*shen*, translated by Mark Elvin as "body-person") is not taken to be a physical or sexual organ alone but is connected with extraphysical attributes and meanings of person, self, and life.[7] There was, of course, extensive discourse about the body in both Confucianism and Daoism, but the objective was above all to preserve long life. Even the sexual act itself, as is well known in the popular Daoist tradition, was considered an act of male physical nourishment. When the human body becomes the object of literary depiction, as in the "pornographic" sections of the famous novel *Jin-Ping-Mei* (sometimes translated as "Golden Lotus"), it becomes an independent object, shorn ironically of human sexuality. Sexual inter-course is treated like a military maneuver, with the male and female organs locked in combat like two soldiers or two generals. "The General's Head" was not directly influenced by *Jin-Ping-Mei*, which Shi had surely read. In fetishizing the body he turned this tradition on its head—first by separating the body from its traditional cultural associations and then by linking it emblematically to human eroticism and sexuality. In this re-gard, the gender issue becomes quite relevant.

In "Kumarajiva" and "The General's Head" the body parts are male; there is hardly any description of the female body in these texts aside from some clichéd descriptions of women's faces. Even when first invok-ing a femme fatale in "The Girl form Fengyang," Shi seems unable to describe her physical attributes adequately; the male protagonist-corre-spondent is more absorbed in his own feelings and in his journey of pursuit. It was not until Shi wrote the story "Shi Xiu" that he began to focus on the trope of the female body under the male gaze. Interestingly, Shi chose for his subject matter a chapter from a misogynist novel, *Shuihu zhuan*, and rewrote it as a study of abnormal psychology—male sadism toward women—as derived from the theory of the marquis de Sade. Shi may be the only Chinese writer to have become so engrossed with the marquis's theory as to use it as the basis of a story.[8]

Why Sade? Shi himself has not provided any explanation, nor can we expect him to have known the place of the marquis in French cultural history or the history of sexuality. But in some ways the use of sadism is perfectly fitting for characterizing the male misogyny in *Outlaws of the Marsh*.[9] The pervasive violence throughout the novel, associated with the machismo of its predominantly male heroes, becomes even more exces-sive when inflicted on females. Shi cleverly pieced together a story based on portions of two chapters of *Shuihu zhuan* (45–46) involving the hero, Shi Xiu, the "sworn brother" of Yang Xiong. In the original plot, Yang's wife, Pan Qiaoyun, carries on an affair with a lewd monk and is discov-ered by Shi Xiu, who then kills the monk and reports the affair to Yang Xiong. To cover herself, Pan Qiaoyun also reports to her husband, accusing Shi Xiu of trying to seduce her. In Shi's modern version, however, this fabricated seduction episode as narrated by Pan is blown up into an elaborate plot of a genuine but unsuccessful seduction on Pan's part that unveils Shi Xiu's repressed desire for his sworn brother's wife. There are detailed descriptions of Shi Xiu's mental agony—his conscious deliberations as well as his unconscious stirrings (the phrase "in an unconscious state," *zai xiayishi zhong,* is used a number of times).

On the thematic surface, the repression is imposed on Shi Xiu by a Chinese "Mafia" morality of male brotherhood and loyalty as glorified in the original novel (hence the title of Pearl Buck's translation of the story, "All Men Are Brothers"). In Shi's modern text, however, the real animus is the protagonist's erotic desire, which is displaced by a feeling of misogynistic revenge when Shi Xiu reports Pan Qiaoyun's amorous tryst with a monk to Yang Xiong. In the original novel this is the central part of the plot; there is no analysis of Shi Xiu's mental state. But Shi Zhecun cleverly uses the old plot to advance his study of abnormal psychology by borrowing the concept of sadism from its originator in order to describe the hero's twisted psyche, in which his repressed desire is displaced by a sadistic lust for blood. The execution of the seductress and her maid thus provides a fitting climax for both the plot and Shi Xiu's sexual desire:

> Shi Xiu gazes at Pan Qiaoyun with longing. Yang Xiong steps forth, twists his sharp knife, and plucks out a tongue first. Blood pours out from her thin lips. Then, scolding, Yang Xiong with one slash cuts from the heart all the way down to the belly, puts his hand in and plucks out the heart and liver and the intestines. Shi Xiu looks at them one by one, feeling a surge of ecstasy with each slice of the knife. It is only when Yang Xiong cuts through Pan Qiaoyun's stomach that he feels somewhat nauseated. Stupid man—after all, he would do such a thing because he comes from an executioner's background. Yang Xiong then cuts off Pan Qiaoyun's limbs and breasts. Looking at such a body tinged with

the residual color of peach red, Shi Xiu feels again a surge of pleasurable satisfaction. What a great spectacle! Upon dissection, each piece of the body is of utmost beauty. If these pieces are put back together to make another live woman, I am going to embrace her and won't care about Yang Xiong.[10]

This gory spectacle is staged ostensibly to punish the "bad woman" for her wanton and immoral behavior and to forge male loyalty and camaraderie. But in fact it becomes a logical consequence of the traditional novel's underlying misogyny. It is clear that Shi Xiu's ecstasy is the result of transference: the onlooker has become the executioner, and in so looking he is finally able to reach sexual orgasm. One wonders how many readers were offended when "Shi Xiu" was first published in the *Short Story* magazine in 1931. With this story Shi Zhecun was well on his way to becoming an established fiction writer with a formidable talent and a most unusual aesthetic sensibility.

In pursuing the motif of eroticism and sexuality in an imaginary (or reimagined) historical landscape, Shi Zhecun certainly pushed his fiction beyond the normal confines of reality. As his attitude toward modern poetry reflects, however (see Chapter 4), he wished to make his stories "express the sentiments felt by modern people amidst the experiences of their modern lives." The setting that best expressed what he considered to be these modern life experiences was, without doubt, urban Shanghai. His historical tales stand as an exceptional subgenre, a "detour" that paves the way for his Shanghai stories written after 1930. In this new urban mode he attempts a delicate balancing act between verisimilitude and fantasy by placing his stories superficially in the realistic setting of Shanghai only to use the urban milieu as a framework to probe the inner thoughts and fantasies of his urban characters. This modern setting in Shi's fiction consists of the familiar sites of public transportation, entertainment, and consumption in Shanghai: railway and tram stations, department stores, restaurants, hotels, coffeehouses, and, above all, movie theaters.[11] In fact, in a few stories Shi has his characters move through these sites in a kind of fictional remapping that becomes a daily ritual of their modern lives. We are reminded of Joyce's mythic remapping in *Ulysses* of the riverbanks, streets, and taverns of his beloved Dublin. In comparison, Shi's intention is much less ambitious and modernistic. Instead of spatializing time by leading two male protagonists on their peregrinations through a myth-encoded city in one day, as in *Ulysses*, Shi uses familiar Shanghai sites and buildings merely as signposts to lend a sense of realism to the background against which the mental experiences of his characters are foregrounded. And instead of employing Joyce's famous technique of stream of consciousness (of which he was aware), Shi experiments with two other devices: interior monologue and free indirect discourse.

Interior Monologue and Arthur Schnitzler

Shi's early story "Ninong," so far neglected by most scholars,[12] offers a good example of his experiments in the narratorial technique of interior monologue. Unlike all his previous stories, it is a work of pure imagination—a stylistic fabrication with no basis in reality. In fact, at first sight "Ninong" reads like a translation from a French story. The French-sounding title, which is the name of a woman and the addressee of the narrator's monologue, is further underscored by the occasional insertion of the French words *hélas* and *non*, the latter sounding almost the same as *nong* pronounced in the Shanghai dialect, which means "you." Thus the exotic name "Ninong" contains, perhaps unintentionally, an aural double take on Chinese second-person address—*ni* in Mandarin and *nong* in Shanghai dialect—rendered somewhat exotic by the similar sound of the French negative, *non*. The narrator's long interior monologue begins with frequent interruptions punctuated by the word *non* as he grapples with difficulties in recapturing the intense personal experience of the death of his beloved, the addressee, Ninong. A strange hypnotic cadence is thus created when the narrator repetitively intones her name: "I look, I look, I look at Ninong, ah! *non!* my Ninong, *non!* She is not Ninong, she is not Ninong! Ah Ninong, whom I once loved, ah *non*, is not such a person. . ." If interior monologue is supposed to be a subjective form of speech—a voice in the head, which speaks out in stream of consciousness fashion (Molly's soliloquy at the end of *Ulysses* comes readily to mind, which may have been Shi's model in this story)—then the story achieves its psychological and linguistic effect in a way seldom encountered in the typical fiction of the time. Even Lu Xun's story "Regret for the Past," which is cast in a partial interior monologue form and partakes thematically of the May Fourth discourse on the liberation of women, does not achieve such an effect. To give an impression of the rhythm of the language in the Chinese original, the following translation is intentionally unpolished. I have also used the French word *non* for the English word "no."

> Evening, for many years, *non*, many hundred years, ah, *non!* how should I say? I have forgotten these long years, before the time when I was able to remember, before, ah! for what seems like the old precedent from ancient times of not counting the years and months, I put my tired, crestfallen, fragile, and thin body [and] gradually sink into these—ah! these soft round chairs, as my eyes like the pale flickering light from a burnt-out candle cast their glance, [as] my heart, *non*, every small tissue of my skin, feels a hundred times over the trembling.

One might say that this passage, which begins the story, is a somewhat crude attempt at setting a general tone for the narrator's interior monologue in order to achieve a lyrical effect. It is an effect in fiction by way of lyrical poetry. In fact, the sentences that constitute the monologue (there are only two instances of quoted speech from the addressee) are liberally touched up with poetic images derived from Baudelaire, Verlaine, and other French symbolists—dead leaves, dark moon in the forest, the shriek of owls, devilish flames, drops of blood from red lips—as the narrator recounts the decay and death of his lover. This lyrical-symbolic landscape is curiously reminiscent of the early works of

Shi's contemporary Li Jinfa, hailed and reviled as China's first symbolist poet—and perhaps also of Baudelaire and Maeterlinck. But the real source of inspiration is Arthur Schnitzler, the turn-of-the-century Austrian novelist for whose works Shi had a particular admiration.

It is not hard to understand why Shi favored Schnitzler, as we read Shi's "Translator's Preface" to Schnitzler's novel *Theresa: The Chronicle of a Woman's Life:*

> The works of Schnitzler can be said to consist entirely of sexual love as their central theme because sexual love is crucial to all aspects of human life. But he does not describe sexual love as a mere fact or behavior, but focuses on the analysis of sexual psychology. We can say that his success in this regard is comparable to his fellow countryman Freud; some say that he may have been intentionally influenced by Freud. In putting Freud's theory into practice, however, thus opening up a new path for modern European literature and paving the way for the appearance of the great psychological masters Lawrence and Joyce in England, the credit must go to him [Schnitzler]. The style of interior monologue as employed in Joyce's famous novel *Ulysses* had been used long before by Schnitzler in his two novellas, *Fräulein Else* and *Leutnant Gustl.*[13]

At the end of the preface Shi adds a bibliography of about twenty works of fiction and drama by Schnitzler, together with their Chinese translations. His own contributions include *Fräulein Else, Leutnant Gustl, Bertha Garlan,* and *Frau Beatrice and Her Son.* In another preface to his translation of *Fräulein Else,* Shi singles out the two reigning themes of Schnitzler's fiction as sexual love and death and once again emphasizes Schnitzler's invention of the interior monologue, to which Joyce was indebted. Then he confesses: "For a while I was passionately in love with Schnitzler's works. I do not read German, but of the English and French translations not a single volume escaped my attention." He also mentions that he had translated three more works but did not have a chance to publish them, and the manuscripts were lost during the war.[14]

It is clear that Schnitzler's works provided an answer to Shi's own quest as a fiction writer. The technical issue confronting Shi's fiction is what may be called subjective narration: how to render a character's subjective voice and perception in a narratorial framework (that is, in the voice of the narrator) which can bring out his or her mental processes. Whereas the theory of Freud was known as early as around 1913, and some of the May Fourth writers—Lu Xun and Guo Moruo included—began to apply it in their own fiction, in particular the use of dreams, no writer before Shi had attempted to develop a new prose style with which to probe the depths of human sexuality and the psyche. He wanted to describe "reality" subjectively through the perceptions of his characters or narrators and by making the third-person or first-person voices more subjective than, for instance, in Lu Xun's short stories. In addition to a Schnitzlerian interior monologue, which incorporates all dialogue, characterization, and plot into one sustained interior narration, Shi also experiments with shifting narrative voices. Another narrative trick used quite often in Shi's fiction is to begin the story in a narrator's third-person voice but then shift imperceptibly to the first-person voice of the character as his or her thinking process unfolds, and then shift back again to third-person narration. This involves so-called free indirect discourse (FID). Two studies have applied this technical concept to modern Chinese literature—one, in fact, to the fiction of Liu Na'ou and Mu Shiying.[15] In my view, a better example can be found in the stories of Shi Zhecun.

Simply put, FID occurs in a subjective narrative in which the narrator's voice still exits but his or her power of perception is rendered indirectly through a character's own perception and voice.[16] Since in the Chinese language there is no rigid tense system and no pure tense marker nor any strict rules governing the agreement between subject and predicate, it allows even more flexibility in the use of FID. This is the major narrative mode used by Shi in *Shan nüren xingping* (Exemplary conduct of virtuous women), a series of psychological portraits of modern or semimodern Chinese women. These stories were also inspired by Schnitzler, for the most interesting protagonists in Schnitzler's novels are women, particularly in those Shi translated—*Fräulein Else, Bertha Garlan,* and *Theresa*—which he published together under a new title, *Fuxin sanbuqu* (A trilogy of woman's heart). Schnitzler's fin-de-siècle Viennese world of bourgeois respectability, in which these women suppress their sexual desires or carry on clandestine affairs in the course of their daily lives only to meet with a tragic fate, must have struck a chord in Shi as he transformed them into urban Chinese women and transferred their world to 1930s Shanghai.

Portraits of "Exemplary" Women

The title of this collection, *Exemplary Conduct of Virtuous Women,* makes a purposeful reference to the traditional hagiographic accounts of chaste women (*jiefu*). The irony lies, of course, in the fact that none of the heroines in this collection can really be considered "exemplary" in their internal conduct, and a few of them indeed harbor unchaste thoughts. Shi's intention is to describe the workings of such unchaste thoughts on their daily lives by a technique of narrative subjectivity that he learned from Schnitzler. This had been his major concern all along, as manifested in some of his early rural stories and historical tales. In this collection he was now ready to display his new talent in its full glory.

How do these urban women think and feel? This simple question poses a daunting challenge for a male writer who does not wish to follow the typical May Fourth tenet about women's liberation. Shi's women characters, though modern and urban, are *not* liberated: one is a widow, another a spinster, but most of them are housewives who have no wish to break away from their husbands and families. It is as if, in reverse response to the "emancipated Nora" syndrome of May Fourth fiction, Shi intentionally kept his would-be Noras at home.

At the same time, anticipating the more sophisticated fiction of Eileen Chang in the early 1940s, Shi chooses to dwell on the small charms of these bourgeoises in their everyday lives. It would have been tempting for Shi to follow in the footsteps of Arthur Schnitzler and uncover their libidos and neuroses beneath the veneer of respectability. This would also have made Shi's fiction a modern case of *épater le bourgeois*, Chinese style. But a reading of the stories does not lead to such a conclusion: the narratorial tone is consistently gentle and sympathetic, though slightly ironic. Like Eileen Chang, Shi is too enamored of his female characters to subject them to a scathing exposé. In contrast to the unbridled eroticism of his historical heroes, the female psyche is portrayed as more delicate and fragile. In one story, "Gangnei xiaojing" (A scene inside the harbor), a wife is bedridden with tuberculosis; her husband tries to leave her for another woman but fails. In another, "Shizizuo liuxing" (A comet in the sign of Leo), a wife who wishes to become pregnant imparts her secret desire to an astrological omen, the reported appearance of a comet, while her fat, insensitive husband snores beside her. In a third story, "Qizhi shengchen" (My wife's birthday), which seems autobiographical, the (implied) author's traditional wife gently nags him to cook a special vegetable soup while he is busy reading a book by Julian Green and translating a series of poems by Richard Aldington. The Western texts mentioned here, we have every reason to believe, were the texts Shi was reading at the time he composed the story. Shi cleverly works a few lines of an Aldington poem into the story's ending as a testimony to the love he feels for his wife:

> The blue smoke leaps
> Like swirling clouds of birds vanishing.
> So my love leaps forth towards you,
> Vanish and is renewed.[17]

Given such gentle romanticism, is it still possible to depict female sexuality and eroticism? If this Chinese version of Victorian society is portrayed less oppressively, does Shi still find Freud relevant?

Two stories in the collection—"Wu" (Fog) and "Chunyang" (Spring sunshine)—portray two women who transform their desires into romantic fantasies. In "Fog" a young widow encounters a gentle-looking man on a train to Shanghai and fantasizes about dating him—only to realize later that he is a famous movie star. The story is told as a straight third-person narrative in which the character's fantasies and perceptions are rendered objectively; her disillusionment comes from her equating the movie star with the lower-class actor (*xizi*) in traditional society. Meanwhile, the narration before closure conjures up the filmlike atmosphere of a romantic encounter, as the movie star, true to his profession, finds himself enacting a role. (This fantasy scenario would be fully played out in Eileen Chang's story "Sealed Off" some ten years later.) The story's title brings to mind a traditional literary allusion, *wuli kanhua*, or "looking at the flower through fog," except that here, "look" contains a double irony: as the heroine looks at the movie actor, she is also looking at herself indulging in a romantic fantasy about him. In this doubly framed deception (the heroine is unwittingly deceived by the actor; the reader is "deceived" by the movielike plot), we are led to witness the gentle process of the heroine's sexual arousal, which, however, is brought to an end by her realization that the man is an actor. Thus, the story's closure also becomes an act of suppression, a modern reworking of the moral endings of countless stories about chaste widows in traditional Chinese literature who dutifully play out their exemplary roles.

A similar treatment can be found in the story "Spring Sunshine," in which the heroine's sensibilities are described by a subtle employment of free indirect discourse as the narrator's commentary imperceptibly blends into the character's own perceptions:

> The mid-February sun, which has not shone on Shanghai for quite sometime, don't you forget, really casts its spell . . . Today, bracing against her face is a puff of hot air, a patch of eye-blinding light, and this makes her feel in high spirits out of nothing. She takes out her gold Elgin watch from ten years ago. Ten minutes to twelve. Quite early. Better walk a little along the streets.

So Auntie Chan of Kunshan walks by herself to Nanking Road in Shanghai, bathed in warm spring sunshine. The women and men passing by all wear such light clothing—so beautiful, and so delicate; and this makes her feel the burden of her own woollen scarf and her *qipao* made of camel's hair. If only I'd known the weather was so warm I would have worn that swallow-feathered *qipao* padded with light wool. As she calculates in her mind, her hand takes off the woollen scarf and folds it over her arm.[18]

In this close-to-literal translation I have supplied only the pronoun "I" and the subjunctive mood in the sentence "If only I'd known the weather was so warm . . ." The lack of verb tenses in Chinese and the omitted subject in the first sentence allow more room for ambiguity and for the natural shift between first- and third-person narration. By taking advantage of this built-in flexibility in Chinese sentence structure, Shi has developed a style that enables him to depict the mental processes of his characters. This story is another study of feminine desire and fantasy that ends in gentle frustration. The plot follows the heroine's wandering in the city in one day: after arriving at the railway station, she goes to her bank and a department store, then eats a solitary meal at a restaurant, where she sees a handsome man and fantasizes about approaching him, and finally returns to her bank to see a young clerk, who turns his attention to another, younger woman. The heroine, frustrated, takes an early train home in the afternoon. She is certainly no *flâneuse*: her activities in the city are nothing more than personal diversions. But the warm sunshine releases her desire, which finds its object as she gently gazes at a male stranger in the restaurant. The ensuing fantasized dialogue, which promises romantic fulfillment, is abruptly interrupted when in her dream scenario he says, "My name is Zhang and I work at the Shanghai Bank." Henceforth her amorous thoughts are immediately transferred to the young clerk she has just seen at the same bank. The transference of her desired object also serves to frustrate her desire, and she is brought back to reality. Thus, although nothing seems to have happened on the surface, she has experienced a lust of the heart, a gentle cycle of amorous arousal and dissipation, without reaching (as Shi Xiu did) a climax through her gaze. It is this vaguely sexual subtext that lends a degree of intensity to Shi's subjective narrative.

As I noted earlier, Shi Zhecun may be called China's first Freudian writer in the sense that some of his stories are conceived in Freudian categories. The stories I have discussed, however, indicate that Shi did not carry his Freudian analysis very far, especially with regard to his female characters. In the *Good Women* collection, Shi seems more interested in the mind than in the body of his female characters. There is no suggestion of any "abnormal" symptom, such as hysteria, that would lend itself to a Freudian analysis of female sexuality. Perhaps, as the collection's title suggests, these are after all "good women," and Shi does not want to derogate their newly gained social status as "modern" Chinese women. But these portraits are by no means "feminist" either: none of the heroines has an identity of her own apart from her man, and Shi's probing of their minds reveals no feminist consciousness. Even without imposing a present-day Western perspective, it is not difficult for the reader to see that Shi's "good women" are semi-traditional in their values, behavior, and even dress code; they are definitely not as foreign and exotic as the fictional heroines of Liu Na'ou and Mu Shiying. Nor, for that matter, are they commodified or objectified into emblems of the modern city itself. They seem to exist in a domesticated space protected against the excessive stimuli of urban life; even the heroine of "Spring Sunshine" returns home unharmed. These women make an intriguing parallel to the image of modern domesticity—of urban woman as wife and mother in a conjugal setting of material comfort—found in the commercial advertisements of the time (see Chapter 2). To these material images of women Shi has given a range of human sensibilities and a degree of psychological depth. It may well be that his contemporary readers could relate to them more easily than to the more fantastic and grotesque heroes of his other stories.[19]

The Erotic, the Fantastic, and the Grotesque

As an avant-garde experimentalist Shi was not, in my view, interested in rendering another Chinese version of the Jamesian "portrait of a lady." From his prefaces we learn that he always wanted to chart new courses. In the same year (1933) that saw the publication of *Exemplary Conduct of Good Women*, another collection of his stories, *Meiyu zhixi* (An evening of spring rain), also appeared. It is a miscellaneous collection that contains ten fictional works dealing with diverse subject matter. In his own preface he admits to their technical limitations, but he also reveals that in at least a few stories he had tried to find a new path, but after repeated efforts he realized that this path had led him astray.[20] This disclaimer is both an honest confession and a beguiling deception. We know that his self-criticism was intended as a modest response to adverse criticism from the leftist camp on account of his radical stylistic departure from social realism. But between the lines he has given us another confession of his experimental impulse. For despite their uneven technical quality, these stories prove quite daringly experimental, as Shi continues his exploration of abnormal psychology first set forth in his historical tales but now returned to a contemporary setting.

The imprint of Schnitzler is clearly visible in the first two stories of this collection, in which a sustained interior monologue is employed as the main narrative framework. Both are portraits of male desire and obsession as narrated by an intensely subjective male voice.

Male erotic obsession is the key motif in the story "Zai Bali daxi-yuan" [At the Paris Theater]. It depicts the narrator's intimate experience watching a film with a young woman companion at the Paris Theater, a movie house in Shanghai which, as the narrator remarks, does not offer the deluxe comfort of the Grand Theater, the Carlton, or the Nanking, and hence is a more fitting place for a tryst. The movie theater provides a realistic setting for an account of the whole ritual experience of going to the movies: buying the tickets, going up the narrow stairway, sitting in the dress circle, reading the plot summary sheets, eating ice cream during the intermission, watching the cartoons and the main feature (a film produced by the German Agfa company), and commenting on the stars (the Russian Ivan Mayukin as compared to Hollywood's Rudolph Valentino). Yet these realistic details of the movie house merely provide the setting for an intense probing of psychological obsession told entirely in a sustained interior monologue by the male narrator-protagonist, in the same vein as Schnitzler's *Leutnant Gustl* and *Fräulein Else*. The first-person narration provides equally lavish details about his subjective experience of going to the movies on a date as a married man. From beginning to end the first-person narrator is constantly deciphering his companion's every move, which he sees as increasingly seductive—a projection of his own sexual arousal. The "climax" is reached when his companion lends him her handkerchief to clean his hands after eating some chocolate ice cream:

> Ah, how fragrant! This really is her aroma—the aroma of perfume mixed with the smell of her sweat. I really want to taste it, it must be very interesting. I could use the handkerchief to wipe my mouth from left to right, and as it passes through I can stick my tongue out and taste it, even suck it, and I won't be discovered. Isn't this wonderful! Good, the lights are out, and the movie begins again. This is a golden opportunity, and let me suck it to my heart's content . . . here it tastes salty, must be the taste of her sweat . . . but what's this, so smelly and pungent? . . . Perhaps it's her spit and snivel. Yes, indeed it is, rather sticky. This is really a marvelous taste! The tip of my tongue is numb with excitement. Strange, I have the feeling that I am embracing her naked body.[21]

The protagonist's rather kinky fetishism in this extraordinary passage is comparable to the sado-voyeurism of "Shi Xiu." It may also contain a deliberate intertextual reference to one of Yu Dafu's stories, in which the male hero experiences a similar taste. In both the metonymic link of orality with sexuality is blatant and daringly depicted. Still, despite all his efforts, the male protagonist is uncertain about the "real" amorous intentions of his woman companion. He is left with the impression that she is still interested in him in spite of his married status, but the complications of his own guilt have yet to be sorted out. This is precisely the theme of "An Evening of Spring Rain," the title story of the collection.

At first glance the story is a mood piece that recalls Dai Wanghsu's famous poem "Rainy Alley," first published in 1928. In Dai's poem, the poet walks down a "rainy alley" and encounters a "lilac maiden" holding an umbrella of oiled paper—a lyrical image that evokes the poet's gentle romantic yearning. In Shi's story the atmosphere is more intense, though equally lyrical. It begins with the first-person narrator-protagonist walking along the familiar streets of Shanghai in a pouring rain. But the familiar sights are subtly transformed into a dreamlike stage for a casual encounter with a young maiden. As the narrator watches her step down from a tram without an umbrella and stand at the street corner waiting for the rain to stop, his interior monologue reveals an inner agitation he can hardly control. As he gingerly offers her his umbrella and walks with her to an uncertain destination, he is besieged with thoughts of desire and guilt as she reminds him of his first girlfriend and his wife. As in Schnitzler's *Leutnant Gustl*, hallucinations begin to play tricks with his perception. "Accidentally, as I look at the roadside, a shopgirl leaning on a store counter is looking at me with melancholic eyes, or perhaps she is looking at her. Suddenly I seem to discover that she is my wife. Why is she here? I wonder."[22] At the story's end, when the narrator reaches home and knocks on the door, he hears a voice that answers his call, a voice not of his wife but of the maiden in the rain, but what he sees, once again, is the shopgirl standing at the half-opened door with her back to the light. "I walk inside in a daze. Under the light I am surprised to find that there is no trace of that girl's illusion on my wife's face."[23] The story can be read as a case of psychological transference, as the maiden elicits desire and guilt, which is transferred back to the maiden and to the shopgirl at the end. But the intrusion of the shopgirl remains enigmatic: why does this figure, who is seen only once in casual glance on the street, reappear at the end? In realistic terms, her presence is purely accidental, and the plot leaves this loose end unresolved. Nor is her symbolic status as something of a double for the wife convincingly portrayed. Rather, she seems to be a mysterious figure, the only one who gazes back at the protagonist—a phantom figure who creates a feeling of unease and fear. It is this inexplicable female figure who reappears in more mysterious and macabre guises to lead the male protagonists in Shi's later stories down a bewitched path.

With the story "Modao" (Demonic way) the dam of plausibility finally breaks and the plot is filled with bizarre incidents encountered both in reality and in the first-person narrator's demented mind. As the story begins, the protagonist-narrator takes a train out of Shanghai one weekend to visit his friend in the country. In the train compartment he sees an old woman in black who makes him uneasy. He arrives at his friend's Western-style house, located in a suburban area of a town (presumably Hangchow). While looking out the window at a bamboo grove in misty rain, he sees the old woman in black again and is stricken with terror. He feels tired, "as if having experienced a war," and takes a nap. Waking up at dusk, he takes a walk. At this point his narration is mixed with hallucinations, as if he were lost in an opium-induced dream, and he begins to talk incessantly about opium. Beside the dark green water of a pond, he recalls an old Chinese folk song as he watches village girls washing clothes, and suddenly he sees the old witch again moving behind the bamboo grove. He returns to the friend's house and sits in the garden with the friend and his beautiful wife. As he bites into a fresh tomato, he is suddenly seized with a desire for her and feels as if the red fruit were her red lips. He takes her kindness for seductiveness. Next morning, as she greets him, he sees her holding a big black cat and perceives her as the old witch reincarnated. As terror and suspicion mount in his mind, he hastily takes the train back home to Shanghai. Upon his arrival, he goes to the Odeon Theater in the evening to catch a movie in order to relax his nerves. At the box office he finds a "Sold Out" sign and sees the last customer entering the theater—an old woman in black. "All old women in black are bad omens! ANYONE! EVERY-ONE!" he exclaims, the last two words in English. He goes to a coffee-house and sees his usual waitress, who gives him black beer, inducing another series of hallucinations in which the waitress, the friend's wife, and the witch are all turned into one temptress whom he kisses. Twenty minutes later he returns home and finds a telegram informing him that his three-year-old daughter has just died. As he looks down from the balcony, he sees beneath a gaslight the solitary figure of an old woman in black turning into a small alley.

The story recalls a number of basic images and motifs from the stories of Edgar Allan Poe, another favorite author of Shi's. The color black figures prominently in the text: the black-clad old woman, black beer, and in particular the big black cat that the friend's wife is holding. Even the sudden, unexplained death of the protagonist's daughter can be read as an added mystical touch in the style of Poe, but it still seems too far-fetched. Again there are several loose ends that remain unresolved in the story. Thus, it seems that the story is not merely a study of abnormal male psychology but an exploration of a new fantastic domain—the powers of the supernatural, which cannot be reined in by rational explanations.

In another story, "Yecha" (Yaksha), a companion piece to "Demonic Way" but more successfully received (as it was first published in the popular journal *Dongfang zazhi*), Shi continues to play with the fantastic. The plot of "Yaksha" was conceived fortuitously as Shi one day saw the head of a woman sticking out from a train compartment window, "with her mouth open, looking just like a woman being choked to death."[24] Thus, he has his male protagonist glimpse a maiden in white on a passing boat near an ancient temple. Bewitched, he mistakes her for a "Yak-sha"—a demon from popular Buddhism that can fly like a witch—and pursues her on a moonlit night until he finds her in a graveyard. In his feverish state he strangles her, only to realize that she is but an innocent peasant woman. As Robert Chi remarks in a perceptive paper, Shi's figures of the deadly-erotic woman "descend directly from Poe's Ligeia and Madeline Usher."[25] Shi must also have derived special inspiration from Poe's famous story "The Fall of the House of Usher," for the maiden spirit in "Yaksha" is likewise conjured up in the narrative by two paintings and then "summoned" by a book of local legends which the protagonist happens to be reading. In fact, this incessant reading by a paranoid protagonist reminds us of Lu Xun's "Diary of a Madman," but unlike Lu Xun's intellectual madman, Shi's protagonist is not ideologically anti-traditional.[26] Still, in both stories the protagonist's act of reading carries a special kind of significance. At the beginning of the protagonist's weekend journey in "Demonic Way," right after his initial encounter with the old woman in black in the train compartment, he tries to settle down and read:

> Let me do some reading. My small leather suitcase carries some books. Ah, well, I'd better not pull out that book, *The Romance of Sorcery*. Is it because I've been reading a few too many books on the occult these past couple of days that I am under their influence? Well, possibly a little bit, but there is something definitely a little odd about that old woman, and even if I had not been reading such books I would still have had the same feeling. Which book should I take out and read? *Strange Tales* by Le Fanu, *Persian Religious Verses, Dossier of Sexual Crimes, Gems of English Poetry?* But I am not in the mood to read these books. What else is in my luggage? . . . Nothing, just these five books . . . I do have a copy of *Psychology Magazine*, but that's not interesting.[27]

This booklist has received some pointed criticism from a Chinese scholar: "The problem lies here: this is a modern educated intellectual. How can he so simply believe in that bunch of superstitions from old books?"[28] Clearly the case points to the contrary: this gross misreading confuses the fictional protagonist with a follower of May Fourth rationality. The significance of the reading list lies elsewhere: Robert Chi has remarked that "it is significant less as a network of intertexuality than as an index of cultural capital."[29] Chi also notes that the first title, *The*

Romance of Sorcery, and the name Le Fanu are printed in Roman letters in the Chinese text; this foreign typography not only lends more exoticism to the visual materiality of the text but also "can allow the narrator, the author, and the reader who can read these words to accrue still more cultural capital."[30]

If indeed Shi wished to show off the "cultural capital" of his Western knowledge, he did not stop at the booklist; the story is peppered with other Western references: ancient Egyptian mummies, catacombs, witches, Leda and the mythic Swan ("What surrealistic eroticism!" the narrator exclaims). Even the words "fantastical" and "grotesque" are written in English. All these textual references can be read as "many signifiers [that] crisscross" in a "terribly self-analytical text," as another scholar, Jingyuan Zhang, argues. "What is signified is the modern sensibility—the embrace of a 'blooming buzzing confusion' (William James's phrase to describe the stream of consciousness) and at the same time a hopeless search for order."[31] If so, some of these "signifiers" do not relate directly to the "signified"—or if they do, they must be mediated by another set of contextual inquiries. To take one example, why does the name Le Fanu appear in bold print in Roman letters in Shi's story—an obscure name that sounds French but is really Irish? What can be gained from flaunting such a name?

Joseph Sheridan Le Fanu (1814–1873) was a mid-Victorian writer whose stories of ghosts are, in V. S. Pritchett's words, like "blobs of the unconscious that have floated up to the surface of the mind"; sometimes the ghost takes the shape of a phantom monkey that suddenly "jumps into the Bible [of a clergyman] when he preaches, and waits for him at street corners, in carriages, in his very room. A very Freudian animal this." Le Fanu's stories are presented, in turn, as case studies by a fictional psychiatrist "whose precise theory appears to be that these fatal visitations come when the psyche is worn to rags and the interior spirit world can then make contact with the external through the holes. A touch of science, even bogus science, gives an edge to the superstitious tale."[32] Is it not possible that this particular name flaunted in the text serves, in fact, as a model for "Maodao," that with "Demonic Way" Shi wants to explore a new fictional path to the supernatural by way of some minor Western "ghost writers" whose own literary fame had been "pushed into limbo by the great novelists with their grandiose and blatant passion for normality"?[33]

During my interviews with Shi Zhecun, he told me that the books carried by the protagonist in the story were books in his own possession at the time. To these he added a long list of his favorite reading matter by a host of authors: Edgar Allan Poe, Jules Barbey d'Aurevilly, James Frazer, Andrew Lang, and Fiona McLeod (William Sharp). As a result of reading these works, he had developed an interest in sorcery, witchcraft, necromancy, and black magic. "Demonic Way" was the first fictional text in which Shi managed to "summon" these readings as his "research aids." In this regard, these foreign works of supernaturalism did not merely equip him with a self-empowering knowledge of the foreign and exotic; they in fact provided the very literary ground for his creative imagination. As sources of his fiction, these Western works were combined with works of the *zhiguai* (strange and bizarre) genre in traditional Chinese literature as well as the more popular strains of Buddhism and Daoism. His story "Yaksha" is clearly inspired by such a native tradition. This combined knowledge of Chinese and Western superstitions certainly does not befit a typical May Fourth intellectual, whose faith in science and rationality must lead him or her to renounce superstitions of any kind. Thus, by foregrounding all his other—and otherworldly—textual sources in his own stories, Shi is determined to convey a crucial message about his new path of writing fiction.

In his bewitched state, the protagonist of "Yaksha" indulges in a peculiar erotic fantasy; he has the sudden urge to make love to the female Yaksha: "In my heart a grotesque desire is burning. I want to experience what was written in the fiction of deities and demons. I want to extend the sphere of human love. I want to discover the natural captivating beauty in an unnatural act. I have totally abandoned reason."[34] This fictional confession can be read as the author's own manifesto of literary intention—to capture and unite in one ecstatic moment or narrative space the forces of the erotic, the grotesque, and the fantastic. And this can be achieved, as the protagonist asserts, again citing as evidence his "ancient books," by the power of words that "can break through the barrier of time and space."[35] Needless to say, the power of words—the language of his fiction—is ultimately the only power that can bewitch both author and reader, both inside and outside the fictional texts.

This writerly intention brings Shi to a position that is not only radically removed from experiential realism as advocated by most May Fourth writers but also close to a postmodern view of literature's self-referentiality. As his reading becomes the source of his writing, his texts are constituted by other texts, and his protagonists are made to be readers also, like himself. As the actual readers of Shi's stories, we are expected to replicate the same reading process and to derive a double pleasure of textual discovery. In other words, Shi invites us to play the dual role of reader and researcher—to serve as both audience to his sorcerer's tricks and scholarly detective of his cited sources. His listing of other titles and authors in his fiction can be read, at least in part, as an extended practice of his cultural enterprise of introducing Western literature in the journals he edited. (In fact, some of the stories in the *Spring Rain* collection were first published in *Les Contemporains*.)

The Urban Uncanny

It seems that with all these quotations from Western literary sources, the fantastic strain of Shi's fiction can be characterized by what may be called the world of the uncanny. In view of Shi's obvious indebtedness to Freud, it may be relevant to discuss Freud's famous 1919 literary essay on the "uncanny" (*das Unheimliche*, or "unhomeliness") as a starting point. In a perceptive analysis of the theme of the uncanny in architecture, the art historian Anthony Vidler has noted that Freud's concept of the uncanny arose "from the transformation of something that once seemed homely into something decidedly not so, from the *heimlich*, that is, into the *unheimlich.*" Generalized as a condition of modern anxiety, the uncanny "finally became public in metropolis." Then, "from the 1870s on, the metropolitan uncanny was increasingly conflated with metropolitan illness, a pathological condition that had, through force of environment, escaped the overprotected domain of the short story." The uncanny "emerged in the late nineteenth century as a special case of many modern diseases, from phobias to neurosis, variably described by psychoanalysts, psychologists, and philosophers as a distancing from reality forced by reality. Its space was still an interior, but now the interior of the mind, one that knew no bounds in projection or introversion. Its symptoms included spatial fear, leading to paralysis of movement, and temporal fear, leading to historical amnesia." Vidler also argues that "the themes of anxiety and dread, provoked by a real or imagined sense of 'unhomeliness,' seemed particularly appropriate to a moment when . . . the entire 'homeland' of Europe, cradle and apparently secure house of western civilization, was in the process of barbaric regression" as a result of the First World War.[36]

As we transpose Vidler's and Freud's insights into a different cultural milieu—though at a time contemporary with Freud's own—several issues immediately suggest themselves. Whether or not Chinese intellectuals were at all affected by the trauma of the European war, Shanghai emerged as the only modern metropolitan city in China in which a writer such as Shi Zhecun could feel a degree of the uncanny—if not in real life, certainly in literature. Most likely Shi had not read Freud's essay, but he was certainly familiar with the literary works in which Freud's concept of the uncanny found its first home: those of E. T. A. Hoffmann and Edgar Allan Poe. As I noted earlier, there are ample traces of the latter in "Demonic Way" and "Yaksha." In the two collections of stories I have discussed, *Good Women* and *Spring Rain*, city and country—a Westernized metropolis and a traditional Chinese landscape of evocative pastoralism—form a spatial matrix for the protagonist's journeys: either he or she arrives in the city already stimulated by a heightened libido, or he or she takes a brief trip to the country and back and goes through an erotic-demonic experience of terror and dread. The themes of anxiety and dread were precisely the ones Shi attempted to (re)capture in his stories. As his fiction indicates, the metropolitan uncanny in China had indeed not "escaped the overprotected domain of the short story"; it had just entered it. The sense of real or imagined "unhomeliness" was a mental state caused by living in a metropolitan island of capitalist splendor in a sea of rural cultural feudalism. We recall that once in the country, the urban protagonist of "Demonic Way" does not feel at home even in his friend's Western-style house. Another urban traveler in the story "Lüshe" (Traveler's inn) curses the poor material conditions of his lodging, only to be plunged into another nightmare of ghosts and demons. For Shi's urban dwellers, the rural countryside becomes the demonic "other," ready to torment and swallow up their already disturbed and deranged psyche.

Vidler's valuable book *The Architectural Uncanny* also reminds us that Shanghai's buildings and spaces in the foreign concessions could be a perfect setting for the metropolitan uncanny. What if Shi's taste for the bewitched had been given free rein, and, instead of losing himself in the countryside, the protagonist-narrator of "Demonic Way" had eventually made his way into a haunted house in Shanghai's French Concession and encountered natural or supernatural "foreign devils"? The story "Xiong zhai" (The haunted house), set in a Dutch-style cottage on Gordon Road in Shanghai's International Settlement, comes close to such a scenario. It is also Shi's only story in which all the characters are foreign. As we saw in Chapter 1, these deluxe houses and mansions were exclusively the domain of rich Westerners and normally beyond the reach of the average Chinese. The story seems to fit into a popular Western genre that is closely associated with the uncanny: gothic romance. Leslie Fiedler has argued that the gothic is, first of all, "an avant-garde genre, perhaps the first avant-garde art in the modern sense of the term."[37] It was designed to shock or titillate its bourgeois readers with its depictions of depravity and horror as well as to affirm the power of the irrational. Fiedler considers the detective story, the ghost story, and science fiction all to be modern descendants of the gothic. Armed with the stories of Poe, Shi Zhecun could have created in "The Haunted House" a Chinese variation on the urban gothic romance—an imaginary site of the urban "un-homely." But he went no farther afield into this alien territory. The plot involves the mysterious deaths of three women in a "haunted" Western house in a Shanghai suburb. Since the story is clearly modeled after the Western detective genre, Shi enlists a host of Western detective writ-ers—from Arthur Conan Doyle and Arsène Lupin to Edgar Wallace—as narratorial aids. In fact, the narrator goes to great pains to quote not only from the charaters' letters and diaries—including one retranslated back into Chinese from a French translation—but also from newspaper ac-counts presumably taken from one of Shanghai's English-language news-papers. But the story ultimately disappoints because it is too concerned with solving the murder case, thus dissipating the spell of the haunted house and the intended effect of suspense.

Another story in which a foreigner plays a major role is "Sixizi de shengyi" (Lucky Four's trade), which introduces another uncanny ele-ment in the form of an erotic gaze that can be further analyzed in terms of gender, race, and sexuality. According to Shi's own account, he wrote the story with great effort but considered it a dismal failure and "un-speakably bad."[38] For the first time Shi attempts to emulate the speech patterns of a lower-class worker, a rickshaw driver who recounts his experience of pulling a foreign woman through the streets of Shanghai. In a carefully designed route Shi maps out Shanghai's key sites and streets—but they are seen from the eyes of a rickshaw man from rural Subei (the northern part of Kiangsu province, where the majority of Shanghai's working class originally came from). With his empty rick-shaw, Lucky Four takes the ferry from north Shanghai to the Interna-tional Settlement. He then makes the rounds and finds himself reaching Nanking Road—"the swankiest thoroughfare in Shanghai"—and heads into trouble.

He eyes the brand-new rickshaws at a shop (perhaps an *hommage* to another writer, Lao She, who wrote a novel called *Rickshaw* set in Beijing), and passes the three big department stores: Wing-On, Sincere, and Sun Company. He stares at the mannequins in the shopwindows and curses the automobiles and tram cars which take his business away. He looks at a jewelry store next to a camera shop. Finally he sees a foreign woman "standing below the big signboard at the corner of Kiangsi Road, on which is painted a foreign man walking with big steps" (Johnny Walker). What follows after the woman steps into his rickshaw is a drama of heightened racial and sexual tension. The white woman, tapping on his shoulder first with the tip of her leather shoe and then with her bare toes, gives him direction to Avenue Joffre in the French Concession by having him wind around the racecourse and the Great World amusement building. As she increases her tapping to hurry him up, he takes the gesture as titillation, and his carnal desire intensifies: he pulls her down to him, she shrieks, and a foreign policeman arrives and arrests him. The story is ostensibly one of Shi's typical studies of male eroticism, but in this situation the object of his desire is presumably a White Russian prostitute acting as if she were his colonial master/mistress. In this vivid reenactment of the master-slave relationship, Lucky Four's thwarted desire, evoked by a highly degrading gesture from the woman, becomes a *ressentiment* that is doubly degrading precisely because he is literally "downtrodden" by a White Russian prostitute whose social status is not much higher than his own. As it is played out against the backdrop of a Western-dominated metropolis, this drama of repressed sexuality takes on the dimensions of class and race: the Chinese rickshaw puller's final outburst is seen as attempted rape from a colonial point of view, but in its irrational way it is also a primitive act of racial revenge—a symbolic lifting of the "white man's burden." As the story ends, the irony of the title is not lost on the reader: this is indeed an unlucky day for Lucky Four.

Shi's elaborately constructed web of racial desire and repression centering on the focal consciousness of an inarticulate narrator-protagonist is another demonstration of his experimental fictional technique. But he was far from satisfied. As he later stated: "In fact, after I wrote 'Lucky Four's Trade,' I could have called it quits, but I was not willing to admit it. I still wanted to use an old news story in order to create something new and exciting. That was 'The Haunted House.' Readers can perhaps see that from 'Demonic Way' to 'The Haunted House' I have virtually written myself into a demonic path."[39]

There is something enigmatic in this confessional passage by Shi Zhecun attached to one of his story collections. What does he mean by the statement "I have virtually written myself into a demonic path"? The sentence seems to spin around an intentional pun on *modao*, which can mean both a devil's trick (hence my translation, "Demonic Way") and a straying path into the bewitched and the bizarre (as in the phrase *zouhuo rumo*, or "playing with fire and getting bewitched"). The former implies a special way with sorcery and magic, which seems to be the original meaning of the story bearing the title. The latter sense is more self-critical, as Shi seems to admit publicly that he has been led astray by his own interest in the former. We now know that he was forced to abandon this line of surrealistic experiments largely because of mounting criticism from leftists.[40] But the double meaning of the word compound *modao* also implies two positions toward fiction writing. In one sense, Shi confesses to going in a wrong (i.e., unrealistic) direction. In another sense, he could also mean that he liked being bewitched by the magic of fiction. In fact, my whole argument in this chapter has been that Shi was well on his way toward evolving his own magic realism—a journey that was cut short all of a sudden.

Shi's last fiction collection, *Xiaozhen ji* (Small treasures), published in 1936 by the Liangyou company (famous for its popular pictorial journal), contains eight stories, all written in a realistic vein with a humanistic touch and without a trace of grotesque and bizarre elements. It seems as if Shi had yielded to leftist pressure and made a complete turnabout from his earlier urban gothic direction. The characters in these stories, while still mostly petty urbanites, are portrayed as pitiable victims of the city. To give one small example, the story "Ou" (Seagull) depicts a Shanghai bank clerk who feels nostalgic for his hometown village by the sea. One evening he takes a walk and comes face to face with Shanghai's finest movie palace, the Grand Theater. As he passes by the "Now Showing" sign (in English, thus enhancing its alienating effect), he suddenly sees a well-dressed modern woman in the company of one of his bank colleagues, a Westernized dandy; she turns out to be the country girl from the clerk's hometown who was his first love.[41] The theme of the modern city as a corrupting influence on the country innocent, which the story clearly follows, had by this time become the prevailing ethos in leftist literature and cinema. Does this story—and the other works in this last collection—indicate that Shi had finally returned to the leftist fold and followed the general trend of social realism? If so, we will have to conclude that for a true urban writer whose budding talent for the erotic, the grotesque, and the bizarre was so quickly nipped in the bud, it is nothing less than a tragedy. But in the collection's postscript we find a note of gentle but sarcastic defiance vis-à-vis his leftist critics:

> It is said that my fiction is not great and that now is the age when we need to read great works. After reading the great works of other "great" writers I felt ashamed, so I couldn't help letting my thoughts turn back to ancient times: I consider my stories to belong to the category of [what the ancients called] unworthy "small pieces by minor writers."
>
> By "small" I mean a minor writer, and "treasure" is meant as in the saying, "Even a shabby broom I can treasure myself." While my works are never great, and never treasured by the "great masses," still I imagine my right of "treasuring" them myself has not been taken away. So I title them a collection of "small treasures" in order to register my feelings of forlorn decline.[42]

The meaning behind this deliberate juxtaposition of the "great" and the "small" could not have been lost even among his contemporary readers. Like Lu Xun, Shi was certainly not impressed by the clarion calls for revolutionary literature. Nor did he wish to follow Lu Xun's road to "greatness" on the leftist front. In fact, his advocacy of the continued relevance of classical literature to students had elicited the master's wrathful critique. In spite of their shared disdain for naive revolutionary slogans, the two writers certainly did not feel the same way toward their age. But even without Lu Xun's animosity, Shi was already under too much external pressure to continue with his creative enterprise.

After his *Xiandai zazhi* folded, Shi edited another short-lived journal, *Wenfan xaopin* (literally, "a literary diet of small essays"), which already leaned toward literary connoisseurship, and published a scholarly anthology of Ming dynasty prose. It would seem that Shi had finally left his modern demons behind and returned to the secure world of premodern Chinese literature. During the war years Shi turned away from creative writing and concentrated on scholarship. He published a sizable number of essays, but no fiction. Then, on the very eve of the war, in June 1937, another respected journal, *Wenxue zazhi* (Literature magazine), published a story Shi had written in March, "Huangxin dashi" (Master Huangxin). This was one of his last works of creative fiction and, like one of his first works, "Ninong," never found its way into any of his fiction collections.

The story has a classical theme and is written in an elegant style with many quotations of classical poetry and prose, but not a single Western reference. In the story the implied author, on an outing with a female companion not his wife, discovers a dilapidated bronze bell in a nunnery. The legend associated with it leads him to scholarly research. He finds in some Qing dynasty books the story of a Song dynasty woman who, after being twice married, became a prostitute and ended her life as a nun, finally plunging into the bronze lava that would forge the bell. Her story is retold by the implied author who, after extensive research into various sources, puts the "facts" in order, which he then "touches up a little bit" by "surmising and imitating" their historical situation. Shi may have heard or read about some old legends in classical literature; after all, as he makes clear, the story does not differ so much from other legends: "a good sword maker sacrifices his life in order to make his sword invincible, or a famous mirror maker sacrifices his life in order to make his mirror show up the ghosts and demons."[43] But why does he go to such lengths in order to bring back the sacrificial story of a nun who was once a prostitute? Is this a failed attempt at reworking the legend of Thaïs? What "secrets" lurk in the depth of her "yellow heart" (as her Buddhist name suggests) and behind the nun's final sacrificial ritual? What ghosts and demons is her forged bell supposed to warn off or scare away? No answer is supplied in the story's research findings or in its indirect narration. The scholarly author even adds a moral sermon at the end: "Although I am not a convert to Buddhism, I believe that when outside power invades a nun of high moral rectitude, she cannot but sacrifice her life in order to protect her dharma. This is the same as the Confucian spirit of sacrificing one's life for moral righteousness."[44]

In view of Shi's former expertise with the unreliability of fictional narration, this disclaimer cannot be taken at face value. By uttering such words the author certainly wishes to maintain a scholarly facade, and his retelling of the legend reveals none of the erotic-fantastic motifs of the protagonist's experience and character, except that the nun is a beautiful woman who can be "morose" for no apparent reason and that she loves to play music. The more we ponder such narrative "teasers" in the text, however, the more we are led to a speculation that is contrary to the author's implied intention: instead of writing another exemplary tale about the moral conduct of another good woman who fulfills her Buddhist vows, Shi may have used this last story to remind his readers that the Freudian ghost of the uncanny had, after all, never really left him.

FACE, BODY, AND THE CITY:

THE FICTION OF LIU NA'OU

AND MU SHIYING

In his classic study *The Country and the City*, Raymond Williams traces the transition in English literary representation from the pastoral "knowable communities" to the "cities of darkness and light."[1] It would be hard to trace a similar transition in modern Chinese literature. Rather, both city and countryside existed side by side as contrasting images and value systems in the modern Chinese consciousness during the first half of the twentieth century. With the triumph of the Chinese Communist Revolution in 1949, the significance of the city was eclipsed by the ideology of rural populism for at least the next four decades. It was not until the late 1980s, as China entered the post-Mao era, that "urban consciousness" was recovered as the central trope in a new discourse of modernity. Thus, unlike the major cities of Paris, Vienna, Berlin, and New York, which became the breeding ground and symbolic universe for Western modernism, as Williams and other scholars have argued, Shanghai played a less predominant and more ambivalent role for the modern Chinese literary imagination. The fictional landscapes of May Fourth literature, as represented by the works of Lu Xun and others, remain anchored in the rural village or the small town. Only in a relatively small number of novels, Mao Dun's *Midnight* being one, does Shanghai emerge as a "city of darkness and light."

In this regard, the two writers I discuss in this chapter, Liu Na'ou and Mu Shiying, are rather special, because for both the city was the *only* world of their existence and the key source of their creative imagination. Known as leaders of the Japanese-inspired neo-sensationalist school, they attempted to project their urban obsession with an experimental technique that both departs radically from the May Fourth tradition of realism and differs from the style of Shi Zhecun. The significance of their contribution to Chinese literature—particularly to the development of literary modernism—has been rediscovered after more than half a century of scholarly oblivion.[2]

Liu Na'ou (1900–1939) was born in Taiwan but grew up in Japan. After his return to Shanghai to study French at Aurora University, he spearheaded two significant avant-garde journals in the late 1920s—*Wugui lieche* (Trackless train) and *Xin wenyi (La Nouvelle Littérature)*—which provided the first showcase for his friends and classmates Shi Zhecun and Dai Wangshu. As his friends became established writers and editors while his bookstore was destroyed during the Japanese bombardment of Shanghai in January 1932, Liu made another trip to Japan and all but disappeared from Shanghai's literary scene. His interest shifted from creative writing to film criticism, and he later edited a film journal, *Xiandai dianying* (Modern cinema), and wrote some penetrating but controversial articles on film aesthetics. In 1939, two years after war broke out against Japan, Liu became the editor of a newspaper under the collaborationist regime of Wang Jingwei and was also making a film when his life was suddenly cut short by assassination, possibly by secret agents of the Guomindang or by the notorious Green Gang, an underground Mafia connected with it.[3]

Mu Shiying (1912–1940) made his first appearance as a fiction writer in Liu's journal *Xin wenyi* in 1930, at the precocious age of eighteen. His early stories, later collected in *Nanbeiji* (Northern and southern poles,

1932), created quite a stir among leftists because they described the world of the lumpenproletariat of river bandits and unemployed workers, although he had no personal knowledge of the subject he described and was concerned only with the question of "how to write."[4] Thus he soon became a protégé of Shi Zhecun and published a series of stories in Shi's journal *Xiandai zazhi (Les Contemporains)*, which exhibited city life in all its splendor and decadence. As a creative writer Mu was even more talented and productive than Liu: within a relatively short span of less than a decade since his fictional debut, he wrote about fifty stories (including one intended for a longer novel), which were published in several collections. Like Liu Na'ou, whose works Mu imitated and surpassed, Mu became an inveterate and "degenerate" urbanite. He openly flaunted a personal style as an avid patron of dance halls, where he reportedly squandered all his money on his nocturnal visits. He pursued a dance hostess with singular devotion from Shanghai to Hong Kong and eventually married her, thus creating something of a legend on the Shanghai literary scene (see Chapter 1). The last years of Mu's life again seemed to imitate Liu's: having returned to Shanghai from Hong Kong to take over the editorship of a newspaper under the puppet regime, he too was assassinated in 1940, apparently by secret agents of the Guomindang.[5]

For his contemporaries and latter-day critics, Mu Shiying's brief and meteoric career represents a process of moral regression—a proletarian realist turned urban decadent. In the early 1930s leftist critics charged that his fiction was utterly divorced from the real "living society" which was "filled with the masses of workers and peasants, with exploitation for profit, and the struggle for tomorrow." In a preface to one of his story collections Mu stated with remarkable candor that he chose to live in the society depicted in his fiction: "Perhaps I have been leading such a life in my dreams, for our critics have said that this is all accidental and separated from society, having to do with my subconscious. No matter whether it is dream, accident, or subconscious, I do not want my own work to be misunderstood and distorted, to be rejected on account of political expediency."[6] The recent revival of scholarly interest in his work may serve to clarify some misunderstandings and redress the imbalance caused by a narrowly politicized judgment.[7] My own reading in this chapter obviously follows the revisionist scholarship of this recent trend.

Since the style and content of Mu's and Liu's works have so much in common, I will discuss their works together as forming a continuum of the urban trope as represented by a modern femme fatale. Liu was the first modern Chinese writer to employ such a trope, which was further fleshed out by the more talented Mu Shiying. I begin with the fiction of Liu Na'ou in order to set up my interpretive framework.

The book cover of Liu Na'ou's only collection of short stories, *Dushi fengjing xian* (Scenes of the city, 1930), features a French word, *scène*, against a stylized background of three flashing spotlights. The vaguely Art Deco design captures brilliantly the book's thematic concern: in the eight stories contained therein a series of city scenes is spotlighted, each drawn from a familiar site of Shanghai's urban life—a ballroom ("tango palace"), a rapidly moving train, a movie house, a street and a flower shop, the observation deck of the racecourse, the Wing On department store, and so on. These familiar scenes are rendered somewhat unfamiliar by a descriptive technique derived from cinema (Liu's favorite medium): the narrative "camera" seemingly moves at random through a bewildering sequence of "shots," sometimes creating a montage-like effect. At the same time, however, most of the stories are also told in the manner of a cinematic voice-over that links together the various shots and scenes in a loose plot. This first-person or third-person narratorial voice is invariably that of a man who occupies a voyeuristic position as he encounters his fantastic heroine, a femme fatale figure who first seduces then overpowers and finally leaves him. She seems to appear from nowhere but is far more at home in the city than the male narrator-protagonist. Above all, she flaunts a free and daringly unrestrained lifestyle that both fascinates and intimidates him.

Such a portrait seems so outlandish as to defy all plausibility, which leads to the inevitable question: on what (urban) cultural grounds are these fictions produced? In my view, Liu's fiction is neither sheer fabrication nor simple derivation from the Japanese school of neo-sensationalism. Rather, it is a fictional projection of the same cultural environment in which it was produced and bears a direct relationship to other genres of Shanghai's print culture. Some of these stories were published in Liu's own journals and in *Les Contemporains*, edited by Shi Zhecun, but Liu and his friends also wrote frequently for more popular magazines with larger circulations such as *Liangyou* (The young companion) and *Furen huabao* (Women's pictorial). Thus, instead of positing an elitist stance of artistic avant-gardism or a political stance of didacticism as found in the leftist works of the time, Liu's fiction evokes a certain visual mood of the city that could prove entertaining to the readers of these pictorials.[8] It therefore also bears a certain resemblance to visual materials. This is especially true of Liu's portrayal of heroines, which draws directly from the female figures in the photos and on magazine covers as well as on calendar posters, to say nothing of the movies. To explore further this intriguing connection between fiction and popular culture, it may be worthwhile to examine a few physical details of Liu's modern heroines.

The Face and Body of the Modern Woman

The modern woman makes her dramatic entry in the very first story of the collection, "Youxi" (Games). This is how she is described under the gaze of her male companion: she has "a pair of easily startled pupils, a rational forehead, and above it her short hair waves in the wind; a thin and straight Greek nose, a round-shaped mouth with a pair of thick lips seemingly ajar."[9] The male narrator also comments ecstatically on her "protruding breasts, and a body soft and smooth like an eel." As she walks down the street, her movements are athletic and agile. The woman in the next story, "Fengjing" (Scenery), has the same small body, bobbed hair, "rational" forehead, and straight nose, but her eyes are "nimble and not easily startled." And she has small, "neurotic" lips "like an overripe pomegranate."[10] In the third story, "Liu" (Flow), the heroine, a revolutionary, is described as "a masculinized" modern woman. Her skin is "light dark," her fully developed limbs are big and strong and full of muscular tension. Her hair is short and neat but, the author tells us, without any trace of "Stacomb"—a popular hair cream for men.[11] In the fourth story, "Liangge shijian de buganzheng zhe" (Two men impervious to time), she appears in the grandstand at the racecourse: "a SPORTIVE modern woman; under her transparent French silk her elastic flesh trembles as if following a gentle movement." (The word "SPORTIVE" appears in English in the original.) She too has a small "cherry-like mouth."[12]

What are we to make of this fleshy, "sportive" modern woman with short hair, "rational" forehead, small mouth, a pair of startled or unstartled eyes, a straight Greek nose, "light dark" skin, protruding breasts, and a small body "as smooth and soft as an eel"? Several features are immediately noticeable in Liu's portrait. It seems that there are more erotic details in the face than in the body; the mouth and lips receive particular attention as the focal points of Liu's eroticism as well as a convenient site for his oral metaphors: the mouth is edible like a fruit but also so avaricious that it can "swallow" a love object. While the "Greek nose" is manifestly Western, the cherry-like small mouth is more characteristic of the traditional Chinese ideal of female beauty. The heroine's eyes and lips, closed or open, are perhaps of more modern origin and derived from Hollywood movie stars, particularly Liu's favorites, Joan Crawford and Greta Garbo. Her bobbed hair may be based on contemporary fashion: it was the popular look among urban young women of the time, especially college students, who chose not to have a permanent wave. The heroine's "light dark" skin is another contemporary hallmark, a by-product of the increasing popularity of athletics in women's education.[13] The color of healthy skin is expected to be tan, in sharp contrast to the classical Chinese ideal of women's skin—white. To be sure, Liu also occasionally eulogizes white skin, which could be seen as a racial fascination.[14] But skin color does not seem to be as predominant a factor in Liu's portraits of his heroines as their "sportive" quality, demonstrated by their agile movements. Obviously these portraits are a composite of diverse elements drawn from both reality and fantasy. If the heroine's facial features bear some resemblance to those of the women in the calendar posters (for instance, the cherry-like mouth of the Ruan Lingyu lookalike in the 1930 poster described in Chapter 2), her body reminds us of the numerous photos of athletic women in *Liangyou* magazine—students or film stars in swim suits or sportswear seen rowing boats, playing ball, or riding bicycles. (The same poses can also be found in the calendar posters.) All in all, these physical details are intended to mark the appearance of a new prototype of the modern woman who also embodies a new aesthetic of beauty. In an essay titled "The Modern Type of Expressive Beauty" (Xiandai biaoqingmei zaoxing), published in *Women's Pictorial* in 1934, Liu made the following revealing remarks:

> This model of beauty can be represented by the movie stars Garbo, Crawford, and Tan Ying. Their behavior and emotional expression from within are bold, direct, and unrestrained. But when not bursting out they automatically suppress them. Crawford, with her big open eyes and closed lips, gazes at men, and that expression perfectly illustrates this [new] psychology: in her heart there is passion racing like a torrent, but this torrent cannot find an outlet but is stifled into a stagnant presence in her eyes and lips. Men's psychological reaction to this kind of expression is: this girl loves me as if she could swallow me in one mouthful, yet pitifully she does not dare to say it. And in this she has a double psychological enjoyment. Modern men are in love with this kind of woman, who passionately looks for—but never seems able to find—a man to love, and who displays such a psychology on her face. Thus, in man's eyes [this kind of] woman appears to be the most beautiful, most modern.[15]

His is a somewhat idiosyncratic theory of sexual repression on which is inscribed a distinctly male point of view. Its male-dominant premise—"this girl loves me . . . [but] she does not dare to say it"—is coupled with a quaint Victorian notion of "stifled" sexuality (passion that "cannot find an outlet") that seems to contradict the "bold, direct, and unrestrained" nature of the heroine's behavior. For all his daring talk, Liu has failed to confront the modern woman's body as the central site of her sexuality. Instead of Crawford's face, he could have chosen Marlene Dietrich's legs, as displayed prominently in *The Blue Angel*, her most famous film, which also proved very popular in Shanghai. Liu's intense reading of Crawford's face also reminds us of what Roland Barthes said of Garbo's face: "Garbo still belongs to that moment in cinema when capturing the human face still plunged audiences into the deepest ecstasy, when one literally lost oneself in a human image as one would in a philtre, when the face represented an absolute state of the flesh, which could be neither reached nor renounced."[16] Liu happened to belong to that moment in world cinema when Garbo's face was the dominant icon. By the early 1930s the faces of Hollywood stars had become a global commodity as a result of massive publicity by the Hollywood studios, which supplied more than a million photos every year to newspapers and magazines worldwide. But Liu was not merely a consumer and film spectator; he was the first modern Chinese writer to have boldly taken possession of such an image and transposed it into his fictional landscape of urban Shanghai. As a result, he has given us not only the exotic "look" of his heroines but also a way of *looking at* them. His stories thus offer a sustained case of male scopophilia—the erotic pleasure derived from looking at women.

The trope of woman as object of the male gaze, together with its implications for gender and sexuality, has been discussed extensively in current American theories of film. As Laura Mulvey argues in her classic essay "Visual Pleasure and Narrative Cinema," "pleasure in looking has been split between active/male and passive/female. The determining male gaze projects its phantasy on to the female figure which is styled accordingly."[17] Peter Brooks has further argued that in Western realist fiction, scopophilia is combined with "epistemophilia," the pleasure of knowing: "The body held in the field of vision is par excellence the object of both knowing and desire, knowing as desire, desire as knowing."[18] Thus, "man as a knowing subject postulates woman's body as the object to be known, by way of an act of visual inspection which claims to reveal the truth—or else makes the object into the ultimate enigma."[19] If we apply this Western gendered model to Liu's fiction, it becomes immediately clear that Liu's fictional male gazers are not up to their scopophilic and epistemophilic tasks. The sexual imbalance in Liu's fictional world is caused not by male activism but by male passivity, thus deflating in the end the erotic energy accumulated by his consistent gaze at the female. Since, as I have noted, the woman in Liu's fiction does not have a full body as an object for visual inspection, what the passive male pursues is rather a phantom image, the embodiment of an exotic ideal with all the accoutrements from foreign sources. Two such sources are especially noteworthy, for upon them Liu apparently drew for inspiration in constructing his modern heroines.

Moga, Morand, Exoticism

In addition to Hollywood stars, the genealogy of Liu's modern heroines can be traced to the "Modern Girl" (*modan gaaru*, abbreviated as *moga*) image that had become a fad in urban Japan in the 1920s. As described by Miriam Silverberg and other scholars, the *moga* also "wore bobbed hair, sheer stockings, high heels, and often a brightly colored one-piece dress in the fashion of American film idols such as Clara Bow, Pola Negri, Mary Pickford, and Gloria Swanson." She was a "glittering, decadent, middle-class consumer who, through her clothing, smoking and drinking, flaunts [sic] tradition in the urban playgrounds of the late 1920s."[20] In a story by Xu Xiacun published in Liu's journal *Xin wenyi* in 1929 titled, most appropriately and in English, "Modern Girl," the heroine is in fact a Japanese waitress. One year earlier, however, the *moga* had already been identified in the *North China Herald* as a "Chinese flapper"—a young woman "dressed in semi-foreign style with bobbed hair . . . short skirt . . . and powdered face" who "has come to stay."[21] Whether or not this "Chinese flapper" image was incorporated directly into Liu's fiction, we can still assume that his fictional heroines are not creatures from a purely private fantasy; they are conceived as "public" figures in the same way that the women portrayed in the pictorial advertisements are displayed in print as public figures.

As well as their connections with print and film culture, Liu's heroines can claim a more literary heritage, as the *moga* image may itself have been indebted to the works of the French writer and diplomat Paul Morand (1888–1976), which Liu was the first to introduce to China. Liu may have first read about Morand in Japanese sources and then read him in French. Morand's novels, such as *Fancy Goods* (*Tendres Stocks*, 1921), *Open All Night* (*Ouvert la nuit*, 1922) and *Closed All Night* (*Fermé la nuit* 1923) are said to have exerted an impact on the Japanese neo-sensationalists.[22] Shu-mei Shih has traced Morand's women characters to the French exoticist tradition from Flaubert to Pierre Loti (1895–1925)—a tradition which Edward Said regards as a clear example of Orientalism—a form of Western domination which tends to relegate the Orient, and in particular Oriental women, to the status of the "subhuman Other."[23] Morand was no stranger to China and Asia; as a diplomat he had traveled widely all over the world. In the summer of 1925 he traveled to Asia and visited Japan, Thailand (Siam), Vietnam (Indo-China, where he fell ill and was visited in the hospital by André Malraux), and China (though I have yet to find any reference to Shanghai). He wrote many travel articles in French and English, some of which later found their way into *Vanity Fair*.[24]

In the October 1928 issue of *Trackless Train*, Liu and his friends managed to translate two short stories by Morand: "Wave of Indolence" (Landuobing, or "Vague de paresse") and "New Friends" (Xin pengy-oumen, or "Les Amis nouveaux"). Both were apparently taken from his 1925 collection *L'Europe galante* (Europe at love). Though quite short, the stories are typical of Morand's work. In the first story, Morand recounts a romantic encounter in London with a Dutch woman born in Java. "I set full value on chance encounters and these expeditions into unknown countries, explorings in human skin," comments the autobiographical hero.[25] Despite taking place in England, the story is suffused with an indolent air of Orientalist condescension. The blatant racism of the following paragraph is faithfully reproduced in the Chinese translation:

> She was a dazzling creature, and wore her black plaits coiled around her ears like the horns of Australian merino rams. She made me think of those signs at country fairs:
> FEMME D'ORIGINE
> ORIENTAL ATTRACTION
> BEAUTÉ—VOLUPTÉ—FÉERIE—LUMIÈRE
> Once again I saw myself obliged to turn to foreign industry for my lovemaking ... And without waking up, as she felt me beside her, she took me to her, closing upon me at once with the instinctive action of a clam.[26]

In the second story, "New Friends," two men find themselves in a restaurant, both having been stood up by the same woman. As the men strike up a conversation, they realize that they both love her for the same reasons. They proceed to enumerate the physical features they both adore: "Her forehead appeared frank, approachable, kind. She was a new creature. She has not got short hair. And her mouth too" as well as her "laughter, her ice-cold hands, her inconstancies—she says that for pure love of faithfulness she is faithful to everybody."[27] It is not hard to trace the imprint of Morand's story on Liu's fiction: the heroine who plays a trick on both men ("'*Très sport*,' she will say"), her facial details and her "not short" hair. Thus, parts of "Les Amis nouveau" are subtly transplanted into Liu's "Two Men Impervious to Time" and "Games." Whereas life for Morand's Agnès "is made up of twelve hours of transgressions and twelve hours of oblivion," Liu's unnamed heroine in "Two Men" surpasses her record by refusing to spend more than three hours with the same man. While in Morand's story the playful heroine's absence serves to bond the two suitors as friends, Liu's femme fatale leaves the two men completely speechless and dejected.

Imitations aside, Liu was quite aware of the colonial implications of Morand's Orientalism. In two stories, titled "Reqing zhi gu" (The bone of passion) and "Liyi yu weisheng" (Etiquette and hygiene), Liu satirizes Western fantasies about Oriental woman by making his Western men (both French) pay for their fantasies. The French protagonist in the first story falls for a Japanese woman, the mirror image of Loti's "Madame Chrysanthemum" (even his name, Biye'er, or Pierre, refers to Loti's), only to be disillusioned in the end when she asks him to pay her five hundred dollars. In the latter story, another French diplomat turned antique dealer gives a lengthy discourse on the difference he perceives between Chinese and Western paintings and women but then admits, "This is probably due to my Oriental fascination."²⁸ But the Chinese protagonist in the same story sounds even more racist as he talks about Slavic women whose flesh has "a wild flavor like lamb's meat from the Caucasus."²⁹ This deprecatory comment refers, of course, to White Russian prostitutes from among the throngs of impoverished Russian émigrés in Shanghai after the Bolshevik Revolution. Liu's Chinese protagonist is a profligate "connoisseur" of prostitutes and a despicable character. Thus, in a surprising turnabout, his wife leaves him for her French-educated lover. To add a final ironic touch, she introduces him to her mute sister for purposes of "hygiene"—that is, to keep him from contracting a venereal disease.

Behind Morand's Orientalism lies the complex issue of exoticism. In the same issue of *Trackless Train* in which the two Morand stories appear there is a much longer article on Paul Morand by the French critic Benjamin Crémieux, as translated by Liu Na'ou himself. The Crémieux article, lengthy and verbose, must have posed a challenge to Liu's knowledge of French, but it contains some unusual insights. As a contemporary of Morand's, Crémieux was fully aware of the charge of "exoticism" (the notion of Orientalism had not yet been conceptualized), but he argues that Morand's brand is somehow different: "His exoticism was intended in a meticulous way to guard against the penetration of romanticized ideas; an exoticism mixed with a practical knowledge about foreign countries through direct contact, [an exoticism that] shows no respect to mankind but boldly lays bare its utmost secrets."[30] Morand himself was said to have "vigorously protested against the use of such a term in criticism of this phase of his art."[31] In the opinion of another contemporary critic, Georges Lemaître, Morand had nothing but contempt for this kind of exoticism, a "gaudy ornament, added more or less artificially to a description for the sake of picturesqueness" or local color. [32] Hence, in Crémieux's opinion, Morand's women characters—such as Clarissa, Delphine, and Aurora in his early novel *Fancy Goods*—serve to unveil the true spiritual state of postwar Europe caught in a modern malaise that "made us aware right away what this modern age of bars, dance halls, and airplanes is all about."[33] Still, despite these protestations, Morand's women characters exude a distinct exotic appeal, especially for his Chinese translators. Liu's fiction can be likewise criticized as a "gaudy ornament"; his heroines are even more exotic creatures than the Dutch woman in Morand's story. In fact, we can charge Liu's entire oeuvre with representing a project of exoticism, an effort to make the figures in his fictional landscape as "foreign" as possible. Whether they also unveil the spiritual state of prewar Shanghai is, however, subject to interpretation.

In Chinese the word "exoticism" is generally translated as *yiguo qingdiao* (literally, the mood and flavor of a foreign country) and carries the connotation of a Western country as "other." The term has in fact been used as the title of two books by Zhang Ruogu and Li Jinfa, both Francophiles. From Heinrich Fruehauf's insightful study we learn that exoticism is precisely the urban cultural code with which writers such as Zhang and Zeng Pu refer to the heady foreign atmosphere of the "Western façade" of Shanghai's concessions, especially the French. Liu Na'ou's *Scenes of the City* is one of the prominent examples of this "newfangled boom of urban exoticism."[34] Other works with a similar urban title and landscape include Zhang Ruogu's *Duhui jiaoxiangqu* (Urban symphonies, 1929) and Xu Weinan's *Dushi de nannü* (City men and women, 1929). In these works "the narrator is generally assigned the role of exoticizing the Familiar by constructing *yiguo*, the Shanghainese vision of a glittering, breath-taking, and at times 'forbidden' Other."[35]

Thus, exoticism can serve as a double mirror. It begins as a Western image of the Orient but ends as an Oriental (i.e., Chinese) image of the West. If Paul Morand's fiction can be regarded as a product of exotic Orientalism from the West, his works were used by French-influenced Japanese and Chinese writers as a reverse mirror with which to exoticize the West. It is, in short, a process of mutual exoticization in cross-cultural reception. Nevertheless, this Chinese phenomenon of what might be called Occidentalism, the construction of the Western "other," does not necessarily imply a Chinese effort to "control" the West—a colonial or imperialist project of "mastery" over the West in knowledge and power, as Morand and a host of other Western writers have applied to the Orient.[36] Rather, it can be argued that exoticism as a phenomenon of urban culture is closely related to a search for a Chinese modernity and provides a partial solution to the paradox that arises between nationalism (a new cultural identity) and imperialism. In the writings of the group comprising the Francophiles Fu Yanchang, Zhu Yingpeng, and Zhang Ruogu, as pointed out by Fruehauf, Shanghai's special status is seen as an intellectual asset: "Shanghai, because it was so 'exotic,' so different from the rest of China, could become a cultural laboratory where, *in vitro*, the experimental restoration of Chinese civilization would be undertaken."[37] For Fu and his friends, *city* is the basis of *civitas*, the center of modern civilization.

Desire, Deceit, and the City

The rich and variegated resources discussed in the preceding section may provide a larger contextual perspective in which to analyze Liu's stories. They may also help us explore some allegorical dimensions of Liu's fiction.

The typical plot of Liu's stories is that of a male protagonist-narrator in hopeless pursuit of a striking-looking modern woman—only to lose out in the end. If the story involves a "love triangle," the woman always manages to outwit and leave both men. Consequently, the woman serves not only as the object of male desire and pursuit but also as the predominant "subject" of the story in the sense that it is her action and personality that propel the plot's progression. A good example can be found in the story "Two Men Impervious to Time."

The love triangle plot begins with one of the male characters—named simply H—meeting the modern girl at the racecourse, one of Shanghai's most popular amusement sites for both Westerners and Chinese and also the site of legal gambling. H has just won by betting on the right horse, thus attracting the attention of the woman. He invites her to an American teashop for ice cream (an omnipresent detail in Liu's stories) and afterwards takes her for a walk, since he "knows that taking a walk is an ineluctable element in modern romance." Their walk takes them through the French Concession, where the rays of the setting sun "[caress] the fresh green leaves of the Western *wutong* trees." At the crossroads (presumably the corner of Nanking Road), H is temporarily sidetracked by a seductive automobile, a Fontegnac 1929, but "he does not forget the FAIR SEX [written in English] beside him" and "with a most graceful gesture" moves her hand from his left to his right arm. Then, the three big monstrous department stores emerge in front of their eyes."[38] It is interesting to note that by this point the male protagonist has been led to believe that he is in charge. The long walk he takes with his "fair sex" is obviously for purposes of display (*chufengtou*). But the more he brags about his gentlemanly behavior, the less stature he has in the eyes of the modern girl. When another man, T, joins them at a dance hall, the two men's pursuit of the woman becomes increasingly pathetic and the modern girl's attitude increasingly playful and condescending. Amidst the rhythms of blues and waltzes, this typical scene of a ménage à trois ends with the heroine leaving both men, but not before she delivers the coup de grâce: "You are just a little boy," she rebukes the hero. "Who tells you to be so awkward and stupid, with all this nonsense of eating ice cream and taking a walk? Don't you know that lovemaking should be done in an automobile racing with the wind? In the suburbs there are green-shaded

areas. Besides, I have never spent more than three hours with a gentleman before. This is an exception."[39]

It is evident that the males are much weaker than the females in
Liu's fiction. Repeatedly the male suitor is described as thin and slender,
in his eager behavior "like a boy." Occasionally he is said to have strong
arms or to have a mustache like Charlie Chaplin's (comical) or Ronald
Colman's (elegant and urbane)—another confirmation of Liu's suscepti-
bility to the impact of the Hollywood image industry—but otherwise no
counterpoint description is provided that would make him either physically or mentally a true match for the woman. While the men may
occupy a position of "internal focalization" in the plot, their own subjective position is precarious, and their efforts are purposely deflated.[40]
Thus, instead of being "knowing subjects" exerting their desire on the
"object" of a woman's body, they seem to be playthings at the mercy of
the self-assured modern heroine.

In a perceptive article on Liu Na'ou's fiction, Shu-mei Shih has
argued that Liu's male protagonists still retain "outmoded patriarchal
moral sensibilities," whereas Liu's prototypical heroine is from the very
outset an urban "product of modernity": "Lodged in her are the characteristics of the urban culture of the semicolonial city and its seductions of
speed, commodity culture, exoticism, and eroticism. Hence the emotions she stimulates in the male protagonist—helpless infatuation and
hopeless betrayal—replicate the attraction and alienation he feels to-
wards the city."[41] The heroine in "Two Men Impervious to Time" is the
very embodiment of this description. Not all of Liu's fictional heroines,
however, are portrayed as modern femmes fatales with an acquisitive
taste for the urban commodities of speed and glamour. It makes an
interesting case if we compare the heroines of this story and "Games."
Both are consummate players in the game of desire and deceit. Both
crave and fetishize automobiles. In "Two Men" the "Fontegnac 1929" in
the male protagonist's field of vision is clearly an object of desire, a
material substitute for the heroine, which is repossessed by the heroine
when she announces her preference for lovemaking in a speedy car. In

"Games," another automobile—a six-cylinder 1929 Viper—is described by the sports car–loving heroine as "really beautiful, its body entirely in green, and harmonizes nicely with the suburban pastures in early summer."[42]

This juxtaposition of cars and women in Liu's fiction has led Shu-mei Shih to argue that "the speed of the city is paralleled by the speed with which the modern girl changes boyfriends and by the modern girl's love of speedy sports cars: transitory scenes and transitory romances, a city of fast cars and brief encounters."[43] The crucial significance of time and speed cannot be overemphasized in any discourse of Western modernity. Cars, like trains, are clearly material markers of modernity as they are a commodity of speed. Liu has underscored this significance even in his story's title: the two male suitors lose to the modern woman precisely because they are "impervious to time." But how much speed do Liu's female characters really crave? The heroine's praise for the Viper in "Games" is based on its six-cylinder power—"it is not even short of breath after running for half a day"—whereas the Fontegnac 1929 in "Two Men Impervious to Time" is a vehicle denoting both speed and novelty, not to mention its obvious signification of wealth. Liu might have found both the brand names and the glossy images of these cars in the advertisements in Shanghai's Chinese and English newspapers as well as foreign magazines such as *Vanity Fair*. His adulation of the automobile betrays a fascination with its materialistic value (money) as much as its symbolic value (speed). At the same time, however, the protagonist of "Games" also compares the crowd of automobiles in the city streets during "RUSH HOUR" (Liu uses the English term) to little monsters (*jiachong*, or "beetles") that "devour" and "vomit" people. It seems that even in the fetishization of this most conspicuous item of modern convenience, both exhilaration and anxiety are implicated.

Another instance of combined exhilaration and anxiety can be found in the descriptions of lovemaking. As if to shock his readers, Liu conspicuously displays scenes of lovemaking in the very first two stories in the collection: "Games" and "Scenery." In fact, the latter story provides a pastoral setting for the lovemaking of hero and heroine, who first meet on a train, then get off at a station and, at the instigation of the heroine, proceed to have sex *au naturel* in the open field before they continue their separate journeys. The heroine is undoubtedly a product of the city; she oozes "that special kind of strong visceral excitement toward the opposite sex, a woman of the metropolis."[44] Their lovemaking is depicted sparely but with a striking metaphor: "On her flesh and skin, shining and smooth like a piece of gauze, flow the blue waves of scores of River Danubes, and her red garter nibs at her snow-white legs."[45] This sensational image, obviously derived from Liu's imitation of Morand and the Japanese neo-sensationalist school, conveys a blatant exotic appeal, but it also defies belief. Is the heroine with a red garter from Shanghai or Paris? On an earlier page, her neck and small round shoulders make her look to the hero like someone who has "just jumped out of the canvas by Dürer [?]."[46] All of these erotic details are meant to lead to the male protagonist's final "meditation" on being shackled by urban "mechanical civilization." The message is as weak and unpersuasive as the plot and characterization.

We should not demand, of course, that Liu follow strictly the dictates of realism in providing plausibility and verisimilitude. His heroine in this story is indeed a fantasy figure. Yet in some other cases she is not so fantastic. The heroine in the story "Games" is depicted in the beginning as equally exotic, with her small, straight Greek nose. Like the heroine in "Two Men," she also has two male suitors: she talks about the one with a Chaplinesque mustache but seduces the other, who is "too absurdly sentimental and romantic." Their lovemaking is described with much revealing detail:

> Above her nose is a pair of flaming eyes, and below it a dark-red cherry. He feels as if touched by electricity and could not extricate himself even if he wanted to.
>
> The snow-white bedsheets are bestirred with waves. Beside his lips he discovers a set of teeth not his own. He senses a surge of

heat from his lower body and he feels that he is having difficulty breathing. A glistening eye gazes at him under his eyes, making him feel pained, but it suddenly disappears. At the same time, [her] broken virginity, like torn white paper, falls under the bed piece by piece, and a pair of small feet, dangling in the air, also fall down. He feels that all has disappeared.[47]

This is a quaint passage about male and female sexuality. While it is narrated—seen and felt—from a male point of view, the "action" comes mainly from the woman, who takes the initiative in seducing the man and whose glistening gaze makes him "feel pained." But there is a strange incongruity in the woman's behavior as well: how can such a free and unrestrained woman have kept her virginity and then chosen to lose it with a man in one night's casual tryst in a hotel room only to leave him for another? The two sides of the heroine's personality—seductress and virgin—simply do not cohere, unless the act of sex is not a crucial factor in her strategies of domination over men, or unless the male narrator-protagonist (or even author) still harbors a hopelessly traditional fantasy that derives the thrill of sexual possession from taking a woman's virginity. Whatever the reason, the sex scene reveals considerable discomfort with bodies, both male and female.

We should also be aware of the fact that not all of Liu's fictional heroines fit comfortably into the image of the free, daring, and possibly promiscuous modern girl. There are also a few who, despite their modern traits, are still attached to men as their possessions and append-ages. This category of women, overlooked by scholars, can be found in the last two works in *Scenes of the City*: "Canliu" (Bereavement) and "Fancheng shi" (Formula). In "Bereavement," the woman is a widow whose husband has just died, and in a series of interior monologues she voices her loneliness and her need for men. As she takes a walk alone, she lets herself be seduced by a foreign sailor—and fulfills his dream to have "A GIRL IN EVERY PORT!" (in English in the original). Thus, she willingly loses her own individuality and subjectivity as a widowed woman and becomes a commodity in the service trade. In "Formula," a man called simply Mr. Y has just lost his wife, who has always prepared fresh SALADE (this and other capitalized terms appear originally in English or French) for lunch. His aunt introduces two modern girls as prospective new wives: a Miss A with "small delicate hands" who listens to Peking opera, and Miss W with a "PERMANENT WAVE" who meets him on a date to watch a "TALKIE." But then he finds himself on a ship with Miss S, whom he met only the day before. Thus the story becomes a "merry-go-round" with four players—one man and three women—who have no identities of their own; even their names are obliterated by capital letters, like numbers. What the story satirizes is the marriage game itself and the impersonal routine of the life of an urban office worker: "Everybody knows that Mr. Y is a product of the city, the possessor of a mathematical brain that is meticulous, clear, and suited for handling all trifling matters."[48] In such a male-dominated, rationalized world, women are but puppet figures or pawns in a chess game, but the male protagonist fares no better.

The story's title, "Formula," proves to be representative of most of Liu's stories. As we read through them, the initial excitement generated by his first published story, "Games" (1928), gradually dissipates as formulaic devices—the futile pursuit, the love triangle—become more evident. And however exotic or symbolic his portrait of the "Modern Girl," it becomes clear that she, like her male suitor, is but a narrative figure in a staged urban landscape. She is made to be superficial precisely because she is made to serve the larger purpose of representing the city. What unites all of Liu's stories is an unabashed fascination with the city itself on the part of both his female and male characters. Thus, Shih is surely right in remarking that "Liu clearly takes great pleasure in describing city scenes, eroticizing them as the objects of his gaze. In almost every one of Liu's stories extended passages in metaphoric language depict aspects of city life and its material culture. Even the moral degradation of the city itself becomes seductive in such linguistic feasts."[49]

As his title indicates, Liu's intention is to create a series of "scenes" of the city. The French word used as the title of the story collection could stand, as Yomi Braester suggests, for both "scenery" (equivalent to the Chinese term *fengjing*) and stage.[50] The characters foregrounded against such "scenery" are like props on a larger stage, the urban "spectacle." Braester considers the "spectacle" to have defined the thematic concerns and literary devices in many of Liu's stories: "Narrative tension often arises from differences in attitudes toward the spectacle. Female characters consistently demonstrate their skill by adjusting to the illusiveness of the spectacle and by moving smoothly from one spectacle to the next. As a result, they often leave their male counterparts behind as victims of their own ignorance of the dangers of the spectacle."[51]

When we come to the stories of Mu Shying, however, these narrative negotiations between male and female characters vis-à-vis the urban spectacle are given more technical polish, although Mu is likewise stranded in the urban spectacle itself. For all their flaunted *modeng* lifestyle, Mu's characters prove to be more "misfit," and hence psychologically more revealing, than Liu's.

If Liu Na'ou can be considered a pioneer—perhaps the first modern Chinese writer to give us an exoticized vision of the city—Mu Shiying is the young master craftsman who completed Liu's city project. Following Liu Na'ou, he brought more flair and fantasy to the descriptions of the modern femme fatale. He pushed the trope of the male-female encounter, awkwardly set up in Liu's work, to its comic and sometimes farcical extremes—so much so that it becomes a devastating satire of commodified modernity. If Liu's description of the female body still betrays a residual traditionalism and seems more focused on the face, Mu is blatantly and brilliantly body-oriented. Finally, Mu portrays scenes of the city with a genuinely cinematic flourish: in his work the city emerges as a veritable panorama of *son et lumière*. It remains to be seen, however, whether such a vision is adequate for an "allegorization" of the city in the same way that Benjamin attributes to the works of Baudelaire.

Portrait of the Female Body

Mu's version of Liu's modern boy-meets-girl plot is both inventive and hilarious. Like Liu, he plays up all the glitter and glamour of the urban landscape, especially the ballroom. His plots, like Liu's, also center on the encounter between the male protagonist and the modern girl as femme fatale. Not only does the encounter lead to the predictable result of the man being outwitted, but the process takes on a more elaborate form and details as well. The story titled "Camel, Nietzscheist, and Woman" (Luotuo, Nicaizhuyizhe yu nüren) can be cited as a tour de force of Mu's characteristic flair. At the beginning of the story, the male protagonist, quoting a passage from Nietzsche's *Thus Spoke Zarathustra* and quickly turning its camel metaphor ("how the spirit shall become a camel") into a consumer item, lights up a Camel cigarette as he saunters past the city's amusement sites: jai alai court, dance hall, gambling joint, bars, "BEAUTÉ EXOTIQUE" (originally in French), and CAFÉ NA-POLI, where he meets an extremely exotic-looking modern woman. "She has eyebrows sharpened like Garbo's, dark tender pupils like velvet, and ripe-red lips."[52] He flirts with her by first presenting a challenge: "Miss, let me tell you something. Your way of drinking coffee and your manner of smoking a cigarette are inexcusably wrong." The woman smiles, invites him to dinner, and then proceeds to instruct him about 373 cigarette brands, 23 kinds of coffee, and 5,000 formulas for mixed drinks. As they ride on the streetcar after dinner, he is aroused with desire, and "as he discards the brown-colored Camel cigarette and throws himself [at her], a vague thought comes to his mind: 'Perhaps Nietzsche is impotent!' Down with all the philosophizing postures and up with the pleasures of the flesh."[53]

Clearly a partial imitation of Liu's "Games" but also a spoof of that story's formulaic encounter, Mu's story is more satisfying because the hero and heroine are in some ways a perfect match, and the ensuing erotic denouement comes as no surprise. But Mu has gone a step further by capitalizing on the erotic symbolism of the cigarette, the most popular of commodities, in ways Liu would never have imagined possible. As the male hero plays a solitary game of "smoking" his Nietzschean quotation by turning metonyms into metaphors and vice versa, the way is paved for him to encounter a modern femme fatale also smoking a cigarette—surely a sight of irresistible sexual invitation. Smoking is combined with eating and drinking to provide a perfect "tease" for sex, which promises to be consummated in a streetcar—not Liu's flaunted sports car, but equally alluring. Compared to Liu's "Games," Mu's scenes of sexual tease are more exhilarating because they are unencumbered by any descriptive awkwardness.

Unlike Liu, Mu concentrates his major efforts on depicting the female body. The "classic" text for this is also one of his best-known stories, "Baijin de nüti suoxiang" (The statue of a female body in platinum). As the title suggests, the story is a "study" of a female body by a medical doctor, a single man who leads a modern-style life marked by punctuality. The woman patient who one day walks into his office is first described as a body "with narrow shoulders, full bosom, fragile waist, slender arms and feet, about five feet and seven inches tall"; once she is seated in the doctor's office, he then notices her face, which looks like "a pale white lotus." She feels weak, has no appetite, and suffers from insomnia. The doctor diagnoses (in an interior monologue marked by parentheses) that she has either tuberculosis at an early stage or "overbearing sexual desire."[54] After some medical questioning, he then asks her to take off all her clothes so that he may examine her body: "With a pair of emaciated feet as base, one leg straight and the other slanting, stands a platinum body statue—a human statue that seems to have no shame, no morality, and no human desire, metallic, with flowing lines, as if the gaze could easily slip past the lines of that body. This unfeeling, insensitive body stands here, waiting for his command."[55]

It is a remarkable portrait: the body, like a sculpted torso, is both cut off from and at odds with the face, whose sick fragility gives little indication of the body's "overbearing sexual desire." Standing like an inanimate object, it becomes the perfect site for the doctor's—and the reader's—voyeuristic gaze. The particular attention to the body's skin color—its platinum whiteness—seems also to add a hybrid touch: a Chinese woman who has the body of a white Western woman. Is she, then, a replica of Liu Na'ou's modern heroine—free, daring, and promiscuous? The story reveals none of her character traits; the body seems grafted onto the face of a rather traditional housewife. Nor is the body made into a material object, a metonymic substitute for automobiles, as in Liu's fiction. In the sanitized office of the doctor, it seems to exist by itself, with no linkage to the city's material culture. As such it becomes a pure object for the doctor's inspection. The resulting sensations could be aesthetic, as in the way an artist looks at a model, an object of lines and shapes, or purely anatomical, as in the way a doctor is supposed to feel about a patient. Yet, as the doctor orders his patient to lie on the examining table, her naked body clearly arouses his desire. Even before her naked body is revealed, the doctor begins to wonder: he has examined many women's bodies and has always "seen through their skins and lines of fat into their intestines and bones, so why does the seductiveness of this woman client today manage to crawl into my mind like bone worms? Enigma—what prescription should be given to her?"[56]

Like the feverish diary musings of Lu Xun's madman about the nature of Chinese culture—also couched as a case for medical study—the doctor's quandary invites analysis. Since the woman shows no sign, much less commits any act, of seduction herself, the doctor's desire must have been induced by his own repressed fantasy. But Mu Shiying is not interested in plumbing the depths of male psychology. Instead, he focuses on the doctor's increased sexual arousal through language. As in Shi Zhecun's device of internal monologue, the doctor's chaotic musings are narrated in purposefully unpunctuated sentences—a kind of stream of consciousness of Mu's own invention at a time when no other writer knew how to do this linguistically in Chinese. Thus, as the doctor looks down at the patient's reclining naked body on the table, the following unpunctuated passage appears in the text in parentheses: "(There is no third person in the room such a gorgeous statue of white platinum have not paid much attention a careless person excessively heightened sexual desire muffled words light stare of the eyes mysteriously senselessly project sublimated passion having lost all obstacles all power of resistance lying there . . .)."[57]

This experiment may be rather primitive by present-day standards (the Taiwan writer Wang Wen-hsing more successfully used this device in his novel *Beihai de ren*—"The Man with His Back to the Sea"—half a century later).[58] Nevertheless, it not only serves to break down the sentence structure of modern Chinese (whose punctuation rules tend to follow those in English, whereas in classical Chinese there is no punctuation), but also, with the omission of personal pronouns, allows enough semantic room for repetition and free association. Thus, when the doctor finally resorts to prayer (itself a markedly Western ritual), his interior monologue becomes a stream of repetitions of a few phrases: "God save me platinum statue ah god save me platinum statue ah god save me platinum statue ah god save me platinum statue ah god save me platinum statue ah god save me . . ."[59] The omission of punctuation easily establishes a chain of equivalences and displacements so that "god" and "platinum statue" become interchangeable in the simulated stream of the protagonist's consciousness as if he were praying to the platinum statue. The misplaced prayer to God thus becomes a deranged worship of the platinum goddess. (Needless to add, the Chinese word for God, *shangdi*, is not capitalized.) For a secular Chinese protagonist who acquires Christianity as part of a modern lifestyle, such "idol worship" does not incur sacrilege but rather enhances the aura of eroticism.

At the linguistic level, however, confusion is created, since the subject "I" (*wo*) in Chinese can also be easily transferred intersubjectively to the "I" of the platinum body—or even to the possessive case—so as to beg the question: who is to be saved from whom? Is the doctor praying for his own salvation from the temptation of the female patient's body (the surface meaning if read as if punctuated)? Or is the real subject of the platinum body, the woman patient, to be saved? Or do we infer that the doctor is already in possession of her body and thus prays for their joint salvation? To me these simple repetitions and wordplays are precisely the stylistic device that creates the satirical-erotic effect that permeates the text. The female body, therefore, becomes a stimulus not only to arouse the male protagonist's desire but also to enhance the authorial desire in language. Yet in spite of such flashes of invention, the story's content is rather traditional and decidedly male chauvinist. This naked encounter results in the bachelor doctor's getting married in the end: his sexual desire, aroused by the body of his female patient, now finds another easy object—or outlet—in his new wife, a "possession" sanctified by the institution of marriage.

In "Craven A," the female body takes on a metaphorical, even allegorical, dimension. The story begins with the first-person male narrator-protagonist looking at a woman at a cabaret who silently puffs away at a "Craven A" brand cigarette. As its "pure aroma slowly floats by amidst the jazz music," he begins to peruse her intently, mapping the features of her face and body with extravagant metaphors so that the body is soon metamorphosed into the map of a nation. His panoramic gaze leads us from the woman's hair (likened to black pine forests), eyes (lakes), mouth (volcano, with a tongue of flame), breasts (twin peaks), and so on to the "fertile plain" of the south (lower body) until it reaches down and his vision is blocked by the table:

> Beneath the table are two strips of ocean embankment, and through the net stocking I see the whitened earth like the belly of a fish. At the tip of the embankments lie two delicate white seagulls with black mouths, deep in their early summer's dreams . . . At the center of the two embankments, surmising from the lay of the land, should be a delta of alluvial plain, and at the seaside an important port, a big commercial harbor, otherwise there would not have been such nicely built embankments. And the nocturnal scene of a metropolis is lovely. Imagine the evening glow at the embankment, the sound of waves at the wharf,

the majestic posture of a big steamship entering the harbor, the
breakers at its stem, and the high-rise buildings on both sides![60]

This "geography" of the female body offers quite an unusual spectacle on which considerable libidinous energy has been concentrated.
Each of its "scenic spots" is so elaborately described as to invite both
viewing and interpretation. Thus, as we follow the protagonist's rambling gaze, we too begin to inscribe our readings onto it. The reading
process, therefore, becomes an excursion into the pleasure of the text
until we reach the body-map's harbor and come to a sudden realization:
if the two embankments can be read as the woman's legs and the seagulls
her shoes, then the "delta of alluvial plain" can only be her "delta of
Venus" (Anaïs Nin notwithstanding). What, then, can the "harbor" signify (the Chinese word gangkou means, literally, "mouth of the harbor") if
not the opening of the woman's vagina? Accordingly, the "majestic posture of a big steamship entering the harbor" cannot but refer to the
penetration of a penis. Never had any Chinese writer dared to go that far
with an erotic fantasy. At the same time, however, Mu's description of the
harbor, with its nocturnal scene and its high-rise buildings, also seems
real: the seaport metaphor is so close to home that this last stretch of the
female body's geography loses its fantastic dimension. Readers at the
time might well have associated it realistically with the city of Shanghai.

At this critical juncture, before the erotic and allegorical potential
of the harbor/city is fully realized, desire is deferred as the narrator's
reverie suddenly stops and the story shifts back to the reality of the
ballroom. The possessor of the fantastic body is a dance hall hostess,
who, as the story develops, turns out to be a lonely figure simultaneously
adored and mistreated by the gigolos who surround her; only the male
protagonist shows her genuine sympathy. The conventional plot thus
deflates the libidinous energy that the body-map has generated. How,
then, do we interpret such an inversion from fantasy to reality? How is
such an extravagant metaphor of the body justifiable in an otherwise
rather conventional story? We can imagine how contemporary Chinese

readers would have received such a "map": since it shows clear traces of the Chinese landscape, they would have considered it offensive to their cherished nationalism.

By the time Mu published this story, a concurrent type of body metaphor by the more patriotic writers Xiao Hong and Xiao Jun—stories of Manchuria being ravaged by Japanese military aggressors like a woman's body[61]—was already being greeted with much acclaim on Shanghai's literary scene, led by Lu Xun himself. By comparison, Mu Shiying's erotic geography of the body looks like an intentional and apolitical putdown of a nationalist cliché. Or perhaps this body-map belongs to a totally different conception—of the *mother*land as a grandiose female myth that dwarfs the male "knowing subject." If so, the story would be quite comparable to Lu Xun's mythological tale "Butian" (Mending heaven), which depicts the gigantic body of the goddess Nüwa as she wakes from a languid dream only to give birth to the petty creature civilization. But the erotic potential in Lu Xun's portrait of this mythic goddess is sidetracked by his cynical satire of civilized hypocrisy; in Mu Shiying's story, only the erotic power of the female body is celebrated.

Can physical attributes alone—a face and/or a body—be sufficient to make a fictional heroine a femme fatale? Mary Ann Doane has commented that the femme fatale is "the figure of a certain discursive unease, a potential epistemological trauma. For her most striking characteristic, perhaps, is the fact that she never really is what she seems to be. She harbors a threat which is not entirely legible, predictable, or manageable."[62] In other words, Doane seems to suggest that the femme fatale is a figure with a mysterious aura, and the unpredictable threat she harbors is most likely directly at men. In this regard, a sense of that aura and that threat can indeed be detected in Mu's platinum body, who proves to be not entirely legible or manageable to the doctor. We could also argue that in "Craven A," the heroine is not really what she seems to be or what her body would lead us to believe. If Mu has succeeded in creating extraordinary women's bodies, he seems to have great difficulty in depicting their psychology and behavior. In a cultural tradition in which women's bodies have not been privileged, Mu's effort can nevertheless be considered more avant-garde than in a modern Western society.

As I noted earlier, Mu pushes Liu Na'ou's formula—the pursuit of an exotic-looking modern woman by one or two weak, sentimental men—to its absurd limit. "Camel, Nietzscheist, and Woman" is one example. Another is a longer story, "Bei dangzuo xiaoqianpin de nanzi" (The man who is treated as a plaything), in which the heroine is characterized as "an amalgam of jazz, machine, speed, urban culture, American taste, epochal beauty . . ." (as if the list were not complete), and her physical appearance is described to the hilt—"a really danger-ous creature."[63] But this femme fatale turns out to be a college student who lives in the dormitory by day and frequents dance halls by night. Following Liu Na'ou, Mu makes all the possible references to Holly-wood stars: she has Vilma Banky's eyes, Nancy Carrol's smile, Norma Shearer's face.[64] Still, the ensuing story of the male protagonist's pursuit and eventual defeat is too drawn out and predictable. In "Wuyue" (The month of May), Mu creates a beautiful Eurasian heroine with a compli-cated family background and a Western education, but she behaves like a demure maiden from a traditional family. Her flirtations with a series of men have none of the femme fatale's flair. In an apparent reversal, her body is hardly described; we find only a portrait of innocence as evoked by the vague contour of a face with "a pair of half-closed eyes, like sleeping lotuses in a clear pond at night, and a nose—such a pure straight nose."[65]

Another extreme case of a discrepancy between body or looks and behavior is the story "He Moudan" (Black peony), in which Mu again creates an exotic heroine "with a high nose and long face," wearing a carnation and long earrings "like two pagodas, hanging down on her shoulders—in the Spanish style." She is a fantasy figure straight out of Hollywood movies—a Garbo playing Mata Hari—and she can shoot as well as she can dance. After some dalliance with the male narrator, followed by a reckless shoot-out with police, she somehow finds herself in the house of a reclusive but well-to-do bachelor; as the narrator visits his friend the bachelor, the woman pretends to be his wife and seems to enjoy it, to the envy of the sexually unrequited narrator.[66] Why should such a fantasy woman be made to play such a traditional role at the end of an utterly unbelievable plot? Why, in spite of their striking bodies and looks, do Mu's female characters (with a few exceptions) seem to harbor a sentimental "soft spot"—a flaw that serves to compromise their fatal attraction?

It would be easy to blame such a flaw on Mu's technical limitations as a novelist, however talented he might have been. But the issues raised by the uneven and discrepant characterization of the modern heroine I have observed in Mu's and Liu's fiction pose questions that cannot be answered by reference to technique alone. We must place this literary and textual problem in a larger context of the cultural background in which such texts were produced. Chinese critics would surely locate a few clues in Mu's personal life, since few modern writers have devoted so much creative energy to the depiction of dance halls and dance hostesses. Mu's friends have confirmed that he indeed led a life very much like that of his male protagonists, with frequent visits to the dance halls in pursuit of his favorite hostesses—one of whom he eventually married.[67] In these familiar accounts art indeed imitates life: Mu's characterization of the fictional heroines was, at least in part, influenced by his association with the real dance hostesses he had known and to whom he could not help offering sympathy. Such sympathy leads in turn to the heavy dose of sentimentalism in his fiction. This conventional interpretation takes for granted a very significant point that needs to be reiterated: if the key woman in Mu's life was a dance hostess, the key "chronotope" for his fiction is the dance hall itself. As a central site of Shanghai's night life (see Chapter 1), the dance hall is crucial in any fictional effort at representing the city. More than any other modern Chinese writer, Mu succeeded in conjuring up the mood and atmosphere of the dance hall with a most fitting technique derived from the cinema. Whereas Liu Na'ou described the dance hall casually as a "lead-in" setting for his heroines, Mu turned it into the key interior set for his film-in-fiction.

The Dance Hall and the City

In a book on modern Chinese cinema, Rey Chow has argued that most modern Chinese writers, steeped in their long written tradition, harbored a "contempt for visuality" and did not pay sufficient attention to the significance and overwhelming impact of film.[68] Mu Shiying is the notable exception, because his fiction is almost all visual and permeated with film culture. Nowhere are his visual talent and cinematic technique better displayed than in two of his most famous stories, "Yezonghui li de wugeren" (Five characters in a nightclub) and "Shanghai hubuwu" (Shanghai fox-trot). In both stories the center of action is the night club or dance hall, and the scenes unfold in a series of whirling panoramic shots as if from a roving camera. Both an expressionistic visual effect and a dancelike rhythm are created by the purposeful repetition of words and images:

> White tablecloth, white tablecloth, white tablecloth, white tablecloth . . . white—
>
> Placed on the white tablecloth are: black beer, black coffee, . . . black, black . . .
>
> Beside the white tablecloth are seated men in black ties and tails: clusters of black and white: black hair, white faces, black pupils, white collars, black cravats, white starched shirts, black jackets, white vests, black trousers . . . black and white . . .
>
> Behind the white tablecloth stand the waiters, white clothes, black hats; on their white pants are black stripes . . .
>
> Joy for whites, sorrow for blacks. The music of the cannibal rites of black Africans, the drums like big and small thunder. A trumpet blows and howls. At the center of the floor a row of de-crowned Slavic princesses are dancing the black's tap dance.

A line of white legs step out under bodies wrapped in black
satin—

  Tip, tip, tip—tip tap![69]

The rhythmic repetition of the prose seems to echo the rhythmic
sound of the dance music; it also conjures up the visual image of a
Western-style nightclub in tones of black and white, an image that
recalls the drawings of the rich and sophisticated urbanites from *Vanity
Fair*, which was one of the favorite American magazines in Shi Zhecun's
circle. A more elaborate variation on the same scene can be found in
"Shanghai Fox-Trot." The paragraph that introduces the cabaret/dance
hall is written in language that is even more evocative. (In this translation
I try to come as close as possible to the sentence structures of the
original):

> A blue dusk hovers over the whole room. A single saxophone
> with its neck sticking out and its big mouth wide open is bellow-
> ing at them. At the center, on the smooth floor, fluttering skirts
> and drifting gowns, exquisite heels, heels, heels, heels, heels.
> Fluffy hair and a man's face. A man's white shirt collar and a
> woman's laughter, arms extended, green jade earrings dragging
> onto the shoulders. Neat columns of round tables, but the chairs
> are scattered around. At the dark corners stand white-uniformed
> waiters. The aroma of wine, the scent of perfume, the smell of
> English ham and eggs, the taste of cigarettes . . . A solitary per-
> son sits at a remote corner, taking black coffee to stimulate his
> nerves.[70]

A few paragraphs later, the entire sequence of the sentences is
reversed, beginning from the very end: "A solitary person sits at a remote
corner, taking black coffee to stimulate his nerves . . ." Thus, the two
paragraphs become linguistic equivalents to a carefully choreographed
dance with the sentences twirling around the "floor" of the text—like a
group of waltzers or fox-trotters—in forward and backward formations.

Or they can be compared to a movie montage sequence of dazzling camera shots with the camera constantly moving, creating a dizzying spell. Either way, these scenes are an audacious demonstration of fictional technique appropriated from other media—dance and film. As in an expressionistic film or painting (a Franz Masreel, for instance), the characters are drawn as cartoon figures, their expression and action purposely distorted. In "Shanghai Fox-Trot," after the scene just quoted, Mu's "camera" moves between two dancing couples in the dance hall—a rich housewife and her stepson and a Chinese movie actress and a Belgian jeweler pretending to be a French gentleman. The entire scene is choreographed and "filmed" in such a way that it resembles a Hollywood screwball comedy or musical in which everything including dialogue is stylized. As the two couples imperceptibly exchange partners, the characters are made to repeat the same words of fake endearment. With such dizzying "camera work" Mu has created a world of make-believe full of surface glitter but signifying little in content.

In both stories the dance floor scenes, while providing the center of action, are framed by scenes of the city. Obviously they are meant to form a continuum of urban visual landscape. It is also in these city scenes that Mu displays his neo-sensationalistic style of prose. The front gate of a building "vomits" a throng of people; an elevator "throws people, like goods, up on the roof garden at a speed of fifteen seconds."[71] These touches of surrealism—a controversial subject for Chinese readers—is in my view but the beginning step in a much more ambitious plan to construct a semiotic world of "floating signifiers" that serves to highlight Mu's vision of Shanghai. In "Five Characters in a Nightclub," for instance, such a semiotic vision is constituted by a swirl of neon signs and advertised sights: a gigantic high-heeled shoe in blue and a bottle pouring out red wine; "Please Drink White Horse Whisky . . . Lucky Strike Cigarette Does Not Harm the Smoker's Throat"; "Alexander's Shoe Store, Johnson's Bar, Rasario Tobacco Company, Dixie Music Shop, Chocolate Candy Store, the Cathay Theater, the Hamilton Hotel . . ."[72] In the story, the list of shops precedes the dance hall sequence, as if it were these very signs that drew the people into the fantasy world of the dance hall. After each of the characters is introduced in a brief vignette, they are made to converge on Saturday evening in a nightclub called Queen, dancing the night away and forgetting their worries, at least temporarily.

This urban scene again reminds us of the intriguing notion of the spectacle. Yomi Braester uses the term "spectacle" to denote "the visual regime that corresponds to capitalist commodification: the spectacle promises that one may acquire what one is looking at and introduces an exchange system to compensate for the inevitable breach of that promise. The spectacle manipulates the spectator's desire through an 'economy' in the psychological sense of the word . . . Desire produced by the spectacle is eventually redirected back at the spectacle; the image turns out to be not the medium but the end."[73] In this sense both the billboards and the dance hall are urban spectacles that seduce, bewitch, and eventually frustrate the spectator. Mu subjects a mélange of his characters—not only the modern heroines—to the spectacle, the ultimate protagonist of his fiction.

Mu harbored even bigger plans for "Shanghai Fox-Trot," calling it a "fragment" of an intended novel to be titled *Zhongguo yijiusanyi* (China 1931), which was never written.[74] In other words, he wished to imbue the urban spectacle with even more meaning as part of a national allegory. The story thus invites immediate comparison with Mao Dun's novel *Midnight*, also subtitled *A Romance of China*. Mu may have intended the novel to be a direct challenge to Mao Dun's work, but from a different perspective. Yet despite the ideological differences between the two authors, the works share a remarkable similarity of fictional design: to make the city a microcosm of the country caught at a critical juncture of time.

Being a professed Marxist, Mao Dun inscribed a "master narrative" of historical development and class conflict in his novel. His ultimate concern was with time and temporality. Mu's fragment-story, by contrast, is structured on the trope of space. It is fragmentary precisely because it is pieced together from a number of scenes with no marked transitions in time. The action supposedly takes place within the span of one night. (The same nocturnal mood pervades *Midnight*, though the novel's time span is longer, lasting several months.) Consequently, "Shanghai Fox-Trot" indeed becomes a modern experiment in "spatial form."[75] But before a national allegory can be constructed from the portrait of a city, the city itself must first be represented artistically as an allegorical vision. Mu gives his story a subtitle in parentheses, "a broken fragment" (*yige duanpien*), also in the literal sense of an episode from a longer piece of fiction or a series of cinematic shots yet to be edited into the final film. Its "narrative" consists of a sequence of scenes—urban spaces envisioned as fictional cinema. Together they conjure up a vision of the city. The following is a fragmentary selection of some highlights of this visionary sequence (words in capital letters are in English in the original):

> Shanghai, a heaven built on hell!
>
> West of Shanghai. A large moon crawls over the sky, shining down on a large plain . . . On the plain the railway tracks draw an arch extending along the sky far into the distant horizon . . .
>
> With a roar, an arch of headlights rises from below the horizon. The railway tracks rumble, and the sleepers on the tracks crawl forward under the light, like a centipede. Telegraph poles emerge and are soon submerged in darkness. The *Shanghai Express* rushes by like a dragon with a bulging belly, da, da, da, dancing to the beat of a fox-trot and holding its luminous pearl, while circling along the arch . . .
>
> The legs of trees painted in white, the legs of telephone poles, the legs of all inanimate objects . . . as in a REVUE, the girls who bare and cross their powdered legs . . . the column of white painted legs, along the quiet avenue, from the windows of residential houses, through their gauze curtains, lights like the eyes and pupils of the city, stealthily sneak out—pale red, purple, green—lights everywhere . . .

NEON LIGHT, extending its colored fingers, writes large characters on the blue-inkish sky. An English gentleman stands in front, wearing a red suit with tails, holding a stick, and walking with such high spirits. Below his feet are written: "JOHNNY WALKER STILL GOING STRONG." On the roadside, on a small patch of grass unfolds a [signboard of] utopia by a real estate company, in which an American smoking a Lucky Strike cigarette gazes down, as if saying: "This is a utopia for the Lilliputians; even the big prairie is not big enough for my foot."

On top of the racecourse building, the golden horse on the weathervane throws its hoofs toward the red moon. Around that large grass-covered ground is a sea of light, surging with waves of crime and evil. The Moore Memorial Church is steeped in darkness, kneeling and praying for the men and women about to go to hell. The spire of the Great World tower refuses its confession and proudly stares at this pedantic preacher while giving off circles of light.[76]

The scene then moves inside the cabaret. The characters leave through the revolving glass door, to be confronted by a sea of rickshaws and automobiles: "Austins, Essexes, Fords, Buick sportscars, Buick compacts, with nine, eight, six cylinders"[77]—the list clearly intended to be an *hommage* to Liu Na'ou. But Mu Shiying's mise-en-scène is more ambitious than Liu's, as the street scene leads to a series of panoramic shots of the city crowd: "drunken-eyed sailors riding on rickshaws and kicking the asses of the rickshaw pullers and laughing," "Indian policemen standing erect" at the traffic lights, waves of cars and people "like headless flies,"

a fashion model wearing clothes from the shop and pretending to be a high-class lady, elevators sending cargo-loads of people up to the rooftop gardens every fifteen seconds, female secretaries standing outside the window of a cloth shop and staring at the all-silk French CREPE while thinking about her boss's laughing mouth with its razor-shaved cuts, ideologues and party members carrying packages of propaganda leaflets . . . blue-eyed girls wearing narrow skirts, dark-eyed girls wearing long *qipao*, both displaying the same coquettish charm at their legs and posteriors.[78]

The human mosaic created in this paragraph brings forth a crescendo of energy and excitement. Readers of the period may well have read these images at the same time that they savored the photographic mosaic in the pictorial magazine *Liangyou huabao*. In both written and visual forms, the city that emerges from these representations exudes an aura of "metropolitan excitement"—*duhui de ciji*, as the Chinese headline proclaims on the magazine's printed page while the smaller English headline on the same page calls it "Intoxicated Shanghai."[79]

In this fictional "cinemascape" neither plot nor character is significant, and human beings are reduced to cardboard figures caught in a whirlwind of the city's "light, heat, power." But the story's symmetrical structure imposes a closure in the very first sentence—"Shanghai, a heaven built in hell!"—an artistic conception that befits the Western modernist paradigm of the "city of darkness and light" as summed up by Raymond Williams. But something of an ideological message is insinuated in the ending: after a night of orgiastic depravity, these urban revelers in the night club wake up to another spectacle that seems to suggest that the image is not the medium nor the end in itself. In a paragraph that may have paved the way for the finale of Cao Yu's famous play *Richu* (Sunrise), written in 1936, a tenor voice is raised in Pudong, "Aye . . . ya . . . aye," followed by the sound of a "heroic chorus," and an awkward and ambiguous panegyric ensues:

> The buildings that lie in slumber are standing up, raising their heads and shedding their gray pajamas. The river flows east again, *huala, huala*. The factory's sirens are roaring.
>
> Singing of a new life, the destiny of the people at the nightclub.

Shanghai has woken up!
Shanghai, this heaven built in hell.[80]

In Cao Yu's *Sunrise*, the singing chorus are the workers at a construction site. The end of the play clearly implies that the new proletarian force is rising and the nocturnal revelers of the capitalist class are doomed. As the heroine Chen Bailu intones in her memorable last lines: "The sun is risen, and the darkness is left behind. But the sun is not for us, for we shall be asleep."[81] In view of Mu's previous feat as the author of a lumpenproletarian collection of stories, *Nanbei ji*, we cannot rule out the possibility of an ending tinged intentionally with leftist ideology. If he had indeed completed his projected novel of China in 1931, would he have echoed Cao Yu and Mao Dun and enshrouded the city in darker shadows? Interestingly, in these urban stories Mu does no more with the urban crowd in the streets than merely sketch its shape in a few scenes, nor does he depict the crowd in political action, as the Japanese neo-sensationalist writer Yokomitsu Reiichi does in his masterly novel *Shanghai 1925*, in which the protagonists—both Japanese and Chinese—lose their mental bearings in the tidal wave of the May Thirtieth demonstrations.[82] To demand of his fiction such a revolutionary commitment would lead us far afield into social realism.

Nevertheless, we could attempt to locate on Mu's fictional canvas the figure of the *flâneur* who roams the city and gazes at the crowd while ruminating about his ambivalent reactions to them. Yomi Braester has suggested that the *flâneur* in Benjamin's conception could be someone with a "seemingly lighthearted attitude, ostensibly indulging in consumption and gambling" as an escape from "the stress caused by the modern urban redefinitions of space and time."[83] If so, the protagonists (male and female) in Mu's and Liu's fiction as well as the authors themselves would qualify as *flâneuers* or *flâneuses* who adhere to the economy of the spectacle. To be sure, the male protagonists in Liu and Mu do take walks, like *flâneurs*, but often in the company of women as a prelude to romance or seduction. The erotic allure of both woman and city could tempt the *flâneur*, but in Liu's stories this urban spectacle proves too overpowering for the men to endure, much less to reflect critically on from a distance. In Mu's fiction the city is given a more complex and multihued imagery in which a more pensive *flâneur* figure would feel at home. We find the trace of such a conception in the minor figure who appears near the end of "Shanghai Fox-Trot," a writer who is trying to find proper subjects for his contemplated chef d'oeuvre on the city. The writer thinks, "The first site of inspection, gambling house; the second site, streetwalkers; the third site, dance hall; the fourth site, I'll see."[84] But as he encounters a young streetwalker and her mother, the writer's thoughts culminate in an illusion of career vanity which soon dissipates in parenthetical self-doubt and self-mockery: "(Isn't it so it's a good subject technique is no problem what she says must be ideologically correct no fear of people saying I am a sentimental humanist . . .)"[85] This revealing passage can be read as a metacommentary on Mu's own planned project of writing a novel about China in 1931, of which the story is intended as a fragment. We know from the writer's self-mocking attitude, however, that Mu would never have been able to finish his novel. Instead of conceiving the writer in the image of a *flâneur*, Mu preferred to use a different mask, that of a Pierrot.

The Writer as Pierrot

In his preface to the story collection *Gongmu* [Public graveyard], Mu mentions that he has written five stories—including "Black Peony," "Craven A," and "Five Characters in a Nightclub"—in order to describe "a few people who have fallen from life, who are fallen PIERROTS."[86] The word "Pierrot" appears in French and is not translated. Mu may have picked up the term from Dai Wangshu, whom he calls a smiling Pierrot and to whom he dedicates the entire story collection. Dai in turn may have discovered this dramatic figure in nineteenth-century French literature, particularly the work of Jules Laforgue, one of his favorite French poets. In Mu's stories, the Pierrot figure has already lost its clownish quality as in the original Italian commedia dell'arte—no longer a figure of derision but, on the contrary, one of sympathy.

According to Robert Storey, the Pierrot figure has undergone a history of transformations. "Among the literati of post-revolutionary France," Storey argues, "the Romantics' sympathies, either real or affected, were with the naively passionate People. And *le peuple* . . . was Pierrot." With the appearance of Laforgue's *Complaintes* in 1885, "the clown discovered his first 'modern' voice and Laforgue an attitude that nearly a whole generation of writers adopted as their own. In all important respects, the voice and the attitude are one" because the Pierrot "is very often a carnival reflection of its creator. He is a figure in whom impulse is frustrated and instinct aggravated by analysis, a figure who has reasoned himself into an attitude of sometimes anguished, sometimes supercilious passivity."[87] That Mu may have inherited the French tradition and used this Laforguean figure in his portraits of people "fallen from life" can be inferred from his remark that "these people who are oppressed by life or fall flat from life . . . do not necessarily show a rebellious, angry, or hateful face; they may wear a mask of happiness on their sad faces."[88] Thus, the Pierrot for Mu is less a comic than a lonely figure who masks his sadness with a happy face. The Pierrot can be either a man or a woman, since some of Mu's femme fatale heroines, such as in "Black Peony" and "Craven A," are also intended to be female Pierrots. And the gallery of dancing figures in "Shanghai Fox-Trot" and "Five Characters in a Nightclub" could also be seen as Pierrots if their happy-go-lucky masks were lifted to reveal their true fragile selves.

This character design creates a curious tension with the femme fatale prototype: if a female Pierrot merely wears the mask of a femme fatale, as is the case in "Craven A," how is it possible for her to be "fatally" attractive to men? And how does she fit the "Modern Girl" image as perpetuated by Liu Na'ou? Mu's usage of the Pierrot figure reminds us that whether as man or woman, it is above all someone with a mask, a theatrical device for the enjoyment of the spectators. As such it should not be taken so seriously as an intellectual figure of social alienation. In Mu's fiction, the Pierrot's relationship with the urban environment is also one of tenuous complexity. We could read his or her exotic mask as a form of mimicry of the Western colonial culture in Shanghai's concessions. If so, the seriousness of the charge is diffused by the theatrical playfulness of the Pierrot characters, whose self-mockery becomes part of their character. We could also read the Pierrot figure, in Shu-mei Shih's formulation, as an "alienated, disillusioned individual in a semicolonial city" who fails to "come up to speed," so to speak, with the metropolis.[89] In Mu's own explanation, however, the Pierrot is a marginalized member of the urban people: his or her alienation is, therefore, more psychological than social, yet the mental anguish of these characters is also diffused by Mu's persistent humanitarian sympathy. In Mu's fiction they have played out their life stories in order to entertain the urban spectators. Thus, we may consider Mu's work "popular" fiction despite his own elitist claims as a gifted but lonely writer much misunderstood by his critics.

If Mu sees himself also as something of a Pierrot figure—for he too wears a number masks in his fiction—this self-image does not contain much of a Laforguean pensive quality. When he tries to be self-analytical, he often becomes farcical, as in a lengthy story titled (in French) "Pierrot," which is dedicated to Dai Wangshu. The protagonist of the story, Pan Heling, is a writer and a solitary figure, who carries a copy of Azorin and hums "Träumerei" or listens to Beethoven's Minuet in G as he yearns for his Japanese Madame Butterfly. He goes to a café and flirts with the waitress, like an "urban nightwalker." He gives lengthy analyses of his own temperament. He goes to a party in a room filled with sundry items: "a statue of Tolstoy, a small radio . . . Pu'er tea, banana peels, cigarette butts and smoke, laughter, historical materialism, American culture, an eight-inch photo of Greta Garbo, walls of books, modernism, sofa, and the smoked-yellow fingers of Mr. Pan Heling who supports the Chinese literary scene together with his neurotic friends."[90] After a lengthy exchange of opinion about Chaplin, Laurel and Hardy, American literature, women's legs, the Pre-Raphaelites, Shakespeare, Mayakovsky, Morand, and of course Garbo's husky voice as a symptom of excessive sexual desire, he gives another analysis of himself, his readers, and his critics. He then goes to his Japanese mistress's house, only to discover that she has a Filippino lover; he forgives her and then becomes ill. After his recovery, he suddenly becomes fascinated with the Bolshevik Revolution, gets involved in the workers' movement, and is arrested. After half a year in jail, he returns to life in the city, only to be ignored by everyone. This long intellectual journey of a pathetic Pierrot in Shanghai reads like a tedious satire. Mu may have intended it as a cynical group portrait of *all* Shanghai writers, or a putdown of another May Fourth posture—that of the romantic writer turned revolutionary. In either case, this Pierrot figure looks more clownish than the fallen-from-life femmes fatales. In an ironic way, the story becomes a carnival reflection of its creator.

That Mu has consciously chosen the Pierrot as the central figure in his urban landscape and as the self-image of a writer, instead of the more aristocratic dandy and the more aesthetic *flâneur*, may be connected with the Pierrot figure's affinity to the Picaro, a roguish figure and tramp made popular by Charlie Chaplin. Both character types are by definition anti-heroes and can be regarded as lower-class counterparts to the *flâneur* and the dandy. We are again reminded of his first story collection, *Nabei ji*, which unveils a world of rural rogues and bandits. Its authentic depiction of lumpenproletarian characters took the leftists by surprise when they later found out that it was all a fabrication by this talented novice. If Mu had no rural lower-class experience to speak of, he might still have brought his rural Picaros into the city and affected some sympathy for the urban proletariat, as another contemporary writer, Jiang Guangci, had done.[91] By following Liu Na'ou, however, he succeeded in creating a different world in which the Pierrot-like figures appear more self-parodistic than self-pitying. And like Liu Na'ou and Shi Zhecun, and even Mao Dun, Mu may have been a little too enamored of the urban pleasures of Shanghai to turn his fictional portrait of this "heaven built in hell" into a truly hellish universe. The city remains a positive source of creative imagination for these writers and several others who will be discussed in the next two chapters.

DECADENT AND DANDY:

SHAO XUNMEI AND YE LINGFENG

It was, above all, out of my exploration of huge cities,
out of the medley of their innumerable interrelations,
that this haunting ideal was born.

—Charles Baudelaire, "To Arsène Houssaye"

The idea of decadence (*la décadence* in French) has been a well-estab-
lished artistic concept in the West, which can be traced to eschatologi-
cal belief in the end of the world in the Judeo-Christian tradition.[1]
What makes it relevant to this study, however, is its connotation as a
"face" of modernity—the "other" face of progress. In Matei Calinescu's
paradoxical formulation, "progress *is* decadence and, conversely, decadence *is* progress."[2] In other words, the concept of decadence grew out
of a counterdiscourse, a sense of dissatisfaction with the results of
progress in the late nineteenth century; it was a manifestation of "aesthetic modernity" that was "radically opposed to the other, essentially
bourgeois, modernity, with its promises of indefinite progress, democracy, generalized sharing of the 'comforts of civilization,' etc."[3] Consequently, the artists and writers who considered themselves decadents
consciously and aggressively cultivated a style of their own alienation,
on both moral and aesthetic grounds, against the complacent human-
ism and hypocritical philistinism of the bourgeois majority. In this
regard, literary decadentism is also closely allied to literary avant-gard-

ism.[4] The style of artistic decadence was famously attributed by Théophile Gautier to Baudelaire's *Fleurs du mal*, though Baudelaire himself was known to be quite ambivalent; he defined his own style as "at once decadent, spiritual, and modern."[5]

Such a formulation becomes immediately problematic if we apply it to the modern Chinese context. For the idea of modernity as linear progress was widely embraced by May Fourth intellectuals who had yet to experience its negative results. With rare exceptions (Lu Xun being one), it was difficult for Chinese modernists to grasp the paradox and adopt a "decadent" position as an aesthetic critique of progress. The first modern Chinese usage of the term was probably by Lu Xun in his translation of a Japanese treatise on literary aesthetics, *Kumon no shōchō* (*Kumen de xiangzheng*, or Symbols of suffering, 1924) by Kuriyagawa Hakuson. The Chinese term Lu Xun used to translate "decadence" is *tuitang* (dejection), whereas Kuriyagawa had used another compound, *tuifei* (dilapidation), also borrowed from the classical Chinese literary vocabulary and later adopted as the standard translation. In a prose poem written in 1925, Lu Xun used a third term as part of its title: "*Tuibai xian de zhandong*" (Tremors of degradation). The three terms—*tuitang*, *tuifei*, *tuibai*—all derive from the same etymological root, *tui*, which carries a general connotation of moral decline and degeneration. Perhaps owing to this etymological factor, decadence has been seen in a negative light.

The strange life of this epithet[6] received a further blow on the Chinese leftist front in the early 1930s, when the League of Left-Wing Writers adopted basically the ideological position of Soviet Marxism, which consistently denounced artistic decadence as corrupt and unhealthy—an anathema to Socialist Realism. Even among non-Marxists on the Chinese literary scene of the 1930s, it was difficult to embrace decadence unreservedly. For a writer such as Shi Zhecun, whose stories demonstrated, at least in part, a decadent imagination, the label was not a welcome one. During my interviews with him, he used words such as "erotic" and "grotesque" to describe his work, but not "decadent." As we

THE MODERN LITERARY IMAGINATION

saw in Chapter 4, Shi and his friends Liu Na'ou and Dai Wangshu characterized their literary journals *Trackless Train* and *Literary Atelier* as "avant-garde," a posture they did not equate with decadence. For the dilemma or contradiction between art and politics, between aesthetic pleasure and ideological commitment, could not be easily resolved in the environment of the 1930s, in which literary production was already threatened by the winds of impending war.

To be sure, writers such as Liu Na'ou and Mu Shiying openly opted for the aesthetic position by flaunting a style of neo-sensationalism in their fiction, for which they were repeatedly castigated by leftist critics, who had drawn upon another book by Kuriyagawa, *Chule xiangya zhita* (Out of the ivory tower), also translated by Lu Xun and first published in 1925. The book's title indicates Kuriyagawa's central thesis, namely, that it was no longer tenable to uphold an "art for art's sake" position, and that artists and writers had to break away from the "ivory tower" of pure aestheticism and return to the concerns and struggles of real life.[7] In Lu Xun's postscript, he has added a quotation from another Kuriyagawa essay which characterizes the modern mind as "wandering at the crossroads."[8] The two phrases had an equally profound impact on Lu Xun and many of his followers. To follow this literary "bible" to the letter, two young writers, Pan Han'nian and Ye Lingfeng (whom Lu Xun later denounced) edited a literary journal, *Huanzhou* (Mirage), which was composed of two parts; the first part was subtitled "Ivory Tower" and the second part "Crossroads."

Given these constrictions on decadence, it would seem that there was no ground for its survival even as a literary term, much less a well-articulated aesthetic doctrine. Still, I would argue that a dimension of what might be called decadent imagination is discernible in a number of literary texts of both poetry and fiction produced in the late 1920s and early 1930s, the result of a series of literary confrontations with Western authors and texts that began with translations of Baudelaire.

Translating Baudelaire

Kuriyagawa's *Kumon de shōchō* is a semi-scholarly treatise on literary creativity and appreciation. His somewhat simplistic theory about creativity
as "symbol of suffering" provided the first major introduction to Freud's
concept of psychoanalysis for a whole generation of modern Chinese
writers. But the references to Baudelaire are casual and scarce, occurring
only in conjunction with Kuriyagawa's discussion of other matters. For instance, a translation of Baudelaire's prose poem "Les Fenêtres" (Windows)
is included as an illustration in the section on the "pleasure of self-discov-
ery." In another section on "the four stages of literary appreciation," he
cites Baudelaire as an extreme case of "sensuous poetry," of which the representative figure is John Keats. "There were poets with an extremely
sharpened sensitivity," he notes, "modern poets of decadence such as
Baudelaire who considered the senses of sight and hearing—color and
tone—insufficient, and they resorted to the unpleasant sense of smell in
their works. But these could be said to be an exception. It goes without
saying that the main sensory factor is hearing, to which music appeals."[9]

This may have been the first time Baudelaire's name was mentioned
in connection with decadence, but the term is left unexplained except to
suggest that it somehow has to do with the "unpleasant sense of smell."
Only in a third instance, as Kuriyagawa discusses the relationship between literature and morality, is Baudelaire described as a "Satanic poet"
(*Emo shiren*), his *Flowers of Evil* a prime example of literary glorification of
the evil and the ugly, which has nothing to do with morality. In his
translation of Kuriyagawa, Lu Xun seems to put more emphasis on the
French poet by inserting as an illustration a painting of Charles Baude-
laire with a caption in German, "Ch. Baudelaire: Selbstporträt (Im
Haschischrausch)," rendered correctly into Chinese as "Self-Portrait of
Baudelaire (in the midst of imbibing Indian hashish)."[10]

Around the same time Lu Xun was translating *Symbols of Suffering*,
the English-educated romantic poet Xu Zhimo also contributed his own

translation of a Baudelaire poem to the prestigious journal *Yusi* (Thread of words), which was edited by Lu Xun and his brother, Zhou Zuoren. The poem Xu translated happened to be "Une Charogne" from *Les Fleurs du mal*. The second stanza contains a striking image which indeed invokes a strong sense of smell:

> Les jambes en l'air, comme une femme lubrique,
> Brûlante et suant les poisons,
> Ouvrir d'une façon nonchalante et cynique
> son ventre plein d'exhalaison.[11]

In Xu's Chinese translation these lines are rendered as follows:

> It opens wide its legs, with the abandon of a wanton woman,
> Oozing foul gas, smeared with a smelly and sticky odor.
> Its rotten bosom and belly have no cover,
> Licentious, filthy lust.[12]

Xu's exceedingly "sensory" translation may have been derived from the English translation by Arthur Symons, the poet and critic of the influential journal *The Yellow Book* and one of the English writers Xu most admired. Symons's translation, entitled "A Carcass," reads:

> Lewd legs in the air, like a lewd woman's passion
> Burning with odious revelations,
> Showing in a sad and cynical and cruel fashion
> Its belly full of exhalations.[13]

Absent from this Victorian translation is any mention of "licentious filthy lust." In parentheses Xu has included the original French phrase "comme une femme lubrique," which Symons translates as "like a lewd woman's passion" (and Richard Howard renders simply as "like a whore").[14] But Xu uses a more expressive Chinese term, *dangfu* (wanton woman), and gives it an air of "licentious abandon" (*fangsi*). While adding "smelly and sticky odor" to the words *poisons* and *exhalaison*, Xu has also further "uncovered" (*ouvrir*, which Symons translates as "showing") the body's bosom and belly but neglects to translate the adjectives *nonchalante* and *cynique*. In short, Xu exceeds the "sensory limits" of both Baudelaire and Symons.

In any event, Xu does not seem to have a clue about the poetic meaning of the title, "Une Charogne," which he renders as "dead body" and locates it "in the tomb of the ancient Greek queen of lust, Clytemnestra." He calls this poem "the most evil and the most gorgeous immortal flower of Baudelaire's collection, *The Flowers of Evil*," and proceeds to praise wildly the "tone and color" of Baudelaire's poetry. Xu also confesses modestly that as a "country bumpkin" he cannot claim to understand Baudelaire's original, but he could still chant it: poetry, like music, is also intended for the pleasure of listening. As a poet himself, Xu says that he can listen to both real music ("music with sound") and the more mystical "music without sound" (*wuyin de yue*), that is, poetry. (This mystical remark provoked Lu Xun to write a sarcastic essay in rebuttal.)[15] In addition to music, Xu has not forgotten about the sensory element of smell in Baudelaire's poetry, which, we recall, is also emphasized by Kuriyagawa. But Xu goes a step further: "His smell is extremely poisonous but also extremely fragrant . . . Literary Europe of the second half of the nineteenth century all smelled his strange odor; many were poisoned to death by him, but still more were intoxicated by his poison."[16]

Xu's extravagant interpretation of Baudelaire produces yet another rendition of the term "decadence"—a transliteration that in both image and sound approximates the French original—*tui jia dang*, or "decadent and wanton," like the dead body of "Une Charogne." With this term Xu also gives a feminine personification to the concept of decadence—as a *dangfu* or wanton woman, a character metonymically close to the femme fatale. It is precisely this romantic image of decadence that is invoked in Shao Xunmei's poetry (which I analyze later in this chapter).

In spite of his attack on Xu Zhimo's interpretation of Baudelaire, Lu Xun was himself deeply attracted to Baudelaire and translated at least one poem on the basis of Japanese and German translations (the latter by Max Bruno).[17] But Lu Xun's sensibility was distinctly different from Xu Zhimo's: he never indulged in romantic excess and would have been loath to impart any flavor or "smell" of wanton depravity. As a leading intellectual of the May Fourth movement, Lu Xun felt strangely alienated from his May Fourth colleagues whose "enlightenment mentality"—the optimistic belief in rationality and progress—seems to have plunged him into the depths of depression. At the same time, he could find no way out of his own spiritual dilemma between hope and despair, between a somewhat self-enforced belief in modernity and a private *ressentiment* of discontent. *Yecao* (Wild grass, or Weeds) offers a rare glimpse into his tormented soul. For Lu Xun, therefore, decadence is truly a tragic reflection and a paradoxical comment on time and progress. As such it offers a rare testimony to the kind of "aesthetic modernity" defined by Calinescu.[18] As I have demonstrated in a previous study, Lu Xun developed a set of poetic images and metaphors endowed with allegorical meaning.[19]

Baudelaire's prose poetry was an important source of creative inspiration for Lu Xun in evolving his own form of prose poetry. Even his conception of this new genre may have been indebted, albeit indirectly, to Baudelaire, who, in a prefatory letter to Arsène Houssaye, said of his *petites poèmes en prose:* "Which one of us, in his moments of ambition, has not dreamed of the miracle of a poetic prose, musical, without rhythm, supple enough and rugged enough to adapt itself to the lyrical impulses of the soul, the undulations of reverie, the jibes of conscience?"[20] The prose poems in Lu Xun's *Wild Grass* have indeed laid bare the lyrical impulses of his soul in a rare revelation of his dark side. Since we know that he read Baudelaire in Japanese and German, he would not have been inspired by the sound of the French master's prose poetry—"musical but without rhythm"—so much as by the possibility of evolving a new "supple and rugged" language that could adapt itself to the "lyrical impulses of [his] soul, the undulations of reverie, the jibes of conscience." These words describe most fittingly what Lu Xun has in mind in conjuring up the dreamlike landscape of *Wild Grass;* his framing of dreams may have been inspired by Kuriyagawa's interpretation of Freud.

There are a few instances of a Baudelairean imprint in Lu Xun's prose poems. None can be seen as direct borrowing, but a certain affinity can still be detected. For instance, the first poem of *Petits Poèmes en prose*, known also as *Paris Spleen*, is titled "The Stranger," a piece cast in the mode of an imaginary catechism in which the stranger, an "enigmatic man," declares that he has no father, mother, sister, brother, or even friends. He does not know his country, hates gold and God; the only thing he cares for is beauty and the clouds—"the clouds that pass . . . up there . . . up there . . . the wonderful clouds."[21]

This "extraordinary stranger" may have served as a partial basis for Lu Xun's "Passer-by," a poetic play much longer and more elaborate than Baudelaire's prose poem. In Lu Xun's play, the passer-by is also a stranger who walks alone and aimlessly in a barren landscape. As he encounters an old man and a young girl, his response to their queries is similar to that of Baudelaire's stranger, though voiced in an "existential" manner, without any allusions to the beauty of clouds:

> Please sit down, stranger. What do they call you?
>
> Call me? That I don't know. Ever since I can remember, I've been on my own; so I don't know how I am called. As I go on my way, people call me by this name or that as they wish . . .
>
> I see. Well, where are you from?
>
> I don't know. Ever since I can remember, I have been walking like this.[22]

These words serve as a portrait of a loner—a central trope in Lu Xun's fiction and, in my view, a self-reflexive metaphor of his own "existential" condition. In another prose poem called "Tremors of Degradation," as noted earlier, decadence is invoked as a lyrical image of degradation. The image is embodied in the figure of an old woman who bears a striking resemblance to the figure in Baudelaire's poem "The Old Woman's Despair":

> A wizened little old woman felt gladdened and gay at the sight of the pretty baby . . . that everyone wanted to please; such a pretty little creature, as frail as the old woman herself; and toothless and hairless like her.

She went up to him all nods and smiles.

But the infant, terrified, struggled to get away from her caress, filling the house with his howls.

Then the old woman went back into her eternal solitude and wept alone, saying: "Ah, for us miserable old females the age of pleasing is past. Even innocent babes cannot endure us, and we are scarecrows to little children whom we long to love."[23]

From this simple scene of an old woman's despair depicted by Baudelaire, Lu Xun constructs an elaborate tableau in the form of a two-part dream. In the first part, the "slight frail body" of a young mother "tremble[s] with hunger, pain, shock, humiliation, and pleasure," as she tries to console her hungry infant while putting her to sleep. In the second part, as the dream continues many years later, an old woman (the young mother grown old) is contemptuously scolded by her daughter for having wrecked her whole life. After this rebuff, the old woman returns to the agonies of her "eternal solitude." In the last paragraphs of the poem, the expression of her sorrow is elongated into a series of surrealistic images, like a montage sequence from a German expressionist film:

> She walked on and on through the depth of night till she reached the boundless wilderness . . . Stark-naked, like a stone statue, she stood in the center of the wasteland and her whole past flashed through her mind: hunger, pain, shock, humiliation, and pleasure . . . she trembled . . . she twitched convulsively . . . Her whole body, great as a statue but already decrepit and ruined, was shaken by tremors. These tremors, small and distinct at first like fish-scales, started seething like boiling water over a blazing fire; and at once the air too was convulsed like waves in the wild, storm-racked ocean.[24]

This passage is a rare instance of Lu Xun's emotion-tinged "purple prose," in contrast to his usual succinct style. With layers of imagery, especially in the last sentence, Lu Xun seems intent on constructing an allegorical tale of decadence as degradation centered on the old woman's "decrepit, ruined" body. He does not succeed, in my judgment, but a certain poetic "inscape" is revealed, a metaphoric landscape of desolation and ruin that forms the background of most of his prose poems in *Wild Grass*. It is nonetheless intriguing that he would choose to have these depressive musings embodied in the decrepit person of an old woman—a figure that may be linked to the image of the corpse of a wanton woman in Xu Zhimo's rendition of "Une Charogne." Of course, the stark landscape of Lu Xun's prose poem is in sharp contrast to Xu's more flowery evocation of Baudelaire.

If decadence can be considered an instance of literary imagination rather than a concept, style, or attitude, we must conclude that it was Xu Zhimo's version, rather than Lu Xun's, that proved to be more in tune with the ebullient mood of the time. Instead of constituting a nihilistic or aesthetic critique of modernity, as in Lu Xun, decadence for modern Chinese writers assumed two different "faces"—"symbolism" and aesthetic hedonism—the former inspired by Baudelaire and French poetry, the latter by a number of English writers, particularly those associated with the Bloomsbury group. More recently, Chinese scholars have done enough research to resurrect the works of a number of Chinese "symbolists"—Li Jinfa, Dai Wangshu, Wang Duqing, Mu Mutian, Feng Naichao, Feng Zhi[25]—but hardly anything has been written about the group of "aesthetes and decadents" led by Shao Xunmei, who will be the subject of my discussion in the next section. Since Shao can be said to be the very embodiment of aestheticism and is so little known, a biographical sketch may be in order.

Portrait of an Aesthete

In the standard histories of modern Chinese literature, Shao Xunmei (1906–1968) is a lesser-known writer than most because he was the least suited to the May Fourth prototype of a writer of social conscience. A poet, essayist, translator, publisher, and flamboyant literary dandy, Shao most closely resembled his friend Xu Zhimo, the eminent poet of the Crescent Moon Society, whose posthumous fame has also served to eclipse Shao's. Born in 1906 to a wealthy family that owned real estate in Shanghai, Shao was sent to a missionary school to study English.[26] In 1924, at the age of eighteen, he enrolled at Cambridge University in England, where he read literature and stayed with the family of the Reverend A. C. Moule, who later became a translator of Marco Polo.[27] He then studied painting briefly in France, where he met Xu Beihong, who later became one of modern China's most renowned painters and with whom he became a "sworn brother" and close friend. Upon his return to Shanghai, he married Sheng Peiyu, the granddaughter of Sheng Xuanhuai, one of the most distinguished industrialists in the late Qing reform movement. He also befriended most of the eminent non-leftist writers, including Xu Zhimo, Shen Congwen, and Lin Yutang, and openly roamed the Shanghai literary scene with his American mistress, Emily Hahn, a reporter for the *New Yorker* and author of *The Soong Sisters* (with research help provided by Shao himself).[28] He also helped her publish an English journal, *Candid Comment*, when their bilingual paper, *Vox*, failed after three issues.[29] For a while they cohabited openly in a small apartment a few blocks from Shao's family home, evidently with his wife's approval. Shao taught Hahn how to smoke opium and apparently became addicted himself.[30]

From all accounts, Shao Xunmei was a handsome man (his name, Xunmei, means literally "truly beautiful"). Apparently he took great pride in his Greek nose—also one of Liu Na'ou's fictional fixations (see Chapter 6)—and went so far as to draw an autograph sketch centering on his exotic nose; he also designed a personal seal combining a horse, his birth sign, with his English name, Sinmay. In her memoir *China to Me*, Emily Hahn devotes several pages to "Sinmay, my Chinese friend." She describes how intimately he knew the city—"every brick in every shop front seemed to have its history for Sinmay"—and how he would drive his "long brown Nash" from his home in Yangtzepoo, across the Soochow

Creek, "up the middle of town where the tempting bookstores were." In Hahn's vivid recollection, Shao was "overwhelmingly curious. He had a mind like a child's, or a puppy's, or an old-fashioned novelist's, prying into everything and weaving stories around whatever caught his attention." He was also a cultivated gourmet and beguiling conversationist: "He would tell long stories about this dish or that, talking first in Chinese to his friends, who liked listening as much as I did, and then remembering suddenly that I didn't understand him and doing a quick interpretation." But with foreign strangers he felt uncomfortable. Only once did he visit Hahn at the *North-China Herald* office, and "his pale face and long gown caused such excitement among the mild British reporters that he became self-conscious and after that made me meet him out in the Bund." They saw each other "almost everyday, sooner or later, mostly later. Time meant nothing whatever to him." She continues, "Then at night, a dinner party or an evening talk at Sinmay's house, or a movie, or reading in bed. I was very happy, even though I began to smell war in the air."[31]

To his Chinese friends, Shao Xunmei was a glamorous figure on the salon circuit, who "added a living attraction to his ornate fin-de-siècle enclave by 'acquiring' a foreign mistress." For Hahn he purchased a snug apartment in the vicinity of Avenue Joffre, where, according to the memory of Zhang Kebiao, "many friends gathered to look at the exotic beauty."[32] The "young master" (*shaoye*) himself, as his friends endearingly called him, lived in a more luxurious mansion nearby, whose exotic interior was comparable to Zeng Pu's salon. This is how one writer, Zhang Ruogu, describes it in a slightly exaggerated fictionalized account:

The young master's residence was one of Shanghai's superior mansions. Entirely built in marble, surrounded by a large garden, and approached by eight pathways wide enough for advancing automobiles, the estate looked like a manifestation of the Eight Diagrams with a tall Western building in the middle. The center of the house formed a hall that was magnificently decorated like an emperor's throne room . . . And there was the host's private

study, where he entertained guests. Here, too, the interior decoration was exceptionally opulent; the wall was adorned by an
authentic bust of the poetess Sappho recently excavated in the
volcanic city of Pompeii—the item alone was worth more than
5,000 dollars. Furthermore, there was a manuscript by the English poet Swinburne that had been acquired for 20,000 pounds in
London . . . In the center of the room stood a Steinway piano . . .
and right next to it there was a pile of music scores that were all
bound in jade-colored snake leather.[33]

This fantastic account leaves out Shao's private collection of a large
number of Western books. Nor does it describe Shao's most significant
contribution to the production of modern Chinese culture: his tireless
efforts in publishing books and journals at his own publishing houses. He
first established Jinwu shudian (La Maison d'or) and published a high-
class literary journal, *Jinwu*, whose yellow cover was clearly modeled after
the famous English journal *The Yellow Book*. He was among the first publishers to pay attention to the design of books: not only the quality of the
paper and binding but also the appearance of the text on each printed
page (often occupying a relatively small space at the center, leaving wide
empty margins all around). He had high standards for the artistic design
and quality of print of his journals, and he spent his family fortune in
setting up his own printing press, which included a rotogravure section,
with the most up-to-date printing machinery ordered from Europe. One
of his clients was also a competitor, the famous *Liangyou huabao*, whose
later issues were printed by Shao's Shidai (Epoch) printing company.

With the new plant as his publishing base, Shao launched three
popular magazines—*Shidai huabao* (Epoch pictorial magazine), *Shidai
manhua* (Epoch cartoons), and *Shidai dianying* (Epoch cinema)—to which
Liu Na'ou also contributed. He had gathered some of the most talented
artists around his journals—Ye Qianyu (b. 1907), Lu Shaofei (b. 1903),
and the brothers Zhang Guangyu (1900–1964) and Zhang Zhengyu
(1904–1970)—who pioneered in the new popular art form of cartoons.

But none of Shao's own journals sold well. Emily Hahn recalls: "Remnants of this former glory could be found in a small bookshop of his in Soochow Road, where 'slim volumes' of forgotten poetry collected dust on the back shelves."[34]

Shao was reportedly also very sociable. It was said that he once made a special visit to the famous Xinya coffeehouse because he heard that this was the gathering place of Zeng Pu and his son Zeng Xubai, as well as Zhang Ruogu, Fu Yanchang, and Zheng Zhenduo; he talked with them from mid-afternoon until dinner, and ended up in Zheng Zhenduo's home.[35] Naturally they all became fast friends. He visited the Zengs at their Zhenmeishan (Truth-Beauty-Goodness) bookstore, which he used as the model of his own Jinwu bookstore, opened in 1928. He held court in his own home or at his mistress's apartment for his numerous literary friends, and made his personal library available to young writers such as Xu Chi and Chen Mengjia, who were college students. He became a contributing member of Xu Zhimo's Crescent Moon Society and helped Lin Yutang found his journal *Lunyu* (Discourse). On his way back from Europe, he stopped in Singapore and bought a copy of a new literary magazine, which he liked very much. As soon as he arrived in Shanghai, he went straight to its offices and befriended all its editors—Teng Gu, Teng Gang, Ni Yide, Fang Guangtao, and Zhang Kebiao, all self-styled "aesthetes"—and write a large number of poems and essays for their journal, *Shihou* (Sphinx).[36] He seems to have had inexhaustible resources of energy, time, literary talent, and money, with which he supported all these endeavors. As a result, he used up all his family wealth and was reduced to utter poverty during the war years. After the Communist takeover, he willingly donated his printing plant, together with all its workers, to the new people's government, which then put him in jail for a year and ruined his health. He finally died in 1968, at the height of the Cultural Revolution. In his last years he tried to support his family by doing commissioned translations such as *The Adventures of Tom Sawyer*, Shelley's *Prometheus Unbound*, *Wuthering Heights*, and three works by Tagore.[37] Some of these were published, presumably for "internal circulation."

I have reproduced these details of Shao's life not only to rehabilitate his name posthumously but also to provide some background for his prodigious knowledge of English, French, and American literature. His record is quite comparable to Shi Zhecun's, and in fact he contributed a learned article on American poetry to Shi's journal, *Xiandai zashi* (see Chapter 4). Even the titles of their journals strike the same modern tone—*Shidai* and *Xiandai*, both manifesting a clear penchant for the modern or contemporary epoch. It behooves us, therefore, to take a brief look at the table of contents of Shao's journals, particularly *Jinwu yuekan*. In its first volume of twelve issues (1929), it featured translations of Pater, Maurois (an essay on Ruskin and Wilde), Hardy (*Jude the Obscure*), Tennyson ("The Lotus-Eaters"), Shakespeare (*Othello*), Katherine Mansfield, Oscar Wilde, George Moore (*Memoirs of My Dead Life*), and Paul Morand, as well as large numbers of original poetry and essays, contributed by Shao and his circle of friends. The list seems rather eclectic, but if we take a closer look at Shao's own essays published there and elsewhere, a profile of his literary tastes begins to emerge.

A most interesting case is his intellectual linkage with George Moore. Shao first read about this English author while in England when one of Shao's acquaintances sent a copy of Moore's new book, *Memoirs of My Dead Life*, to Shao for translation. In his lengthy article on Moore, Shao gives an account of the intellectual peregrinations of this author in a most empathetic manner, as if he were writing his own memoir. He talks about Moore's experiences as a young man in Paris, where he tried to study painting and met a host of French artists and writers. After Moore returned to London, he befriended Arthur Symons, W. B. Yeats, and J. M. Synge, with whom he "planned to promote Irish literature," and wrote a three-volume autobiographical work, *Hail and Farewell*. He also became close to another circle of literary friends, including Walter Pater, Henry James, Edmund Gosse, and Walter de la Mare. Most of these English writers were themselves admirers of French symbolist poetry. Shao reports that the English writer whom Moore most admired was Water Pater, whose *Marius the Epicurean* awakened Moore "like a spring breeze." Thus it was through Moore that Shao probably acquired his first taste of French poetry and an abiding interest in the English fin-de-siècle aesthetes and decadents.[38] In his article Shao reproduces a quotation in French, which turns out to be Moore's quotation of Walter Pater quoting Théophile Gautier: "Je trouve la terre aussi belle que le ciel, et je pense que la correction de la forme est la vertu."[39] The inclusion of so many names and quotes in English and French must have baffled Shao's many readers.

Shao's account of Moore presents the image of a bohemian aesthete—an image at great odds with the standard view of Moore as a realist writer who also adapted French naturalism into the Victorian novel.[40] This aesthetic-decadent hallmark was incorporated into Shao's own self-image, and fortified by more self-proclaimed affinities with Western writers. In another article he announces that on the walls of his own study hung two pictures: a portrait of the ancient Greek poetess Sappho and another of Swinburne as painted by Rossetti. He then gives a reminiscent account of his journey of discovery. On his way to Cambridge he disembarked in Naples and visited a museum, where he saw a fresco painting of a beautiful woman who beckoned to him with a lover's gaze: "Come to me, my Sinmay!" He was totally bewitched and seduced.[41] Upon arriving in Cambridge, he asked Reverend Moule about this beautiful woman, Sappho, and was in turn introduced to a classics scholar, L. M. Edmonds of Jesus College, who recommended that if he wished to have a taste of Sappho's poetic beauty, he should read Swinburne, who was the first modern English poet to use the Sapphic form.[42] Shao followed his advice and wrote a long essay about Swinburne while in Cambridge. Later he translated (from English) four poems by Sappho, with notes, and wrote another essay on his poetic idol for his fraternal journal *Sphinx*.[43]

In a preface to a collection of his own poems, Shao establishes a clear genealogical line: from his admiration for Sappho he learned of Swinburne, from whom he then learned of Baudelaire and Verlaine.[44] One of the first books published by his Jinwu bookstore was his collection of essays with an exotic title, *Huo yu rou* (Fire and flesh), inspired by a line from Swinburne: "Hands that sting like fire." The collection contains six essays, one on Sappho, two on Swinburne, and the other three on Verlaine, Gautier (a translation of Arthur Symons), and the love poetry of the ancient Roman poet Catullus. The volume can be seen as a summing-up of his education in Western literature at Cambridge University, where a few years earlier Xu Zhimo had been exposed to a similar influence and had acquired similar tastes. Both tend to emphasize the rebellious ethos and romantic sentiment in these works.[45] Thus in his first essay on Swinburne, Shao paired Swinburne's *Poems and Ballads* (1866) with Baudelaire's *Fleurs du mal* (1857) as milestones and hailed the two poets as "revolutionaries and liberators of all the literature imprisoned by religion, morality, and custom. The two are creators and protective deities of all the poetry of truth, beauty, feeling, music, and sweetness. Their poetry always finds fragrance from stench, truth from falsehood, goodness from evil, beauty from ugliness, diversion from life's depression, happiness from a world of melancholy, in short, 'consolation from sin.'" He carefully differentiates the Swinburne of the early decadent phase from the later revolutionary phase in a second essay, "Songs before Sunrise" (after the title of a Swinburne poetry collection).[46] The same romantic strain recurs in his essay on Verlaine, a figure he discovered through reading Moore's memoir, and he praises both as hedonists, not decadents: "Others call him the saddest of poets, but I think where he is sad is precisely where he finds pleasure."[47]

Shao Xunmei's "reading list" offers an interesting case study of cultural encounter between China and the West. From a Western perspective, the genealogy he traces reflects a common line of English decadence that began with Swinburne and culminated in the group of Pater, Symons, and Oscar Wilde—the writers of the so-called Yellow Nineties, so named after the famous journal *The Yellow Book*, which inspired Shao's own journal *La Maison d'or* in both its color design and aesthetic content. Yet his particular fixation on George Moore's memoirs led him to adopt what Richard Gilman has called a "romantic, even apocalyptic" view and a "ludicrous and even excessive" misreading of Baudelaire and decadence. This is what Gilman says of Moore in his famous study on decadence: "His words show us what it was like for an impressionable young writer, raised in the Victorian atmosphere of re-pressed passion, moral hypocrisy, and fear of 'dangerous' art, to come upon Baudelaire and the whole startling line of *poètes maudits*."[48] This assessment could just as well be applied to Shao Xunmei himself if we replaced "Victorian" with "traditional Chinese." Gilman's view of Swin-burne is likewise uncharitable. He calls him "a highly unstable personal-ity, intellectually a peculiar combination of schoolboyish bravado and subterranean priggishness," a combination he sums up as "a particular sort of cultural adolescence." He quotes T. S. Eliot's well-known remark about Swinburne that he "knew nothing about Evil, or Vice, or Sin," otherwise "he would not have had so much fun out of it." [49] Yet it was Swinburne who first translated selections from Baudelaire's *Fleurs du mal* into English, from which his young Chinese disciples Xu Zhimo and Shao Xunmei first learned about Baudelaire. If Gilman is harsh on Swin-burne, how much harsher would it be if we applied the same high standards to these "adolescents" from another culture who had to grapple with a totally alien language (two if we add French) to begin with? How much spiritual profundity could we expect from this novice effort? And how much could a young Chinese in his early twenties be expected to know about the long tradition of Western decadence?

In an essay on Verlaine, Shao attempts to distinguish between two styles—"decadent" (Oscar Wilde) and "hedonist" (George Moore)—and clearly favors the latter. He then proceeds to read Verlaine in the hedon-istic light of Moore! Clearly Shao is incapable of probing the depths of "a moral or spiritual order" or examining "the forbidden, the tainted, in a realm of injured or arrested souls and of voluptuous blasphemy," as Gilman writes of Baudelaire.[50] Shao spoke admiringly of Baudelaire, but never translated him. At the same time, he admired even more Baude-laire's spokesman Théophile Gautier. In Gilman's view, if for Baudelaire decadence "was primarily a matter of metaphysical inquiry and learning, for Gautier it was a style, a coloration, and an attitude." Gautier was the chief progenitor of the "secular side" of decadence—less spiritual and more physical and romantic, as manifested "in a penchant for the colorful and the outlandish . . . and in bohemianism and artistic snobbery."[51] Shao would certainly take Gautier's side and would not hesitate to endorse noncomformity and individual rebellion. To that extent, decadence is not far from avant-gardism, especially in this Chinese context.

"Flower-like Evil"

As we examine Shao's own poetry, this impression is further borne out. He had worked very hard on writing poetry. As he states in the preface of his *Shi ershiwu shou* (Twenty-five poems): "The first time it was shameless imitation, then it was the temptation of words and phrases, and then, the intoxication in sound and tones," but he nearly forgot about "something more important, poetic imagery." He criticizes these early poems as rather "ornately colorful," "decorative and delicate things which aside from being pleasing to the eyes and ears express only meanings that are on the surface of words."[52] Yet, this weakness can also be said to be the strength of Shao's style: it contains a profusion of ornate and colorful images built with "things"—natural or artificial objects, especially flowers, vegetation, water, and precious stones—that constitute a world of "elemental reverie," an important feature of the "decadent imagination" in European art.[53] In the following excerpt from a poem with an autobiographical title, "Xunmei's Dream," we find a typical succession of such colorful objects:

> From the pale red and pale green lotuses is grown
> A warm tender dream, as she leans against my soul.
>
> In the poet's flesh, there are no foul sprouts.
> The embryo is naturally a pure crystal;
> It will turn into emeralds as it falls in love with green leaves,
> And into bright corals as it falls in love with red flowers.[54]

The poem is clearly the work of a novice trying to find his own poetic image and tone. There are lingering traces of traditional Chinese poetry, as in the cliché pair of red flowers and green leaves. In fact, the end rhymes in some lines still imitate traditional patterns. Here is a short poem titled "To Sappho" with its end rhymes adhering strictly to the rhyming structure of classical Chinese four-line poems (carrying the same rhyme in lines 1, 2, and 4, as approximated in my English translation):

> From a flower bed, amidst fragrances you are awake,
> A virgin's naked body, a bright moon it does make—
> I see again your fire-red flesh and skin,
> Like a rose, opening for my heart's sake.[55]

Shao's modest claim to "originality," as shown in these two samples, lies in his technique of weaving natural objects into an artificial world of sensuality in which the central figure is invariably a woman, who becomes both a personification of these objects and a projection of desire. The flower imagery also shows traces of Swinburne's imprint. What gives Shao's poetry certain notoriety for his contemporary audience is its exhibition of the "voluptuous blasphemy" of the female body and sexuality—a poetic equivalent, as it were, of the femme fatale figure in the stories of Liu Na'ou and Mu Shiying. But the poetic landscape is pastoral and mythic, shorn of all the paraphernalia of urban material culture. In the midst of such artifice of nature the poet celebrates or otherwise indulges his amorous reverie in the sensuality of the female body. The eroticism is derived not only from some pointed metaphors of the flesh but also from an assumed position of male gaze or fantasy. Shao's erotic evocations are still male-centered; one searches in vain for a woman's voice inspired by Sappho's poetry. The following examples are drawn mostly from his collection *Hua yiban de zui'e* (Flower-like evil)—named after Baudelaire's *Flowers of Evil*, with a side reference possibly to George Moore's *Flowers of Passion*:

> A peony also dies
> But her virgin-like redness,
> Shaking like a harlot
> Is enough to make you and me go crazy in the day
> And have wild dreams at night

> She may lack fragrance,
> Though she has added a sweet taste in poetry,
> And some deceit in tears.
> But I can never forget her wet soft flesh,
> Her clear red skin
> And that squeezed feeling of inebriation.[56]

> The dew on the grass mattress of a tree tent,
> Is like the sweet tears of a virgin on her wedding night;
> Or the hot sweat on a seductress's lower body,
> That makes so many souls drunk with her spell.[57]

The boldness of these lines lies, of course, in turning a familiar flower-and-grass trope, almost a cliché in classical Chinese poetry, into the shocking metaphoric pair of virgin and harlot. In the first poem, "Peony," the poet's free association turns the flower into an object of lustful desire. The flower's "red skin" and "wet soft flesh" thus become transferred into images of the female sexual organ. The second poem, "Flower-like Evil," uses the same variation, pairing the virgin's "tears" and the harlot's "hot sweat," likening them to the wetness of the dew on the "grass mattress" in the first line. Thus, we are ushered into Shao Xunmei's "decadent" world—*tuijiadang*—a world in which the erotic motifs are given a decorative dressing of "wanton depravity." In fact, he wrote a poem with the title "Decadent Love" (Tuijiadang de ai), which describes the act of lovemaking in the image of the coupling of clouds:

> Ah, coupling with this cloud,
> With another he becomes also intertwined;
> In the midst of such music and color,
> He has thus lost his soul.[58]

There is nothing new in this image, which draws upon a cliché of classical Chinese poetry—"clouds and rain"—for lovemaking. The use of celestial beings and imagery is more erotic and seductive in the poem "Snake":

On the palatial steps and the temple tiles
You let down your softest part—
Like a loosened sash of a woman
And wait for the trembling boldness of a man.

I don't know, your blood-red forked tongue tip—
Which side of my lips will it sting?
They are waiting, waiting
For the double pleasure of this moment!

I never forget your slipperiness that I cannot hold
That has smoothed over so many bamboo strips;
I know there is pain in my bliss,
And I know there is fire in the icy cold.

Ah, I wish you could let the other part of you
Entwine my body which I cannot hold tight,
And when the sound of bells sneaks into a cloud's net,
Warmth will crawl all over the thin satin blanket in this cold
   palace![59]

The poet's lovemaking partner here is the snake, a metaphoric figure rich
with familiar associations in Western literature and mythology—desire,
evil, and temptation. In Chinese literature it can also refer to a femme
fatale, as in the phrase "a beauty as vicious as a snake and a viper" (*shexie
meiren*). These rich associations thus imbue the poem with a kind of
mythological aura and intensity: the lovemaking becomes a coupling of
ecstasy and death and an allegory of love seeking death. The orgiastic
intensity so created is framed at the beginning and the end by an image
drawn from traditional Chinese poetry—a reference to the "cold palace"
of the moon made immortal by the Sung dynasty poet Su Shi: "I would
ride the wind up there / but fear those marble domes and onyx galleries /
are up so high I couldn't bear the cold."[60] Interestingly, the heat of love's
passion generated by Shao's Western-derived "wanton depravity" has
succeeded in bringing warmth to the cold palace.

Shao's poetry was not well received in his time. Some adverse criticism was leveled at his collection *Flower-like Evil*. His critics charged that in devoting his entire energy to the creation of beauty, Shao had "gone down a wrong path with his poetry"—a charge similar to the leftist criticism of Shi Zhecun's fiction. They also charged that his poetry was nothing but a pile of sensual words—fire, flesh, kiss, poison, rose, virgin—with no clear clue to its overall meaning.[61] This negative reception provoked Shao's ire, and in his response he faulted his critics for failing to understand his poetry. He was most distressed by their preconceived moral attitude, whereby they mistook the eroticism of his poetry for self-confession. "We can be sympathetic to a bandit or a harlot," he writes, "but it does not mean that we approve the conduct of a bandit or a harlot . . . or become bandits or harlots ourselves."[62] He argues that the "Weimei pai" or "beauty for its own sake" school, to which he was consigned, was not what its Chinese name implied but had its own set of aesthetic principles drawn from a distinguished pedigree—referring, of course, to Swinburne, Ruskin, and Rossetti, about whom he had written long articles. To illustrate his position that "beauty is boundless," he cites two Western figures: "We cannot say that Jesus' virgin mother can be called beautiful whereas the seductive Salome cannot be called beautiful."[63] But it also reveals, perhaps unwittingly, an artistic preference of his own, one that his critics called immoral: just as he compared "the sweet tears of a virgin on her wedding night" to the "hot sweat on a wanton woman's lower body," he certainly favored the harlot over the virgin and Salome over Mary as his preferred personification of beauty. There is in his poetry a persistent fascination with the harlot figure as an embodiment of wanton depravity. Although he does not write about Salome as much as he does about Sappho, it was in fact the Salome figure—particularly as depicted by Oscar Wilde and Aubrey Beardsley—that became the center of attraction in a number of literary journals published by Shao and other Chinese writers who shared a "decadent" imagination. One writer who played a prominent role in this regard was Ye Lingfeng (1905–1975).

Salome and Beardsley

Oscar Wilde's play *Salome* was translated into Chinese by the dramatist Tian Han and performed in the 1920s. The published translation, in a nicely bound volume, included the famous drawings of Salome by Aubrey Beardsley. Tian Han also used Beardsley's drawings to grace the covers of his own magazine, *Nanguo zhoukan* (Southern country weekly).[64] The name of this fin-de-siècle English artist also became known through his contributions to the magazine *The Yellow Book*, which was first introduced to Chinese readers by Yu Dafu, who published a long article in *Chuangzao yuekan* (Creation monthly) even before Shao Xunmei was able to purchase an expensive copy of the journal itself. A younger member of the Creation Society and a student of painting, Ye Lingfeng learned about Beardsley and Wilde through his two senior colleagues and immediately fell under their spell. He purchased an original volume of Beardsley's *Salome*, which remained one of his favorite books, and began to imitate the ornate decorative style of Beardsley's drawings, which somehow reminded him of the work of the Tang poet Li He.[65] Thus, through his active promotion and imitation Ye earned for himself the infamous sobriquet "China's Beardsley."[66]

It was Ye's self-promotion in the name of Beardsley that aroused Lu Xun's moral wrath. In a series of articles he launched a frontal attack on Ye and his ilk. At the same time, however, Lu Xun was himself interested in the art of Beardsley; he selected sixteen Beardsley drawings for publication in a special volume which was intended to be a "correction" of Ye Lingfeng's faddish misconceptions about this English artist. This curious move reveals one of the many contradictory facets of Lu Xun's life: his personal taste in art seemed at odds with his public stance of political commitment. It appears that this doyen of Chinese letters, a committed leftist known for his untiring espousal of Soviet Marxism and social realism, was also drawn, almost in spite of himself, to the artistic style of decadence.[67] In the bedroom of his own house in Shanghai we find, in fact, two drawings of female nudes by a European artist (yet to be identified) whose style bears some resemblance to Beardsley's. This re-markable contradiction in Lu Xun has never been recognized in the iconography of Lu Xun scholarship, just as it fails to take note of his fascination with Baudelaire's prose poetry. Partly as a consequence of Lu Xun's acrimonious attack, Ye Lingfeng has never regained his reputation on the Shanghai literary scene. During the war years he moved to Hong Kong, where he died in 1975.

Like Shao Xunmei and Shi Zhecun, both of whom he knew well, Ye was an avid reader of modern Western literature and a collector of Western books. He gradually built up a personal collection amounting to nearly ten thousand volumes by constantly ransacking Shanghai's used bookstores. In one such store he even bought an original copy of Joyce's *Ulysses* published by the Shakespeare and Co. bookstore in Paris.[68] Ye was also an indefatigable editor of journals. As I mentioned earlier, he edited with his friend Pan Han'nian a left-leaning literary journal called *Huanzhou* (Mirage, 1926–1928). Its contents were divided into separate two parts: aesthetic articles in "Ivory Tower" and ideologi-cal matters in "Crossroads." It is a perfect reflection of Ye's own intellec-tual profile. In the early 1930s Ye became Shi Zhecun's colleague at the Xiandai publishing company, where he edited a journal, *Xiandai xiaoshuo* (Modern fiction), and made it a showcase of recent literary trends and authors in Europe and America. Like Shi, he read a large number of literary journals and reviews published in the United States and England and freely translated or incorporated the materials contained therein into his own journals. With Mu Shiying and others he edited another journal, *Wenyi huabao* (Literature illustrated), which contains a special section of photos featuring famous or new Western authors lifted di-rectly from these foreign sources: for instance, a photograph of James Joyce accompanied by a news item that the American ban on *Ulysses* had just been lifted, or another photograph of the young American poet Paul Engle taken from the front page of the *New York Times Book Review*, which hailed the emergence of a major new talent.[69] Together with the illus-trated journals published by Liu Na'ou and Shao Xunmei—*Shidai huabao*,

Shidai manhua, Xiandai dianying (Modern cinema), *Furen huabao* (Women's pictorial)—they provided a window on Western literary trends and fashions.

Portrait of a Dandy

Ye Lingfeng always tried to be à la mode—to stay abreast of what was going on abroad. On the home front, he wished to be a trendsetter. With his bibliophile habit, Ye was one of a small number of Shanghai writers to own a sizable collection of Western literature; another was his friend Shao Xunmei. Ye had a sufficient background in painting to become a semiprofessional sketch artist and to imitate Beardsley's style in his own drawings. While he was certainly not rich or handsome like Shao, he was nevertheless able to create in his fiction an elaborately dressed dandy modeled after Oscar Wilde.

The dandy is of course a well-known figure in French and English decadent literature. The best-known dandy in literature is found in Joris-Karl Huysmans's novel À *Rebours*, generally considered "the Bible of the Decadence," which in turn "bears the mark of Baudelaire throughout."[70] As Richard Gilman has perceptively remarked about this novel, it is "a structure of the most precise artifice," an aesthetic quality which its protagonist, Des Esseintes, proclaims "to be the distinctive mark of human genius." Thus, in the novel "life is carried on at its most artificial, which is to say its most 'invented' and refractory to imposed moral and social obligations."[71] I have no idea if Ye Lingfeng or Shao Xunmei ever read Huysmans's novel, but they certainly knew of Wilde's *Picture of Dorian Gray*, in which the hero's "education in vice is helped along by a poisonous book in a yellow cover which Wilde later acknowledged had been inspired by Huysmans's À *Rebours*, as indeed had the whole narrative."[72] Wilde's reference to a "book with a yellow cover" may have given rise to the title of the English journal with which he was associated, *The Yellow Book*, which in turn became a model for Shao Xunmei's *Maison d'or*. This literary genealogy would not have served much purpose if it had not inspired Ye Lingfeng to create one of the most "artificial" dandy figures in modern Chinese literature in his incomplete novel, titled "Jindi" (Forbidden zone), which deserves some attention.

At the beginning of the novel Ye introduces his male protagonist by focusing on his face—a face "with a modern handsome look as if touched up artificially" that would "make men jealous and women fall for it." The face is "oval-shaped, with a rosy complexion touched with a wan look which, upon closer inspection, rather enhances its beauty." He wears a pair of rimmed glasses, has thick and well-shaped eyebrows, thin lips, and eyes with "not too crystal-clear eyeballs but a pair of nimble pupils" that "surpass what the epithet 'autumn water' has [insinuated] for women's eyes."[73] This is close to a summation of the ideal of feminine beauty found in Shanghai's advertising posters; the semi-traditional features also provide an intriguing parallel with the face of the "Modern Girl" in Liu Na'ou's stories. But Ye's effeminate hero is more narcissistic than Liu's more masculine-looking heroine. He gazes at himself in the mirror and smiles, "making a coquettish gesture, but then avoids his own glance, takes off his glasses, and empties some facial powder from a box on the wardrobe and applies it carefully to his face and hands." Following this act of narcissism is a lavish description of his array of cosmetics. "We would never imagine," the narratorial voice comments, "that they belong to a young bachelor."[74] Ye gives a detailed description of the hero's dressing table in his bedroom (words in capitals are in English or French in the original):

> At the center is an ivory-rimmed mirror carved with exquisite modern-style patterns. On the left side of the mirror are five perfume bottles of various sizes; three of them carry the brand-name of HOUBIGANT, two colored light yellow and one pure white . . . We can see that the two light yellow bottles are LOTION and PERFUME, the white bottle is [eau de] TOILET [sic] . . . On the right side of the mirror, the first item is a box of face powder . . . Next to it are two cube-shaped paper boxes, one

in ivory color with minuscule red patterns, the other has yellow and black lines and a gold strap across it. The ivory one EN BEAUTÉ is for facial use, and the yellow one is the currently popular hair lotion STACOMB. The last item on the right is a black square box gilded on two sides with silver. This is CUTEX, used for trimming nails. On top of the box is another small box of nail polish. These two items are seldom seen even on the vanities of the most fashionable women, but are now found in the room of a young bachelor. This proves that the hero's character is most unusual.[75]

All these details must have been intended to establish the background for the protagonist, a young, foppish, but passive and androgynous dandy. He pays meticulous attention to dressing himself, wearing a black padded dressing gown—"when the wind blows you can see the yellow satin lining inside"—and a pair of brown leather shoes with rubber soles.[76] All of these are obviously derived from the French prototype but drawn with some Chinese characteristics. Ye's hero clearly does not embody sufficiently la psychologie morbide with which Huysmans endowed his fictional hero, whose cult of artificiality reflects the author's equation of modernity-artificiality-decadence. As Matei Calinescu comments on Huysmans's portrayal of Des Esseintes: "Attracted by all that is aberrant, his imagination will voluptuously explore the realm of the abnormal in search of a beauty that is supposed to be both antinatural and absolutely new. The appeal of decadence comes as no surprise in such a context."[77]

But Ye Lingfeng's portrait is more peculiar and inconsistent. His protagonist is a writer who is trying to write a novel. After a few pages of lavish description of his cosmetics collection, however, we quickly move on to the story that the protagonist himself is writing about another young writer, which reads like his autobiography. This metafictional device could have served as a mirror for some critical self-reflection on the hero's own character and morbid psychology. Instead, the reader is ushered into an unfinished story of a triangular affair in which the young man is involved with an older married woman and his male friend, the editor of a journal called *Satan*, who has published his first novel, which he publicizes as "China's *Camille* or a second *Manon Lescaut* or *Sappho*." Since from Ye's own book notes we learn that *La Dame aux camélias* and *Manon Lescaut* were among his favorite reading (because in Dumas's story Marguerite and Armand pick up a copy of *Manon Lescaut*) we are given another display of intertextuality that is nothing more than Ye's showing off his book knowledge.

Unlike "decadence," the word "dandy" is not an intellectual epithet and did not receive a proper translation in Chinese. Most English-Chinese dictionaries render the term by invoking Chinese equivalents such as *wanku zidi* (literally, a scion wearing brocade pants) or *huahua gonzi* (literally, flowery young master), both of which connote a profligate or debauched son from a rich family. It carries a further modern implication of foppishness and, in contemporary parlance, refers to a "rich playboy." Shao Xunmei might fit this popular dandy image, but not Ye Lingfeng. Still, none of these meanings carries the full aesthetic and philosophic measure of eccentricity and unconventionality that has distinguished Huysmans's Des Esseintes. Instead of Huysmans's dandy hero, Ye probably modeled his writer hero after Oscar Wilde and *his* hero, Dorian Gray. But he stopped short of delineating an "alternative lifestyle" based on the hero's latent homosexuality. He was familiar with Wilde's scandals and trials but frankly admitted that he liked Beardsley's illustrations even more than Wilde's play about Salome.[78] Thus, it seems that after having introduced his dandy hero with great descriptive fanfare about his cosmetics collection, Ye did not know how to proceed with the plot of a love triangle. Ye may indeed have harbored an ambition to touch on the "forbidden zone" of homosexuality, as the story's title suggests, but the work was left unfinished. It ends just at the point when the hero's male friend is praising his looks:

> "It's not flattery. If I were a woman I would have been crazy for you. Even now I am. . . ."

Juxuan suddenly blushed with shyness.

"Ju, I am just joking. Don't be angry. Tonight's movie at the Feilington is very good, let's go out." Pinqiu quickly changed his tone.[79]

Had the action proceeded further, a more decadent dandy character might have emerged from this story within a story. One wonders why Ye could not complete the novel. Was it because he had no time or no courage to "transgress" into the forbidden zone—or because the character's potential sexuality lay beyond the confines of his limited technique? As the plot stands, the young hero is still under the spell of an earlier affair with an older woman, though the memory is beginning to fade. The reason for the work's failure may have less to do with the crudities of fictional technique than with the author's own "cultural memory." At the level of technique, Ye seems capable of depicting only the hero's face but not his behavior and thought. In fact, it is the face of the writer who is writing the story rather than the hero he is writing about that has received the most lavish attention. One wishes that the author in the story would forget about writing his story and get into some action himself.

Whatever its peculiarities, Ye's fascination with the male face, in my view, must be traced to classical Chinese literature and aesthetics—in particular, to Jia Baoyu, the young and equally androgynous hero of the famous eighteenth-century Chinese novel *The Dream of the Red Chamber*, who is indeed the handsome and talented scion of a large aristocratic family. One could in fact write a separate monograph about this great novel as a work of "Chinese decadence" which has exerted an enormous impact on all subsequent writers.[80] In the person of Jia Baoyu, the novel has bequeathed the aesthetic ideal of a Chinese dandy in the image of a young, handsome, and extremely sensitive "pale-faced scholar" (*baimian shusheng*). Thus, Ye Lingfeng's fictional dandy is neither defiant of social convention nor debauched in pursuit of wanton depravity. He is, rather, a Baoyu-like hero with touches of a modern urbanite—a traditional *caizi* (talented man) transformed by Shanghai's modern material culture into a foppish dandy who likes to frequent the cinemas and dance halls in order to meet the "beautiful ladies" (*jiaren*) who are either dance hall hostesses or social butterflies (*jiaoji hua*). Their encounter and ensuing romance thus becomes the formulaic theme of Ye's popular novels. As Ye himself admits, what his contemporary readers expected most from him were precisely those modern "talent-meets-beauty" romances with "extremely strong sexual titillation or extremely sentimental romantic plots."[81]

The Dandy and the Modern Girl

Two of Ye's long novels, both serialized in the Shanghai newspaper *Shishi xinbao*, are worth discussing for the way in which Ye brings the city landscape to bear on the romance between his "dandy" and "beauty" characters. In *Shidai guniang* (Modern girl, 1933) the plot involves a young woman from a rich family in Hong Kong who leaves her boyfriend and arrives in Shanghai to seek excitement and become a "Modern Girl." She seduces a Shanghai dandy who is already married. Just as his wife finds out and threatens divorce, her devoted boyfriend from Hong Kong comes to Shanghai to find her. He is escaping the scandal of his involvement with her, only to read about another scandal involving her in the newspaper. As a result, he commits suicide. The newspaper, therefore, serves as the crucial plot device and allows Ye to imitate its journalistic style, thus rewriting the same scandals in different ways.

In the second novel, *Weiwan de chanhuilu* (Unfinished confession, 1936), the author (Ye himself in fictional guise) meets a Shanghai dandy who recounts his love affair with a famous socialite: they meet, fall in love, live together, and finally part, and he becomes ill. The banal plot is given a literary twist by the author's purchase of an illustrated copy of *La Dame aux camélias* at a foreign bookstore. Thus, before the author proceeds to read the hero's diary, he makes a conspicuous association between the heroine's diary in the French novel and the diary of this "self-styled sentimental dandy."[82] In so doing, Ye also manages to sneak into his novel a plot twist borrowed from the French work: just as

Marguerite decides to leave Armand, Ye's socialite heroine apparently decides to leave her possessive dandy for his own good. Yet despite these intertexual references, both of Ye's novels are written in a style designed for serialization in the newspaper, in which each installment must have a subtitle and a subplot consisting of a complete episode. Ye took great pride in his accommodation to popular "taste," declaring that he purposefully left out all the "artistic descriptions" in the style that characterizes his short stories. At the same time, he also argued that writing a "novel for the masses" (*dazhong xiaoshuo*) represented his "attempt to lure readers of popular fiction into the field of New Literature."[83]

His cleverness in straddling the fence between the elite and the popular does not conceal the paucity of his own imagination, but it did achieve a semblance of reality which appealed to his readers. One of them wrote to Ye that he saw a couple coming out of the China Hotel and wondered if they were Lili and Mr. Xiao from Ye's novel *Modern Girl*. Ye responded by quoting Upton Sinclair to the effect that real people and incidents are given real names but fabricated names are given to fictional figures. Hence "the China Hotel in Shanghai is real, but Miss Qin Lili who lives there is—"[84] With this dangling tease of an incomplete sentence, Ye succeeded in luring his readers to a world of make-believe constructed out of the real urban environment of Shanghai. In other words, Ye compensated for the weakness of his fictional technique with his pointed evocations of the sites and sounds of the city based on his own familiarity—as if he, too, were playing urban dandy and *flâneur* via his own fiction. The "Feilington" (a fictional name for the Carlton?) and Cathay movie theaters, the restaurant Xinya, and the coffeehouse Sullivan's are recurring sites where his characters meet, date, become intimate, or while away the time. Another favorite site of his is Shanghai's foreign bookstores, where, for instance, a male "BIBLIOMANIAC" (Ye uses the term in English) meets his female match as they both stare at the title of a new Hemingway novel, *Men without Women*.[85] Needless to add, Ye considered himself not only "China's Beardsley" but also China's earliest promoter of Hemingway as well.[86]

This sense of familiarity with Shanghai's cultural milieu can be a double-edged sword: it serves to establish a common ground with the "life world" of his urban readers, but it also intrudes upon—and detracts the reader's attention from—the achieved world of his fiction. In the story "Forbidden Zone," discussed earlier, the effect of the hero's eccentricity is all but dissolved in the gallery of brand names: Houbigant, En Beauté, Stacomb, Cutex. These material signifiers, while lending a certain atmosphere to the protagonist's dwelling, read like advertisements that lure the reader into another world—the world of real commodities in the big department stores. The effect could be compared to that of the American daytime soap opera, in which the fashionably coiffed and dressed actors and actresses who play out the romantic fantasies also play out the commodity fetish of the viewer's subconscious. One can imagine Ye's urban female readers reading about these fashionable brands of lotion and perfume and rushing out to buy them at the nearest Wing On or Sincere.

Apparently Ye's story did *not* create a massive craze for male fashion, as German readers in a different era responded to *The Sorrows of Young Werther* by wearing yellow scarves. Nor are other material objects—automobiles in particular—worked into the descriptive fabric of his fiction to help create a kinetic energy and rhythm, as we found in some of Liu Na'ou's and Mu Shiying's stories (see Chapter 6) In one story Ye tries to imitate Mu and Liu by equating a woman with a car: "She, like a new 1933 car . . . glides like an eel into the throngs of people . . . Facing the wind, [she] cuts a 1933 healthy figure, [with] a V-shaped water-tank, two front lights shaped like half-globes, and short-hair swaying back like Isadora Duncan's."[87] But he does not succeed in creating a really alluring femme fatale to embody the city. Instead, it seems that Ye has intentionally made the heroine of his novel *Modern Girl* not so modern but rather traditional in her loyalty and subservience to a possessive hero. When compared to the ironic, self-mocking heroes we find in Liu's and Mu's stories, Ye's male protagonists seem hopelessly narcissistic and weak-willed as they play the game of flirtation and deceit but without much sexual energy. The fictional dandy Ye tried to create thus degenerates into a dandy manqué in his popular novels. This may have been an unexpected consequence of Ye's own literary decadence.

Zhang Kebiao, a founding member of the journal *Sphinx*, which Shao Xunmei also joined as a sponsor, wrote a retrospective essay about his group of former colleagues:

> People like us were all "half neurotic," indulging ourselves in the school of aesthetic beauty—one of the most fashionable artistic schools of the time. We espoused a style that is bizarre, grotesque, and self-contradictory, that seeks to transcend convention and mores and shock society. Something like this was also promoted in Western Europe by Baudelaire, Verlaine, Wilde, and Maeterlinck. We were goaded by curiosity and vogue-consciousness. We pretended ostentatiously to discourse about creating wonders out of rottenness, about ugly flower petals and flower-like evil, and about the beauty and beatitude of death etc. etc. in a language that pulls in the opposites and dissolves the contradictions. This was what the *Sphinx*'s tenets were like: advocating novelty, adulating the grotesque, emulating ugliness, viciousness, rottenness, and darkness, denigrating light and glory, and opposing the convention of richness and pomposity, castigating high officials and wealthy lords of the gentry.[88]

The same summary judgment can be leveled, to a large extent, at the works of Shao Xunmei and Ye Lingfeng and a host of like-spirited lesser writers as well. Had they succeeded in accomplishing what they pretended to achieve—artistic novelty, grotesque imagery, eccentric behavior, defiance of authority and convention—they would have accomplished a great deal. In a curious twist on Baudelaire's famous statement about modern art, they were all too enamored of the "contingent" to worry about the "permanent"—and too happily basking in the urban "light and glory" of their city to contemplate the artistic significance of "ugliness, viciousness, rottenness, and darkness." To coin a phrase, they all seemed to be *les fleurs* malgré *mal*—young and talented men (*caizi*) who lived and thrived in a Chinese "belle époque" on the eve of war and revolution that would soon nip their burgeoning literary talent in the bud.

EILEEN CHANG:

ROMANCES IN A FALLEN CITY

The death of Eileen Chang (Zhang Ailing, b. 1920) on September 8, 1995, in Los Angeles made headlines in all the Chinese newspapers. In the Chinese-speaking areas of Taiwan, Hong Kong, and mainland China, a veritable mystique has been built around her by both the public media and her large number of devoted readers (who called themselves Changmi, or "Chang's fans"). In the last twenty-three years of her life, Chang lived quietly and incognito in Los Angeles, shunning all social contact and escaping publicity by constantly changing her residence in numerous hotels, motels, and small apartment houses until her death in an obscure apartment building in the Westwood section of Los Angeles. The "mystery" of her last years only adds more glamour to her legend: she was like a retired movie star past her prime, like Greta Garbo.[1]

Chang had a meteoric early career as a writer. Born in Shanghai in 1920 to an illustrious family, she was a precocious and oversensitive child, partly as a result of the divorce of her parents when she was ten years old and her virtual imprisonment by her tyrannical father for half a year in the family home in the French Concession when she was seventeen.[2] She published her first story at age twelve in her school journal and her first essay in English (describing her experience) in a Shanghai newspaper at age eighteen. She passed the examination to study at the University of London but enrolled at the University of Hong Kong instead in 1939, owing to the outbreak of war in Europe. In December 1941, shortly after Pearl Harbor, Japanese troops occupied Hong Kong, and Chang had to cut short her university studies the next year with only one semester to finish before graduation. When she returned to Shanghai, her own city had also been occupied by the Japanese, and the foreign concessions had lost their protective autonomy.

Yet it was precisely under these extraordinary circumstances that Chang felt inspired to write: more than a dozen short stories and numerous essays were published within a brief span of two years (1943–44) in several popular magazines, including *Ziluolan* (Violet), a leading journal of the Butterfly school edited by Zhou Shoujuan, who first discovered her talent, and *Wanxiang* (Panorama) edited by the distinguished dramatist Ke Ling. By the precocious age of twenty-three, Eileen Chang had become an instant literary celebrity. She married and then divorced Hu Lancheng, a learned and stylish litterateur who served under the Wang Jingwei puppet regime. The first printing of her short story collection *Chuanqi* (Romances) sold out in four days. For the second edition, she wrote a preface and announced unabashedly: "To be famous I must hurry, otherwise when it is too late I won't be so happy . . . Hurry, hurry, otherwise it would be too late, too late!"[3] Her premonition proved prophetic: like a meteoric star that suddenly blazed over Shanghai's literary firmament and then vanished, her glory faded abruptly after she left China in 1952. During the next forty years she lived in obscurity, mostly in the United States, marrying an American writer, Ferdinand Reyher. While her name was totally erased in her native Shanghai after Liberation, in Taiwan and Hong Kong her writings have continued to be best-sellers and have gone through numerous editions since the 1960s. Her legend has continued to grow in spite of—or even because of—her death.

Neither her life nor her legend is my central concern in this chapter. Rather, I find her Cassandra-like stance in her writing extremely intriguing as it runs counter to the prevailing ethos of nationalism and revolutionary progress at the time. I am interested in the ways in which Eileen Chang was able to draw a kind of allegorical closure by bringing to an end an entire era of urban culture that had nurtured her creativity—an era that began in the late 1920s, reached its height of urban glory in the early 1930s, and thereafter declined until its demise in the early 1950s, the time when Chang decided to leave her beloved city and country and become a permanent exile. Thus, her writing also forms the perfect closure for this book.

In order to trace such an allegorical trajectory, I begin with some aspects of living reality—the urban life of Shanghai to which Chang repeatedly professed her devotion and from which she drew so much inspiration for her own writing.

Shanghai through the Eyes of Eileen Chang

In her many essays Eileen Chang always portrayed herself as a Shanghai "petty urbanite" (xiao shimin). During the first half of her life, aside from two years in Tianjin and three years in Hong Kong, she lived in Shanghai. Her loyalty to this metropolis was enhanced after she returned from war-ravaged Hong Kong in 1942, when she began to write. As she openly acknowledged to her readers, even when she was writing a series of stories set in Hong Kong, she was mainly thinking about her beloved Shanghai readers, to whom they were dedicated: "I love Shanghai people; I hope they like my books."[4] She characterized them as clever, sophisticated, good at flattery and chicanery but not to excess. "Shanghai people are distilled from traditional Chinese people under the pressure of modern life; they are the product of a deformed mix of old and new culture. The result may not be healthy, but in it there is also a curious wisdom."[5] She enjoyed the sights and sounds, the smells and tastes, of her beloved city, which she described in nuanced detail in a large number of essays. For instance, in her essay "The Joy of Apartment Living" (Gongyu shenghuo jiqu), she confessed that she loved the "city sound"—the sound of tram cars—and could not go to sleep without its accompaniment. She also loved the taste of Western sweets and the strong smell of "stinky bean curd." The shouts of street hawkers and vendors were music to her ears. She even commented at length on the wisdom of the elevator operator in her apartment building, whose international clientele she tried to capture in a brief panoramic "shot" very much like the beginning sequence in Hitchcock's film *Rear Window*.[6] She saw herself as a bourgeois consumer and loved clothes and cosmetics: she spent her first earnings—five dollars, for a cartoon she drew that was published in an English-language newspaper—on a tube of lipstick.[7]

Such urban tastes also reveal Chang's penchant for the world of everyday life. It is a world of small public and private spaces—alleys and side streets off the main thoroughfares, dark attics or balconies, rooms in old houses stuffed with old furniture, passageways used for kitchens in a crowded residential building. Once we enter these small spaces, we are immediately drawn into the congested world of the Shanghai petty urbanites. In a remarkable essay titled "The Days and Nights of China" (Zhongguo de riye), which was appended to her short story collection, Chang presents a rambling portrait of this street-corner society observed with her own eyes as she goes shopping for groceries. It is a scene filled with the daily activities of ordinary Chinese: street vendors, children, maids, a Daoist priest; an apprentice in a butcher's shop cuts and sells meat to an aging prostitute as the butcher's wife complains about her husband's sister in a melodious Shanghai dialect, while a radio in another shop is blasting away with the singing of the local *kunqu* opera, as the sound rises over the red walls of an elementary school.[8] This is Eileen Chang's urban China—"a country of patchwork" like the patchy blue clothes its people wear. At the end of her portrait she writes: "I am happy to be walking under the sunshine of China. I am also happy that my hands and feet are young and energetic. And these are all somehow connected. I don't know why, but when I am happy I feel as if I had a part in the radio sound and the street colors. Even when I have a sinking feeling of melancholy, I sink onto the muddy ground of China. After all, this is China."[9]

All of these elements are transformed by her fictional art into a unique urban vision that is in sharp contrast to that of Liu Na'ou and Mu Shiying: whereas these neo-sensationalists portray a fantastic urban world of modern glitter as embodied in equally fantastic female figures, Chang's quotidian world is more sensuously local and immediate. In this more localized world the rhythm of life seems to "beat to a different time scale," and the people in it seem to have too much time to spare. A typical character from her fiction is like "a dreamer from the ancient romances, except that he just wakes up from sleep without a dream—and he feels all the more lost."[10] This odd dis-location of time and space evokes a different urban sensibility—a sensibility closer to that of the semi-traditional fiction of the Butterfly school than to Western modernism. How does Chang relate this small world of Shanghai to the modern metropolis, with its advertising signs and shops and honking automobiles?

In her perceptive analysis of Eileen Chang's fiction, Rey Chow has focused on "details," defined as "the sensuous, trivial, and superfluous textual presences that exist in an ambiguous relation with some larger vision such as reform and revolution, which seeks to subordinate them but which is displaced by their surprising returns."[11] Chang's "world of detail," Chow continues, "is a part that is always already broken from a presumed 'whole.' It is this sense of wholeness—as that which is itself cut off, incomplete, and desolate, but which is at the same time sensuously local and immediate—rather than the wholeness of idealist notions like 'Man,' 'Self,' or 'China' that characterizes Chang's approach to modernity."[12] Whereas Chow considers the presence of details as having a special bearing on women and domesticity, I believe that the significance can be extended beyond the private realm to Shanghai's urban life as a whole. With her details Chang forces our attention to those material "signifiers" that serve not only to tell a different story about Shanghai's urban life but also to reconfigure the spaces of the city—private and public, small and large—in accordance with her own vision.

We can reconstruct the spaces of Chang's everyday world by piecing together a few details from her fictional works. Her characters live in two kinds of interior spaces: either a typical Shanghai alleyway courtyard (*nongtang*) with old-fashioned houses inside stone gates (*shikumen*), or a rundown Western-style house or apartment building. A good example of the former can be found in her later novel *Bansheng yuan* (Destined for half a lifetime), in which one of the heroines lives in a *nongtang*: "It is situated in a crowded section; along the street are shops, their front doors taken off and put one by one against the back doors. A group of maids and servants gather around the public tap cleaning rice or washing clothes, splashing water on the cement ground. Among them a maid is washing her feet . . . baring her toes which are colored red with Cutex."[13] As her suitor enters for the first time, he has the instinctive feeling that the maid works in the heroine's house, and he is right. The atmosphere inside the two-story house is warm and familiar: as he is led upstairs to the family's crowded rooms, he also enters into her family and eventually becomes a familiar presence who can drop by without prior notice, since he is recognized by the servants who are the guardians and gossips of the *nongtang*.

By contrast, a Western-style house or apartment building is often the site of estrangement and disturbance. In this novel the heroine's sister marries a speculator and moves to a Western-style building in a deserted suburb. It is in this house that the heroine is raped by her sister's husband and kept in an upstairs room for half a year. This "madwoman in the attic" device is lifted almost directly from English gothic romances, which makes the house doubly alienating. In "Xinjing" (Sutra of the heart), the story of a daughter's obsession with her father, the action takes place in a Western-style apartment building with a roof garden, rooms with glass doors, an elevator, and a long stairway where the electric light happens to be out. All these architectural details serve to accentuate the characters' psychological tensions. Most of the negative associations with Western-style buildings may have stemmed from Chang's own childhood experiences, as she lived in an old Western-style house with her father and stepmother, from which she eventually escaped to live in an apartment building with her mother and aunt. But Chang never lived for any length of time in a *nongtang*, and her empathy goes beyond personal experience.

Sometimes, "old" and "new" elements are interwoven as the characters move from one space to another, hence creating a mixed effect. In the story "Liuqing" (Traces of love), a middle-aged couple, Mr. and Mrs. Mi, both twice married, visit a relative's house. Their pedicab first passes "a dark brown house with faded blue venetian blinds standing quietly in the rain. For some reason it looked distinctly foreign. Mr. Mi was reminded of the days when he studied abroad," where he met his first wife, and he recalls their bad marriage. The pedicab then passes another house across from the post office, "an old, gray, Western-style house where a macaw was usually hung out squawking miserably." Every time they pass this house, Mrs. Mi is reminded of the home of her first husband and her past failed marriage, even more traumatic than Mr. Mi's. Their relative, Mrs. Yang, lives in "an upper-middle townhouse off a small alley"—that is, in a *nongtang*. As they enter, "Mrs. Yang [is] at the mahjong table in the dining room." At her husband's urging, Mrs. Yang "became a lovely mistress of the house; her sitting-room had the feel of a salon." It was in this old-fashioned house of a new-style mistress that Mr. and Mrs. Mi had first met. As they leave the house after the visit, the surroundings of the *nongtang* serve to "patch over" their strained relations. The story ends with this description:

> They said good-bye and walked out to the alley. Under the sheltered walkway someone had set a small stove on a patch of dry pavement. It was standing and crackling like something alive. In the empty alley one could easily have mistaken it for a dog, or even a child.
>
> They walked out of the alley onto the road. There were few pedestrians, as if it was early morning. Most of the buildings in this area had yellow walls which had turned black and moldy

because of the damp. Parasol trees lined the road; their yellow leaves looked exactly like flowers blossoming in the spring. Set against the dark gray walls, the small yellow trees looked particularly brilliant. The leaves at the top of the trees waved in the wind and then took off, drawing an arc in the air before overtaking the two of them. Even after the leaves touched ground, they drifted a long way off.[14]

Thus, on their way home, Mr. and Mrs. Mi realize that they love each other. Walking over the fallen leaves that so resemble fallen petals, Mrs. Mi reminds herself to point out the macaw when they pass the post office.[15] The subtle use of colors and details sustains both the story's autumnal atmosphere and the emotional mood of the couple in the autumn of their age. The small stove on the dry pavement, smoking and crackling like "a dog, or even a child," brings a human warmth to the *nongtang* surroundings in a way that reminds us of the public tap where maids wash clothes and clean their feet in *Half a Lifetime*. It is in these familiar spaces that human relations are frayed and patched up with the aid of yellow autumn leaves that look like flowers in the spring despite the desolate intimation of "the dark gray walls." In contrast, "the dark brown house with faded blue venetian blinds" and the "old, gray, Western-style house" across from the post office seem alienating and haunted with bad memories.

As Chang's fictional characters move from one house to another in this quotidian world of the Shanghai bourgeoisie, they take rickshaws and pedicabs or go by tram. Only on special occasions or in emergencies do they order a taxi. If they become rich, they may buy an automobile and hire a chauffeur, who then joins the household service ranks of guards and servants. In Mrs. Yang's house there is a private telephone, but in the usual *nongtang* world several families have to share one. In *Half a Lifetime*, Chang makes successful use of the telephone as another human link, which renders coincidences plausible and connections possible. In the Yang house in "Traces of Love," even the old lady's room is stuffed with modern furniture and modern conveniences: "a green metal desk, a metal armchair, a metal filing cabinet, a refrigerator and a telephone." This is because the Yangs come from a "progressive tradition," and thus "even the old lady was fond of new, foreign things." But the family still uses a charcoal brazier, an almost omnipresent object in all of Chang's fictional homes. What really strikes Mr. Mi during his visit is "an old-fashioned clock with a rectangular red leather case, a gilded face, and very slender hands that susurrated; one couldn't tell the time very clearly."[16] If the charcoal brazier is an old, familiar utensil for yielding (human) warmth, the old-fashioned clock is an outmoded emblem of time and a reminder of the old lady's inability to catch up with modern days. Chang uses clocks frequently in her stories, together with old mirrors, antique screens, curtains, old photo albums, dried flowers, and various other objects, to punctuate the special poignant moments in the lives of her transitional characters—moments in which they must wrestle with their emotional entanglements with memories of the past in an attempt to face new realities.

This wealth of objects—the old juxtaposed with the new—bespeaks a deep-seated ambiguity toward modernity that is the distinct hallmark of Eileen Chang's fiction. Nevertheless, this sense of ambiguity should not be mistaken for nostalgic traditionalism. In both fiction and real life, Chang's attachment to modern (*modeng*) life can likewise be traced through aspects of Shanghai's material culture. As her characters move from the domestic and semi-public space of the *nongtang* and enter into the public arena, they frequent restaurants, Chinese and Western, as well as coffeehouses. For example, the last scene of *Half a Lifetime* takes place in a secluded room in a restaurant where the hero and heroine, long separated by trials and tribulations, finally meet again only to realize that it is too late to marry. But the most ubiquitous public site in Chang's fiction is surely the cinema and going to the movies the most popular pastime.

Movies and Movie Palaces

Chang was an inveterate fan of the movies. According to her brother's reminiscences, during her student years she subscribed to a number of English-language fan magazines such as *Movie Star* and *Screen Play* as bedside reading. In the 1940s she saw practically every Hollywood film starring Greta Garbo, Bette Davis, Gary Cooper, Clark Gable, Shirley Temple, and Vivien Leigh, whose performance in *Gone with the Wind* she adored (though she did not like Greer Garson in *Pride and Prejudice*). She also liked Chinese films and film stars such as Ruan Lingyu, Tan Ying, Chen Yanyan, Shi Hui, Zhao Dan, and others.[17] She contributed movie reviews in English and Chinese and later wrote screenplays for several notable films made in Shanghai and Hong Kong. This personal hobby was incorporated into her fiction and became a key element in her fictional technique. In her stories the movie theater is both a public space and a fantasy land, and the intertwining of their functions creates its own narrative magic. As an illustration, we can look at the beginning section of the novella "Duoshao hen" (Evermore sorrow), written in 1947:

> The modern movie theater is the cheapest palace, a magnificent structure of glass, velvet, and imitation stone. As one enters this one, the floor is fresh yellow—the whole place is like a yellow glass magnified ten thousand times, giving off a clean and glittering illusion of beauty. The movie has already been under way for quite sometime. The hallway is empty and deserted—it turns into a scene of palatial sorrow, and from another palace is heard the distant sound of pipes and drums.[18]

Chang calls the movie theater the "cheapest palace" for good reason: by this time there were quite a number of movie palaces in Shanghai, and movies had become an established institution of popular entertainment. It is therefore a most appropriate setting for this story, which tells about a woman who falls in love with a married man—the stuff of countless movie tearjerkers. According to Chang, the novella was a fictional rewrite of one of her film scripts, called "Never Ending Love" (Buliao qing). In a remarkable touch of self-reflexivity, the movie theater becomes the backdrop for the first scene in a movie/story which introduces the heroine: "In front is a colorful signboard, raised high up, advertising the coming attraction . . . on which appears a gigantic cut-out picture of a woman with tears in her eyes. Another tragic figure, much smaller, who is wandering underneath the signboard, is Yu Jiayin."[19] These opening lines read like a sequence of shots by a movie camera; they give us a distinctly visual sense of a woman set against an urban commercial landscape emblematized by the advertising sign. At the same time, however, the gigantic cut-out face of a woman on the sign is also a material sign that frames the heroine and turns her story into a movie fantasy. As such it becomes linked with another signifier, a classical literary reference which is introduced almost imperceptibly near the end of the paragraph—"palatial sorrow" (gongyuan), a phrase that immediately conjures up the image of the palace ladies and imperial concubines in ancient China who pine away in cold palaces while the emperor is making merry with "pipes and drums" and his favorite concubine. An average Chinese reader would be able to pick up this familiar reference to the legendary romance between Emperor Minghuang of the Tang dynasty and his imperial concubine, Yang Gueifei, a legend made even more popular by the famous narrative poem written by Bai Juyi titled "Everlasting Sorrow." It is astonishing to see how in one sentence Chang manages to turn the empty lobby of the movie theater into an allegorical "cold palace" resonant with echoes from classical literature.

In focusing on the theater's lobby, Chang has perceptively seized on the most salient interior space that defined the wonder of the modern for Shanghai audiences. In the newly renovated movie palaces such as the Grand Theater, it was not so much the exterior magnificence of the building as the lush interiors—in particular the lobby, with its Art Deco designs and marble (or fake marble) floors shining like mirrors—that attracted the moviegoer as he or she first entered and was immediately ushered into a different world, one that set the scene for the exotic fantasy on the screen. The modern movie theater has, therefore, become both a real and a symbolic presence in the text that bridges the gap between film and literature.

We have reason to believe that Chang's cinematic models were mostly taken from American—not Chinese—movies, of which her favorite genre may well have been the sophisticated screwball comedy: such as *Bringing up Baby* (1938), *The Philadelphia Story* (1940), and *The Lady Eve* (1941). One of her later screenplays was an adaptation of *The Tender Trap* by Max Shulman, which Chang retitled "Courtship Is Like a Battlefield" (Qingchang ru zhangchang).[20] As the new title suggests, the central trope is courtship and marriage, rendered as a field of play, contention, and performance. Common to all Hollywood screwball comedies—and a mark of their sophistication (especially in films directed by Preston Sturges and Howard Hawks)—is the incessant talk and clever repartee between the courting, battling partners. (Hawks's *His Girl Friday* is a good example.) As Stanley Cavell has reminded us, "these films are themselves investigations of (parts of a conversation about) ideas of conversation." The emergence of this genre may have had something to do with advances in sound in Hollywood filmmaking, but, more significantly, as Cavell has argued, it had to do with "the creation of a new woman, or the new creation of a woman . . . and this phase of the history of cinema is bound up with a phase in the history of the consciousness of women."[21] The relevance of the genre for Chang could likewise be that it provided a new space for delineating the sensibility and consciousness of women in urban Shanghai. Thus, by introducing the heroine in a "cinematic" setting in "Evermore Sorrow," Chang has also placed the heroine's consciousness at the center of the story's plot, which determines its feminist ending: instead of agreeing to be a modern concubine to the married man she loves—as her traditional good-for-nothing father urges her to do—Yu Jiayin decides rather to leave him and finds a new teaching job in another city.

But the issues are far more complicated than can be inferred from the beginning and ending of one story. What transpires in the plot, as is the case with most of Chang's stories, touches on the whole matrix of human relationships revolving around marriage and the family. In adapting this Hollywood genre into a Chinese story, Chang in fact adds a number of other elements which are not sufficiently foregrounded in Hollywood comedies: the conflicts between mother and daughter-in-law, the chicanery of relatives, and above all the philandering of males. In other words, the Hollywood model is given an ethical dimension centered on the family *(jiating lunli)*.[22] In this familial context, Chang's heroines are made to undergo a human experience of courtship and marriage (or remarriage in the case of "Love in a Fallen City," to be discussed later) that is not so far from the familiar "sorrow and joy, parting and reunion" *(beihuan lihe)* trope in popular Chinese novels. At the same time, however, Chang's stories, like Hollywood comedies in Cavell's interpretation, invite us likewise to "think again, what it is Nietzsche sees when he speaks of our coming to doubt our right to happiness, to the pursuits of happiness"—except that it is not Nietzsche but Chang herself who "calls for us to have the courage of our sensuality," of our repressed right to happiness.[23] Interestingly, in an essay "On Woman," Chang makes fun of Nietzsche and men on behalf of women in a different context:

> Ever since it was invented by Nietzsche, the term "Superman"
> has been cited quite often. Before Nietzsche, we can find similar
> ideals in ancient legends. It's funny that our idealized Superman
> is always a man. Why? Probably because the civilization of the
> Superman is more advanced in achievement than our civiliza-
> tion, which is merely men's civilization. Moreover, the Super-
> man is a crystallization of pure ideal, but it's not hard to find a
> "Superwoman" in practical life. In any stage of culture, women
> are always women. Whereas men tend to develop in some spe-
> cial areas, women are the most universal and fundamental, and

they embody the cycle of seasons, the land, [the human life cycle of] birth, aging, illness, and death, as well as eating, drinking, and procreation. Women have fastened all the wisdom required of flying to outer space to the pole grounded in reality.[24]

Clearly, for all the intentional or unintentional "putdowns," women still occupy center stage in Chang's fictional universe. Precisely because they are so well grounded in real life, they are given all the agony and pathos of life in their pursuits of happiness.

"Contrast in De-cadence": Eileen Chang on Her Writing

Whether or not Chang was truly indebted to Hollywood comedies, she had certainly developed a personal style and sensibility that made her fiction liable to severe criticism. Shortly after she published her first major stories in 1943, a long critical essay appeared in the journal *Wanxiang* early the next year in which the pseudonymous author (who turned out to be Fu Lei, the famed translator of French literature) praised her talent and art but attacked the content of her fiction, citing her story "Love in a Fallen City" (Qingcheng zhilian):

> Nearly half of the story's space is taken up by flirtation: it's all a spiritual game of cynical hedonists. . . . All this pretty dialogue and the games of make-believe and hide-and-seek—they float on the surface of the heart; luring and teasing, the trivial battles of attack and defense—all conceal a falsehood. The man is empty of heart, doesn't want to anchor his heart, and takes romance as an appetizer, like golf or whisky. And the woman, she is worried all day that her last capital—her youth at age thirty—may go bankrupt. Her pressing desire for material life gives her no time to care for her soul. This kind of comedy, so bloodless at gut level, of course can come to no good end.[25]

(The same criticism can certainly be leveled against Preston Sturges's comedies.) From the specific target of one story, Fu Lei then moves on to an all-embracing attack on Chang's fiction as a whole:

> Love and marriage is the author's central theme, at least up to now. These six or seven short or long works are but VARI-ATIONS UPON A THEME [in English in the original]. Old fogies and leftovers from the old dynasty, and petty bour-geois—they are all pestered by this nightmare of a romantic problem between man and woman. And in this nightmare it's always autumn, with its rainy drizzle, wet, gray, dirty, and with the suffocating smell of decay, like the room of a dying patient . . . The nightmares are boundless, and hence there is no escape. And those piecemeal trials and the tribulations of life and death are nothing but an unnamable waste. Youth, passion, fantasy, hope can find no place . . . and on top of it all there is a gigantic hand beyond one's vision, opening its palm and crashing down from nowhere on everyone's heart. Such a picture, as printed on bad-quality newsprint with its lines and black-white contrast all besmeared, should convey the same atmosphere as Miss Chang's short stories.
>
> Why should I use such a metaphor? Because her somber prose is sometimes tinged with a light touch or flippant talk. It's like a flicker of phosphorescent light, making us unsure whether the pale light is dusk or dawn. Sometimes a dosage of humor is excessive, and a tragicomedy becomes farce. Farce is all right, but when touched with flippancy the art is ruined.[26]

This well-meaning but devastating critique all but killed Eileen Chang's creativity; she withdrew a serialized novel from a journal and did not publish another story until December of that year. But Fu Lei's florid prose and metaphors also elicited a long and nuanced response from Chang herself which shed a great deal of light on her fictional technique and on her outlook on life. In this widely quoted essay called "My Own Writing" (Ziji de wenzhang), Chang made a lengthy self-defense:

> In my fiction . . . my characters are not heroes but they carry the general burden of this age. Although they are not absolute they are serious. They have no tragic grandeur; they have only desolation. Tragic grandeur is a form of closure, but desolation is revelation . . .
>
> I know that my works lack force, but since I am a fiction writer I can only express the energy of the characters in my fiction but cannot create force on their behalf. Besides, I believe that although they are weak—the average people are not as forceful as heroes—it is precisely these average people who can better represent, more so than heroes, the sum total of this age.
>
> In this age, old things are crumbling and new things are growing . . . People feel that things in their daily lives are just not right—even to the point of terror. They live in this age, but this age is sinking like a shadow, and people feel themselves abandoned . . .
>
> I would rather write nothing except the trivial matters between a man and a woman. There is neither war nor revolution in my work, for I believe that when people are in love they become more innocent and more abandoned than in war and revolution . . . I like plainness and simplicity, but I can only describe the basic human simplicity that filters through modern fashions and ideas . . . I don't make falsehood and truth into stark opposites. Instead, through *cenci de duizhao* I show truth amid the falsehood of our times, and simplicity amid the sumptuousness of superficial appearances.[27]

This rumination is rather astounding for a young writer in her early twenties at the beginning of her career. For it is more than a self-defense; it is the initial articulation of her aesthetic principles. The key to her aesthetics is what she calls the technique of *cenci de duizhao*, a term that is hard to render, as it implies both an aesthetic concept and a narrative technique of contrasting two things not in a mutually oppositional way but in a sort of uneven, mismatched fashion.[28] It is a term of her own creation which is never fully explained but merely insinuated. Karen Kingsbury deems it "not only a means of elaborating theme and character, it also operates at the level of narrative style, in the teasing voice of the narrator, and the frequent shuttling between, for instance, self-mockery and self-indulgence, fantasy and reality, satire and sympathy."[29] I would like to borrow a term from the Hong Kong critic Ackbar Abbas and call it a contrast in "de-cadence"—an intentional pun on the concept of decadence which, as I shall demonstrate, is also closely related to Eileen Chang's aesthetics.

To illustrate, Chang uses the example of colors: a contrast in "de-cadence" is a contrast between the colors of scallion and peach as compared to the "strong" contrast between red and green, whose effect is more exciting than revealing. A strong contrast gives off a sense of strength, a "de-cadenced" contrast beauty; the former happiness, the latter sorrow. And this feeling use of colors becomes one of the most salient features of her technique. For instance, this is how she describes Shanghai's colors: "The prevailing colors in the city cannot be named: they are neither blue nor gray nor yellow: they serve only as background, they are a neutral color, a protective color, also called a civilized or mixed color."[30] In the story "Traces of Love," Chang gives this subdued mixture a more colorful display: *pale yellow* walls that have turned *dark gray* owing to dampness; charcoal burning from *dark green* to *dark red*; two vases of *dried red* chrysanthemums; rainy weather "like a big *dark brown* dog, fluffy and sticky, its icy-cold *black* nose nudging and sniffing at a human face." Only occasionally do we see a "residual patch of rainbow appearing in a *pale blue* sky, short and straight, in *red, yellow, purple,* and *orange*," and even it appears only "in a flash, and rather late."[31] Such a typical sampling, in Chang's view, certainly does not give rise to a feeling of tragic glory (*beizhuang*) or sublime grandeur (*zhuanglie*), which is manifested only in "strong" oppositions and is a characteristic of revolution and war. But

Chang prefers the aesthetic state of "cold desolation" (*cangliang*), which can be a "revelation"—an epiphany that discloses a plain truth. This intriguing formulation also reveals a gendered contrast: if the power and glory of war and revolution are manifestly masculine, then the aesthetic state of sorrowful desolation is certainly feminine. It is only with this in mind that we may be able to delve into her fictional characterization and narrative style.

A Technique of Popular Fiction

In spite of her desolate outlook, Eileen Chang claimed to be a "popular" writer. Like all writers of popular fiction, she was very concerned with audience reception: she speaks a great deal about how fiction appeals to its readers. She argues that if a writer "places herself in the midst of readers, naturally she knows what the readers want, and what they want she will give, plus a little extra."[32] She is most emphatic in her identification with her readers, who were mostly the "petty urbanites" of Shanghai whose reading habits had been nourished by traditional popular novels and plays as well as the works of the Saturday school of Mandarin Ducks and Butterfly fiction instead of works of the New Literature or translations from Western literature. How, then, does she "match" her unique outlook of desolation with the demands of popularity? In one of her testimonials about her "inexplicable fondness" for Chinese popular fiction, she says of the characters depicted therein: "Those characters do not need much explanation—if their sorrow, joy, parting, and reunion are said to be too superficial, then the same [can be said] for frescoes, which are an art. However, I think it is very difficult to write [popular fiction]."[33] How to chisel artistic "frescoes" out of the raw material of everyday life and use them to conjure up a desolate vision? How to give this "something extra" to her readers without damaging the tried-and-true formulas of Chinese popular fiction? This is obviously the challenge she sets for herself.

Of the four tropes that constitute the basic plot structure in traditional fiction, Chang seems to prefer sorrow the most: "This thing called happiness is lacking in interest—especially other people's happiness." The average reader is more likely to be moved by sorrow, especially when it is caused by "conflict, hardship, and trouble," which is also the source of drama.[34] In other words, sorrow and parting must be the "precondition" to joy and reunion, since otherwise there would be no emotional or cathartic effect on the reader. This means that in traditional Chinese fiction the characters are normally made to go through a series of trials and tribulations before they can be reunited and rewarded with joy and happiness. Most of Chang's stories and novels, however, do not have a happy ending. Rather, her ordinary characters are put through a course of gentle suffering marked by the all-powerful trope of *qing* (feeling or emotion), especially as manifested in love and marriage between men and women caught in a transitional age. But then, near the end of the story, illness and death always loom large (in the familiar human life cycle of birth, old age, illness, and death—*sheng lao bing si*). Chang seems to repeat the story of unrequited love and unhappy marriage time and again: "They can be written from countless different angles and can never be exhausted in one's lifetime."[35]

A technical "extra" in Chang's stories—something that is not often found in other popular fiction—is an almost omniscient narratorial voice that not only hovers over or enters into the characters effortlessly but also constantly comments on them with an intimate and bemused tone. The voice may sound slightly condescending, as if it came from a seasoned observer, but it also dwells on a trivial detail or appearance, sometimes when least expected. At such moments the narrative language takes sudden and unexpected flights into imagery and metaphor. For instance, a woman's face is "flat and unwrinkled, like a newly made bed, but once the weight of worry is added, it's like someone sitting with his ass on it."[36] Or another woman's arm is "white, like squeezed-out toothpaste; in fact her whole body is like squeezed-out toothpaste: it has no form."[37] Such digressions may be no more than a display of wit such as is also found in Somerset Maugham, P. G. Wodehouse, Aldous Huxley, and other English writers whom Chang admired. But occasionally they can be quite philosophical, as in this passage from the story "Red Rose and White Rose": "An ordinary life is at best like a 'peach blossom fan.' One bumps one's head and blood spills over the fan, and it can be touched up and painted as a peach blossom. But Zhenbao's fan is still blank: the brush is filled with ink, the desk and the studio nicely set, all waiting for him to apply the brush."[38] To describe a character's emotional experience as a tabula rasa on which the whole weight of a renowned historical play from the early Qing is brought to bear may be excessive. But in my view this is precisely how Chang wields her fictional magic on the reader: the narrative voice places itself both inside and outside the world of the fictional characters, deriving its inspiration from both the narrative situation in the story and an external vantage point above it. Leo Tolstoy, another author Chang read and discussed, used the same "meta-commentary" device in *War and Peace*. The danger, as Chang warns, is that such a voice can easily become didactic and message-ridden; "it is better to let the story explain itself than follow a predetermined theme." She cites the example of Tolstoy's novel to show that originally the author wanted to expound "the attitude to life of a prevailing religious group," but after seven revisions "the story itself triumphs over the thesis," hence making *War and Peace* an immortal classic.[39]

But the "attitude" of Chang's omniscient narrator is harder to define and decipher. It certainly does not advocate any philosophy or religion, nor does it, as in a traditional Chinese novel, conform to the prevailing mores of the reading public. As it moves inside and outside the character's thinking processes, its "words of wisdom" gradually take on a certain intellectual weight, until we begin to realize that it implies nothing less than the author's own attitude toward life, a philosophy of desolation.[40] As Kingsbury points out, this voice serves to define "the writer's vision of her own mental position, her own site of growing consciousness, as it is reflected back to her through the act of writing."[41] We must therefore pursue further the larger implications behind this narratorial voice of desolation.

A Philosophy of Desolation

As I mentioned earlier, in her preface to the second edition of *Chuanqi* (Romances), her only collection of short stories, the young Eileen Chang made a peculiar plea: "Hurry, hurry, otherwise it would be too late, too late." At first sight, this seems to be a plea concerning her need for instant fame. But her comments are intended to be more broadly philosophical: "Even if an individual can wait, time is in a hurry; it is in the midst of destruction, and greater destruction will come. One day our civilization, whether sublime or superficial, will be [a thing] of the past. If my most commonly used word is 'desolation,' it is because I feel this amorphous threat in my intellectual background."[42] To link one's own fame with a vague sense of "desolation" is rather odd, especially in the preface of a popular best-seller.

The immediate background to Chang's remarks was of course the Sino-Japanese War of 1937 and the fall of the city of Shanghai to the Japanese in 1942. But when she talks about the desolate state of "our civilization," the implications loom much larger. It seems that she is also referring to the hurried march of modernity—of the linear, deterministic notion of history as progress that would eventually make the present civilization a thing of the past by the force of its destruction. As a writer with a special gift for metaphors, she likens this "grand narrative" to a symphony, with all its polyphony and bombast, but she would rather hear the plaintive tunes of a female singer in a local opera. In the preface she describes with great fondness her experience of watching a perform-ance of the *bengbeng xi*, an opera for lower-class audiences, telling how the actress's vivid and earthy language and singing cast such an endearing spell that they made her totally at one with the mass audience below the stage. Chang then concludes with the following observation: "In the wilderness of the future, amidst the ruins of buildings and walls, only a woman like the heroine from a *bengbeng* opera can survive and live on peacefully, because there is a home for her in any era, any society, anywhere."[43]

This is an exceptional preface on several counts. If we read Chang's statements allegorically, we can interpret this example as indicating not only a reaction against modernity but also a return to native Chinese sources for intellectual nourishment and aesthetic pleasure. At the same time, however, her meditation on "civilization"—"whether sublime or superficial"—is all-embracing: it seems to refer to both aesthetic and material culture, both the native folk tradition and the urban cultural environment in which she lived. In other words, in Chang's "intellectual background," tradition and modernity are always juxtaposed in ways never anticipated by the "symphonic" conductors of the May Fourth movement.

As we read this preface, we begin to realize that tradition and modernity have already made their appearance in a sort of mismatched and "de-cadenced" contrast in the very cover design of *Chuanqi*. Drawn by her close friend Yan Ying, it shows the profile of a modern woman leaning out a window as she peers into a boudoir scene from what looks like a portrait painting of the late Qing period, in which a traditionally dressed lady is seated at a round table playing solitaire mahjong, with an amah holding a child keeping her company. The intrusion of a disproportionally large upper torso of a modern woman and her curious gaze make this otherwise tranquil boudoir scene rather disquieting: "This is precisely the atmosphere I hope to create," Chang announces in her preface.[44] In Chang's description, the modern woman's torso, in light green, is like a ghostly presence, her detached gaze the source of disturbing incongruity. But the traditional picture under her gaze looks equally odd, as if lost in a time and space that belong to another era and another world. The tradition of *Chuanqi*, or "accounts of the extraordinary," as a literary genre can be traced back to the Tang dynasty prose *chuanqi* as well as to the popular genre of Ming drama. In the Tang genre in particular, the accounts of extraordinary happenings often involve ghostly figures or legendary heroes and heroines. The Ming *chuanqi* drama deals, among other subjects, with historical romance, such as *The Peach Blossom Fan* (Taohua shan). Chang must have been conscious of this distinguished genealogy when she declared in the same preface that her purpose in writing fiction is "to find the ordinary in the extraordinary and also to find the extraordinary in accounts of the ordinary."

How, then, do we account for the ordinary and the extraordinary in Chang's fiction, and in what ways are they related to the larger issues implicated in Chang's ruminations on tradition and modernity, history and fiction? The stories contained in *Chuanqi* offer numerous examples, of which I would like to discuss two—"Fengsuo" (Sealed off) and "Qing-cheng zhilian" (Love in a Fallen City)—toward at least a partial illumination.

Romancing the Ordinary

"Fengsuo" (Sealed off), published in 1943, is one of the few stories in which the principal action takes place not indoors but in a tram car in Shanghai during an air raid. But this popular form of Shanghai public transportation is soon transformed into the most private of indoor spaces, a setting for a romantic fantasy that owes its existence to an air raid:

> If there hadn't been an air raid, if the city hadn't been sealed, the tram car would have gone on forever. The city was sealed. The alarm bell rang. Ding-ding-ding-ding. Every "ding" was a cold little dot, the dots all adding up to a dotted line, cutting across time and space.
>
> The tram car ground to a halt . . . Inside the tram, people were fairly quiet . . . Gradually, the street also grew quiet . . . The huge, shambling city sat dozing in the sun, its head resting heavily on people's shoulders, its spittle slowly dripping down their shirts, an inconceivably enormous weight pressing down on everyone. Never before, it seemed, had Shanghai been this quiet—and in the middle of the day![45]

Read somewhat allegorically, the tram car is a vehicle of modernity, like the trains (the familiar symbol, we recall, in Liu Na'ou's and Mu

Shiying's fiction), which operates in close observance of time.[46] Chang was herself clearly enamored of trams: as we saw earlier, she claimed that she could not go to sleep without hearing the sound of tram cars pulling into the terminus. In this story the "real" is combined with the allegorical to give us both a sense of historical time and space and a feeling that transcends it by means of a "transcription" of sound into sign—the ding-ding of the tram car's bell into dotted lines that cut across time and space. Thus, in one stroke Chang establishes the atmosphere for a fantastic story to unfold. A man nudges his way in the tram car and finds himself seated next to a woman; they strike up a conversation, fall in love, and begin to talk about the possibility of marriage. A few hours later, as the air raid is lifted, the tram starts again. "The lights inside the tram went on, she opened her eyes, and saw him sitting in his old seat, looking remote. She trembled with shock—he hadn't gotten off the tram, after all! Then she understood his meaning: everything that had happened while the city was sealed was a non-occurrence. The whole of Shanghai had dozed off, had dreamed an unreasonable dream."[47] The plot is, therefore, a dream framed by reality, a fantasy narrative framed by a realistic setting. Thus framed, the inner "core" of sentiment is also "sealed off," at least for a moment, from the inexorable pressures that external reality has imposed on the human psyche. This is made possible by the transposition of time into space: as time stands still, the halted tram becomes a strange space removed from everyday reality.

Again we may compare the story to a film: the language of modern fiction, like the film medium, can be manipulated to break up the normal duration and sequence of time through the use of stream of consciousness or montage. Chang never resorts to the technique of stream of consciousness in her narrative language, but the effect achieved by her prose style is comparable. At the same time, however, Chang's story is anchored in Shanghai's material reality. As Rey Chow has observed in her analysis of this story, the modern metropolis is the key to its plot and background: "Without this metropolis, without its tram cars, and without all its modern material culture, the story of 'Sealed Off' would never have been possible."[48] Historical "reality" also intrudes on the story: the air raid that seals off Shanghai temporarily is a clear time marker that reminds us that such an incident could take place only in Japanese-occupied Shanghai around 1943, when the story was written. It was this particular conjunction of time and space that enabled Chang to turn this ordinary story into an extraordinary romance, but it also cuts short the characters' romantic fantasy and brings them back to reality.

The "sealed-off" state of the story, in which time and space are suspended, is also an artificial frame created by the author's narrative technique in which people's sensory perceptions become sharpened and small details take on a many-splendored presence. In Chow's view this aesthetic space is what gives the heroine of the story a freedom to imagine a romance that cannot exist in reality. Such a sealed-off space is also a perfect metaphor for the state of Eileen Chang's women characters as they yearn for love and romance within the confinement of their own existence, even though they remain aware of the ephemerality of love and the unreliability of men.[49] What is implied is a gendered allegory: that "normal" time and space are defined by men, whose linear conception of continuous history has also dominated the nation-building project of modern China. Thus in making her fictional heroines struggle to overcome this male-dominated chronotope within the narrative structure of the story, Chang as a *woman* author also seeks to transcend the very historical circumstances in which her fiction was produced, through the aesthetic resources contained in her own fiction. In other words, Chang's fiction represents a *subversion* of the grand narrative of modern Chinese history by virtue of her art.

The story that in my view best exemplifies Chang's aesthetic subversion of the "master narrative" of history is also the story singled out in the devastating critique by Fu Lei, quoted earlier. Yet in spite of Fu's moral outrage, "Qingcheng zhilian" (Love in a fallen city) proved to be one of Chang's most popular works: published in 1943 shortly before "Sealed Off," it was adapted for the stage the next year and later for the screen.

At first sight, the story seems contrary to Chang's usual mode of popular fiction: it takes place mostly in Hong Kong on the eve of the Japanese invasion; it has a happy ending; and its characters seem unusually sophisticated. The story's exotic setting of Hong Kong's Repulse Bay Hotel, in which the romance between a British-educated playboy and a young divorcee from Shanghai unfolds, is itself like a stage setting or film location. The romance between this elegant couple unfolds in a long series of flirtations at restaurants and dance halls, in the hotel's lobby and on the nearby beach, and in the heroine's room. It is in such scenes that we see a clear debt to Hollywood screwball comedies. By a remarkable coincidence, it is also a story of remarriage, a genre in Hollywood films in which Stanley Cavell has invested a special significance: "The conversation of what I call the genre of remarriage is . . . of a sort that leads to acknowledgment; to the reconciliation of a genuine forgiveness; a reconciliation so profound as to require the metamorphosis of death and revival, the achievement of a new perspective on existence; a perspective that presents itself as a place, one removed from the city of confusion and divorce."[50] There cannot be a better or more fitting perspective on Chang's story than these words of appreciation by an American philosopher.

"Love in a Fallen City" begins like a staged play, in the style of the local Shanghai opera. As the plaintive tune of a *huqin* (Chinese violin) wails in the night, the narrator's voice intones: "A *huqin* story should be performed by a radiant entertainer, two long streaks of rouge pointing to her fine, jade-like nose as she sings, as she smiles, covering her mouth with her sleeve."[51] The heroine, Bai Liusu, is then introduced as if she were a role played by the "radiant entertainer." Chang's use of this folk-dramatic device is in a way quite fitting because the Bai household is described as a traditional family that is lagging behind time and out of step with Shanghai's modern world. But a few scenes later, as Liusu cries kneeling next to her mother's bed, the scene takes on a cinematic quality and suddenly "dissolves" to the past, "when she was about ten years old, coming out of a theater, and in the midst of a torrential downpour she was separated from her family."[52] When she goes upstairs and looks at herself in front of a mirror, the scene becomes a "close-up," and she is transported to another stage: "Following the undulating tune, Liusu's head tilted to one side, and her hands and eyes started to gesture subtly. As she performed in the mirror, the *huqin* no longer sounded like a *huqin*, but like strings and flutes intoning a solemn court dance . . . Her steps seemed to trace the lost rhythms of an ancient melody."[53] The accumulated effect of these "shots" prepares the reader for more film-like sequences set in the exotic locale of Hong Kong as Liusu travels to meet her playboy suitor, Fan Liuyuan.

By the time they meet in the Repulse Bay Hotel, the scene has changed totally: their romance takes place therefore in a most fittingly romantic atmosphere. In Chang's description, Hong Kong is a thoroughly alien colony with none of the native sights and sounds of Shanghai to which the reader has become so accustomed in Chang's fictional world. Consequently it is a natural background for an "extraordinary" romance to take place—a romance that begins with sophisticated flirtation and witty repartee which, for Liusu, a traditional, nearly illiterate woman, seem almost out of character. In the scale of realism, it would be hard to imagine a more incompatible couple, given such diverse backgrounds. It would not be hard to argue that only in the movies could their romance be possible. It is likely that Chang appropriates the narrative formula of Hollywood screwball comedies in order to bring out the mistaken intentions and personality clashes in the initial courtship. The narrative formula of such films calls for both hero and heroine to be cleverly on their guard, playing a long and intricate courtship game with mutual mistrust and misunderstanding, and only at the last moment, when the film's plot reaches its denouement, do they *really* fall in love with each other and get married.

In Chang's story, however, such a "reconciliation of a genuine forgiveness" is not achieved until the couple have gone through a real "metamorphosis of death and revival" caused by the Japanese invasion. The war experience is notably different from the Great Depression background of Hollywood comedies in that it refuses to be erased by a make-believe setting of luxury and leisure. Fan Liuyuan and Bai Liusu court each other on "borrowed time" and, especially on Liusu's part, cannot afford such luxury and leisure. The circumstance of the story is also more extraordinary in that the couple are made to fall in love *because of* the war background and not, as in Hollywood comedies or musicals of the thirties, in spite of it. It is also under such extraordinary circumstances that Eileen Chang chooses to evoke the ultimate state of love's desolation beyond forgiveness and reconciliation. How is this done? We must begin from a conventional point of departure, by reexamining the story's plot and characters.

In "Love in a Fallen City," remarriage is not an individual choice but a social necessity. The character of the "gay divorcée" never exists, and there is nothing glamorous about Liusu's position. As a divorcée who lives with her own family, Liusu is constantly ridiculed by her relatives for her failure in marriage. This traditional set of circumstances forces her to seek a new marriage prospect. In the scene in which she looks at herself in the mirror at home in Shanghai, her gaze may be interpreted as an act of narcissism, but as she "performs" in the mirror, a subtle transformation also takes place: "Suddenly, she smiled—a private, malevolent smile—and the music came to a discordant halt." The traditional tales from the *huqin*—"tales of fealty and filial piety, chastity and righteousness," become distant: they "had nothing to do with her."[54] She seems ready to plunge into a new world and assume a new role. Thus, role-playing becomes not merely a structural ingredient in a screwball comedy plot but, more significantly, a necessary act in Liusu's search for identity. When relatives introduce her to Fan Liuyuan, a rich playboy who has just returned from England, Liusu is so eager to extricate herself from her family bondage that she takes the extraordinary step of meeting him in Hong Kong, a place "removed from the city of confusion." The value system is thus radically changed. The ethical web of human relations that characterizes her traditional family is no longer operative. She is on her own, playing a totally nontraditional role alien to her own personality—that of a "gay divorcée" who is setting a "tender trap" to catch her man. Without family ethics, Liusu is also compelled to define her individual subjectivity as a nontraditional woman (since most women characters in traditional Chinese fiction are not divorced). Thus, in embarking on the quest for a new marriage prospect, Liusu is concurrently in search of her own identity as a woman torn between two worlds.

How does Liusu define herself, now that she is all alone in an alien place? Her "acting" has the incongruity of an actress in a Shanghai local opera who is suddenly thrust onto the modern stage of a "spoken drama" (*huaju*) or a Hollywood comedy. As she tries to cope with all the modern social rituals—dancing, dining in a Western restaurant, walking on the beach, even dealing with Liuyuan's "old flame," an Indian princess—she is being constantly watched by others and by a bemused male suitor who seems to know all about her role-playing and treats her as an exotic Oriental woman under his "colonial" gaze. Still, Liuyuan finds himself gradually falling in love with her. How is it possible? Romantic love is, of course, a modern luxury and a prerequisite in screwball comedies. In traditional Chinese fiction, however, love is but one facet of human relations, which is buttressed by an all-embracing human ethos, feeling (*qing*). The courtship between Liuyuan and Liusu combines the elements of both plus a little extra which seems added to the regular plot. Yet it is precisely this "extra" element that makes the story extraordinary. In order to explicate its significance, I must quote several courtship scenes in full. The first takes place when the two are taking a walk:

> "Let's walk over there a bit," said Liuyuan.
>
> Liusu didn't say anything. But as he walked, she slowly followed. After all, it was still early, and lots of people went out for walks on the road—it would be all right. A little way past the Repulse Bay Hotel, an overhead bridge arched through the air. On the far side of the bridge was a mountain slope; on the near side there was a gray brick retaining wall. Liuyuan leaned against the wall, and Liusu leaned too, looking up along the great height,

a wall so high that its upper edge could not be seen. *The wall was cool and rough, the color of death* [emphasis added]. Against it her face looked different: red mouth, shining eyes, a face of flesh and blood and feeling.

"I don't know why," said Liuyuan, looking at her, "but this wall makes me think of the old sayings about the end of the world. Someday, when human civilization has been completely destroyed, when everything is burnt, burst, utterly collapsed and ruined, maybe this wall will still be here. If, at that time, we can meet at this wall, then maybe, Liusu, you will honestly care about me, and I will honestly care about you."[55]

This episode is a bit odd because of one small detail that bears hardly any relation to the plot: the "gray brick retaining wall," cool and rough, the color of death, like a leftover object from another era. The confrontation with this odd object marks an epiphanic moment and lends Liuyuan—a playboy with no sense of culture or history—to imagine the end of the world with a half-remembered phrase from an old Chinese poem: "Dilao tianhuang buliao qing," literally, "aged earth and deserted sky, and love is endless." This poetic line was so frequently used as a panegyric to eternal love that it had become almost a cliché (and later would be used as the Chinese title for a Hollywood film, *The Magnificent Obsession*). Liuyuan's remark is profoundly ironic. On the one hand, it is made all the more poignant because for the first time in his prolonged flirtations it is touched with feeling. The emotional force is derived from the vivid imagery of the original poetic line—the earth has grown old and heaven is deserted and ruined—but it implies an inverted meaning: only *then* can true love begin. Liuyuan's language is filled with apocalyptic sentiments: he talks about "when human civilization has been completely destroyed, when everything is burnt, burst, utterly collapsed and ruined." Such ominous evocation of a wasteland is not only out of sync with Liuyuan's character but also, given the circumstances, so out of place as to suggest the very opposite of the original meaning: that in the modern world love has no finality or end result, and hence there is no such thing as "endless love." With Liuyuan's unwitting omission, the phrase "endless love" thus becomes, by its very absence, intensely suggestive and ironic: genuine love can begin only at the end of the world, at the end of time, when time itself no longer matters. It is at such a moment that we can imagine Chang's aesthetic state of desolation—*cangliang*, literally, "gray and cold," the color of the wall.

If it is only at this penultimate *fin-du-monde* moment that the truth of feeling can be affirmed, then it is surely too late, as the intimation of death is already literally written on the wall, and eternal love can only mean death. Given such an ironic logic, would Liuyuan and Liusu be able to meet again when the world comes to an end? We are once more reminded of Eileen Chang's remarks in her preface to *Chuanqi*, quoted earlier: "In the wilderness of the future, amidst the ruins of buildings and walls, only a woman like the heroine from a *bengbeng* opera can survive and live on peacefully, because there is a home for her in any era, any society, anywhere." A woman like Liusu, since she is very much modeled after such a heroine, will likewise survive, but not Fan Liuyuan. It seems that in this larger allegory of life, Chang has reserved a special place for her half-traditional heroine, not necessarily for reasons of her gender but for what her gender represents in Chinese culture in this transitional era.

For readers of traditional Chinese fiction, the wall image also recalls an episode in *Dream of the Red Chamber* (Chapter 23), when the heroine Lin Daiyu suddenly hears two lines from an aria from the Ming play *Moudan ting* (The peony pavilion) and is transfixed: "Here multiflorate splendor blooms forlorn / Midst broken fountains, mouldering walls."[56] The novel was Chang's own favorite literary work, on which she later wrote a scholarly book. Her indebtedness to this classic novel can be detected not only in the traces of direct literary quotation but also in a kind of modern reenactment of its sentiment, a "re-presentation" against a totally different background: 1940s Hong Kong versus eighteenth-century Beijing. If linear time and history can be transcended, however, we can easily locate similar intimations of doom—by the parallel portraits in both works of a culture in the last splendor of its afterglow before darkness descends. In *Dream of the Red Chamber*, the love between hero and heroine, Baoyu and Daiyu, is played out against the author, Cao Xueqin's, own autobiographical background of the decline of family fortune and the end of refined aristocratic culture as represented in "The Garden of Grand Vision" (Daguanyuan). With such intimations overshadowing its plot, the two young protagonists, especially Daiyu, are torn with self-torment and an amorphous sense of doom. Their search for emotional fulfillment is ultimately unfulfilled, but it has left a wealth of lyrical testimonials in the form of poetry and drama.

Chang's story "Love in a Fallen City" evokes a similar aesthetic sentiment that is, so to speak, cut off from its original source by the passage of time and changed space. The beginning of the story implies that the inexorable movement of history steps to a quicker and grander march or symphony, and will soon drown out the plaintive tunes from a *huqin*. Chang's heroine, however, is not bemoaning the passing of an era but rather wishes to liberate herself from it. Nostalgia is *not* the key motif in the story. On the contrary, the past is evoked only as a mythic presence to prophesy the cataclysm of modernity: the world that is doomed is not that of traditional China but the modern world of war and revolution. Chang's aesthetics of desolation thus runs counter to the mainstream of modern Chinese literature and history. But instead of utter nostalgia (the stance of an archconservative) or utter pessimism (that of a cynic or nihilist), Chang has opted in this story for comedy and irony.

After the wall episode, a crucial flirtation scene takes place in the hotel; it in turn builds to a climactic scene of seduction that consummates the courtship. Thus, the emotional denouement is reached well *before* the story's end. For the flirtation scene the author cleverly resorts to the modern convenience of a telephone in the hotel room, so the protagonists do not even see each other face to face. As if watching a film, we see Liusu lying in bed at night unable to sleep. Just as she drifts off, the phone suddenly rings: it is Liuyuan, who says, "I love you," and then hangs up. But just as Liusu puts down the receiver, the phone rings again and Liuyuan says: "I forgot to ask you—do you love me?" This abrupt phone call serves as a prelude to Liuyuan's proposal of marriage. He seems compelled to voice the cliché line that appears in all romantic comedies (but never in traditional Chinese fiction): "I love you." But the scene does not stop here, nor does it end in the typical Hollywood fashion, with the requisite kiss (since the two are in separate rooms). For Liuyuan, quite out of character, proceeds to quote a verse from the ancient Chinese classic *Shijing* (The book of songs):

> "I don't understand that sort of thing," Liusu cut in.
>
> "I know you don't understand," Liuyuan said impatiently. "If you understood, I wouldn't need to explain! So listen: 'Life, death, separation—with thee there is happiness; thy hand in mine, we will grow old together.'
>
> "My Chinese isn't very good, and I don't know if I've got it right. I think this is a very mournful poem which says that life and death and parting are all enormous things, far beyond human control. Compared to the great forces in the world, people are very small, very weak. But still we say 'I will stay with you forever, we will never, in this lifetime, leave one another'—as if we really could decide these things!"[57]

Liuyuan's suddenly quoting the *Shijing* is indeed enigmatic and hard to understand. How can someone born and educated abroad, whose "Chinese isn't very good," suddenly remember a line from an ancient classic written in the classical language (*wenyan*), not in the modern vernacular as used in the story's narration and dialogue? Why this particular quote out of some hundreds of lines? Following the romantic formula, we can consider this to be a form of wedding vow—at least this is what the story's English translator believes it to be, for it could likewise be rendered in a more commonly accepted interpretation as: "In life and death, here is my promise to thee: thy hand in mine, we will grow old together"[58]—and, one might add, "till death do us part." But then Liuyuan himself says that "this is a very mournful poem," and his ensuing com-

ment clearly resonates with the desolate outlook and sentiment manifested in the wall episode. As a superficial and foppish man, Liuyuan is
incapable of uttering such comments, even at the height of emotion. For
a cynical playboy is not likely to swear eternal vows of love and devotion. This is precisely how Liusu receives his message: "Why not go
ahead and just say, flat-out, that you don't want to marry me, and leave it
at that! Why beat about the bush, with all this talk of not being able to
decide things?!"[59] Such talk does not decide a marriage, for marriage as a
traditional institution is not necessarily the final outcome of romance in
Chang's own scale of things.

In romantic comedies, flirtation can only lead to seduction, and the
story's scene of seduction is so carefully scripted and described with such
detail that it looks like a "shot-by-shot" film sequence. As Liusu gets
ready for bed in her hotel room, she stumbles over a shoe and finds
Liuyuan in her bed, and he is soon kissing her: "He pushed her into the
mirror, they seemed to fall down into it, into another shadowy
world—freezing cold, searing hot, the flame of the forest burning all
over their bodies."[60] These "shots" could have come from a number of
Hollywood movies, in which the mirror on the woman's vanity is a
common prop and the mirror shot of the heroine by a hidden camera is
an usual trick, a "double take" of visual narcissism. But the mirror is also
one of those decorative details that frequently occur in Chang's stories,
particularly in "Love in a Fallen City." The earlier episode in which Liusu
looks at herself in a mirror naturally paves the way for the "mirror shot"
in this scene: the image of herself as a woman subject is now being
"transgressed" as a man pushes her "into the mirror." But once they fall
down into the mirror, they enter another world in which reality ceases to
count: it is the shadowy world of desire and desolation, of desire *as*
desolation. It becomes, in other words, a mythic world of *cangliang* in
which burning passion is reflected in the "freezing cold" mirror. Read in
sequence with the earlier quoted phrase about "aged earth and deserted
sky," the present image can only lead us to thoughts of melancholy: when
the "searing hot" passion is burned out, its ashes (another favorite meta-

phor of Chang's) can only decorate the "freezing cold" landscape of "the aged earth," the world at its end. In Chang's world of desolation, passion can only be, to use a Lu Xun metaphor, a "dead fire."

Nevertheless, in spite of all these desolate implications, Chang allows the outcome of marriage—a result not of the couple's romance but of the external intervention of war. The next day, right after their love-making, Liuyuan tells her that he is going to England in a week, apparently intending to keep her as a mistress in Hong Kong. At this critical juncture of the plot, history again intervenes, as in the case of the story "Sealed Off," but this time things turn out "happily." His trip is halted by the outbreak of the war, and they decide to get married. At the end of "Love in a Fallen City," the narratorial voice comments amidst layers of irony:

> Hong Kong's defeat had given her victory. But in this unreason-
> able world, who can say which was the cause and which the
> result? Who knows? Maybe it was in order to vindicate her that
> an entire city fell. Countless thousands of people dead, countless
> thousands of people suffering, and what followed was an earth-
> shaking revolution . . . Liusu did not feel that her place in history
> was anything remarkable. She just stood up smiling, and kicked
> the pan of mosquito incense under the table.
>
> The legendary beauties who felled cities and kingdoms were
> probably all like that.[61]

In concluding the story with this reference to "legendary beauties who felled cities and kingdoms," Chang has delivered her ultimate critique of history and her affirmation of fiction in the form of a generic irony. If *chuanqi* as legend is a romantic genre which has traditionally been considered beyond the pale of historical writing and beyond belief, why can it not intervene in a fictional work when history itself is beyond belief? Who knows what will happen with the earth-shaking revolution? In granting Liusu's pursuit of happiness a happy ending, Chang once again pays tribute to the local opera heroine and to the legendary beauties of China. In writing a modern fiction, however, she has reversed their fortune in the well-known classical legend. It is said that there was once an ancient king (presumably the last king of the Shang dynasty) who wanted so much to please his beautiful imperial concubine that he lit a bonfire at the Great Wall to trick his troops into believing that the barbarians were invading. When his troops arrived, the hoax made the concubine laugh. But when, after a couple of these foolish games, the real invasion came, his troops did not come to the rescue, and his kingdom fell. Hence the familiar line: "One smile felled a city, another smile toppled a kingdom." Chang's modern sensibility certainly would not allow this traditional bias about beautiful women being the "flood of evil" to prevail. Like the *Shijing* quotation, she gives this familiar legend an ironic twist by applauding Liusu's victory: as if a city had fallen just to complete her romance and give her story a happy ending! In these extraordinary times of war and revolution, her women characters—and Liusu in particular—deserve some happiness, no matter how ephemeral.

A year after Chang published "Love in a Fallen City," she wrote an essay, "From the Ashes" (Jingyu lu), about her own experience when the city of Hong Kong was besieged. She was then a student, living in the university dormitory. As portrayed in the essay, her classmates' reaction—and hers—to the bombardment was, surprisingly, one of indifference: her friend Yan Ying even ventured out to catch a movie. To maintain one's calm in danger and adversity may be courageous; Chang's portrait of indifference, however, has nothing to do with courage but signifies something else:

> Throughout the eighteen-day siege, everybody had that horrible four-in-the-morning feeling—the shivering dawn, the confusion, the huddling up, the insecurity. You couldn't go home. If you did, your home might no longer be there, the house could have been demolished, money could have been wastepaper in

the blink of an eye, people could have died, and you were even less sure of living the day out. I am reminded of two lines: "Aggrieved I bid my dear farewell, and drift off into hazy mists." But somehow the lines don't reflect the indifferent emptiness, the hopelessness. It was intolerable and, in a desperate bid to cling to something dependable, people got married.[62]

The sentiment in the last sentence certainly applies to Liuyuan and Liusu when they decide to get married. "Love in a Fallen City" was the fourth story Chang wrote about Hong Kong. They were evidently written because her memories of this fallen city remained fresh after her return to Shanghai in 1942, and she wished to dedicate these Hong Kong stories to her beloved city of Shanghai. Obviously in both her life and art Hong Kong was a complement to Shanghai, standing as its "other" in her fictional representation. This self-reflexive linkage is also relevant for our purposes, because the more she exoticizes Hong Kong, the more Hong Kong, like a mirror, reflects back upon her own city of Shanghai. With her usual prescience, Chang has invested in this "tale of two cities" so much cultural significance that it is still being felt today. Thus, in the concluding part of this book, I bring the larger story of Shanghai up to date by offering my own historical reflections on this remarkable "tale of two cities," with a little help from Eileen Chang's fiction.

REFLECTIONS

SHANGHAI COSMOPOLITANISM

The Chinese who lived in and around these foreign enclaves were in effect a colonial population, the "natives" of a regime complete with all the trappings of the European colonial system, including the discriminations, exclusions, and racial attitudes practiced by the foreign masters and the submissive acceptance of the "treaty-port mentality" by great numbers of Chinese in their role as subjects. For many shame and anger remained near the surface of this acceptance. It was the older more deeply rooted Chinese chauvinistic pride more than anything else that fueled the nationalist revolution that challenged this state of affairs in the 1920s.[1]

These remarks by Harold Isaacs, himself an old Shanghailander, would certainly ring true for a postcolonial reader of this book. Nevertheless, at the end of this study we must ask a slightly different question from that inspired by Isaacs: In what ways could Chinese writers, living as "submissive subjects" in a city with all the trappings of European colonialism, still proclaim themselves to be Chinese? Wasn't the claim itself a sign of self-deception? And what constituted the "older more deeply rooted Chinese chauvinistic pride" that fueled their nationalism and revolution? In fact, the same impression of colonial exploitation was shared by Mao Zedong himself and served as the impetus for his famous revolutionary strategy (popularized by Lin Biao) of "the countryside surrounding cities." Mao's anti-urbanism also drew its ideological force from the deep-seated ambivalence, even personal guilt, of Chinese leftist intellectuals who lived in Shanghai in the 1930s, who, in spite of their "shame and anger" at the colonial domination of Western powers, did *not* want to leave because they enjoyed the city's material conveniences and the protection of the treaty port concessions. The configurations of colonialism, modernity, and nationalism are surely more complex than what may have appeared near the surface to a sympathetic observer. They are the larger issues against which all the literary figures and texts treated in this book must be reexamined. Thus in this concluding chapter I offer a discussion of these larger issues, based on a summary of my readings of both historical data and literary texts as presented in the preceding chapters.

The Colonial Condition

The issue calls, first of all, for a reexamination of postcolonial discourse itself in this particular historical context.

All postcolonial discourse, it seems to me, assumes a colonial structure of power in which the colonizers have the ultimate authority over the colonized, including their representation. It is a theoretical construct based on the situation of former British and French colonies in Africa and India. It also assumes that the colonizer is the "subject" of the discourse, for which the colonized can only serve as the "object" or "other." In Shanghai, Western "colonial" authority was indeed legally recognized in the concession treaties, but it was also conveniently ignored by the Chinese residents in their daily lives—unless, of course, they got arrested in the concessions.[2] The writers treated in this book seemed to have been well adjusted to living in this bifurcated world of China's largest treaty port. Although they had little personal contact with Westerners, they were also among the most "Westernized" in their lifestyle and intellectual predilections. Yet none of them ever conceived himself or herself as serving in any way as the colonized "other" to a real or imagined Western colonial master; in fact, with a few exceptions—Shi Zhecun's "Haunted House" and some stories by Eileen Chang readily come to mind—the Western "colonial masters" do not even appear as central characters in their fiction. Rather, it was the Chinese writers' fervent espousal of Occidental exoticism that turned Western culture itself into an "other" in the process of constructing their own modern imaginary. This process of appropriation was crucial to their own quest for modernity—a quest conducted with full confidence in their identity as Chinese nationalists. In fact, in their minds modernity itself was in the service of nationalism.

This is evidently not the same situation as in colonial India. Rather it arises from a different historical legacy: despite a series of defeats after the Opium Wars, China was victimized but never fully colonized by a Western power. The treaty port may be considered a "semi-colony"—not necessarily in the Maoist double-negative sense (that is, of colonial status aggravated by being combined with "semi-feudalism") but in the hybrid sense of a mixture of colonial and Chinese elements. As such it presents an intriguing test case for what Homi Bhabha has called "mimicry," which he defines both subtly and opaquely. According to him, "colonial mimicry is the desire for a reformed, recognizable Other, as a subject of a difference that is almost the same, but not quite . . . a desire that, through the repetition of partial presence . . . articulates those disturbances of cultural, racial, and historical difference that menace the narcissistic demand of colonial authority." Thus, Bhabha's theory suggests that even the "partial representation" of the colonial object can be both submissive and subversive. Although the "mimic man" is created by a colonial education—"almost the same but not white"—his very "partial presence" and his "gaze of otherness" give the lie to the post-Enlightenment beliefs of British colonial policy makers.[3] Obviously, such a phenomenon is a product of a long history of total colonization.

In a country in which Western colonialism was not a total system governing the entire nation, the situation might be more complicated, even worse. One might find a species of Bhabha's "mimic men" among the compradorial and commercial elite who had close personal and business relations with Westerners. They could have been willing colonial subjects even if they still carried Chinese citizenship papers—because of their desire for total Westernization. Still, I would argue that such a world of financial capitalism is qualitatively different from the field of cultural production and consumption in literature, in which such a "colonized" species is not well represented.[4] The obvious reason lies in the fact that in spite of their reading knowledge of foreign literatures, modern Chinese writers did not use any foreign languages to write their work and continued to use the Chinese language as their *only* language.

This obvious point nevertheless harks back to a long and deeply entrenched tradition of written Chinese unchallenged by any foreign language throughout Chinese history. Unlike some African writers who were forced by their colonial education to write in the language of their colonial masters, the Chinese never faced such a threat. Their works of poetry and fiction continued to be written in Chinese, in which the syntactic structures of the modern vernacular are preserved, and in some cases enriched (some would say adulterated), by translated terms and phrases. No one wrote fiction in English or French or experimented with the possibilities of bilingual writing. Thus, in the rare case of a story or novel involving a Western character, the Chinese diction remains unchanged. Several characters in the popular novel *Feng xiaoxiao* (The whirling wind) by Xu Xu, which has Japanese-occupied Shanghai as its background, are Western—an American agent, his wife, another young American woman who falls in love with the Chinese protagonist-narrator, and her mother—and all presumably speak English. Yet in no way are we led to believe that English is somehow implicated in the dialogue—even the love letters show no traces of translation—whereas at several key junctures the protagonist repeatedly claims that he does not understand Japanese, and some of the Japanese spies (including a femme fatale) speak only halting Chinese. Clearly the foregrounded text makes sure that the language of the enemy—Japanese—must be "alienated," yet it allows no such linguistic mediations as far as English is concerned. The same can be said about Eileen Chang's story "Aloe Ashes—Second Burning" (Chenxiangxie, dierluxiang), in which all the main characters are British, as the story takes place in colonial Hong Kong. Their repressed sexuality is framed in a third-person narratorial voice (presumably Chinese) that has subtly humanized and "Sinicized" them. Thus, while the landscape is unmistakably Western, the characters' speech patterns are unmistakably Chinese. There is hardly an "alienation" effect.

But Chang is also the only one of the Chinese writers who was capable of writing bilingually. (Another famous writer, Lin Yutang, published essays in Chinese in his journals in Shanghai and shifted to writing in English only after he went to live in New York.) Chang wrote her first essay in English as a schoolgirl and continued to contribute English essays to Shanghai's Western newspapers. Still, Chang did not write fiction in English until much later, in the early 1950s, after she left Shanghai. Two novels in English, an anticommunist work, *The Rice-Sprout Song*, and *The Rouge of the North*, are both based on her work in Chinese. But for all her bilingual talent, Chang's effort to make her name in America by writing in English failed. This was due largely to the relative provincialism of the American market, but certainly different linguistic sensibilities are also at work in Chang's Chinese and English writings. A casual examination of her English essays written in 1942 which she then rendered into Chinese has made me aware that the Chinese versions have a more acerbic, but also more intimate, tone than the English ones. The intimacy of her Chinese essays is related, it seems, to a presupposition of a Shanghai readership with whom Chang is in easy communion. For instance, in her Chinese essay "Gengyi ji" (On changing clothes) she can survey the changes in women's fashion with more facility and greater attention to detail than in its English version (titled "Chinese Life and Fashions"), because she and her readers share the same familiar history. In an essay called "As a Foreigner Looks at Peking Opera and Other Matters" (Yangren kan jingxi ji qita), Chang purposefully wishes to adopt the perspective of a foreigner looking at Peking opera. Yet throughout the essay she cites one example after another to show that "Westerners can never understand" the popularity of this art form which combines the sublime and the ridiculous all in one play.[5] This Chinese essay, like her essays in English, is a roundabout defense not only of Peking opera but of China as well. Thus, even in this most "foreign-flavored" essay, Chang nevertheless takes the subjective position as a Chinese.

I would therefore put forth the argument that for all their flaunted Westernism, the Shanghai writers treated in this book never imagined themselves, nor were they regarded, as so "foreignized" (yanghua) as to become slaves to foreigners (yangnu). From their works I draw the obvious conclusion that their sense of Chinese identity was never in question *in spite of* the Western colonial presence in Shanghai. In my view it was only because of their unquestioned Chineseness that these writers were able to embrace Western modernity openly, without fear of colonization. Research on an earlier period has also indicated that for all their anxieties and perplexities, Shanghai residents welcomed the arrival of modernity in its concrete "mechanical" forms—railways (after an initial fiasco), telegraphs, tram lines, electric lights, automobiles.[6] This does not mean, however, that in China as a whole the national project of modernity was "completed." It was not. But for a time in the early 1930s a collective ethos of national subjectivity (derived from the claim of national sovereignty) did, for better or worse, infuse the urban culture of Shanghai and other treaty port cities (notably Tianjin, Qingdao, Wuhan, and Guangzhou, with the notable exception of Hong Kong, which remained a British colony) to an extent that was unsurpassed before. As we saw in Chapter 1, Shanghai had just reached a new height of urban development in the 1930s, with the construction of skyscrapers, department stores, and movie theaters. This new cityscape became the setting for most of stories by the Chinese neo-sensationalist writers, who were apparently dazzled by its novelty and magnificence. By the time Eileen Chang returned from Hong Kong in 1942 to a Shanghai under Japanese occupation, this spectacle of an urban skyline had become part of a world that she had taken for granted.

A Chinese Cosmopolitanism

Instead of colonial mimicry, I see this phenomenon of Chinese writers eagerly embracing Western cultures in Shanghai's foreign concessions as a manifestation of a Chinese cosmopolitanism, which is another facet of Chinese modernity.

One could argue that cosmopolitanism is also a by-product of colonialism. Hence in the anti-colonial national struggles, cosmopolitanism is also a target for attack. This is certainly explicit in Mao's revolutionary strategy. At the same time, as Joseph Levenson has argued, from a different angle, the Confucian world had also been internally cosmopolitan. This traditional cosmopolitanism was deemed too provincial by those May Fourth intellectuals who wanted to open up China to the world. In Levenson's view (against his personal sympathies), the advocates of this new "bourgeois cosmopolitanism" were doomed to failure because their membership was so tiny and looked so provincial: "The very cosmopolitanism of some Shanghai Chinese, looking out from China, seemed a provincial variant, at the end of the line, to men who were looking in. The coin wavers, one side with the face of sophistication, the other with the face of questing, diffident innocence." The example he gives and criticizes is that of the Chinese translators of Western plays, who seemed unable to "assimilate the play[s] into Chinese needs and experience."[7]

Writing at the beginning of the Cultural Revolution in 1966 shortly before he died, Levenson witnessed the rising tide of another revolution that threatened to wipe out whatever traces of urban cosmopolitanism still remained in Shanghai. Naturally he was discouraged, and this pessimism about the prospects of cosmopolitanism seems to have influenced unduly his assessment of the drama translations. His research (conducted in only one library in Hong Kong) did, however, unearth a large number of translations from an immensely diverse array of Western authors—Schiller, Shakespeare, Corneille, Molière, Fielding, Wilde, Schnitzler, Pirandello, and Goldoni—all during the relatively short period of the 1920s and 1930s. No matter whether they were performed or not, the effort of these "questing, diffident" innocents set an all-time record in terms of the quantity and diversity of translations. As Levenson belittled this effort, he also lamented its obvious futility: who cares if a Chinese translator of a Schnitzler play tried to make a fine distinction between the Berlin spirit and the Viennese sensibility?[8]

In my view, precisely the reverse question should be asked: given such lack of background, how was it possible for Chinese writers and translators to have found such differences in Western authors and literature? Had Levenson been able to read more about Schnitzler in China, he would have realized that almost all the important works by this Viennese writer were either translated or introduced in the journals edited by Shi Zhecun. As we saw in Chapter 4, Shi had himself translated *Fräulein Else*, *Berthe Garlan*, and other novels; he had also purchased a number of Schnitzler's works in German and English, including *Fräulein Else*, *Leutnant Gustl*, and *Daybreak*. Schnitzler's plays were mostly translated by Zhao Baoyan. How did this tiny segment of the Chinese intelligentsia succeed in translating such a wealth of Western literature in such a short period? The easy answer is that there was obviously a demand from the urban reading public, no matter how small compared to the Chinese population as a whole. More important, this massive translation and production of texts served to constitute the very cultural space in which the implications of cosmopolitanism must be measured. Instead of taking the guise of an outsider looking in, as Levenson seems to have done, I have chosen the reverse procedure of trying to position myself as an insider looking out. A sophisticated outsider at a later age, such as Levenson, is particularly prone to ex post facto intellectual condescension.

Thus, I disagree with Levenson's interpretation and argue the opposite position: that if cosmopolitanism means an abiding curiosity in "looking out"—locating oneself as a cultural mediator at the intersection between China and other parts of the world—then Shanghai in the 1930s was the cosmopolitan city par excellence, which had earned from Western tourists the popular epithet of the "Paris of the Orient." Despite the "Orientalist" implications, the epithet nevertheless served to underscore Shanghai's international significance and to connect it in the Western popular imagination to the other metropolises in Europe and America. In Asia, Shanghai replaced Tokyo (damaged by an earthquake in 1923) as the center of a network of cities linked together by ship routes for purposes of marketing, transportation, and tourism. As the branch offices of the bookstore Kelly & Walsh indicates, the book traffic mapped out a closely linked chain connecting Shanghai, Hong Kong, Tientsin, Yokohama, Singapore, New Delhi, and Bombay. While the imprint of British colonialism is clearly discernible, this chain of cities nevertheless formed an international cultural space in which not only Britain and France but also Japan played a significant role.

The Japanese Connection

The North China Sea was traversed constantly by Chinese and Japanese intellectuals, writers, and students from around 1900 on. The Japanese "concession" in the northern part of Shanghai was another enclave in which writers such as Lu Xun had their residences, together with a population of Japanese expatriates who outnumbered the British and the French. As is well known, this "Japanese connection" provided a key to Chinese leftist literature, as most Chinese leftists including Lu Xun had been educated in Japan and translated most of the works on Marxism and revolutionary theory from the Japanese originals or retranslations from German or Russian sources. But the Japanese impact was not limited only to leftist literature and thought. Most of the seminal terms and concepts of Western literature came from Japan. Terms such as "symbolism" and "repression" as crucial elements of artistic creativity were first discussed in the works of Kuriyagawa Hakuson, of which Lu Xu translated three volumes into Chinese: *Kumen de xiangzeng* (Symbols of suffering), *Chule xiangya zhita* (Out of the ivory tower), and *Shanshui sixiang renwu* (Landscape, ideas, and figures).[9] Kuriyagawa's rather eclectic and wide-ranging discourses—from English romanticism to French realism and Symbolism, from Sigmund Freud to Henri Bergson (in *Symbols of Suffering*), from self-expression to national character, from hedonism to the literature of labor (in *Out of the Ivory Tower*), and from Western writers and politicians to places in his own travels (in *Landscape, Ideas, and Figures*)—provided the essential background reading for a whole generation of Chinese writers, leftists and non-leftists alike. As I mentioned in Chapter 7, it was from the first volume of Kuriyagawa's work as translated by Lu Xun that the concept of decadence, via Baudelaire, was first derived.

At the same time, Shanghai also offered a special meaning for Japanese intellectuals, especially during the crucial period from the late 1920s to the late 1930s when most of them went through an ideological conversion *(tenko)* from aestheticism and proletarianism to Japanese imperial nationalism. Shanghai, which many of them visited, provided both a real and a fictional setting for them to negotiate their own mental ambivalences and ambiguities between nationalism and internationalism. In this regard we must give attention to a masterly novel, *Shanghai* by Yokomitsu Reiichi, the leader of the Japanese neo-sensationalists, in order to shed some comparative light on the complexities of cosmopolitanism.

Yokomitsu himself visited Shanghai in 1928 and spent about a month there. His novel about Shanghai was first serialized in seven installments in the literary journal *Kaizo* (Reconstruction) from November 1929 through November 1931, by which time his neo-sensationalist school (1924–1927) had disbanded and some members had turned to proletarian literature. This may be the reason why Liu Na'ou and Mu Shiying made no specific references to the novel, nor was the work translated, although traces of Mu's imitation can still be discerned. In the

novel Yokomitsu creates a large number of characters—Japanese, Russian, British, American, and Chinese—each identified in terms of his or her social status in order to focus on "the feeling and sensation specific to the relationship of character to the given social reality." In other words, Yokomitsu goes beyond the depiction of subjective sensations of the characters in order to grasp "the sensation of almost tactile immediacy about the environment and things in Shanghai."[10] Interestingly, in sharp contrast to the glittering modern metropolis as portrayed by his Chinese followers, Yokomitsu's Shanghai is a dark, poverty-stricken underworld of squalor. This is the scene described at the beginning of the novel:

> A neighborhood of crumbling brick. In the narrow byways, crowds of Chinese wearing black garments with long sleeves filled the area quite spiffily, like seaweed sedimented on the bottom of the sea. The beggars squatted on the road paved with pebbles. In the storefronts above their heads, fish bladders, hacked sections of carp dripping with blood, things like that were hanging. In the fruit stand to the side mangos and bananas were piled up flowing over even to the pavement. Then there was the character to the side of the fruit store where endless numbers of skinned pigs, with hoofs hanging down, were hollowed out into dark flesh-colored caves.[11]

This is a scene in which one of the Japanese characters is taken to a Chinese communal bathhouse. It is a mild evocation when compared to other scenes of "filthy slums filled with opium smokers and brothels." As Emanuel Pastreich has remarked, "Yokomitsu's language leaves us with a weird, surreal impression we can well imagine [in] a Dali painting . . . Shanghai serves as a defamiliarized landscape in which the Modernist author can explore the limits of his new sensations, his *Shinkankaku.*"[12] One wonders why, after a month-long stay in Shanghai presumably as a tourist, Yokomitsu preferred to zero in on such slum scenes of squalor instead of the more magnificent evocations of heat, light, and power, especially in view of his interest in evoking the subjective sensations aroused by the excitements of material modernity. Perhaps such evocations were already commonplace in Japanese neo-sensationalist literature, and he wished to define a world totally different from modern Japan. If so, China was already marked in Yokomitsu as an *alien* country (the name he uses for China is the more traditional and disparaging Shina rather than the more modern Chūgoku)—an Oriental "other" to Japan and to the Japanese characters in Yokomitsu's Shanghai.

There can be no better way to describe this "alien country" than to evoke a mass movement as a wave or avalanche of anonymous energy, like the sailors in the battleship *Potemkin* in Eisenstein's classic film (which also begins with a scene of incredible filth and squalor).[13] It is a most fitting device because the Chinese masses could remain a faceless mob only insofar as China was seen as an alien "other" for the Japanese protagonists. One character, Sanki, assumes the post of a temporary managerial assistant at the textile factory, thus occupying a position, as Naoki Sakai observes, "similar to that of colonial administrator to whom the workers should appear characterless"; Yokomitsu's *Shanghai* thus "succeeded in presenting the 'sensorial' equivalents for subjective positions in colonial, class, and racial hierarchies."[14] What is suggested in Sakai's insightful analysis is that in Yokomitsu's fictional evocation, Shanghai has emerged as a city fraught with complex tensions, a testing ground for the various colonial characters to negotiate their own personal feelings of self-esteem or shame as connected to their social status, economic privilege, race, and nationality, which dictate how one would behave in relation to people of other nationalities and races. "Nationality is like a bank account . . . In Shanghai, perhaps, British and French nationalities meant the highest deposits, while pre-revolutionary Russian nationality . . . meant a deficit. The imperialist hierarchy of the world was nakedly apparent."[15] Given this imperialist imprimatur, the central question for the Japanese "subjects" in *Shanghai* then becomes, in Sakai's words, "How would one negotiate with the perceived contradiction between one's belonging to that nation and the awareness of one's affiliation with its imperialism?"[16] Yokomitsu's novel is fascinating precisely because he has created a fictional space, Shanghai, in which such a contradiction is fleshed out with all the convoluted twists of human relations among the key characters.

Interestingly, there is only one leading character who is Chinese: Fang Qiulan works by day as a factory girl in the Japanese textile plant but shows up at night in the dance halls; in fact, she is a revolutionary and labor organizer. Much "Oriental" mystery seems to hover over this character, who contrasts sharply with the factory women in Mao Dun's novel *Midnight*, who have no "secret life" at all. Her mysterious allure thus confirms her "inscrutability" as a Chinese revolutionary, who is made to lead the workers' strike at her factory, the Oriental Cotton Mill, which is modeled after the real cotton mill where on May 15, 1925 "Japanese guards fired on a group of Chinese workers who invaded the temporarily closed mill, demanding work and smashing machinery. One of the leaders, a communist, died from his wounds."[17] This incident led to more demonstrations by workers and students that culminated in an incident on May 30, when a British police officer ordered his Sikh and Chinese constables to shoot at the demonstrating crowd at the Lousa Police Station in the International Settlement; four died on the spot, and eight more died later of their wounds. Five or six among the dead demonstrators were students.[18] This nation-shaking event is the real subject of Yokomitsu's novel. The tidal wave of the mass demonstrations is described with great dexterity and with all the visual flourishes that Yokomitsu could summon from his neo-sensationalist technique. At the same time, the sheer magnitude of the mass movement somehow made Yokomitsu feel humbled as a novelist, and he attached this preface to the first edition of the novel, published by the Kaizo publishing house:

> With regard to the landscape that appears in this work, it concerns the May 30th incident: in the modern history of the Far East, the first new battle between Europe and East Asia. Writing profoundly on that unending maelstrom which swirled around the issue of the foreign presence, that is to say, the very act of

writing itself, has been not only problematic, but the publication of what I have written has also proven equally difficult. Although I have tried to stick faithfully to the historical facts as much as possible, the closer I approach them, the more I cannot help feeling the inconvenience of having nothing left to me but to limn the general events with my pen.[19]

The preface seems to give the impression that historical reality proves more formidable than fiction—a typical dilemma for a writer of realist fiction. But history also took an unexpected turn. By the time this preface was written in 1932, much had changed in the "modern history of the Far East." The first Japanese bombing of Shanghai heralded the coming of Japanese militarism. Although the attempt was repulsed, largely as a result of negative world opinion, it did not forestall the trend of ideological transition from international leftism to native fascism among Japanese writers and intellectuals. Since the 1930s, Yokomitsu himself had been making his own transition: as he fled from a cosmopolitan stance in addressing the effects of imperial nationalism and anti-colonial nationalism in Shanghai, his later novels indicate clearly that he had abandoned his avant-gardist flourish and moved to a more rigid position of fixity, to a culturalist endorsement of Japanese nationalism.[20] As Maeda Ai has noted, the "inconvenience" and "difficulty" Yokomitsu felt may have been imposed on him by the changed circumstances.[21] In the eyes of the new Japanese nationalists, the May 30 incident "as the first new battle between Europe and East Asia" in modern history assumed a totally different meaning: it signaled the necessity for a greater East Asian collaboration effort led by Japan to resist Western imperialism.

On the Chinese side, the situation was also changed radically. The mass agitations which had gathered enormous force and impact came to an abrupt end with Chiang Kai-shek's "liquidation" of all communists in April 1927. The Chinese Communist Party was forced to retreat to the countryside, thereby both relinquishing its urban base and gradually renouncing an urban strategy based on the labor movement. As Chiang's

Nationalist Party (Guomindang) consolidated its power in Nanking in 1928, it, too, began to establish ideological control in the name of nationalism. Shanghai's concessions, therefore, became a haven for leftists of all hues—underground CCP agents, Marxists, Trotskyists, and advocates of "revolutionary literature," as well as left-leaning avant-garde artists and writers such as Shi Zhecun, Liu Na'ou, and Dai Wangshu, who had just begun to publish their small journals in the late 1920s. As I showed in Chapter 4, in their short-lived journals such as *Trackless Train* and *La Nouvelle Littérature*, they equated artistic avant-gardism with radical politics; in both they considered themselves leftists but not communists. Their bookshops—with names such as Froth and Frontline—were watched by both the concession police and Guomingdang agents. As we saw in Chapter 6, Liu Na'ou, in particular, continued to promote his "mixed" brand of artistic modernism, a combination of Japanese neo-sensationalism with French exoticism (Paul Morand) and Hollywood cinema.

In view of all these political complications and ideological ambiguities, the issue of the Japanese presence in Shanghai was not easily resolved. On the one hand, some Chinese leftists would regard Japanese aggression as the new wave of imperialism which had begun with Western colonialism. On the other hand, other Chinese leftists, Lu Xun included, continued to learn from Japanese leftists, translating their treatises and slogans and trying to figure out what had really transpired in Soviet Russia through Japanese sources,[22] until the entire proletarian scene in Japanese literature came to an end with the massive "conversion" to Japanese imperial nationalism. In short, by 1937, when war finally broke out, the nature of nationalism itself had changed in both China and Japan.

The End of a Cosmopolitan Era

Thus, from a leftist point of view, the decade from 1927 to 1937 was also the period in which a cosmopolitan atmosphere prevailed in Shanghai almost by default, because the more conservative nationalisms in both

Japan and China had ironically facilitated the growth of a loose alliance of left-wing intellectuals against Japanese imperialism in Asia and fascism in Europe, which the urban wing of the underground CCP exploited to its great advantage. Several international bodies, including the Comintern, sent their delegates to Shanghai to meet with Chinese followers and sympathizers in the concessions. Thus, a kind of informal international brotherhood was forged. The French writer Henri Barbusse took a leading role in this movement; he was, however, unable to visit China and sent his former classmate Paul Vaillant-Couturier, an editor of the French leftist newspaper *L'Humanité*, instead. Shi Zhecun and Du Heng visited him at his hotel and published his article written especially for Chinese readers, "To the Chinese Intelligentsia," in their journal *Les Contemporains* (4, no. 1, November 1933). Vaillant-Couturier also attended an "Anti-War Congress"—anti-imperialist war, that is—under the secret sponsorship of the CCP "that was publicly announced and conspiratorially held right in the heart of the city."[23] Fifty Chinese delegates from all part of the country, including those from the "Red Army districts," attended. Other foreign delegates included Lord Marley of the British Labour Party, a Belgian communist named Marteau, a French socialist named Poupy, and an American journalist, Harold Isaacs, editor of the English-language journal in Shanghai, *China Forum*, which duly reported the proceedings. Soong Ching-ling opened the meeting and Lord Marley presided. This brand of cosmopolitan leftism conforms to the general ideological temper of the literary scene at the time—a leftism reinforced by patriotic sentiment against Japanese aggression among writers in China on the one hand combined with a vague feeling of internationalist alliance against fascism in Europe on the other.[24] Even after war was declared in 1937, clandestine anti-Japanese activities could still be conducted in Shanghai under the legal protection of the Western concessions.

Thus, despite—or because of—all these special circumstances, Shanghai reached the pinnacle of its urban glory in the early 1930s. It continued during the "insulated island" period of 1937–1941, when

Shanghai was only partially occupied by Japan while the concessions still maintained legal autonomy and even after the Japanese occupied the entire city in 1942, the time when Eileen Chang returned from Hong Kong to begin her writing career. Shanghai under Japanese occupation was already on the wane, but it was not until after the Sino-Japanese War ended in 1945, when the chaos caused by inflation and civil war had reduced the city's economy to a shambles, did Shanghai's urban glory come to an end. The triumph of the rural-based Communist Revolution further reduced the city to insignificance. For the next three decades in the new People's Republic, Shanghai was dominated and dwarfed by the new national capital, Beijing, to which it had also to contribute more than 80 percent of its annual revenue. Moreover, despite its growing population, Shanghai was never allowed to transform its physical surroundings: the city remained largely the same as in the 1940s, and its buildings and streets inevitably decayed as a result of neglect and disrepair. Under the stern gaze of an authoritarian government, the city lost all its glitz and glamour, its dynamism and decadence. And Mao Dun's "midnight" world of "light, heat, and power" seems also to have vanished. Taking its place is the rapidly developing former colonial city of Hong Kong.

EPILOGUE:

A TALE OF TWO CITIES

"The presence of this touch of oriental color is obviously meant for foreigners. The English came from far away to take a look at China, and we must give them a China to look at—a China in Western eyes: exotic, delicate, ludicrous."

This remark appears in "Aloe Ashes—First Burning," a story Eileen Chang wrote about Hong Kong: it was the first story she submitted to the Shanghai journal of Butterfly fiction *Ziluolan* (Violet) in 1943, and surprised its editor. Once published, the story and its sequel ("Second Burning") took the Shanghai literary scene by storm. Why would an editor and a readership of Butterfly journals, who were habitually steeped in a more traditional Chinese world of culture, be interested in a story about a young woman who becomes a prostitute in Hong Kong? What was the appeal of Hong Kong to Shanghai residents? If this British colony represented China in Western eyes—exotic, delicate, ludicrous—can we say the same about the treaty port Shanghai?

At the beginning of the story, Chang describes a mountainside "white house"—constructed with "streamlined geometric designs, like a modern movie theater"—and its odd combination of Western and "Orientalist" motifs in interior decor. It is a high-class house of prostitution run by the heroine's aunt. The corruption of innocence seems to be the initial theme of the story, but we soon realize that Ge Weilong, the young heroine, willingly joins this "exotic, delicate, and ludicrous" world as if out of a certain fatal attraction and fully aware that "she herself is a part of this peculiar Oriental color of the colony." She meets with a variety of her aunt's clientele, often competes with her aunt for their favors. "She considers her aunt to be a most capable woman who can hold off the grand wheels of time and, in her own world, keeps up the depraved atmosphere of the last years of the Manchu dynasty and plays the role of a small-scale Empress Dowager behind closed doors." At a lavish garden party, some elegantly clad British "ladies" sing "The Last Rose of Summer" while flirtation goes on everywhere behind the bushes. The narrative voice intones: "Hong Kong society imitates the British in every respect, but they go a little overboard and lose its authentic face. Mrs. Liang's garden party really plays up the heavily local color, with five-foot-tall 'Lucky' lanterns planted on the grass everywhere, which are lit in the evening, creating delicate shadows—like the inevitable set of a Hollywood movie about 'The Secret History of the Qing Palace.'" It is in such an exotic atmosphere that Ge Weilong befriends a woman of mixed ancestry—"in her complicated genealogy can be found seven or eight types of blood, such as Arabic, Negro, Indian, English, and Portuguese"—and soon falls in love with her brother, another handsome hybrid who alternately speaks English and Portuguese as he seduces her by *not* promising marriage. But they get married anyway and seem to find happiness amidst all the uncertainties.[1]

Never before have we encountered such an exotic cast of characters and such a bizarre setting—a colonial island and (from the Chinese perspective) the product of a humiliating history. In Chang's fiction, Hong Kong is subject to a double gaze: that of the English colonialists and that of the Chinese from Shanghai. In her essay titled "I Am after All a Shanghai Person," Chang says of the series of "Hong Kong romances" written for her Shanghai readers, "When writing them I was constantly thinking about Shanghai people, because I was trying to look at Hong Kong from a Shanghai person's point of view."[2] This admission nevertheless raises some thorny questions for a latter-day reader: Is the extravagant display of Orientalism in Chang's fiction about Hong Kong intended as a satire or a realistic description of a colonized society? What is a Shanghai person's point of view? How does it differ from that of an English colonialist? And what can we say about the intricate relationship between these two cities, both products of a history of English colonial aggression in Asia? With her unusual perception, Eileen Chang has also perceived an unusual connection between the two cities, which is worth pursuing further so as to bring my own narrative down to the present day.

Hong Kong as the "Other" of Shanghai

In the quoted passages from "Aloe Ashes—First Burning" (Chenxiang xue—diyilu xiang), Hong Kong first emerges as a cinematic representation, in a way similar to that in "Love in a Fallen City." Ge Weilong, like Bai Liusu, is a young woman from Shanghai who has to play out a role that does not befit her original status (a student), as if she were suddenly thrust into an Orientalist Hollywood movie. The self-reflexive reference to a "modern movie theater" is the same device used at the beginning of "Evermore Sorrow": the story begins in a white house that looks like a movie theater and becomes itself a plot for a movie yet to be made. In short, for the average Shanghai reader of the time, perhaps the initial reaction would be that the story, like some Hollywood movie, is appealing precisely because it is unbelievably exotic. But exoticism is a part of Chang's fictional technique that helps the text achieve a "defamiliarizing" effect. Realism is certainly *not* one of Chang's favorite literary tenets. Thus the story, like several of Chang's other stories, is more suggestive of an allegory—a story about a city that is the "other" of Chang's home city of Shanghai. If it takes the "other" to understand the self, the city of Hong Kong is also crucial to our understanding of Shanghai. This point may be implicit in Chang's stories set in this colonial island.

What light can we expect a city like Hong Kong to shed on a city like Shanghai? The question can be rendered from a more postcolonial perspective: To what extent can we consider Shanghai a colonial city like Hong Kong? Is the difference between the two cities merely one of degree and not of substance, of Western colonization? Chang's compli-cated response, gathered from her essays and stories, seems to be that whereas the Hong Kong of her time (circa 1940) was unabashedly colonial, Shanghai was not, or at least not exactly, because Hong Kong did not have Shanghai's "cultivation" (*hanyang*), a word that originally referred to the cultured sophistication of a person who has the elegant appearance of self-restraint. As the description of Mrs. Liang's garden party suggests, Hong Kong is too blatant, too vulgar and flamboyant in its Western imitation, hence producing cultural kitsch. Hong Kong is also, in Chang's description, too eager to "prostitute" itself to the desires of its colonial master. Thus, the city presents itself, purposely, as the object of a Western Orientalist gaze by materializing what existed only in the colonist's fantasies. True to Chang's fictional technique, however, this picture of Orientalist exoticism is negotiated through the narratorial voice of an outsider, one who belongs not to Hong Kong but to Shang-hai. In other words, the colonial world of Hong Kong is viewed from a distance by a somewhat bemused Chinese observer.

There is also much psychological trauma to be found in this alien place: a young British couple's Victorian sexual repression on their wed-ding night ("Aloe Ashes—Second Burning"); a young student's abnormal fascination with his mother's former lover, who is his teacher, and the resulting "incestuous" love he feels for the teacher's daughter ("Fragrant Jasmine Tea"); the life of a lower-class Chinese woman as seen through her affairs with a series of men—the Indian businessman who bought her, a Chinese shop clerk, a British officer ("Locked Circles"). Only when the heroine has a thorough Shanghai background but is compelled by circumstances to "cross over" to Hong Kong, such as Bai Liusu in "Love in a Fallen City," do we find a more humane experience in spite of the alienating environment. In this story Liusu has to compete with a "colonial" rival, an Indian princess, but manages to "win" her man. Obviously, for Eileen Chang, whereas Hong Kong is almost hopelessly colonial, Shanghai for all its foreignness is still Chinese. What in the history of the two cities made Chang feel this way?

When Eileen Chang went to Hong Kong as a student in 1939–1941, the island had been a British colony for a century and remained largely unchanged in its colonial appearance. All of the official buildings were constructed as exact replicas of the official Palladian style derived from the original model of the Queen's House in Greenwich, built in 1616.[3] Although the twelve-story Shanghai and Hong Kong Bank building (1935) stood out as the most advanced commercial building in Asia,[4] the island did not go through an architectural transformation in the 1930s as Shanghai did. It is no wonder, then, that Chang was so condescending in her fictional portraits of Hong Kong. As a student she lived in an old-fashioned castle-like building that was a variant of the colonial style—an example of the so-called classical revival eclecticism of Gothic and Renaissance architecture.[5] It was only after the Japanese surrendered the island to the British in 1945 that Hong Kong began to develop into a metropolis of culture and commerce.

The outbreak of the Sino-Japanese War had a direct impact on Hong Kong's cultural development. The Japanese occupation of Shanghai in 1938 forced a massive exodus of Chinese intellectuals, including most of the writers treated in this book. As the majority left for the hinterland areas of Chongqing and Yan'an, some took a roundabout route via Hong Kong, and a few stayed. Mao Dun was in Hong Kong in 1938 and served briefly as editor of the literary supplement of *Libao*, a newspaper with a large circulation founded by Cheng Shewuo in 1935 and moved to Hong Kong in 1938. Mu Shiying also arrived in 1938 to make a film and to court and marry the dance hall hostess he had met in Shanghai. Reportedly he accumulated too much gambling debt and had to return to Shanghai at the invitation of his friend Liu Na'ou, who had become an important figure under the puppet regime.[6] Mu was assassinated in 1940, shortly after Liu had met with the same fate. A Japanese literary journal published a number of memorial articles, including one written by Yokomitsu Reiichi, the leader of the Japanese neo-sensationalist school.[7]

While Mu did not make much of a contribution to Hong Kong's literary scene, his friend and brother-in-law Dai Wangshu did. (Dai was married to Mu's sister.) Dai came to Hong Kong in 1936 and spent a total of thirteen years there. He edited a number of journals and literary supplements of local newspapers, the most famous being *Xingzuo* (Constellation), the literary supplement of *Xingdao ribao*, for which he solicited contributions from a wide circle of writers, including his friends Shi Zhecun, Mu Shiying, Xu Chi, and Ye Lingfeng. He also wrote profusely, including poetry, translations, and scholarly research on traditional Chinese vernacular fiction.[8] He had been jailed briefly by the Japanese but otherwise lived comfortably in a hillside villa on Pokfulan Road with a view on the sea. Eventually his marriage broke up and he was invited by leftist writers to return to China in 1949, where he died the next year.[9] Dai's younger friend, the poet Xu Chi (who was Dai's best man at his wedding), came to Hong Kong in 1938 and visited him frequently. While in Hong Kong Xu also saw Mu Shiying, who joked about this cultural backwater and the primitive conditions for filmmaking.[10] Xu later made several trips between Hong Kong and Chongqing and befriended a large number of writers and artists, including the leftists Xia Yan and Qiao Guanhua, and gradually became converted to Marxism.[11] Perhaps the Shanghai writer most identifiable with Hong Kong (aside from Eileen Chang) is Ye Lingfeng, who left Shanghai in 1938 in partial disgrace (having been evicted from the League of Left-Wing Writers), and spent the last twenty-seven years of his life in Hong Kong, where he first took over the editorship of *Libao*'s literary supplement after Mao Dun left and then succeeded Dai Wangshu in editing *Xingzuo*, where he continued to publish a large number of essays and articles until he retired at age seventy. He died in 1975. But he had stopped writing fiction; instead, he had indulged his lifelong bibliophilic habit and had become a book collector.[12]

The arrival of these and other writers in Hong Kong in the period 1938–1941 marked the first wave of "southern movement." They formed two organizations—the Hong Kong branch of the All-China Resistance Association (1938–1941) and the Chinese Cultural Association (1939–1941)—to promote literary activity and spread anti-Japanese propaganda.[13] When Japan occupied Hong Kong in December 1941, many of them returned to Shanghai or the hinterlands. The outbreak of civil war in 1947 triggered a second wave of writers moving south to Hong Kong. By this time Hong Kong was no longer a Chinese "cultural desert" or an exotic colony. The massive influx of immigrants from the mainland brought a sharp increase of Hong Kong's population: from 1 million in 1945 to more than 2 million in 1950. It also brought money and capital from Shanghai. While the majority of the refugees lived in dire poverty in the outskirts of the city, Hong Kong's commercial and cultural elite underwent what might be called a process of "Shanghainization": it was no longer a city to visit or to take a vacation but a place to stay. Thus by the early 1950s Hong Kong had become Shanghai's "retreat" and sanctuary. Tycoons from the Shanghai film industry relocated their companies to Hong Kong, where they were joined by other companies such as the Shaw Brothers, Cathay, and Dianmau (which provided Eileen Chang with needed income as a screen writer). Department stores such as Wing On and Sincere had already established Hong Kong branches. Restaurants, Chinese and Western, claimed origins in Shanghai or Beijing or Tianjin. As textile industries established with Shanghai capital began to thrive, real and imitation "Shanghai tailors" also set up their shops.

But in spite of this obvious "Shanghainization," Hong Kong in the 1950s remained a poor copy of the fabled metropolis. As it slowly made its recovery after the ravages of war, Hong Kong was in no position to cope with the sudden onslaught of refugees from the mainland. The Hong Kong government's early measures of housing construction were woefully inadequate and lacked overall planning. Most of the major construction projects during the 1960s took place in the private commercial sector. By the mid-1960s a number of new twenty-story skyscrapers had appeared; some of the high-rise hotels were built on newly filled land in the harbor area.[14] Following the suppression of a leftist-instigated uprising in 1967, Governor Murray Maclehose launched in 1972 a ten-year plan for public housing[15] and initiated several public construction projects, thus changing the long-established colonial policy of exacting local revenues for London. When the first harbor tunnel linking Kowloon to Hong Kong was completed in 1972, Hong Kong was finally on its way to becoming a metropolis that would surpass Shanghai.

Economically Hong Kong took off in the 1970s, whereas Shanghai was paralyzed by the Cultural Revolution, which also resulted in another wave of illegal refugees to Hong Kong. By the early 1980s, Hong Kong had become Britain's "crown" colony, replacing India as its "jewel" in the East. A series of major constructions were under way: the first harbor tunnel in 1972, the Connaught shopping center (fifty-two stories) in 1974, and the new railway station in 1977 (the Gothic-eclectic tower was retained as a historic relic of the old station). A modern subway system linked to the Kowloon-Canton Railway with electric trains was also completed in the early 1980s.[16] With public transportation in place and housing problems addressed, the 1980s also witnessed the mushrooming of cultural activities—film, television, experimental theater, musical performances, and print journalism—which necessitated the construction of a performing arts center in Hong Kong and a large culture center in Kowloon. By this time Hong Kong had not only supplanted Shanghai but surpassed it.

Nostalgia: Shanghai as the "Other" of Hong Kong

We could simply read this narrative of urban development as a typical example of Hong Kong's speedy "modernization." In the midst of this mad race toward economic development, however, a curious cultural

phenomenon was observable: while Hong Kong left Shanghai far behind, the new metropolis has not forgotten about the old; in fact, one
could discern an increasing nostalgia for old Shanghai perpetuated
largely by the mass media. In the 1980s a welter of consumer goods
began to appear: compact disk reissues of old Shanghai popular songs
(one titled "Shanghai at Night," sung by a famous actress of the 1930s,
Bai Guang), "old Shanghai-style" clothes marketed as the latest chic
items in expensive boutiques, exhibitions of photos and memorabilia,
and above all films and two popular television drama series called *Shanghai tan*, or "Shanghai Bund."[17] In these manifestations of the popular
imagination, as Daisy Ng observes, "Shanghai is a strange place of superficial prosperity and deep-seated rottenness, a capitalistic society
where extraordinary wealth exists side by side with extreme poverty, a
semi-colony where a small group of foreign imperialists walk over the
mass body of common Chinese people, a chaotic place where the gun
rules over the fist, a gigantic dye vat where the new immigrants from the
countryside are corrupted by money, power, and lust in no time. In short,
the 'old Shanghai' is a city of fin-de-siècle splendor."[18] Ng sees in this
popular image of old Shanghai an obvious analogy to Hong Kong: "The
lost prosperity of Shanghai easily becomes a parable for the predetermined course of [Hong Kong's] history, especially in light of the fact that
Hong Kong has superseded Shanghai in its economic development over
the last century and replaced Shanghai as the major international city
and gateway to the world."[19] In other words, the "fin-de-siècle splendor"
signifies Hong Kong's "predetermined" reversion to China in 1997; it is,
in the words of the local poet Leung Ping-kwan, a "city at the end of
time."[20] Ng also remarks that if, as the Hong Kong scholar Ackbar Abbas
observes, "until a decade ago all stories about Hong Kong tended to turn
into stories about somewhere else," then "ironically by the same token
stories about other places (such as Shanghai) within the Hong Kong
mass media are inclined to be parables about Hong Kong."[21]

One indeed finds what Ng calls a "back-to-the-future syndrome" in
present-day Hong Kong. The juxtaposition of past and future cannot be

better illustrated than by the buildings of the Shanghai and Hong Kong Banking Corporation (designed by Norman Foster, 1986) and the seventy-story Bank of China building (designed by I. M. Pei, 1989), which stand side by side as two architectural emblems of the city. The former's postmodern "high-tech" style, a fitting tribute to the "late capitalist" stage of the firm's long colonial lineage, contrasts with the modern palatial magnificence of the latter, a hegemonic presence which is surely a reminder of China's dominance in Hong Kong's future. But I see a more intricate cultural significance behind this obvious self-absorption—an inscription of Hong Kong's own anxieties onto a Shanghai of the past.

As Hong Kong did for Eileen Chang's Shanghai of the 1940s, it takes an "other" to define the self. Colonial Hong Kong had always been a reminder of the "semi-colonial" anxieties of Shanghai's Chinese residents, especially in view of the increasing traffic in goods, money, tourism, and colonial hobbies such as horse racing.[22] But Eileen Chang and the Shanghai urbanites she described were certainly less appreciative of what Hong Kong could offer compared to what the cultural producers of Hong Kong's mass media have made of Shanghai. In my view, the old Shanghai craze in Hong Kong's mass culture scene is not merely a reflection of Hong Kong's narcissism, its obsession with its own identity. Rather, Shanghai's past glory represents a genuine mystery which cannot be explained by the official master narratives of history and revolution. It is a mystery the people of Hong Kong wish to unravel, and in so doing forge a symbolic link between the two cities that transcends history. This is particularly the case in some of the notable films made about Shanghai in recent years: Tsui Hark's *Shanghai by Night* (Shanghai zhiye) and Stanley Kwan's *Ruan Lingyu* and *Red Rose and White Rose* (Hongmeiguei yu baimeiguei), the last an adaptation of one of Eileen Chang's stories.

Hong Kong Films about Old Shanghai

At first glance, all these films belong to the category of what Fredric Jameson has called "nostalgia film," which as a stylistic manifestation of pastiche and parody seems to "involve imitation or, better still, the mimicry of other styles and particularly of the mannerisms and stylistic twitches of other styles."[23] Tsui Hark's *Shanghai by Night* consciously imitates the film *Shizi jietou* (Crossroads, 1937), especially its comic plot turns involving the hero and heroine in the narrow interior space of a small room with a partitioning curtain. But this "reinvention of the feel and shape of characteristic objects of an older period" does not necessarily "reawaken a sense of the past associated with those objects."[24] For Tsui Hark's film, Shanghai is no more than a prop or set, made all the more artificial by the primitive conditions in which the sets were constructed. But it is this very artificiality that Tsui seizes as a way to reflect on a symbolic link between the two cities through a kind of semiotic self-reflexivity. In one scene we see a gigantic billboard advertising a movie about Shanghai against which the hero and heroine run for shelter during an air raid. It seems as if Tsui has purposely jettisoned the film's diegetic realism in order to lay bare the purposeful flatness of its filmmaking. Above all the scene accelerates the film's rhythm to such excess that there are hardly any melodramatic or sentimental elements left from the earlier film; what we see instead is an exhilarating comedy of errors enacted on a barely believable "stage."

Thus, the Hong Kong film is a parody in both style and content, and as such it keeps the viewer at an ironic distance from the reality depicted in the film: the more the characters cry, the more we laugh. In one sense we could say that Tsui Hark's film spoofs Shanghai's leftist film tradition by imitating not its ideologically correct or emotionally meaningful content but the primitive conditions of its filmmaking. What was once hailed as realistic art now looks unbearably comic as a commercial commodity. But this stylistic reading cannot explain the film's popularity and that of the television series based partially on it. For whatever reason, once Shanghai is invoked, even as a stylistic spoof, it seems to trigger some "other" deep response from the Hong Kong audience. Does the film's superficial plot about the outbreak of war in Shanghai elicit an analogous anxiety about Hong Kong's future?

The Hong Kong director Stanley Kwan's nostalgia for Shanghai is already noticeable in his early film *Yanzhi kou* (Rouge), in which a female ghost from an earlier era descends on present-day Hong Kong in search of her former lover. While the scenes of her life as a famous courtesan called Fleur are presumably set in Hong Kong of the 1930s, they could easily serve as a reminder of old Shanghai. Whatever the real identity of the old city, the film presents the intriguing thesis that the allure of a bygone era drenched in decadence can be invoked but not fully recaptured. Fleur's quest for love ends in failure: she does find her former lover, who has become a decrepit old man who works as an extra on a movie lot and is utterly incapable of love. Thus, in one sense the film can be read as a lamentation on love and romance couched in the popular Chinese formula of a ghost story. But I think more is at stake in the film's representation. Its flashback sequences of old Hong Kong are done in a style of lavish opulence with elaborately composed shots, but the film abruptly shifts to a simple, unadorned realistic mode in describing the present.[25] The allure of the female ghost does not seem to stop at the plot level. It is as if a heroine lifted from a story by Eileen Chang and purposely placed in present-day Hong Kong encounters an ordinary Hong Kong couple and begs them for help in finding her former lover so as to complete the meaning of her own past. Nostalgia is certainly involved in her quest. But as the story unfolds in the present, this spirit from the past becomes embroiled in the present. What can the modern Hong Kong couple who lead a normal, everyday life say to the ghost? That her era is gone forever and any romantic quest for love is doomed to failure? Or that the romance of her past still offers meaning to the present? While the couple become increasingly engrossed in the ghost's affairs and help her find her old lover, they realize in the process that they will never be able to match the intensity of her passion, which led her to commit suicide. This sober realization serves to inflame their sexual passion as they make love under the bemused gaze of the ghost. The couple seem to treasure this moment, which can barely approximate what we imagine Fleur once experienced in her previous life. Still, their momentary passion reaffirms not only their mutual attachment but also the value of their shared mystery, for a figure from another era has not only intruded upon their life—a contemporary life that seems to leave no room for the past—but also connected them to an era of their own history. In one scene the journalist protagonist searches the antique shops for relics of this bygone era and finds an old newspaper for sale in which an article about the double suicide of Fleur and her lover is printed. This may seem an ordinary discovery, but to him the object is a revelation because it enables him to seize upon a piece of another reality. Nostalgia in this case has gone beyond pastiche and parody to offer a historical allegory: if the past no longer exists—a common metaphor for a place such as Hong Kong—it must be reinvented in order to make a new connection with the present. Unlike Tsui Hark's *Shanghai by Night*, this film is not a parody of old Shanghai but a tribute and an affirmation. In the guise of popular entertainment, the director's intention is dead serious.

In another film about Ruan Lingyu, the famed Shanghai movie star who committed suicide in 1935, Stanley Kwan adds an ironic dimension to his romantic quest. In a bold act of self-referentiality, Kwan frames his film as the making of a film about Ruan Lingyu. The Hong Kong actress who plays Ruan Lingyu is interviewed several times about her own feelings, while segments of the present film in which she reenacts some of the famous scenes in Ruan Lingyu's films are juxtaposed with real footage from the old movies. The achieved verisimilitude between the original and the imitation serves only to underscore their historical distance. Nostalgia, therefore, means that which can never be attained, and in the process of evocation it inevitably idealizes the past. But the visual medium of the film itself becomes the crucial intermediary which not only re-presents the past (the reenacted scenes) for the present but also brings the past (Ruan Lingyu's old film footage) literally into the present. Like the female ghost in *Rouge*, the "real" Ruan Lingyu, by way of her own films, is allowed to enter the framed reality of the present film by Stanley Kwan. Her haunting presence thus becomes a reminder not only of Kwan's own indebtedness to the films made in Shanghai but also of the haunting mystery of Shanghai itself that continues to hold Hong Kong audiences spellbound. Naturally Kwan shot most of his film on site in present-day Shanghai, as he did with his next film, *Red Rose and White Rose.* Having brought his crew to Shanghai, however, Kwan ended up using very few shots of real sites, as if the present reality no longer held any attraction. The old Shanghai allure is gone and must be re-created by the magic of filmmaking itself. Most of the action takes place indoors, and the interior scenes—particularly those in the dance hall—are re-created with an authentic atmosphere complete with Art Deco designs and intimate lighting. Kwan must have read Eileen Chang's essays about Shanghai apartment living, too, since the film constantly makes reference to the sound of tram cars.

As a film *Red Rose and White Rose* is not entirely successful. It may be that Kwan remained too faithful to Chang's story, which concerns the love affairs of a rather selfish man with two women. Chang's narration is filled with her sardonic commentary, and Kwan reproduces some of the lines faithfully on the screen like the written titles in a silent film. Obviously, the film's narrative mimics the short story—an attempt that fails because the story relies so heavily on the characters' psychological interaction, which the film cannot replicate. Moreover, the actor who plays Zhenbao, the male protagonist, has too much of the easygoing manner of a young man from present-day Hong Kong or Taiwan to fit Eileen Chang's 1930s Shanghai cosmopolitan with a conservative, male-chauvinist bent. The same charge of failed characterization may be leveled at Ann Hui's film adaptation of "Love in a Fallen City," in which Fan Liuyuan is played by the well-known Hong Kong actor Chow Yuen-fat, and the acting of the female lead seems forced, lacking the air of elegance and make-believe sophistication that we find in the fictional Bai Liusu. This superficial comparison of film and fiction leads us to the obvious conclusion that "old Shanghai" is lost forever and cannot be reproduced by whatever means.

This realization is not due to any material inadequacy: in terms of population and physical scale, Hong Kong has far surpassed the Shanghai of the 1930s. What has been lost is rather a cultural and aesthetic sensibility that Eileen Chang so naturally embodies and so vividly represents in her fiction. That sensibility, analyzed earlier, is first of all derived from various physical details: the Art Deco arch over a bandstand in a dance hall, the smell of coffee and sweets at Café Renaissance, the vendors' voices in a narrow alley, the bells of tram and trolley cars. These and many other details are the stuff that made Shanghai so endearing to Eileen Chang. As we saw in Chapter 8, to do justice to her city Chang evolved a prose style with which she managed to recapture its sights and sounds. It might seem that the visual medium of film is even more appropriate for such a purpose, and Stanley Kwan tries valiantly to (re)construct a few filmed images of such details. But he has at most given us an incentive to imagine what living in Shanghai might have been like. In my view Kwan's failure reveals the earnestness of his effort to reconnect with Shanghai: following Eileen Chang, he has created an allegorical romance of a "tale of two cities," like Marguerite Duras's *Hiroshima Mon Amour* without its sexual mystique but more in the spirit of a cultural and historical *hommage*.

Our sense of loss is exacerbated if we compare Kwan's serious attempt with the utter insensitivity to nuance and detail in a lavishly made film, *Shanghai Triad* (Yaoyaoyao yaodao waipoqiao), by Zhang Yimou, an otherwise talented director whose rural upbringing, in my view, renders him incapable of dealing with an urban cosmopolitan subject such as old Shanghai. As if aware of his project's inadequacy, Zhang had to insert a long but unrelated rural sequence in order to revitalize his "urban" narrative. The film's cabaret scenes, staged in a pseudo-spectacular style, do not even qualify as a poor imitation of a Hollywood musical. From an old Shanghailander's point of view (as Eileen Chang surely would have remarked), it must be said that half a century of revolution has indeed destroyed in toto China's urban culture, together with its cosmopolitan sensibilities. The only cosmopolitan city that remains outside the revolutionary maelstrom is Hong Kong, and it takes one city to understand another.

Whatever may have been their intentions, Tsui Hark's and Stanley Kwan's obsession with Shanghai must be accounted for in a larger perspective. What Hong Kong and Shanghai have shared in common is not only the historical background of colonialism or semi-colonialism but also an urban cultural sensibility rooted in cosmopolitanism. History has dealt its most ironic coup de grâce by making the cities important once again as cultural and commercial centers after half a century of rural revolution promoting the triumph of the countryside over the cities. As a century of China's search for modernity comes to an end, the specters that hang over the not so distant horizon are cities such as Shanghai and Hong Kong.

A Shanghai Revival

Despite his pessimism about the prospects for cosmopolitanism, Joseph Levenson nevertheless afforded himself a glimmer of optimism when he wrote these comments in 1966:

> The provincialism of the culture of the Cultural Revolutionaries is a mark of loneliness, too, a cutting off from their past and the contemporary world around them. They try to speak to the world, as our men of the foreign theater tried to speak. Some people are listening. Maybe some peoples are listening. One way or another (the choice of ways is fearful), China will join the world again on the cosmopolitan tide. Cultural intermediaries, Cultural Revolutionaries—neither will look like stranded minnows or stranded whales forever.[26]

He would have been heartened to know that China has indeed joined the world again "on the cosmopolitan tide" of transnational market capitalism. Some people are indeed listening. Since the late 1980s, thanks to investors from Hong Kong and other countries, Shanghai has been undergoing an exhilarating urban reconstruction—so much so that the new skyline in the Pudong area bears a remarkable resemblance to that of Hong Kong. Meanwhile, some of the old colonial companies that once occupied the buildings on the Bund, such as Jardine, Matheson & Co., have rented back their old dwellings from the Communist Party bureaucracies. A new Paramount hotel and ballroom has been built, reportedly with design advice from Hong Kong architects. All of this construction has spurred a massive research project on Shanghai's history and culture under the sponsorship of the Shanghai Academy of Social Sciences (with publications which have in turn facilitated the writing of this book). And a new generation of young Shanghai writers and poets have begun to explore in their fiction and poetry what they call a new "urban consciousness" (dushi yishi)—a subject of which they had known practically nothing. A journal called *Shanghai Culture* (Shanghai wenhua) was launched in 1993. In its prefatory statement to its readers, it reaffirms the "deep and solid foundation of the school of Shanghai culture, with its splendid tradition of assimilating outside cultures with an open mind." Included in this inaugural issue is an essay titled "Reconstructing Shanghai's Urban Image," a scholarly article on the cultural consumption of books in old Shanghai, and an interview with Shi Zhecun, in which Shi is said to have completed a three-volume compendium of his past translations, which will come to several million Chinese characters.[27]

Perhaps the most surprising phenomenon is the rediscovery of Eileen Chang: in the memorial articles written shortly after her death, young scholars and writers on the mainland openly shared their sense of wonder and admiration with their colleagues in Taiwan, Hong Kong, and abroad. The prolific young writer Su Tong, now internationally known, was among the group of writers who raved about Chang's fiction. In his own novels Su has attempted to reinvent a world of the prerevolutionary era that has all the decadent veneer of an Eileen Chang story, but without her urban—and urbane—sophistication. The recurring images of decay, squalor, and death in his fictional world seem to accentuate a lacerating sense of sordid provincialism that, by contrast, makes Chang's fabled Shanghai even more remote and unreal in the imagination of this postrevolutionary generation.

Now that Shanghai is not only reborn from the ashes of a century of war and revolution but also seized with nostalgia for its own glorious past of the 1930s (as evidenced by the sudden mushrooming popularity of old photos and other memorabilia), what would Chang have to say to these ironies of history in which the fortunes of her city have been subjected to such unexpected reversals? How would she react if she were to see this urban spectacle of a new Shanghai that looks like the reflection of a reflection—a modern or postmodern replica of a Hong Kong that has for so long modeled itself after old Shanghai? How would she respond to my own interpretive reconstruction in this "tale of two cities" which is itself inspired by her work? In an essay titled "China Day and Night" (Zhongguo de riye), she describes a typical Shanghai street scene which includes a Daoist priest begging. The sight of this anachronistic figure leads Chang to muse:

> Time, like space, has its expensive sections and also large patches
> of barrenness . . . Now this Daoist priest carries some worthless
> surplus of time and comes to this high-speed metropolis where
> he is surrounded by the hurly-burly swelter of advertising bill-
> boards, shops, and automobiles blowing their horns. He is like
> someone from an ancient romance who wakes up from a dream,
> except that he merely wakes up from a deep sleep with no
> dreams—and feels even more at a loss.[28]

If she were to return to the new metropolis of Shanghai in post-socialist China half a century later, she would surely assume the reincarnated role of that Daoist priest.

NOTES

1. Remapping Shanghai

1. Mao Dun, *Midnight*, trans. Sidney Schapiro, 2nd ed. (Beijing: Foreign Languages Press, 1979), 1.

2. H. J. Lethbridge, introduction to *All about Shanghi: A Standard Guidebook* (Hong Kong: Oxford University Press, 1983), x; the original edition was published by Oxford University Press in 1934–35.

3. An old version of the dictionary was also translated and published in Shanghai around this time by the Commercial Press. A representative account of the Shanghai legend for Western tourists can be found in the following: "In the twenties and thirties Shanghai became a legend. No world cruise was complete without a stop in the city. Its name evoked mystery, adventure and licence of every form. In ships sailing to the Far East, residents enthralled passengers with stories of the 'Whore of the Orient.' They described Chinese gangsters, nightclubs that never closed and hotels which supplied heroin on room service. They talked familiarly of warlords, spy rings, international arms dealers and the peculiar delights on offer in Shanghai's brothels. Long before landing, wives dreamed of the fabulous shops; husbands of half an hour in the exquisite grip of a Eurasian girl." Harriet Sargeant, *Shanghai* (London: Jonathan Cape, 1991), 3.

4. Mao Dun, *Ziye* (Hong Kong: Nanguo Reprint, 1973), 1–66; Mao Dun, *Midnight*, 34.

5. In a response to a magazine's request to envision the future of Shanghai, Mao Dun stated in 1934 that he was quite optimistic that with all the goods and rich consumers flocking to the city, "Shanghai will become the number one metropolis in the world, a metropolis specially for consumption." See *Xin Zhonghua* fankan (New China magazine supplement), ed., *Shanghai de jianglai* [The future of Shanghai] (Shanghai: Zhonghua shuju, 1934), 23–24. All translations are my own unless otherwise attributed.

6. Betty Peh-t'i Wei, *Old Shanghai* (Hong Kong: Oxford University Press, 1993), 31. For a description of Westerners in Shanghai, see Nicholas R. Clifford, *Spoilt Children of Empire: Westerners in Shanghai and the Chinese Revolution of the 1920s* (Hanover, N.H.: Middlebury College Press, published by University Press of New England, 1991), esp. chaps. 3–4.

7. For studies of the histories of the concessions, see *Shanghai shi ziliao congkan*, reprint, *Shanghai gonggong zujie shigao* [History of Shanghai's International Settlement] (Shanghai: Shanghai renmin chubanshe, 1980); Louis des Courtils, *La Concession française de Changhai* (Paris: Librairie du Recueil Sirey, 1934); Ch. B.-Maybon and Jean Fredet, *Histoire de la Concession française de Changhai* (Paris: Librairie Plon, 1929).

8. Tang Zhenchang, "Shimin yishi yu Shanghai shehui" [Bourgeois consciousness and Shanghai society], *Ershiyi shiji* [Twenty-first century, Hong Kong] 1 (June 1992): 12.

9. Ibid., 13. See also, Tang Zhenchang, ed., *Jindai Shanghai fanhua lu* [The splendor of modern Shanghai] (Hong Kong: Shangwu yinshu guan, 1993), 240. The first automobile was imported by a Hungarian named Lainz.

10. There is extensive scholarly literature in Chinese on Shanghai's political, social, and economic history. Two authoritative volumes are Tang Zhenchang, ed., *Shanghai shi* [History of Shanghai] (Shanghai: Shanghai renmin chubanshe, 1989), and Zhang Zhongli ed., *Jindai Shanghai chengshi yanjiu* [A study of the modern city of Shanghai] (Shanghai: Shanghai remnmin chubanshe, 1990). For a discussion of Western scholarship, see Wen-hsin Yeh, "Shanghai Modernity: Commerce and Culture in a Republican City" (unpublished paper). I am most grateful to the author for her criticism and advice in my writing of this chapter. Another useful guide is the collection of scholarly papers edited by Frederic Wakeman, Jr., and Wen-hsin Yeh, *Shanghai Sojourners* (Berkeley: Institute of East Asian Studies, University of California, Berkeley, 1992). The topics studied range from Shanghai's bankers' associations, markets, and native-place organizations to student protests, prostitution reform, Subei migrants, the Green Gang, and silk-weavers' strikes. Only Yeh's paper, on "progressive journalism and Shanghai's petty urbanites," bears on my focal interest in the culural dimension. A number of essays in an earlier volume, *The Chinese City between Two Worlds*, ed. Mark Elvin and G. William Skinner (Stanford: Stanford University Press, 1974), also deal with Shanghai's socioeconomic institutions but not its cultural artifacts. Another masterly study by Marie-Claire Bergère, *The Golden Age of the Shanghai Bourgeoisie* (Cambridge: Cambridge University Press, 1989), remains useful as a comprehensive economic study. A more

recent book by Christian Henriot, *Shanghai, 1927–1937: Municipal Power, Locality, and Modernization* (Berkeley: University of California Press, 1993), deals with the laws, policies, finances, and political power of Shanghai's municipal government.

11. Tess Johnston, *A Last Look: Western Architecture in Old Shanghai* (Hong Kong: Old China Hand Press, 1993), 9.

12. For a detailed discussion of the issue, see Robert A. Bickers and Jeffrey N. Wasserstrom, "Shanghai's 'Dogs and Chinese Not Admitted' Sign: Legend, History, and Contemporary Symbol, " *China Quarterly* 142 (June 1995): 443–466. In June 1928 public parks were finally open to the Chinese; it was said that "far from taking umbrage, the Shanghai Chinese responded to this new state of affairs with great enthusiasm and in good humour." Wei, *Old Shanghai*, 31.

13. Lethbridge, *All about Shanghai*, 33–34. According to Wakeman, the Chinese population in the International Settlement alone grew from 345,000 to 1,120,000 between 1900 and 1935. See Frederic Wakeman, Jr., "Licensing Leisure: The Chinese Nationalist Regulation of Shanghai, 1927–1949," *Journal of Asian Studies* 54.1 (February, 1995): 22 n. 1.

14. Wei, *Old Shanghai*, 31.

15. The phrase *yangchang* is defined in one Chinese-English dictionary as "metropolis infested with foreign adventurers (usu. referring to preliberation Shanghai)," and the phrase *yangchang e'shao* as "rich young bully in a metropolis (in old China)." See *The Pinyin Chinese-English Dictionary*, ed. Wu Jingron, Beijing Foreign Languages Institute (Beijing: Commercial Press, 1979), 800.

16. These and other buildings on the Bund have been carefully studied by Jon Huebner in his two articles, "Architecture on the Shanghai Bund," *Papers on Far Eastern History* 39 (March 1989): 128–163, and "Architecture and History in Shanghai's Central District," *Journal of Oriental Studies* 26.2 (1988): 209–269.

17. For a comprehensive study of the architectural history, regulations, and firms of Shanghai, see Lai Delin, "Cong Shanghai gonggong zujie kan Zhongguo jindai jianzhu zhidu" [The institutions of modern Chinese architecture as seen from Shanghai's International Settlement], *Kongjian* [Space magazine], nos. 41–43 (January–March 1993).

18. Huebner, "Architecture on the Shanghai Bund," 140.

19. Johnston, *A Last Look*, 53.

20. "There is also the belief (unverified) among the Chinese that gold was accidentally used in the casting of the figures." *All about Shanghai*, 46.

21. Quoted in Huebner, "Architecture on the Shanghai Bund," 138. See also

Yang Bingde, ed., *Zhongguo jindai chengshi yu jianzhu* [Modern Chinese cities and architecture] (Beijing: Zhongguo jianzhu gongyi chubanshe, 1993), 54.

22. Johnston, *A Last Look,* 53.

23. Thomas R. Metcalf, *An Imperial Vision: Indian Architecture and Britain's Raj* (Berkeley: University of California Press, 1989), 177–178.

24. A crucial book on Shanghai architecture is Muramatsu Shin, *Shanhai tōshi to kenchiku, 1842–1949 nen* [The metropolitan architecture of Shanghai 1842–1849] (Tokyo: Parco, 1991), esp. chap. 3 on skyscrapers.

25. Hudec was born in 1893 in Czechoslavakia, graduated in 1914 from the Royal University of Budapest, and was elected to the Royal Institute of Hungarian Architects in 1916. He arrived in Shanghai in 1918, joined the firm of R. A. Curry, an American architect, and later opened his own firm. See Johnston, *A Last Look,* 86. See also *Men of Shanghai and North China* (Shanghai: University Press, 1935), 269. The Park Hotel was twenty-two stories high, with an additional two-story basement, totaling eighty-two meters in height. It remained the tallest building in East Asia for some thirty years. Modeled after the American skyscraper, the building was one of Hudec's prized designs, his having won the commission in open bidding over two other firms. The actual construction, as with most new buildings, was done by Chinese companies. It took three years (1931–1934) to complete. See *Jindai Shanghai jianzhu shihua* [Historical accounts of modern Shanghai architecture] (Shanghai: Shanghai wenhua chubanshe, 1991), 91–99.

26. Johnston, *A Last Look,* 86; "Wudake jiangzhushi xiaozhuan" [Brief biography of Hudec the architect], *Jianzhu zazhi* (Architecture magazine) 1.5 (May 1933): 13.

27. Johnston, *A Last Look,* 70; see also the photographs of the theaters, 88–89. Photos of the renovated Grand Theater and the Majestic Theater can also be found in Chen Congzhou and Zhang Ming, eds., *Shanghai jindai jianzhu shigao* [Draft history of modern Shanghai architecture] (Shanghai: Sanlien, 1988), 207–209.

28. For New York skyscraper architecture and Art Deco, see Robert Stern et al., *New York, 1930: Architecture and Urbanism between the Two World Wars* (New York: Rizzoli, 1987); Cervin Robinson and Rosemarie Bletter, *Skyscraper Style: Art Deco New York* (New York: Oxford University Press, 1975); Don Vlack, *Art Deco Architecture in New York, 1920–1940* (New York: Harper & Row, 1974); and Robert Messler, *The Art Deco Skyscraper in New York* (New York: Peter Lang, 1986). Despite Jeffrey Wasserstrom's ingenious essay, "Comparing the 'Incomparable' Cities: Postmodern Los Angeles and Old Shanghai," *Contentions: Debates in Society, Culture, and Science* 5.3 (1996), I still prefer

the comparison with New York, in view of the cultural significance of the skyscraper for a discourse on Chinese modernity, over any postmodern comparisons that can be made.

29. See, for example, the musical *Broadway Melody* (1938) with Eleanor Powell and the comedy *The Magnificent Flirt* (1928), in which Loretta Young "bedded down in Art Deco comfort." Richard Striner, *Art Deco* (New York: Abbeville Press, 1994), 9, 72. At the same time, the Art Deco style was meant to evoke the fantasy and charm of the movies rather than real life. See Robinson and Bletter, *Skyscraper Style*, 40.

30. Patricia Bayer, *Art Deco Architecture: Design, Decoration, and Detail from the Twenties and Thirties* (New York: Harry N. Abrams, 1992), 8. Bayer also refers to the international influence of Art Deco as evidenced in some famous hotels and mansions in Shanghai (85).

31. Ibid., 12.

32. One writer finds that the facilitating factor in Art Deco's own mediational role in Western architecture—"its function as a middle range between conservative and radical design—is especially apparent in municipal and public buildings." See Striner, *Art Deco*, 86. Striner lists the following characteristics of the Art Deco style: "the synthesis of classical symmetry and modernist simplification of form; zigzag terracing and projecting ziggurats on buildings; design symbolism that suggested both the ancient past and the distant future; an ornamental repertoire of simple motifs such as sun-bursts, fountains, and leaping gazelles; the combination of new machine-age materials with far more traditional ones; and, by the early 1930s, the pervasive appearance of curvilinear streamlining" (15). The last feature—curvilinear streamlining—is easily noticeable in Shanghai's cinemas such as the Grand Theater.

33. In Xiao Jianqing, *Manhua Shanghai* [Shanghai in cartoons] (Shanghai: Jingwei shuju, 1936).

34. Zhang Guangyu, "Pai yungchang" [Used for occasion], *Shidai manhua* [Epoch cartoon] (1933?).

35. Xiao Jianqing, *Xianhua Shanghai* [Random talks about Shanghai] (Shanghai: Jingwei shuju, 1936), 2, 8.

36. Ann Douglas, *Terrible Honesty: Mongrel Manhattan in the 1920s* (New York: Farrar, Straus, Giroux, 1995), 434–436.

37. Wang Dingjiu, *Shanghai menjing* [Keys to Shanghai] (Shanghai: Zhongyang shudian, 1932), chapter on "living" (*zhu de menjing*), 11–12.

38. For a vivid description, see Frederic Wakeman, Jr., *Policing Shanghai, 1927–1937* (Berkeley: University of California Press, 1995), 105–106.

39. David Au, "Shanghai Department Stores Have Unique History of Their Founding," *China Weekly Review* 12 (November 17, 1934): 41.

40. Ibid., 42, 69.

41. *Jindai Shanghai jianzhu shihua*, 82.

42. Ibid., 84. For another account of the Wing On department store, see Yang Jiayou, "Baihuo jupi Yong'an" [The giant department store Wing On], in Ye Shuping et al., *Bainian Shanghaitan* [One hundred years of Shanghai Bund] (Shanghai: Shanghai huabao chubanshe, 1990), 54–56.

43. Lethbridge, *All about Shanghai*, 31.

44. *Jindai Shanghai jianzhu shihua*, 86.

45. Clifford, *Spoilt Children of Empire*, 61.

46. Reverend C. E. Darwent, *Shanghai: A Handbook for Travellers and Residents* (1920; rpt. Taipei: Ch'eng Wen Publishing Company, 1973), 10–12.

47. Ibid., 14.

48. Ibid.

49. In a special "automobile edition" of *Shen Bao* (August 1923), we find photos of cars such as the British Steyr and Austin, and three models of American Ford cars—Hudson, Essex, and the Ford itself, advertised as the cheapest car in which one could "drive all over the world," a slogan that is still being used to sell Fords in Taiwan.

50. Tang Weikang and Du Like, eds., *Zujie yibainian* [One hunded years of the treaty concessions] (Shanghai: Shanghai huabao chubanshe, 1991), 128.

51. Darwent, *Shanghai: A Handbook for Travellers and Residents*, 77.

52. Zhongguo tushu bianyi guan, ed., *Shanghai chunqiu* [Shanghai annals], 2 vols. (Hong Kong: Nantian shuye gongsi, 1968), 2:88.

53. Quoted in Heinrich Fruehauf, "Urban Exoticism in Modern and Contemporary Chinese Literature," in *From May Fourth to June Fourth: Fiction and Film in Twentieth-Century China*, ed. Ellen Widmer and David Der-wei Wang (Cambridge, Mass.: Harvard University Press, 1993), 144. For this section of the chapter, which is entirely based on Fruehauf's article, I am obviously indebted to his pioneering research. Heinrich Fruehauf completed his doctoral dissertation on the same subject at the University of Chicago in 1992 under my supervision.

54. Quoted ibid., 145.

55. Ibid., 141.

56. Zhang Ruogu, "Cha, kafei, maijiu" [Tea, coffee, ale], *Furen huabao* [Women's pictorial] (1935): 9–11.

57. Zhang Ruogu, "Xiandai duhui shenghuo xiangzeng" [The symbol of modern urban life], in *Kafei zuotan* [Café forum] (Shanghai: Zhenmeishan shudian, 1929), 3–8.

58. Zhang Ruogu, introduction to *Kafei zuotan*, 6.

59. Zhang Ruogu, "Xiandai duhui shenghuo xiangzeng," 4–11.

60. The coffeehouse was, of course, very popular in Taishō Japan, being

"among the symbols of Taisho high life," according to Edward Seiden-sticker, who writes that the café was "the forerunner of the expensive Ginza bar. Elegant and alluring female company came with the price of one's coffee, or whatever. The Plantain was the first of them, founded in 1911." See Edward Seidensticker, *Low City, High City: Tokyo from Edo to the Earthquake* (Cambridge, Mass.: Harvard University Press, 1991), 104, 201.

61. Ibid., 8.

62. Personal letter from Xu Chi, February 26, 1986.

63. Zhang Ruogu, "E'shang fuxing guan" [The Russian business Café Renais-sance], in *Zhanzheng, yinshi, nannü* [War, drink, food, and sex] (Shanghai: Liangyou chubanshe, 1933), 143, 146.

64. Zhang Ruogu, *Kafei zuotan*, 24, 74.

65. Wakeman, *Policing Shanghai*, 108.

66. The legendary Paramount Ballroom is immortalized in modern Chinese literature in a story by Pai Hsien-yung, "Jindaban de zuihou yiye" (The last night of Taipan Chin), in which the protagonist, an aging dance hostess from Shanghai, finds herself in a cheap dance palace in Taipei: "What a cheap creep! Nuits de Paris, Nuits de Paris indeed! It may not sound polite, but even the john at the Paramount must have taken up more room than the Nuits de Paris dance floor!" See Pai Hsien-yung, *Wandering in the Garden, Waking from a Dream: Tales of Taipei Characters*, trans. Pai Hsien-yung and Patia Yasin, ed. George Kao (Bloomington: Indiana University Press, 1982), 51.

67. Tu Shimin, *Shanghai shi daguan* [Panorama of Shanghai], 56. This source also indicates that in 1946, when dance hostesses were required to register with the city police, there was a total of 3,300 of them in the city (57).

68. Wakeman, "Licensing Leisure," 27; see also his *Policing Shanghai*, 108. Wakeman calculates that "toward the end of the 1930s Shanghai would have 2,500 to 5,000 taxi dancers, more than 60 percent of whom were believed to be practicing prostitutes" (*Policing Shanghai*, 108.)

69. Yu Muxia, *Shanghai linzhao* [Shanghai tidbits] (Shanghai: Hubao chubanbu, 1935), 37–38.

70. Maurine Karns and Pat Patterson, *Shanghai: High Lights, Low Lights, Tael Lights* (Shanghai: Tridon Press, n.d.), 27–29.

71. Ding Baigao, "Hua xiao wuchang" [Talking about small dance halls], *Xian-dai manhua* [Modern cartoons] 2 (February 1934). The piece is accompa-nied by two small cartoons by the famous artist Ye Qianyu.

72. Piaopo Wang [King of wanderers], "Wuqiong de xiwang" [Endless hope], *Shidai manhua* 9 (September 1934).

73. "Modeng tiaojian" [Conditions of being modern], *Shidai manhua* 2 (Febru-ary 1934).

74. Mu Shiying, "Luoto, Nicaizhuyizhe yu nüren" [Camel, Nietzscheist, and woman], in *Xin ganjue pai xiaoshuo xuan* [Selected stories from the neo-sensationalist school], ed. Li Ou-fan (Taipei: Yunchen wenhua, 1988), 191–197.

75. Pan Ling, *In Search of Old Shanghai* (Hong Kong: Joint Publishing Co., 1982), 36; Wu Guifang, *Songgu mantan* [Random talks on old legends about Shanghai] (Shanghai: Shanghai renmin chubanshe, 1991), 193; see also Bickers and Wasserstrom, "Shanghai's 'Dogs and Chinese Not Admitted' Sign," 446.

76. Betty Peh-T'i Wei, *Shanghai: Crucible of Modern China* (Hong Kong: Oxford University Press, 1987), 231–232.

77. Ibid., 232.

78. See, for instance, the popular guide complied by the Commercial Press, *Shanghai zhinan* [Guide to Shanghai] (Shanghai: Shangwu yinshuguan, 1926), chuan 5:17–21.

79. Mao Dun, *Midnight*, 239.

80. *Shanghai zhinan*, 16.

81. Austin Coates, *China Races* (Hong Kong: Oxford University Press, 1983), 26.

82. Ibid., 34.

83. Ibid., 121.

84. Ma Xuexin et al., *Shanghai wenhua yuanliu cidian* [Dictionary of Shanghai's cultural sources] (Shanghai: Shanghai shehuikexueyuan chubanshe, 1992), 50; Wakeman, *Policing Shanghai*, 99.

85. Yomi Breaster, "Shanghai's Economy of the Spectacle: The Shanghai Race Club in Liu Na'ou's and Mu Shiying's Stories," *Modern Chinese Literature* 9.1 (Spring 1995): 41–42. According to another Chinese source it was four stories high, but the tower was ten stories high; see Ma Xuexin et al., *Shanghai wenhua yuanliu cidian*, 639.

86. Wakeman, *Policing Shanghai*, 98; Braester, "Shanghai's Economy of the Spectacle," 41.

87. Braester, "Shanghai's Economy of the Spectacle," 42.

88. Ibid., 49.

89. Harold Isaacs, *Re-encounters in China: Notes from a Journey in a Time Capsule* (Armonk, N.Y.: M. E. Sharpe, 1985), 7.

90. In the other treaty ports such as Tientsin and Wuhan, the concessions were smaller in size, though Tientsin had more Western concessions and thus offers a different case for further research and comparison.

91. Weijen Wang, "The Transformation of the City Fabric of Shanghai in the 1980s" (unpublished paper).

92. Ma Xuexin et al., *Shanghai wenhua yuanliu cidian*, 513.

93. Luo Qingwen, *Shikumen: xunchang renjia* [Stone-gate houses: ordinary living] (Shanghai: Shanghai renmin chubanshe, 1991), 59–59. This is part of a five-volume series, "Da Shanghai" (Great Shanghai), edited by Yao Bingnan et al.

94. For a study of the writers and their lifestyle in the "pavilion rooms," see Zhang Qing, *Tingzijian: yiqun wenhua ren he tamen de shiye* [The pavilion room: a group of men of culture and their careers] (Shanghai: Shanghai renmin chubanshe, 1991). This is also part of the "Great Shanghai" series.

95. Ibid., 5.

96. Ibid., 3.

97. Ye Lingfeng, *Dushu suibi*, [Random notes on reading], 3 vols. (Beijing: Sanlian, 1988), 1:115.

98. Most Westerners' accounts do not give us much detail about the everyday lives of Chinese writers (and for that matter most Chinese residents) because even if they knew them, their social activities were conducted mostly in public places such as restaurants. On the few occasions when a Westerner did go to a Chinese writer's home, such as when Harold Isaacs visited Lu Xun at his, the episode seems to have been easily forgotten. Isaacs claims that "that was a time of many comings and goings and perhaps it is reasonable of me not to have remembered this [visit]" ("Re-encounters in China," 115). The only Westerner who has written about her Chinese friends' living quarters in some detail is Emily Hahn, who was in fact Shao Xunmei's mistress (see Chapter 7). Of course, the same can be said about Chinese writers' lack of any detailed knowledge of the lives of Shanghai's foreigners; again their depictions are likewise limited to public places.

99. Walter Benjamin, *Charles Baudelaire: A Lyric Poet in the Era of High Capitalism*, trans. Harry Zorn (London: Verso, 1983), 170.

100. Ibid.

101. Ross King, *Emancipating Space: Geography, Architecture, and Urban Design* (New York: Guilford Press, 1996), 38.

102. See Paul Rabinow, *French Modern: Norms and Forms of the Social Environment* (Cambridge, Mass.: MIT Press, 1989).

103. Ye Lingfeng, "Luoyen" [Fallen wild goose], in *Lingfeng xiaoshuo ji* [Stories of Linfeng] (Shanghai: Xiandai shuju, 1931), 32–33.

104. See Susan Buck-Morss, *The Dialectics of Seeing: Walter Benjamin and the Arcades Project* (Cambridge, Mass.: MIT Press, 1991).

105. Benjamin, *Charles Baudelaire*, 36–37.

106. Ibid., 54.

107. Bruce Mazlich, "The *Flâneur*: from Spectator to Representation," in *The Flâneur*, ed. Keith Tester (London: Routledge, 1994), 49.

108. Wakeman described *yeji* as "streetwalkers who wore gaudy clothes and were thought to go here and there like wild birds" (*Policing Shanghai*, 112).

109. Michel de Certeau, *The Practice of Everyday Life*, trans. Steven Randall (Berkeley: University of California Press, 1988), 97–98.

110. For a brief discussion, see my book *The Romantic Generation of Modern Chinese Writers* (Cambridge, Mass.: Harvard University Press, 1973), 280–281.

111. Fruehauf, "Urban Exoticism," 144.

112. Ibid., 148.

113. Recent scholars in the West have also pointed out that even "in Benjamin's carefully compiled notes on the *flâneur* there are very few references to a living person who may be seen as a personification of the myth or one of its sources"; the *flâneur* should thus be seen as "a mythological ideal-type found more in discourse than in everyday life." See Rob Shields, "Fancy Footwork," in Tester, *The Flâneur*, 65, 67.

114. Zhang singles out the protagonist-narrator of *Feng xiaoxiao* (The blowing wind, 1946), an urban man who plays detective in Japanese-occupied Shanghai and is involved with three women, as a perfect fit to Baudelaire's ideal type, as described in his famous essay "The Painter of Modern Life" (1863). In my view, however, the novel's protagonist is a self-styled intellectual who evinces much narcissism but little cultural bearing or sensibility. Midway through the novel he is suddenly turned into a spy against the Japanese—a rather ridiculous role and posture which has nothing to do with the figure of the urban detective from the fiction of Edgar Allan Poe that both Baudelaire and later Benjamin admired so much. See Yingjin Zhang, *The City in Modern Chinese Literature and Film* (Stanford: Stanford University Press, 1996), 226–228.

115. Lee, *The Romantic Generation of Modern Chinese Writers*, 280–283.

116. Yingjin Zhang, "The Texture of the Metropolis: Modernist Inscriptions of Shanghai in the 1930s," *Modern Chinese Literature* 9.1 (Spring 1995): 19.

117. Ibid., 19–20.

118. Benjamin, *Charles Baudelaire*, 170.

119. Ibid., 304.

2. The Construction of Modernity in Print Culture

1. Leo Ou-fan Lee, "In Search of Modernity: Reflections on a New Mode of Consciousness in Modern Chinese Literature and Thought," in *Ideas across Cultures: Essays in Honor of Benjamin Schwartz*, ed. Paul A. Cohen and Merle Goldman (Cambridge, Mass.: Harvard East Asian Monographs, 1990), 110–111.

2. This term is included in Appendix D, "Return Graphic Loans: Kanji Terms

Derived from Classical Chinese," in Lydia Liu, *Translingual Practice: Literature, National Culture, and Translated Modernity—China, 1900–1937* (Stanford: Stanford University Press, 1996), 308.

3. Benjamin Schwartz, *In Search of Wealth and Power* (Cambridge, Mass.: Harvard University Press, 1964), 238–239.

4. Rengong [Liang Qichao], "Hanman lu" [Record of travel toward the unknown], *Qingyi bao* [Pure discussion news] 35 (1899): 2275–78.

5. Benedict Anderson, *Imagined Communities: Reflections on the Origin and Spread of Nationalism* (New York: Verso, 1983), 30.

6. Ibid., 31–36.

7. Jürgen Habermas, *The Structural Transformation of the Public Sphere*, trans. Thomas Bürger (Cambridge, Mass.: MIT Press, 1989), 40–41, 50–51.

8. But this "community" is not the same as Habermas's "public sphere," as China did not share the same preconditions that prevailed in Europe in the eighteenth century. Thus I differ from the view that there was a Chinese public sphere or civil society. Still, the idea of a reading "public" does open up notions of the "public space" as well as urban space, which may constitute a "semi-public sphere" within the framework of urban society. But even so, some of the standard manifestations Habermas sees in eighteenth-century French salons or English pubs and journals did not occur in China.

9. Homi K. Bhabha, "Dissemination: Time, Narrative, and the Margins of the Modern Nation," in *Nation and Narration*, ed. Homi K. Bhabha (London: Routledge, 1990), 291–322.

10. Robert Darnton, *The Business of Enlightenment: A Publishing History of the "Encyclopédie"* (Cambridge, Mass.: Harvard University Press, 1968).

11. There has already been scholarly treatment in Western languages of both *Dongfang zazhi* and the Commercial Press. Thus I do not go into their background. For a comprehensive study of the press, see Jean-Pierre Drege, *La Commercial Press de Shanghai, 1897–1949* (Paris: Institute des hautes études chinoises, Collège de France, 1978). See also the valuable collection of reminiscences, *Shangwu yinshuguan jiushinian* [Ninety years of the Commercial Press] (Beijing: Shangwu yinshuguan, 1987).

12. Ma Xuexin et al., eds., *Shanghai wenhua yuanliu cidian* [A dictionary of cultural sources in Shanghai] (Shanghai: Shanghai shehui kexueyuan chubanshe, 1992), 199.

13. Jing Cang, "Jinhou zazhi jie zhi zhiwu" [The duty of the magazine world from now on], *Dongfang zazhi* [hereafter *DZ*] 16.7 (July 1919): 3–5.

14. Lu Lu, "Jiqi yu rensheng" [Machines and life], *DZ* 16.10 (October 1916): 47–54.

15. *DZ* 8.1 (March 1911): 38.

16. Apparently English-Chinese dictionaries were in great demand, and the

Commercial Press had to make an all-out effort in order to beat other publishers to the market. Most dictionaries were patchwork assembled from English and Japanese dictionaries. In the case of publishing *Webster's Dictionary*, the Commercial Press had to pay a sizable sum as a result of the lawsuit brought by the original company. See Xie Juzeng, *Shili yangchang de ceying*, [Silhouettes on the Bund] (Guangzhou: Huacheng chubanshe, 1983), 50.

17. Actually Zhu's editorship was in name only; the real editor was a man, Zhu Yunzhang, a member of the press's staff, who nominally consulted her and wrote some articles under her name. See ibid., 38.

18. See "Jiaokeshu zhi fakan gaikuang" [The general situation in the publication of textbooks], in *Zhongguo jindai chuban shiliao chubian* [Historical materials of early modern Chinese publishing, 1st ser.], ed. Zhang Jinglu (Shanghai: Zhonghua shuju, 1957), 220.

19. Ibid, 228. The Japanese connection proved to be a mixed blessing, and the press eventually severed it. This may have been the reason, though undocumented, why the Japanese bombarded and detroyed the press's printing plant and other buildings during an air raid on Janaury 28, 1932.

20. This announcement and the advertisements for the photo and postcards can be found in *DZ* 8.11 (November 1911).

21. Zhang Jinglu, *Zhongguo jindai chuban shiliao chubian*, 243–244.

22. *Zhongguo jiaoyu daxi* [The grand compendium of Chinese education], 5 vols. (Wuhan: Hubei jidoyu chubanshe, 1994), 2:2221–22.

23. Zhang Jinglu, *Zhongguo jindai chuban shiliao chubian*, 242–243.

24. Ibid., 246.

25. Ibid., 221.

26. Wang Yunwu, "Wangyou wenku di yierji yinxing yuanqi" [The background for the publication of the first and second series of the Wanyou wenku], in Zhang Jinglu, *Zhongguo xiandai chuban shiliao yibian* [Historical materials of modern Chinese publishing, 2nd ser.] (Shanghai: Zhonghua shuju, 1954), 290–291. Drege discusses Wang Yunwu's reorganization efforts (*Commercial Press*, 89–94), and lists the periodicals distributed by the Press, as well as *congshu* (collectanea) and dictionaries (185–198) but not textbooks.

27. Wang Yunwu, "Wangyou wenku di yierji yinxing yuanqi," 290–291.

28. Ibid., 293–294.

29. Wang Yunwu, "Wanyou wenku bianyi fanli" (Guidelines for the compilation of *Wanyou wenku*), in *Wangyou wenku diyiji yiqianzhong mulu*, [catalogue of one thousand titles of Wanyou wenku, 1st ser.] (Shanghai: Shangwu, 1929) 2.

30. The relevance was noted by Li Shizeng, a renowned intellectual of the

time, who is reported to have remarked that he admired two historical figures: Ji Xiaolan, the Qing dynasty compiler of the *Siku quanshu*, and Denis Diderot, the French philosophe of the *Encyclopédie*. See Qian Huafo and Zheng Yimei, *Sanshinian lai zhi Shanghai* [Shanghai of the past thirty years] (1946; rpt. Shanghai: Shanghai shudian, 1984), 46–47.

31. *Shanghai wenhua yuanliu cidian*, 379. For an analysis of the making of the *Compendium of New Chinese Literature*, see Liu, *Tranlingual Practice*, 214–238.

32. Huang Kewu, "Cong Shenbao yiyao guanggao kan minchu Shanghai de yiliao wenhua yu shehui shenghuo" [Shanghai's medical culture and social life as seen in Shenbao's medicine advertisements], *Zhongyang yanjiu yuan jindai shi yanjiu suo jikan* [Quarterly journal of the Modern History Institute, Academia Sinica], no. 17 (December, 1988): 141–194.

33. *Liangyou huabao* 6 (July 15, 1926): 18.

34. Ibid., 14 (April 15, 1927); see also Figure 15.

35. Mark Elvin, "Tales of Shen and Xin: Body-Person and Heart-Mind in China during the Last 150 Years," *Zone 4: Fragments for a History of the Human Body*, pt. 2 (1989): 275.

36. Ibid., 277.

37. Ibid, 295.

38. Talk at the Workshop on Chinese Cultural Studies, Fairbank Center, Harvard University, March 9, 1995.

39. Elvin, "Tales of Shen and Xin," 268.

40. See, for instance, Henri Lefebvre, *Everyday Life in the Modern World*, trans. Sacha Rabinovitch (London: Transaction Publishers, 1990). But Lefebvre's interpretive scheme is too contemporary and Western to be relevant to the Chinese materials treated in this book.

41. *Liangyou huabao* 85 (1934): 14–15.

42. Ibid. 103 (1935): 34–35. My student Ezra Block wrote a senior thesis at Harvard (June 1996) on the journal: "Modeling Modernity: The *Liangyou huabao* in the 1930s."

43. Zhang Yanfeng, *Lao yuefenpai guanggao hua* [Advertising paintings in old calendars] (Taipei: Hansheng zazhi, 1994), 1:65.

44. Cai Zhenghua and Fan Zhenjia, "Yuefenpai" [Calendars], in *Bainian Shanghai tan* [One hundred years of Shanghai port], ed. Ye Shuping and Zheng Zu'an (Shanghai: Shanghai huabao chubanshe, 1990), 120–122.

45. This was a gift from William Tay, who purchased it in Hong Kong. A photo reproduction is included in Zhang Yanfeng, *Lao yuefenpai guanggao hua*, 1:18. Apparently a widespread nostalgia for these old artifacts is sweeping Hong Kong, Taiwan, and mainland China.

46. Ibid., 1:10.

47. Ibid., 1:42.

48. Francesca Dal Lago has written a master's thesis on the subject. Contrary to my sedate and conservative reading, she argues that the central figure in the poster is the "New Woman" who looks morally loose; hence the figure is associated with concubines or high-class prostitutes. See her paper, "Modern Looking and Looking Modern: 'Modern Woman' as Commodity in 1930s Shanghai Calendar Posters," delivered at the symposium "Visual Cultures and Modernities in China and Japan," Institute of Fine Arts, New York University, October 26, 1996.

49. Anderson, *Imagined Communities*, 30.

50. As advertised in *Liangyou huabao* 87 (April 1934) for the second edition. Its first printing of three thousand copies quickly sold out.

3. The Urban Milieu of Shanghai Cinema

1. C. J. North, *The Chinese Motion Picture Market*, Trade Information Bulletin no. 467, U.S. Department of Commerce, Bureau of Foreign and Domestic Commerce (1927), 13–14.

2. Ibid., 15.

3. *Motion Pictures in China*, Trade Information Bulletin no. 722, U.S. Department of Commerce (Washington, D.C.: U.S. Government Printing Office, 1930), 7.

4. An article in the *Shanghai Evening Post and Mercury* touting "the new gadget at the Grand" ran under the headline "'Sino-phone' Great Boon to Native Movie Fans" (November 18, 1939, sec. 3, 1).

5. Ye Shuping and Zheng Zu'an, eds., *Bainian Shanghai tan* [One hundred years of Shanghai Port] (Shanghai: Shanghai huabao chubanshe, 1990), 119. See also Cao Yongfu, "Shanghai Daguangming dianying yuan gaikuang" [General account of Shanghai's Grand movie theater], *Shanghai dianying shiliao* [Shanghai film historical materials] (Shanghai: Shanghai shi dianyingju shizhi bangongshi) 1 (October 1992): 207–211.

6. Du Yunzhi, *Zhongguo dianying shi* [History of Chinese cinema] (Taipei: Shangwu yinshuguan, 1972), 1:17–24.

7. Shanghai yanjiu zhongxin, ed., *Shanghai qibainian* [Seven hundred years of Shanghai] (Shanghai: Shanghai renmin chubanshe, 1991), 360.

8. Betty Pei-t'i Wei, *Old Shanghai* (Hong Kong: Oxford University Press, 993), 31.

9. See "Shanghai dianying yuan de fazhan" [The development of Shanghai movie theaters], in *Shanghai yanjiu ziliao xuji* [Research materials on Shanghai, sequel collection], ed. Shanghaitong she (Shanghai: Zhonghua shuju, 1939), 532. The article also gives a detailed list of some fifty theaters and eleven open-air cinemas (541–551), plus discussion of the architecture and

equipment of three leading theaters: the Nanking, the Grand, and the Metropole (553–554).

10. Yang Cun, *Zhongguo dianying sanshinian* [Thirty years of Chinese cinema] (Hong Kong: Shijie chubanshe, 1954), 168. According to Yang, the decline was caused by the Japanese bombing of Shanghai in January 1932. He lists a total of some forty movie theaters in Shanghai: eight in the Chinese city, twenty-four in the International Settlement, and twelve in the French Concession, not including the movie theaters inside amusement halls.

11. For instance, a "combine" of six companies controlled the Zhongyang chain of five theaters in Shanghai (Zhongyang, Enpeiya or Empire, Huguang, Xingguang, and Jincheng) and built new movie theaters in other cities. (ibid., 21). A one-page ad for these theaters can be found in issue 2 (1940) of the magazine *Xinhua huabao* (New China pictorial).

12. In the 1932–1934 period, Lianhua produced twenty-five films, Mingxing nineteen, Tianyi twenty-one, and Yihua ten; see Yang Cun, *Zhongguo dianying sanshinian*, 169.

13. Zhang Wei, Ying Xian, and Chen Jing, "Zhongguo xiandai dianying chubanwu zongmu tiyao" [A concise listing of modern Chinese film publications], *Shanghai dianying shiliao* 1 (October 1992): 212–234; 2/3 (May 1993): 289–344.

14. Yang Cun, *Zhongguo dianying sanshinian*, 9, 24.

15. Wang Dingjiu, *Shanghai menjing* [Keys to Shanghai] (Shanghai: Zhongyang shudian, 1932), 14.

16. Ibid., chapter titled "Seeing" [Kan de menjing], 20.

17. Ibid., 15–22.

18. I have obtained a bilingual plot sheet for the film *The Perfect Marriage* (starring Loretta Young and David Niven) from the Cathay Theater. The front side advertises the film in English and Chinese. On the back side, the English and Chinese versions of the plot are printed side by side, but the contents are not identical. At both top and bottom are ads for cigarettes (Million), cognac (Joseph Guy), and cotton and brocade fabrics. Another plot sheet for the film *Random Harvest* (starring Ronald Colman and Greer Garson) gives only the Chinese version, but the summary is quite detailed and written in an elegant style. On one side is a short piece explaining how Loretta Young became a star. These two plot sheets may have been from the same theater and distributed together. A third sample, from the Majestic Theater, gives three pages of plot summary of the film *The Constant Nymph* (starring Charles Boyer and Joan Fontaine), with a credits column on the last page. It also includes ads for a raincoat, a movie journal, and another film, *The Egg and I*. Given the dates when these Hollywood films were first released these sheets must have been used in the 1940s.

19. According to Gongsun Lu, those who wrote plot sheets for silent films were mostly well educated in literature, including such Butterfly writers as Yao Sufeng, Fan Yanqiao, Zheng Yimei, and Zheng Zhengqiu. One writer, Dan Duyu, went to excess, writing in an elegant classical style beyond the comprehension of the average filmgoer. See Gongsun Lu, *Zhongguo dianying shihua* [Historical notes on Chinese cinema] (Hong Kong: Nantian shuye gongsi, 1961), 219–220. One famous writer of Butterfly fiction, Zhou Shoujuan (1894–1968), wrote movie columns in his own journals and even served as advertising adviser to movie theaters.

20. For a detailed discussion of Lin Shu's translations of Dumas and Dickens, see my book *The Romantic Generation of Modern Chinese Writers* (Cambridge, Mass.: Harvard University Press, 1973), chap. 3.

21. Interview, October 22, 1984.

22. See *Xiandai dianying* [Modern cinema] 1.2, 1.5, 1.6, 1.7 (1933–34). (These are some of the issues I was able to locate in my research in Shanghai.) Liu's praise of Garbo and Crawford can be found in *Furen huabao* [Women's pictorial] 18 (May 1934): 16. For the relationship of this topic to Liu's own creative writing, see Chapter 6.

23. For a compendium of views, including attacks on Liu, see Zhongguo dianying yishu yanjiu zhongxin [Center for the study of Chinese film art], ed., *Zhongguo zuoyi dianying yundong* [Chinese leftist cinema movement] (Beijing: Zhongguo dianying chubanshe, 1993), 142–162.

24. *Xiandai dianying* 1.2 (1934): 1.

25. Liu Na'ou, "Dianying xingshi mei de tanqiu" [The search for the formal aesthetics of film], *Wanxiang* [Panorama] 1 (1934). Predictably, Liu's views received scathing criticism from leftist critics of the time. For a typical sample, see Chen Wu, "Qingsuan Liu Na'ou de lilun" [Liquidating Liu Na'ou's theory], in *Zhongguo zuoyi dianying yundong*, 162–167.

26. North, *Chinese Motion Picture Market*, 2.

27. Miriam Hansen, *Babel and Babylon: Spectatorship in American Silent Film* (Cambridge, Mass.: Harvard University Press, 1991), 15.

28. Ibid., 123.

29. The tradition of the woman on the front cover was established in the late Qing courtesan journals, of which the female star covers of the 1930s can be regarded as a form of commercial and aesthetic displacement. The film historian Jay Leyda has remarked: "Only on Chinese calendars of modern beauties can one find counterparts of the ladies who were 'developed' to attract film audiences of the treaty ports in the 1930s, and these standards have changed little since then." See Jay Leyda, *Dianying: An Account of Films and the Film Audience in China* (Cambridge, Mass.: MIT Press, 1972), 86.

30. Liu Yiqing, "Cong modeng shuodao xiandai qingnian funü" [From the

modern to the young women of the present era], *Linglong* 3.44 (December 13, 1933): 2439–42.

31. Leyda, *Dianying*, 49.

32. Ibid., 49–50.

33. Xu Changlin, "Zaoqi Zhongguo yinmu shang de minzu tese" [The national characteristic in early Chinese cinema], *Zhongguo dianying yanjiu* [Studies in Chinese cinema], Hong Kong Society of Chinese Film Studies, 1 (December 1983): 20–21.

34. Shu Zi, "Fengyu zhai yingxi tan" [Talking about movies from the Wind-and-Rain Studio], *Banyue* 2.4 (1922): 3–4. Enjoying Western films was by no means a hobby only for the Westernized upper classes but was eagerly embraced by the authors and readers of this supposedly traditional school as well. In the same issue, the magazine's editor, Zhou Shoujuan, himself a translator of Western fiction, raves about another film, *The Four Horsemen of the Apocalypse*, in an editorial comment; and in a subsequent issue he quibbles over the translation of film titles. See *Banyue* 3.2 (1923): 13.

35. North, *Chinese Motion Picture Market*, 2.

36. Ibid., 3–4.

37. See Zheng Shusen [William Tay], *Cong xiandai dao dangdai* [From modern to contemporary] (Taipei: Sanmin, 1994), 64–65, 77–78, 83–84. The Chinese title of *The Tender Trap* is *Qingchang ru zhanchang* [The field of romance is like a battlefield], included in Zhang Ailing [Eileen Chang], *Wangran ji* [At a loss] (Taipei: Huangguan, 1991), 171–239.

38. Hansen, *Babel and Babylon*, 16.

39. Ibid., 15.

40. Ibid., 161.

41. Ibid., 141. According to Hansen, this is the modern narrative which Griffith had both contributed to and departed from in his films.

42. Paul Pickowicz, "Melodramatic Representation and the 'May Fourth' Tradition of Chinese Cinema," in *From May Fourth to June Fourth: Fiction and Film in Twentieth-Century China*, ed. Ellen Widmer and David Der-wei Wang (Cambridge, Mass.: Harvard University Press, 1993), 298.

43. See *Tansuo de niandai* [Early Chinese cinema: the era of exploration] (1984): 3, a catalogue for a festival of films of the 1930s, sponsored by the Hong Kong Arts Center and the Hong Kong Chinese Film Association. These categories were first proposed by the literary scholar Huang Jichi.

44. Cheng Jihua, Li Shaobai, and Xing Zuwen, *Zhongguo dianying fazhan shi* [History of the development of modern Chinese cinema] (Beijing: Zhongguo dianying chubanshe, 1963), 2 vols.; see vol. 1, chap. 3, esp. 171–244.

45. *Xin Shanghai* 1.1 (1933): 67.

46. Ibid., 68.

47. Ibid., 67–73.

48. Pickowicz, "Melodramatic Representation," 304–305.

49. Ibid., 324.

50. Nick Browne, "Society and Subjectivity: On the Political Economy of Chinese Melodrama," in *New Chinese Cinemas: Forms, Identities, Politics*, ed. Nick Browne et al. (Cambridge: Cambridge University Press, 1994), 40.

51. Ibid., 41.

52. Pickowicz, "Melodramatic Representation," 301–303. Both Browne and Pickowicz draw from Peter Brooks's book *The Melodramatic Imagination* (New York: Columbia University Press, 1985), which is a study of the fiction of Balzac and Henry James.

53. Xia Yan, *Lanxun jiumeng lu* [Too lazy to seek old dreams] (Beijing: Sanlian shudian, 1985), 224–231. Xia's friend Qian Xingcun was a close friend of Zhou Jianyun, the manager of Mingxing; their first meeting with the Mingxing in-house directors, Zhang Shichuan and Zheng Zhengqiu, took place in the popular DD's Café in the French Concession. Zhang was old-fashioned, but Zheng admired Hong Shen and had more influence.

54. Ibid., 232–233.

55. Ibid., 233.

56. Leo Ou-fan Lee, "The Tradition of Modern Chinese Cinema: Some Preliminary Explorations and Hypotheses," in *Perspectives on Chinese Cinema*, ed. Chris Berry (London: British Film Institute, 1991), 12. Some of the scripts of the silent films are slightly more elaborate in technical clues, which include scene-by-scene and even shot-by-shot directions.

57. Lin Niantong, *Jingyou* [The roving mirror] (Hong Kong: Suye chubanshe, 1985), 3–6.

58. Lee, "Tradition of Modern Chinese Cinema," 14.

59. Hansen, *Babel and Babylon*, 23.

60. Ibid., 79.

61. Ibid., 82, quoting the critic Frank Woods.

62. Since the celebrated theorist André Bazin, the "long take" aesthetic has been seen as more characteristic of the European tradition, from Italian neorealism to the films of Jean-Luc Godard and Chantal Ackerman. For an insightful application of Bazin's theory of "documentary realism" to Chinese films, though not of the 1930s, see Li Tuo, "Chang jingtou he dianying de jishixing" [The long take and film's documentary realism], in *Dianying meixue: 1982* [Film aesthetics: 1982], ed. Zhong Dianfei (Beijing: Zhongguo wenyi lianhe chuban gongsi, 1983), 94–131.

63. Noël Burch, "Narrative/Diegesis—Thresholds, Limits," *Screen* 23 (July–August 1982): 22.

64. Huang Ailing, "Shilun sanshi niandai Zhongguo dianying danjingtou de

xingzhi" [On the nature of the single long take in 1930s Chinese cinema], *Zhongguo dianying yanjiu*, 1:47.

65. Ibid., 1:44, 49.

66. Ma Ning, "The Textual and Critical Difference of Being Radical: Reconstructing Chinese Leftist Films of the 1930s," *Wide Angle* 11.2 (1989): 23.

67. Ibid., 26.

68. The film starred Janet Gaynor and was directed by Frank Borzage, whose sentimental style may have endeared himself to Chinese audiences. I was unable to find the video version of the film. The following plot summary and assessment is taken from a current guide to old movies on television: "Italian girl fleeing from police joins traveling circus, meets and falls in love with young painter who finds her an inspiration. Followup to success of *Seventh Heaven*, is actually much better, a delicate, beautifully photographed romance." Leonard Maltin, ed., *1979–80 TV Movies* (New York: Signet, 1980), 669. *Seventh Heaven*, translated as *Qichong tian*, was apparently also a box office hit in Shanghai.

69. Leyda, *Dianying*, 106.

70. Ma Ning, "Textual and Critical Difference of Being Radical," 24.

71. Quoted in Leyda, *Dianying*, 117.

72. *Xiaocheng zhichun*, made in the 1940s, is an awesome accomplishment which in my view differs from and towers above all the thirties films in its mastery of the form in the service of a deeply psychological drama of ethical conflict and sexual repression. In his short biography of Fei, Leyda does not even mention this film. Since I saw the film only once, in Hong Kong, and have not been able to find a video version, I cannot offer an extensive analysis.

73. Leyda, *Dianying*, 86.

74. Huang Ailing, "Shilun sanshi niandai Zhongguo dianying," 42.

75. Ibid., 43.

76. *Zhongguo zuoyi dianying yundong*, 555.

77. Cai Chusheng, "Bashisiri zhihou—gei *Yukuangqu* de guanzhongmen" [Eighty-four days later—to the audience of Fisherman's song], ibid., 364–365.

78. Song Yizhou (Song Zhidi), "Dianying xinshang yu guanzhong xinli" (Film appreciation and audience psychology), ibid., 215.

79. Shen Xiling, "Zenyang zhizuo *Shizi jietou*" [How was *Crossroads* made], ibid., 395.

80. The Hong Kong director Tsui Hark (Xu Ke) later made a spoof of this story by turning the ménage à deux situation into a ménage à trois in one of his own films. See Chapter 10.

81. We could even compare such sequences intergenerically with the opening

pages of Mao Dun's novel *Midnight*, which likewise evokes such a contradictory atmosphere of the exhilarating modernity of (as Mao Dun wrote in English) "LIGHT, HEAT, POWER" and wanton depravity.

82. For a brief but perceptive analysis, see Rey Chow, *Primitive Passions: Visuality, Sexuality, Ethnography, and Contemporary Chinese Cinema* (New York: Columbia University Press, 1995), 23–26. In this film, as Chow remarks, "words, whenever they are used, are used very sparingly, so that the audience must learn to see the film through the visual composites that we conventionally call images" (25). This is precisely what makes this particular film so exceptional. Chow sees elitist resistance to visuality by both writers and scholars of modern Chinese literature. My own position is to find linkages and mutual mediations between visuality and the written word.

83. Chen Huiyang, *Mengying ji* [Dreaming of movies] (Taipei: Yunchen, 1990), 77–79.

84. This remark and other information is taken from *Early Chinese Cinema: The Era of Exploration*, the program booklet of a festival of 1930s films held in 1984, published by the Hong Kong Arts Center and the Hong Kong Chinese Film Association.

85. The film was shown for thirty-four consecutive days and attracted an audience totaling more than 100,000. See Luo Suwen, *Shikumen: xunchang renjia* [Stone-gate houses: ordinary living] (Shanghai: Shanghai renmin chubanshe, 1991), 235. Its popularity also "benefited a lot from the producer's aggressive promotion [of it] in the newspaper as 'the first horror film' and outside the theaters with giant posters and eerie lights that scared the passers-by." I am grateful to Yingjin Zhang for this reminder in his editorial review of the first draft of this chapter. See also Jin Shan, "Yi wangshi nian wangyou" [Reminiscing about the past, thinking of my deceased friends], *Dazhong dianying* 139 (1956): 25.

86. Cheng Jihua, Li Shaobai, and Xing Zuwen, eds., *Zhongguo dianying fazhan shi*, 1:460–461, 490. *The Desert Island* is considered reactionary, and one of the faults Cheng finds in *Singing at Midnight* is the director's "direct copying" of *The Phantom of the Opera*.

87. Giuliana Bruno, *Streetwalking on a Ruined Map: Cultural Theory and the City Films of Elvira Notari* (Princeton: Princeton University Press, 1993), 48–49.

88. Ibid., 50–51.

89. Ibid., 38.

90. Leyda, *Dianying*, 2–3.

91. Ibid., 23. I have corrected some minor errors in Leyda's English translation.

92. Ibid., 22. Du Yunzhi, *Zhongguo dianying shi*, 1:28–29.

93. From my interviews with Wei Shaochang, a famous scholar of Butterfly fiction and himself an avid filmgoer and patron of Shanghai's local operas,

it would seem that the only difference was in the price range, with balcony seats costing almost twice as much as orchestra seats. While foreign audiences may generally have been seated in the balcony, there is no shortage of accounts about Chinese couples having romantic trysts in the balcony also. Shi Zhecun's story "At the Paris Cinema" is a good case in point (see Chapter 5).

94. It would still be intriguing to explore whether there was de facto segregation in the seating arrangements inside the movie theaters. It is said that at the Shanghai racecourse the Chinese spectators were allowed to occupy only the lower viewing platforms, with the upper stands reserved for foreigners, though the natives participated in this colonial sport with equal enthusiasm by betting on the horses. In the tram cars, the first-class compartments were often occupied by foreigners, with second class for native passengers. Unlike racial segregation in the American South, however, these colonial divisions were not enforced (except at the racecourse); they reflected, in my view, more a hierarchy of status and money.

95. Bruno, *Streetwalking*, 49. In particular, the train can be seen as "the mechanical double for the cinematic apparatus"; in both, "the spectator travels through and along sites in a perceptual machine ensemble. In a movie theater, as in a train, one is alone with others, traveling in time and space, viewing panoramically from a still sitting position through a framed image in motion" (50).

96. Ibid., 50. Bruno here quotes Mary Ann Doane.

4. Textual Transactions

1. Shanghai yanjiu zhongxin, ed., *Shanghai qibainian* [Seven hundred years of Shanghai] (Shanghai: Shanghai renmin chubanshe, 1991), 334.

2. Xie Juzeng, *Shili yangchang de ceying* [Silhouettes on the Bund] (Guangzhou: Huacheng chubanshe, 1983), 84.

3. Xu Chi, *Jiangnan xiaozhen* [A small town on the southern Yangtze] (Beijing: Zuojia chubanshe, 1993), 104.

4. My interviews with Shi Zhecun took place at his house in Shanghai in 1985, 1986, and 1994.

5. Xu Chi, *Jiangnan xiaozhen*, 115.

6. Ibid., 134. The currency values in Shanghai circa 1930 are based on Frederic Wakeman, Jr., *Policing Shanghai, 1927–1937* (Berkeley: University of California Press, 1995), xi.

7. Dust jacket of *Bulfinch's Mythology* (New York: Modern Library, n.d.).

8. From the edition I have purchased from Shi. Book 2, *Easy Parsing and Analysis* (1928), was designed "for the lower classes in secondary schools."

9. This was one of the first grammar books that Dai Wangshu studied, according to the bookstore owner from whom I purchased the book in June 1994.

10. Half a century later, when I first met Shi, he inquired about *Vanity Fair* and asked me to send him copies of the most recent reincarnation of the journal, which he found disappointing.

11. Xu Chi, *Jiangnan xiaozhen*, 124, 182.

12. Ibid., 126.

13. They were collected in a volume edited by Dai's close friend Shi Zhecun, *Dai Wangshu yishi ji* [Collection of Dai Wangshu's translated poetry] (Changsha: Hunan remin chubanshe, 1983).

14. Interviews with Shi Zhecun, October 1986 and June 1994.

15. Harriet Sergeant, *Shanghai: Collision Point of Cultures, 1918–1939* (New York: Crown Publishers, 1990), 4–5.

16. Shi Zhecun, "Xiandai zayi" [Memoirs of the Contemporary], *Xinwenxue shiliao* [Historical materials on new literature] 1 (1980): 213–220; 2 (1981): 158–163; 3 (1981): 220–223. Shi later claimed that he had in fact been a closet leftist and one time member of the Communist Youth League. Though not striking any political stance in particular, he refused to publish works by the Guomindang writers. At the same time, he got into trouble in the early 1930s with the Left-wing League and Lu Xun because he advocated the usefulness of reading Zhuang Zi and *Wenxuan*, which aroused Lu Xun's anti-traditional wrath. The episode has since become a bone of contention in Shi's political background, for which he was persecuted during the Cultural Revolution; at the peak of Red Guard radicalism anyone Lu Xun had attacked in the 1930s became ipso facto a "class enemey." After the Cultural Revolution, Shi was fully rehabilitated, and began to write his memoirs of *Xiandai* magazine, partly because a younger generation of scholars and critics, now influenced by the new tide of modernism from the West, suddenly discovered Shi's literary past and declared him a pioneer of Chinese modernism.

17. All this information was obtained during my last interview with Shi Zhecun at his home in Shanghai on June 7, 1994.

18. Ying Guojing, "Shi Zhecun nianbiao" [Chronology of Shi Zhecun], in *Zhongguo xiandai zuojia xuanji: Shi Zhecun* [Selections from modern Chinese writers: Shi Zhecun] ed. Ying Guojing (Hong Kong: Sanlian, 1988), 313–314.

19. For a detailed account, see Shi Zhecun, "Women jingyingguo sange shidian" [We have operated three bookstores], *Xinwenxue shiliao* 1 (1985): 184–190.

20. Paul Morand (1888–1976) was a diplomat, a traveler, and a very popular

writer in Europe and America in the 1920s and 1930s. He later became a collaborationist under the Vichy regime, but was finally elected to the Académie française in 1968. His literary fame was established by the publication of his two story collections, *Tendres Stocks* (1921) and *Ouvert la nuit* (1922), which were translated by no less a modernist than Ezra Pound into English; Marcel Proust had written a preface to *Tendres Stocks*. The English translation was never published because of Pound's feuds with the publishers. The books were finally published in 1984 under the title *Fancy Goods; Open All Night* (New York: New Directions, 1984); see the introduction by Breon Mitchell, vii–xxiv. The two stories translated into Chinese—"Les Amis nouveaux" (New friends) and "Vague de paresse" [Wave of indolence]—are apparently not taken from these collections. An English translation of Morand's "Turkish Night" also appeared in the September 1921 issue of *The Dial*, to which Shi and his friends had access. Morand, who had received his education in English at Oxford, also contributed essays and stories to *Vanity Fair*, which was, as I noted before, Shi's favorite American journal. Thus, his case again illustrates the importance of textual connections through the traffic in literary journals.

21. According to Shi himself, the story is an imitation of a Soviet story called "Flying Osip" from an English collection of Soviet short stories that he purchased at one of Shanghai's Western bookstores. See Shi Zhecun, "Wo de chuangzuo shenghuo zhi licheng" [The journey of my creative life], in *Chuangzuo de jingyan* [Expriences in creative writing], ed. Huang Jiamuo (Shanghai: Xiandai shuju, 1933), 78–79.

22. This is mentioned in most Chinese studies but I have yet to find a copy of such a book. The journal *Wenyi gongchang* also seems to have been lost. Issues of *Wugui lieche* and a complete set of *Xin wenyi* can be found in the Shanghai municipal library.

23. Shi Zhecun, "Wo de chuangzuo shenghuo zhi licheng," 79.

24. See the study of these two works by Elena Hidveghyova, "The Decadent Obsession: Eros versus Celibacy in the Work of Shi Zhecun and Anatole France," *Asian and African Studies* (Bratislava) 4.1 (1995): 47–70.

25. Personal letter from Shi, January 13, 1993.

26. Those that regularly published translations of Western literature included *Xiaoshuo yuebao* (Short story monthly, 1921–1931), *Wenxue zhoubao* (Literature monthly), *Wenxue xunkan* (Literature biweekly) and *Wenxue* (Literature, 1921–1929), *Xiandai xiaoshuo* (Modern fiction, 1928–1930), *Jinwu yuekan* (*La Maison d'or*, 1929–1930), *Beixin* (1926–1930), *Huanzhou* (Mirage, 1926–1928), *Wenxue* (Literature, 1933–1937), *Xiandai wenxue* (Modern literature, 1930), *Yiban* (General, 1926–1929), *Zhongguo wenxue* (Chinese literature, 1934), *Xin xiaoshuo* (New fiction, 1935), *Benliu* (Running torrent,

1928–29), *Wenyi yuekan* (Literature and art monthly, 1930–1937), and *Xinyue* (Crescent moon, 1928–1933). Shi himself later edited two short-lived journals after *Xiandai zazhi* folded: *Wenyi fengjing* (Literary landscape, 1934) and *Wenfan xiaopin* (Literary vignettes, 1935). This list was prepared by Shumei Shi in her dissertation "Modernism in China" (UCLA, 1993), 3–4.

27. Shi Zhecun, "Xiandai zayi," *Xin wenxue shiliao* 3 (1987): 221.

28. *Xiandai* 1.1 (May 1932): 2.

29. Shi Zhecun, "Xiandai zayi," *Xin wenxue shiliao* 1 (1981): 217.

30. *Xiandai* 5.6 (October 1934): 834–837.

31. Shao Xunmei, "Xiandai Meiguo shitan gaiguan" [An overview of the contemporary American poetry scene], ibid., 886.

32. Zhao Jiabi, "Meiguo xiaoshuo de chengzhang" [The growth of American fiction], ibid., 854–858.

33. Ling Changyan, "Fukena—yige xinzuofeng de changshizhe" [Faulkner—an experimentalist of a new style], ibid., 1009.

34. This is in sharp contrast to the unquestioned admiration for these two writers by the editors of *Xiandai wenxue* [Modern literature] in Taiwan in the early 1960s, which introduced Western modernism to Taiwan with youthful zest and bravado, beginning with an inaugural issue on Franz Kafka. Interestingly, both journals feature introductory articles as well as translations of original fiction and poetry. Whereas *Xiandai zazhi* in the 1930s relied mostly on general literary journals as sources, the latter-day *Xiandai wenxue* was more scholarly and used articles by famous critics such as Philip Rahv and Robert Penn Warren. A far as I know, the latter's young editors had no knowledge of the former.

35. Mu Mutian, "Xinjingzhuyi de wenxue" [Literature of psychologism], *Xiandai* 4.6 (April 1934): 936–938.

36. Ling Changyan, "Fukena," 1002.

37. Ibid., 1003.

38. Ironically, half a century later, in the early 1980s, history would repeat itself as some veteran poets criticized the poetry by a younger generation as "obscure." Consistent with his earlier principles, Shi did not take the veterans' side. It was these younger poets and writers who "discovered" Shi as a pioneer of their own modernism.

39. Shi Zhecun, "You guanyu benkan zhong de shi" [Again concerning the poetry in this journal], *Xiandai* 4.1 (November 1933): 6–7.

40. Shi Zhecun, "Zhijiage shiren Ka'er Sangdebao" [The Chicago poet Carl Sandburg], *Xiandai* 3.1 (May 1933): 115.

41. Xu Chi, *Jiangnan xiaozhen*, 125.

42. Interviews conducted in China and in the United States, 1982–1984.

When Xu visited the United States as a guest of the International Writing Program at the University of Iowa, I took him to Chicago for a visit. Among the Chinese writers from the People's Republic, he was the only one who was ecstatic upon seeing Chicago's skyscrapers; the other writers all preferred the rural landscape of Iowa City, and not a few remarked that the Chicago architecture was ugly. Xu was also among the first to venture the timely, though theoretically dubious, argument in the early 1980s that modernism in art and literature would be a perfectly fitting superstructural manifestation of the government's new policy of the "Four Modernizations." He committed suicide in 1996 by jumping from the window of his residence in Wuhan, reportedly out of ennui with old age.

43. Walter Benjamin, "The Task of the Translator," in *Illuminations*, trans. Harry Zohn (New York: Schocken Books, 1969), 71.

44. *Xiandai* 4.1 (November 1933): 7.

45. Matei Calinescu, *Faces of Modernity: Avant-Garde, Decadence, Kitsch* (Bloomington: Indiana University Press, 1977), 41–42.

46. For a study of Freud's reception in China, see Jingyuan Zhang, *Psychoanalysis in China: Literary Transformations, 1919–1949* (Ithaca, N.Y.: Cornell University East Asia Program, 1992).

47. Zhou Yang, "Guanyu shehuizhuyi de xianshizhuyi yu geming de langmanzhuyi" [Concerning socialist realism and revolutionary romanticism], *Xiandai* 4.1 (November 1933): 27–28. This may well have been the first Chinese formulation of a slogan later popularized by Chairman Mao himself in 1958.

5. The Erotic, the Fantastic, and the Uncanny: Shi Zhecun's Experimental Stories

1. Ying Guojing, ed., "Shi Zhecun nianbiao" [Chronology of Shi Zhecun], in *Zhongguo xiandai zuojia xuanji: Shi Zhecun* [Selections from modern Chinese writers: Shi Zhecun] (Hong Kong: Sanlian, 1988), 32–313.

2. These were collected in *Juanzi guniang* [A girl named Juanzi] (Shanghai: Yaxiya shuju, 1928) and *Shangyuan deng* [Lantern festival] (Shanghai: Xin Zhongguo shuju, 1932).

3. These are collected in *Shangyuan deng* (Shanghai: Shuimo shudian, 1929). For a scholarly treatment of some of the stories, see Chen Guoqiu, "Cong 'wangran' dao 'chouzhang': shilun *Shangyuan deng* zhong de ganjiu pianzhang" [From "loss" to "melancholy": on some nostalgic pieces in Lantern festival], *Zhongguo xiandai wenxue yanjiu* [Studies of modern Chinese literature] 4 (1993): 83–95.

4. Shi Zhecun, "Zixu" [Self-preface], in *Jiangjun de tou* [The general's head] (Shanghai: Xin Zhongguo shuju, 1932), 1.

5. Shi Zhecun, *Jiangjun de tou*, 104.

6. Jingyuan Zhang, *Psychoanalysis in China: Literary Transformations, 1919–1949* (Ithaca, N.Y.: Cornell University East Asia Program, 1992), 112–113.

7. Mark Elvin, "Tales of Shen and Xin: Body-Person and Heart-Mind in China during the Last 150 Years," in *Zone 4: Fragments for a History of the Human Body*, pt. 2 (1989): 275.

8. When I first met Shi in 1981 in Shanghai, I asked him what books he would like me to find for him in the United States. To my surprise he answered without hesitation: a copy of the new *Vanity Fair* (which he found disappointing) and any book by the marquis de Sade.

9. For a discussion of misogyny in the novel, see Sun Shuyu, *Shuihu zhuan de laili xintai yu yishu* [The origins, mentality, and art in *Men of the Marshes*] (Taipei: Shibao, 1981), esp. pt. 3.

10. Shi Zhecun, "Shi Xiu," in *Xin Ganjuepai xiaoshuo xuan* [Selected stories from the neo-sensationalist school], ed. Li Ou-fan (Taipei: Yunchen wenhua chubanshe, 1988), 84–85.

11. This begs the further theoretical question of whether these sites from the real world are the same once they enter the fictional world of Shi's stories. Of course not, from a technical point of view; but the real Shanghai does enter into fiction as raw material in the production of the texts and as figures and signposts in the fictional world itself. In this cutural study of Shi's fiction, I am not willing to separate the two worlds entirely, though I am aware of the difference in theory. Shi once told me that his stories are set in the real Shanghai, whereas Liu Na'ou's stories are set in some city that looks like Shanghai but is more like Tokyo.

12. This story is not included in any of Shi's published fiction collections, perhaps because it does not fit into any of the content categories Shi used to compile his collections.

13. Shi Zhecun, preface to Arthur Schnitzler's *Boming de Dailisha* [Pitiable Teresa] (Shanghai: Zhonghua shuju, 1937). Shi also mentions Schnitzler's countryman the dramatist Hugo von Hofmannsthal, whose works he considered to be "filled with the color of mysticism," whereas Schnitzler was more of a "neoromanticist," his works permeated with a southern European–flavored realism.

14. Shi Zhecun, foreword to *Aiersai zhisi* [The death of Else], translation of Arthur Schnitzler, *Fräulein Else* (Shanghai: Fuxing shuju, 1945), 1–2.

15. Elly Hagenaar, *Stream of Consciousness and Free Indirect Speech in Modern Chinese Literature* (Leiden: Leiden University, 1992); Anthony Wan-hoi Pak, "The School of New Sensibilities in the 1930s: A Study of Liu Na'ou and

Mu Siying's Fiction" (Ph.D. diss., University of Toronto, 1995), esp. chap. 3.

16. Pak, "School of New Sensibilities," 126.

17. Shi Zhecun, *Shannüren xingpin* [Exemplary conduct of good women] (Shanghai: Liangyou, 1933), 87. The original poem, titled "Images," can be found in *The Complete Poems of Richard Aldington* (London: Allan Wingate, 1948), 38.

18. Ibid., 98–99.

19. The edition of *Shannüren xingpin* I have obtained from the Harvard-Yenching Library is the second printing of a 1940 popular edition *(pujiben)*. It may have been a modest best-seller.

20. Shi Zhecun, "Ziba" [Self-postscript], in *Meiyu zhixi* [Evening of spring rain] (Shanghai: Xin Zhongguo shuju, 1933), 1–2.

21. Shi Zhecun, "Zai Bali daxiyuan" [At the Paris Cinema], in *Meiyu zhixi*, 36.

22. Ibid., 15.

23. Ibid.

24. Shi Zhecun, "Ziba," in *Meiyu zhixi*, 2.

25. Robert Chi, "It Goes without Saying: On the Gothic Fiction of Poe and Shi Zhecun," seminar paper, Harvard University, 1996.

26. Jiangyuan Zhang, *Psychoanalysis in China*, 113. Zhang also gives a detailed analysis of the story as Shi's parody of Henry James's "Turn of the Screw" and calls it "a deliberate attempt by Shi to juggle literature and psychology" (113–114).

27. Shi Zhecun, "Modao," in *Meiyu zhixi*, 46. English translation by Robert Chi, with my slight revision.

28. Yan Jiayan, *Lun xiandai xiaoshuo yu wenyi sichao* [On modern fiction and artistic trends] (Changsha: Hunan renmin chubanshe, 1987), 164.

29. Chi, "It Goes without Saying," 50.

30. Ibid.

31. Jingyuan Zhang, *Psychoanalysis in China*, 114–115.

32. V. S. Pritchett, "An Irish Ghost," in *The Living Novel* (Oxford: Oxford University Press, 1944), 96–97.

33. Ibid., 95.

34. Shi Zhecun, "Yecha" [Yaksha], in *Meiyu zhixi*, 152.

35. Ibid., 147.

36. Anthony Vidler, *The Architectural Uncanny: Essays in the Modern Unhomely* (1992; rpt. Cambridge, Mass.: MIT Press, 1994), 6–7.

37. Leslie Fiedler, *Love and Death in the American Novel* (New York: Anchor Books, 1992), 135; quoted in Chi, "It Goes without Saying," 19.

38. Shi Zhecun, "Ziba," in *Meiyu zhixi*, 2.

39. Ibid.

40. In interviews Shi still spoke with bitterness and disdain about a minor leftist critic, Lou Shiyi, who castigated his fiction, together with that of Liu Na'ou and Mu Shiying, as decadent and immoral. In a personal letter to a friend (who showed it to me), Lou has recently recanted and mentioned the whole incident with remorse.

41. Shi Zhecun, "Ou" [Seagull], in *Xiaozhen ji* [Small treasures] (Shanghai: Liangyou, 1936), 90.

42. Shi Zhecun, "Bianhou ji" [Editorial postscript], ibid., 193–194.

43. Shi Zhecun, "Huangxin dashi" [Master Huangxin], *Wenxue zazhi* [Literature magazine] 1.2 (June 1937): 58.

44. Ibid.

6. Face, Body, and the City: Liu Na'ou and Mu Shiying

1. Raymond Williams, *The Country and the City* (London: Chatto & Windus, 1973).

2. In the United States it has been the subject of dissertations by Randy Trumball (Stanford University, 1989) and Anthony Wan-hoi Pak (University of Toronto 1995; see chap. 6, n. 15), part of another dissertation by Shu-mei Shih (UCLA, 1992), and a book by Zhang Yinjin, *The City in Modern Chinese Literature: Configurations of Space, Time, and Gender* (Stanford: Stanford University Press, 1996). In China the pioneer scholar was Yan Jiayan, who compiled China's first post-Mao collection of *Xinganjuepai xiaoshuo xuan* [Selected stories of the neo-sensationalist school] (Beijing: Renmin wenxue chubanshe, 1985) and wrote extensively about the school, though his critical judgments are clearly based on a position of moral realism. Another valuable study is Wu Fuhui, *Dushi xuanliuzhong de haipai xiaoshuo* [Shanghai school fiction in the urban vortex] (Changhsha: Hunan jiaoyu chubanshe, 1995), which includes a special appendix (321–340) giving brief biographies of some twenty Shanghai writers and lists of their works, including all those discussed in this book.

3. Biographical information about Liu Na'ou and Mu Shiying remains sketchy. For a pioneering study of Liu and other writers of the school, see Yan Jiayan, introduction to *Xinganjuepai xiaoshuo xuan*. The introduction is also included in his *Zhongguo xiandai xiaoshuo liupai shi* [A history of schools and trends in modern Chinese fiction] (Beijing: Renmin wenxue chubanshe, 1989), 125–174. A recent discovery was Liu Na'ou's diary by the Taiwan scholar Peng Xiaoyan, who is arranging to have it published.

4. Mu Shiying, preface to the revised edition, *Nanbeiji* [Northern and southern poles] (Shanghai: Xiandia shuju, 1934), 1.

5. Yan Jiayan, "Lun sanlingniandai xinganjuepai xiaoshuo" [On the neo-sen-

sationalist fiction of the 1930s], in *Xinganjuepai xiaoshuo xuan* [Selected stories from the neo-sensationalist school], ed. Li Ou-fan [Leo Ou-fan Lee] (Taipei: Yunchen, 1988), 348–349. Yan also quotes a source who says that Mu was killed for the wrong reason, as he was himself an underground Guomindang agent.

6. Mu Shiying, "Zixu" [Self-preface], in *Gongmu* [Public graveyard] (Shanghai: Xiandai shuju, 1933), 2–3.
7. The first effort to restore Mu's stature was made in the Hong Kong journal *Siji* [Four seasons] in 1972, which contains a seminal article by the Hong Kong writer Liu Yichang (himself an early modernist) on Mu's "double personality" and an interview with Mu's friend Ye Lingfeng, as well as other studies.
8. Peng Xiaoyan, "Xinnüxing yu Shanghai dushi wenhua" [The New Woman and Shanghai's urban culture], *Zhongyang yanjiuyuan Zhongguo wenzhe yanjiu jikan* [Bulletin of the Institute of Chinese Literature and Philosophy, Academia Sinica, Taipei] 10 (March 1997): 25–28.
9. Liu Na'ou, "Youxi" [Games], in *Dushi fengjingxian* [Scenes of the city] (Shanghai: Shuimo shudian, 1930), 6–7.
10. Liu Na'ou, *Dushi fengjingxian*, 23.
11. Ibid., 47.
12. Ibid., 93.
13. The fashion even made its way to films, as in *Tiyu huanghou* [The sports queen], directed by Sun Yu (1934).
14. The colonial implications of this fascination is powerfully dissected in Frantz Fanon's well-known treatise *Black Skin, White Masks* (1952). But in Liu's case I do not think that race is a crucial factor, nor does Liu's fiction reveal any particular racial bias against blacks. When the heroine of "Games" demands that her old lover buy her a Viper convertible and hire a couple of "black-faced chauffeurs," this does not necessarily refer to blacks; if it does, the image comes from Hollywood movies. If there is one facial feature of which Liu clearly favors the Western prototype, it is the straight Greek nose. As the next chapter will show, the decadent poet Shao Xunmei took great pride in his own "Greek nose" and used a drawing of it as his personal signature.
15. Liu Na'ou, "Xiandai biaoqingmei zaoxing" [The modern type of expressive beauty], *Furen huabao* [Women's pictorial] 18 (May 1934): 16.
16. Roland Barthes, "The Face of Garbo," in *Mythologies* (New York: Hill and Wang, 1972), 56, as quoted in Mary Ann Doane, *Femmes Fatales: Feminism, Film Theory, Psychoanalysis* (New York: Routledge, 1991), 47.
17. Laura Mulvey, "Visual Pleasure and Narrative Cinema," in *Visual and Other*

Pleasures (London: Macmillan, 1989), 19. The definition of scopophilia is from Peter Brooks, *Body Work* (Cambridge, Mass.: Harvard University Press, 1993), 98. In these theoretical discourses the face is very much connected to the body, since in the pause of a cinematic close-up the face becomes the center of attention for the spectator. Although the face is "that bodily part not accessible to the subject's own gaze," it is the "most articulare sector" and "the most readable space" of the body. As Susan Stewart observes, "If the face reveals a depth and profundity which the body itself is not capable of, it is because the eyes and to some degree the mouth are openings into fathomlessness . . . The face becomes a text, a space which must be 'read' and interpreted in order to exist." Susan Stewart, *On Longing: Narratives of the Miniature, the Gigantic, the Souvenir, the Collection* (Baltimore: Johns Hopkins University Press, 1984), 125–127, as quoted in Doane, *Femmes Fatales*, 47. But Stewart's observations do not seem to apply to Liu's fiction, as his heroine's face reveals little depth and profundity.

18. Brooks, *Body Work*, 99.

19. Ibid., 97.

20. Shu-mei Shih, "Gender, Race, and Semicolonialism: Liu Na'ou's Urban Shanghai Landscape," *Journal of Asian Studies* 55.4 (November 1996): 947–948, quoting studies by Barbara Hamill Sato and Miriam Silverberg.

21. Cited in ibid., 948, quoting Harriet Sergeant, *Shanghai* (London: Jonathan Cape, 1991), 271.

22. Ibid., 947.

23. Edward Said, *Orientalism* (New York: Vintage Books, 1979), 184–190.

24. For instance, "A Chinese Curio Hunt" (March 1926), "A Chinese Ghost Story" (August 1926), and "Chinese Phantoms" (September 1926). I happened on these *Vanity Fair* articles while advising a senior thesis at Harvard on *Liangyou huabao* by Ezra Block.

25. Paul Morand, *Europe at Love* (New York: Boni and Liveright, 1927), 38. This volume does not give the name of the translator; it may have been rewritten in English by Morand himself.

26. Ibid., 37. Chinese translation in *Wuguei lieche* [Trackless train] October 25, 1928), 161–162.

27. Morand, *Europe at Love*, 47, 49. Chinese translation in *Wuguei lieche* (October 25, 1928), 163–175.

28. Liu Na'ou, "Liyi yu weisheng" [Etiquette and hygiene], in *Dushi fengjingxian*, 131.

29. Ibid., 112.

30. Benjamin Crémieux, "Bao'er Muhang lun" [On Paul Morand], trans. Nana'ou [Liu Na'ou], *Wugui lieche*, October 25, 1928, 153. Crémieux's article was most likely published in *Revue de Paris* around 1924.

31. Georges Lemaître, *Four French Novelists: Marcel Proust, André Gide, Jean Giraudoux, Paul Morand* (London: Oxford University Press, 1938), 385.

32. Ibid.

33. Crémieux, "Bao'er Muhang lun," 147.

34. Heinrich Fruehauf, "Urban Exoticism in Modern and Contemporary Chinese Literature," in *From May Fourth to June Fourth: Fiction and Film in Twentieth-Century China*, ed. Ellen Widmer and David Der-wei Wang (Cambridge, Mass.: Harvard University Press, 1993), 150.

35. Ibid.

36. For more explorations of this phenomenon in contemporary China, see Xiaomei Chen, *Occidentalism: A Theory of Counter-Discourse in Post-Mao China* (New York: Oxford University Press, 1995), esp. chap. 1.

37. Fruehauf, "Urban Exoticism," 141.

38. Liu Na'ou, "Liangge shijian de buganzheng zhe" [Two men impervious to time], in *Dushi fengjingxian*, 97–99.

39. Ibid., 104.

40. For a discussion of the use of "internal focalization" as a method of expressing subjectivity, see Anthony Wan-hoi Mak, "The School of New Sensibilities in the 1930s: A Study of Liu Na'ou and Mu Shiying's Fiction" (Ph.D. diss., University of Toronto 1995), chap. 4.

41. Shu-mei Shih, "Gender, Race, and Semicolonialism," 947.

42. Liu Na'ou, *Dushi fengjingxian*, 10.

43. Shu-mei Shih, "Gender, Race, and Semicolonialism," 948.

44. Liu Na'ou, *Dushi fengjingxian*, 26.

45. Ibid., 31.

46. Ibid., 23.

47. Ibid., 14.

48. Ibid., 167.

49. Shu-mei Shih, "Gender, Race, and Semicolonialsm," 943.

50. Yomi Braester, "Shanghai's Economy of the Spectacle: The Shanghai Race Club in Liu Na'ou's and Mu Shiying's Stories," *Modern Chinese Literature* 9.1 (Spring 1995): 50.

51. Ibid., 40. Braester also sees both male and female characters in Liu's fiction behaving as *flâneurs*: they assume "a seemingly light-hearted attitude, ostensibly indulging in leisure-consumption and gambling," and "the flaneur's gaze" is what "restructures the space around him." But in my view they merely strike up a pose—a *flâneur*'s gaze *manqué*—in order to display themselves (*chufengtou*), as the male protagonist in "Games" clearly states. There is hardly any self-reflexivity or ambivalence in their observations about the city, since neither they nor their creator is sufficiently detached from it.

52. Mu Shiying, "Luotuo Nicaizhuyizhe yu nüren" [Camel, Nietzscheist, and woman], in *Sheng chunü de ganqing* [A saintly virgin's feelings] (Shanghai: Liangyou, 1935), 56.

53. Ibid., 59.

54. In Mu Shiying, *Baijin de nüti suoxiang* [The statue of a female body in platinum] (Shanghai: Fuxing shuju, 1934), 3–5.

55. Ibid., 13.

56. Ibid., 11.

57. Ibid.

58. See the translation by Edward Gunn, *Backed against the Sea* (Ithaca, N.Y.: Cornell East Asian Series, 1993); see also his article "The Process of Wang Wen-hsing's Art," *Modern Chinese Literature* 1.1 (September 1984): 29–42.

59. Mu Shiying, *Baijin de nüti suoxiang*, 15.

60. Mu Shiying, "Craven A," in *Gongmu*, 110.

61. See Lydia Liu's analysis of Xiao Hong's *Shengsi chang* [Field of life and death] in *Translingual Practice: Literature, National Culture, and Translated Modernity, China, 1900–1937* (Stanford: Stanford University Press, 1995), 199–213.

62. Doane, *Femmes Fatales*, 1.

63. Mu Shiying, "Bei dangzuo xiaoqianpin de nanzi" [The man who is treated as a plaything], in *Gongmu*, 12.

64. Ibid., 13.

65. Mu Shiying, "Wuyue" (The month of May), in *Sheng chunü de ganqing*, 117–118.

66. See Mu Shiying, "He Moudan" [Black peony], in *Gongmu*, 215–234.

67. See, for instance, He Ying, "Wo Jiandao de Mu Shiying" [The Mu Shiying I saw], *Xinwenxue shiliao* [Materials on new literature] 3 (August 22, 1989): 142–145. See also Ye Lingfeng, "Sanshiniandai wentan shang de yike huixing—Ye Lingfeng xiansheng tan Mu Shiying" [A meteor on the literary scene of the 1930s—Ye Lingfeng on Mu Shiying], *Siji* [Four seasons, Hong Kong] 1 (November 1972): 27–30.

68. Rey Chow, *Primitive Passions: Visuality, Ethnography, Sexuality, and Contemporary Chinese Cinema* (New York: Columbia University Press, 1995), 4–18.

69. Mu Shiying, "Yezonghui li de wugeren" [Five characters in a nightclub], in *Gongmu*, 75.

70. Mu Shiying, "Shanghai hubuwu" [Shanghai fox-trot], in *Gongmu*, 201–202.

71. Ibid., 205.

72. Mu Shiying, "Yezonghui li de wugeren," 72–73.

73. Braester, "Shanghai's Economy of the Spectacle," 40.

74. Mu Shiying, preface to *Gongmu*, 3. These remarks were deleted by the editor when the story was first published in *Les Contemporains*.

75. The term is taken, of course, from Joseph Frank's famous study of modern

Western fiction, *The Idea of Spatial Form* (New Brunswick, N.J.: Rutgers University Press, 1991).

76. Mu Shiying, "Shanghai de hubuwu," 194–204.

77. Ibid., 204.

78. Ibid., 204–205.

79. *Liangyou huabao* [The young companion] 85 (1934): 14–15.

80. Mu Shiying, "Shanghai de hubuwu," 214.

81. Cao Yu [Tsao Yu], *Sunrise*, trans. A. C. Barnes (Peking: Foreign Languages Press, 1960), 187.

82. For a more detailed discussion of this novel, see Chapter 9. For an analysis of the novel in terms of its portrait of city space, see Maeda Ai, *Doshitsu kunkian no naka no bungaku* [The literature of city space] (Tokyo, 1982), 365–401.

83. Braester, "Shanghai's Economy of the Spectacle," 46.

84. Mu Shiying, "Shanghai de hubuwu," 208.

85. Ibid., 210.

86. Mu Shiying, preface to *Gongmu*, 3–4.

87. Robert F. Storey, *Pierrot: A Critical History of a Mask* (Princeton: Princeton University Press, 1978), 109, 139, 153.

88. Mu Shiying, preface to *Gongmu*, 4.

89. Shu-mei Shih, "Gender, Race, and Semicolonialism," 945.

90. Mu Shiying, "Pierrot," in *Baijin de nüti suoxiang*, 199.

91. Jiang Guangci wrote a novelette called *Shaonain piaopo zhe* (The young drifter) in 1926 about another Pierrot as he narrates his picaresque experiences from the countryside to the city in letters sent to a leftist activist. But Jiang proved to be a less talented writer, and the hero of his novelette "has more self-pity than confidence and appears a grumbling, incoherent sufferer rather than disdainful, Satanic misanthrope." See Philip Williams, "The Pierrot as a Variety of the Picaro in Modern Chinese Fiction," presented at the Association for Asian Studies annual meeting, Los Angeles, 1993.

7. Decadent and Dandy: Shao Xunmei and Ye Lingfeng

1. Matei Calinescu, *Faces of Modernity: Avant-Garde, Decadence, Kitsch* (Bloomington: Indiana University Press, 1977), 153.

2. Ibid., 155.

3. Ibid., 162.

4. Ibid., 162–163.

5. Ibid., 164–165.

6. The phrase "strange life of an epithet" is taken from the subtitle of Richard

Gilman's famous book *Decadence* (New York: Farrar, Straus, and Giroux, 1979), which has inspired the conception, though not the argument and content, of this chapter.

7. Lu Xun, trans. *Chule xiangya zhita* [Out of the ivory tower], in *Lu Xun quanji* [Complete works of Lu Xun], 20 vols. (Beijing: Renmin wenxue chuban-she, 1973), 13:156.

8. Ibid., 374.

9. Lu Xun, trans., *Kumen de xiangzeng* [The symbols of suffering], in *Lu Xun quanji*, 13:86.

10. Ibid., 76–77, 118. The illustration is on 86. The first edition of Kuriya-gawa's book contains no such illustration.

11. Charles Baudelaire, *Les Fleurs du mal*, bilingual ed., trans. Richard Howard (Boston: David Godine, 1983), 213.

12. Xu Zhimo, "Sishi" [Dead body], *Yusi* [Thread of words] 3 (December 1924): 6.

13. In Joseph M. Bernstein, ed., *Baudelaire, Rimbaud, Verlaine: Selected Verse and Prose Poems* (Secaucus, N.J.: Citadel Press, 1947), 30.

14. Baudelaire, *Fleurs du mal*, 35.

15. Lu Xun, "Yinyue?" [Music?], *Jiwaiji* [Extraneous collection], in *Lu Xun quanji* [Complete works of Lu Xun], 16 vols. (Beijing: Renmin wenxue chuban-she, 1981), 7:53–54.

16. Xu Zhimo, "Sishi," 5–6.

17. The poem's Chinese title is "Ziji fajian de huanxi" (The joy I have discov-ered myself). I have not been able to identify Baudelaire's original. See Lu Xun, *Yiwen xuba ji* [Collection of translation prefaces and postcripts], in *Lu Xun quanji*, 10:237.

18. Calinescu, *Faces of Modernity*, 151–221.

19. For a detailed discussion of *Wild Grass*, see my book *Voices from an Iron House: A Study of Lu Xun* (Bloomington: Indiana University Press, 1983), chap. 5.

20. Charles Baudelaire, *Paris Spleen*, trans. Louise Varèse (New York: New Directions, 1970), ix–x.

21. Ibid., 1.

22. Lu Xun, *Yecao* [Wild grass], in *Lu Xun quanji*, 2:189–190. English translation by Yang Xianyi and Gladys Yang, *Wild Grass* (Peking; Foreign Languages Press, 1974), 30–31. I have made some alterations.

23. Baudelaire, *Paris Spleen*, 2.

24. Lu Xun, *Wild Grass*, 48; translation slightly revised.

25. See Sun Yushi, *Zhongguo chuqi xiangzeng pai shige yanjiu* [A study of early symbolist poetry in China] (Beijing: Beijing daxue chubanshe, 1988), 29–62.

26. My biographical account is based on two crucial sources: a long reminis-

cence by Shao's wife, Sheng Peiyu, "Yi Shao Xunmei" [Remembering Shao Xunmei], *Wenjiao ziliao* [Materials on literary education, ed. Nanjing Normal College] 5 (1982): 47–72, and another similar essay written in 1984 by Sheng, "Wo he Shao Xunmei" [I am Shao Xunmei] and published in an obscure journal, *Huzhou shizhuan xuebao* [Academic journal of the Huzhoa Normal College, Zhejiang province], no. 5 (1982): 47–72. In addition, Shao's former friend and colleague Zhang Kebiao wrote an article, "Haishang caizi gao chuban—ji Shao Xunmei" [A Shanghai talent getting involved in publishing—remembering Shao Xunmei], *Shanghai wenshi* [Shanghai literature and history] 2 (1989): 4–10.

27. Shao Xunmei, "Jinwu tanhua" [Talk at La Maison d'or], *Jinwu yuekan* [La Maison d'or monthly] 1.1 (January 1929): 157. Moule's translation, done together with Paul Pelliot, was published as *Marco Polo: The Description of the World* (London: Routledge and Sons, 1938).

28. In her dispatches to the *New Yorker*, Hahn wrote several times about a certain Mr. Pan, who is clearly Shao Xunmei. These articles were later collected and published in a book titled *Mr. Pan* (Garden City, N.Y.: Doubleday, 1942).

29. Emily Hahn, *China to Me* (Boston: Beacon Press, 1988), 23–24, 27.

30. Zhang Kebiao, "Haishang caizi gao chuban—ji Shao Xunmei," 8.

31. Hahn, *China to Me*, 8–9, 12.

32. Zhang Kebiao, "Haishang caizi gao chuban," 8.

33. Zhang Ruogu, *Duhui jiaoxiangqu* [Urban symphonies] (Shanghai: Zhenmeishan, 1929), 13–14; quoted in Heinrich Fruehauf, "Urban Exoticism in Modern and Contemporary Chinese Literature," in *From May Fourth to June Fourth: Fiction and Film in Twentieth-Century China*, ed. Ellen Widmer and David Der-wei Wang (Cambridge, Mass.: Harvard Contemporary China Series, 1993), 147. Fruehauf is the only Western scholar who has studied Shao and the group of aesthetes; see his dissertation, "Urban Exoticism in Modern Chinese Literature, 1910–1933" (University of Chicago, 1990).

34. Hahn, *China to Me*, 23.

35. Shao Xunmei, "Jinwu tanhua liuze" [Six talks from La Maison d'or], *Shihou* (Sphinx) 10 (November 16, 1928): 32.

36. For research on this group, see Zhang Wei, "Shihou she chulun" [Preliminary discussion of the Sphinx group], *Zhongguo xiandai wenxue yanjiu* [Research on modern Chinese literature] 3 (1993): 124–132. See also Xie Zhixi, *Mei de pianzhi: Zhongguo xiandai weimei—tuifei zhuyi wenxue yanjiu* [Extremities of beauty: a study of the literary trends of aestheticism and decadence in modern China] (Shanghai: Shanghai wenyi chubanshe, 1997), chap. 4. These are among the very few studies on this "decadent" group of writers in China.

37. These titles and other such information, unless otherwise noted, are all based on the accounts by Sheng Peiyu and Zhang Kebiao cited in n. 26.

38. Shao Xunmei, "George Moore," *Jinwu yuekan* 1.1 (January 1929): 211–215. *Aesthetes and Decadents of the 1890s,* an anthology of British poetry and prose edited by Karl Beckson (New York: Vintage Books, 1966), includes selections by most of these writers, together with sixteen illustrations by Aubrey Beardsley.

39. Shao Xunmei, "George Moore," 216. In another article, "Chuncui de shi" [Pure poetry], he quotes more of Moore's views in English; see *Shihou* 4 (August 1928): 1–3.

40. *The Columbia Encyclopedia* (New York: Columbia University Press, 1975), s. v. "George Moore."

41. Shao Xunmei, "Liangge ouxiang" [Two icons], *Jinwu yuekan* 1.5 (May 1929): 55–56.

42. Ibid., 59.

43. Shao Xunmei, "Shafo," *Shihou* 2 (1927): 29–41.

44. Shao Xunmei, "Zixu" [Self-preface], in *Shi ershiwu shou* [Twenty-five poems] (Shanghai: Shidai toushu gongsi, 1936), 7.

45. For a full discussion of Xu Zhimo and the romantic sentiment, see my book *The Romantic Generation of Modern Chinese Writers* (Cambridge, Mass.: Harvard University Press, 1973), esp. chaps. 7, 8, 14.

46. Shao Xunmei, *Huo yu rou* [Fire and flesh] (Shanghai: Jinwu shudian, 1928), 19–20, 40.

47. Ibid., 54.

48. Richard Gilman, *Decadence: The Strange Life of an Epithet* (New York: Farrar, Straus, and Giroux, 1980), 113, 116.

49. Ibid., 117–118.

50. Ibid., 91.

51. Ibid., 90–91.

52. Shao Xunmei, *Shi ershiwu shou,* 8.

53. See Jean Pierrot, *The Decadent Imagination, 1880–1990* (Chicago: University of Chicago Press, 1981), chap. 8.

54. Shao Xunmei, "Xunmei de meng" [Xunmei's dream], in *Shi ershiwu shou,* 3–5.

55. Shao Xunmei, *Hua yiban de zui'e* [Flower-like evil] (Shanghai: Jinwu shudian, 1928), 23.

56. Shao Xunmei, "Moudan" [Peony], in *Shi ershiwu shou,* 39–40.

57. Shao Xunmei, *Hua yiban de zui'e,* 49.

58. Shao Xunmei, "Tuijiadang de ai" [Decadent love], in *Hua yiban de zui'e,* 14.

59. Shao Xunmei, *Shi ershiwu shou,* 55–56.

60. Su Shi, "Shui-diao ge-fu" [Song for the river tune], trans. Stephen Owen in his *Anthology of Chinese Literature* (New York: W. W. Norton, 1996), 577.

61. Shao Xunmei, "Guanyu Huayiban de zui'e de piping" [Concerning the criticism of Flower-like evil], *Shihou* 1 (revived issue, July 1928): 2–3.

62. Ibid., 1.

63. Ibid., 3.

64. Ye Lingfeng, "Biyasilai Wang'erde yu Huangmianzhi" [Beardsley, Wilde, and the Yellow book], in *Dushu suibi* [Random jottings on reading], 3 vols. (Beijing: Sanlian shudian, 1988), 1:283–284.

65. Ye Lingfeng, "Yu Dafu xiansheng de Huangmianzhi he Biyasilai" [Yu Dafu's Yellow book and Beardsley], in *Dushu suibi*, 1:342–343.

66. Ye Lingfeng, "Guanyu Biyasilai" [About Beardsley], in *Dushu suibi*, 2:295–296.

67. I have discussed this interesting paradox in an article, "Lu Xun yu xiandai yishu yishi" [Lu Xun and artistic consciousness], which is appended to the Chinese translation of my book *Tiewu zhong de nahan* [Voices from the Iron House] (Hong Kong: Sanlian shudian, 1991), 222–248.

68. Ye Lingfeng, "Qiaoyisi jiahua" [Legends about Joyce], in *Dushu suibi*, 1:115. See also his accounts of Shanghai's bookstores as a source for rare or used books (137–138).

69. See photo pages in *Wenyi huabao* 1.2 (1933); 1.4 (1934).

70. Gilman, *Decadence*, 103, 105.

71. Ibid., 105.

72. Ibid., 115.

73. Ye Lingfeng, "Jindi" [Forbidden zone], in *Lingfeng xiaoshuo ji* [The stories of Lingfeng] (Shanghai: Xiandai shuju, 1931), 422–423.

74. Ibid., 426–427.

75. Ibid., 427–428.

76. Ibid., 423.

77. Calinescu, *Faces of Modernity*, 172.

78. Ye Lingfeng, *Dushu suibi*, 1:287.

79. Ye Lingfeng, "Jindi," 474.

80. I have attempted an analytic sketch about the novel's decadent elements in my essay "Mantan Zhongguo xiandai wenxue zhong de tuifei" [General thoughts on decadence in modern Chinese literature], first published in *Jintian* [Today] and included in my book of scholarly essays, *Xiandaixing de zhuiqiu* [In search of modernity] (Taipei: Maitian chubanshe, 1996), 191–225. Some of my ideas for this chapter were first developed in that essay.

81. Ye Lingfeng, "Qianji" [foreword], in *Lingfeng xiaoshuo ji*, iii.

82. Ye Lingfeng, *Weiwan de chanhuilu* [Unfinished confession] (Shanghai: Jindai shudian, 1936), 20–21, 44.

83. Ye Lingfeng, "Ziti" [Self-preface], ibid., 1–3. See also his "Qianji" [Self-

preface] to *Shidai guniang* [Modern girl] (Shanghai: Sishe chubanbu, 1933), 1.

84. Ye Lingfeng, *Shidai guniang*, 3–4.

85. Ye Lingfeng, "Liuxingxing ganmao" [Contagious flu], *Xiandai zazhi* 3.5 (September 1933): 655.

86. Ye Lingfeng, *Dushu suibi*, 2:250. To his credit, he was also among the first to introduce Joyce and Kafka to Chinese readers. See *Dushu suibi*, 1:115–120, 352–354. Thus his effort predated by some thirty years the more formal championship of all three modernist writers by the journal *Xiandai wenxue* (Modern literature) in Taiwan in the early 1960s.

87. Ye Lingfeng, "Liuxingxing ganmao" [Influenza], *Xiandai zashi* 3.5 (September 1933): 653–654.

88. Zhang Kebiao, "Huiyi Shao Xunmei" [Reminiscing about Shao Xunmei], *Wenjiao ziliao* 5 (1982): 68.

8. Eileen Chang

1. In fact, a movie has been made about her life, written by another legendary woman writer from Taiwan, San Mao, who shortly thereafter committed suicide. For a reliable account of Chang's death, see Lin Shitong (who was executor of her will), "Youyuan deshi Zhang Ailing" [I had the fortune to know Zhang Ailing], *Huangguan* [Crown], no. 504 (February 1996): 98–135.

2. This brief biographical account is based on two very valuable publications, Zhang Zijing, *Wo de jiejie Zhang Ailing* [My sister Eileen Chang] (Taipei: Shibao, 1996), edited with a chronology by Ji Ji; and Sima Xin [Stephen Cheng], *Zhang Ailing yu Laiya* [Eileen Chang and Ferdinand Reyher] (Taipei: Dadi chubanshe, 1996).

3. Zhang Ailing, "Chuanqi zaiban zixu" [Self-prefce to the second edition of Romances], in *Zhang Ailing duanpian xisoshuo ji* [The collected stories of Eileen Chang] (Taipei: Huangguan, 1980), 3.

4. Zhang Ailing, "Daodi shi Shanghai ren" [I am after all a Shanghai person], in *Liuyan* [Gossip] (Taipei: Huangguan, 1984), 57.

5. Ibid., 56.

6. Zhang Ailing, "Gongyu shenghuo jiqu" [The joy of apartment living], in *Liuyan*, 27–33.

7. Zhang Ailing, "Tongyan wuji" [Childish words], in *Liuyan*, 7.

8. Zhang Ailing, "Zhongguo de riye" [The days and nights of China], in *Chuanqi zengding ben* [Romances, expanded edition] (Shanghai: Shanhe tushu gongsi, 1946), 388–393.

9. Ibid., 392–393.

10. Ibid., 390.

11. Rey Chow, *Woman and Chinese Modernity: The Politics of Reading between West and East* (Minnesota: University of Minnesota Press, 1991), 85.

12. Ibid., 114.

13. Zhang Ailing, *Bansheng yuan* [Destined for half a lifetime] (Taipei: Huang-guan, 1980), 41. This novel was written in the late 1940s and rewritten in the 1970s.

14. Zhang Ailing, "Liuqing" [Traces of love], in *Chuanqi*, 3–5; English translation by Eva Hung in *Renditions* 45 (Spring 1966): 114–115.

15. Zhang Ailing, "Liuqing," 20–21. *Renditions*, 127.

16. Zhang Ailing, "Liuqing," 8, 10; *Renditions*, 118–119.

17. Zhang Zijing, *Wo de jiejie Zhang Ailing*, 117–119.

18. Zhang Ailing, "Duoshao hen" [Evermore sorrow], in *Wangran ji* [At a loss] (Taipei: Huangguan, 1991), 97–98.

19. Ibid., 98.

20. Included in her *Wangran ji*, 172–239.

21. Stanley Cavell, *Pursuits of Happiness: The Hollywood Comedy of Remarriage* (Cambridge, Mass.: Harvard University Press, 1981), 7, 16.

22. See Zheng Shusen [William Tay], *Cong xiandai dao dangdai* [From the modern to the contemporary] (Taipei: Sanmin, 1994), pt. 2.

23. Cavell, *Pursuits of Happiness*, 131.

24. Zhang Ailing, "Tan nüren" [On woman], in *Liuyan*, 84.

25. Xun Yu [Fu Lei], "Lun Zhang Ailing de xiaoshuo" [On Eileen Chang's fiction], in *Zhang Ailing yanjiu* [Studies on Eileen Chang], ed. Tang Wenbiao (Taipei: Lianjing, 1986), 124–125.

26. Ibid., 128.

27. Zhang Ailing, "Ziji de wenzhang" [My own writing], in *Liuyan*, 21–23; English translation taken in part from Karen Kingsbury, "Eileen Chang's 'Cenci de duizhao' and Eurasian Culture-Creation," delivered at the International Conference on Eileen Chang, Taipei, May 25–27, 1996, 17.

28. Karen Kingsbury translates the term somewhat heavily as "off-set opposition" and "uneven, unmatching contraposition" (ibid., 17–18).

29. Ibid., 18.

30. Zhang Ailing, "Tongyan wuji," 14.

31. Zhang Ailing, "Liuqing," esp. 1, 4, 20; emphasis added.

32. Zhang Ailing, "Lun xiezuo" [On writing], in *Zhangkan* [As Chang looks] (Taipei: Huangguan, 1976), 271.

33. Zhang Ailing, *Wangran ji*, 97.

34. Zhang Ailing, "Lun xiezuo," 272.

35. Zhang Ailing, "Xie shenmo" [What to write], in *Liuyan*, 125.

36. Zhang Ailing, "Hungluan xi" [Wedding happiness], in *Chuanqi*, 24.

37. Zhang Ailing, "Fengsuo" [Sealed off], in *Chuanqi*, 382.

38. Zhang Ailing, "Hong meigui yu bai meigui" [Red rose and white rose], in *Chuanqi*, 37.

39. Zhang Ailing, "Ziji de wenzhang," 23–24.

40. For a reading of Chang's desolation as a countergesture to the sublime figure of history and perceptive analyses of her stories, see Ban Wang, *The Sublime Figure of History: Aesthetics and Politics in Twentieth-Century China* (Stanford: Stanford University Press, 1997), 89–100.

41. Kingsbury, "Eileen Chang's 'Cenci de duizhao,'" 18. Kingsbury is here defining Chang's method of *cenci de duizhao*, but I think it is a more fitting description of Chang's narratorial voice and state of desolation.

42. Zhang Ailing, "Chuanqi zaiban zixu," 3.

43. Ibid., 5.

44. Zhang Ailing, "You jiju hua tong duzhe shuo" [A few words to tell the reader], in *Chuanqi*, 1.

45. Zhang Ailing, "Fengsuo," 377; English translation by Karen Kingsbury in *The Columbia Anthology of Modern Chinese Literature*, ed. Joseph Lau and Howard Goldblatt (New York: Columbia University Press, 1995), 188.

46. Zhang was of course aware of such references, as she once remarked that "the vehicle of the era moves forward roaringly." See her "Jingyu hui" [From the ashes], in *Liuyan*, 54.

47. Zhang Ailing, "Fengsuo," 387; English translation, *Columbia Anthology*, 197.

48. Rey Chow [Zhou Lei], "Jiqiao, meixueshikong, nüxing zuojia" [Technique, aesthetic chronotope, and woman writer], paper presented to the International Conference on Eileen Chang, Taipei, May 25–27, 1996, 9.

49. Ibid., 8–10.

50. Cavell, *Pursuits of Happiness*, 19.

51. Zhang Ailing, "Qingcheng zhilian" [Love in a fallen city], in *Chuangqi*, 152; English translation by Karen Kingsbury in *Renditions* 45 (Spring 1996): 61.

52. Ibid., 156; *Renditions*, 65.

53. Ibid., 158–159; *Renditions*, 67.

54. Ibid., 159; *Renditions*, 67.

55. Ibid., 170; *Renditions*, 76–77.

56. Cao Xueqin, *The Story of the Stone*, 4 vols., trans. David Hawkes (Baltimore: Penguin Books, 1976), 1:466.

57. Zhang Ailing, "Qingcheng zhilian," 177; *Renditions*, 82.

58. See Kingsbury's footnote, *Renditions*, 82.

59. Zhang Ailing, "Qingcheng zhilian," 177; *Renditions*, 82.

60. Ibid., 181; *Renditions*, 85. I have discussed at length Chang's technical affinity with cinema and also, somewhat playfully, concocted a series of cinematic shots for this scene. See my paper "Buliao qing: Zhang Ailing he

dianying" [Endless love: Eileen Chang and movies] for the International Conference on Eileen Chang, Taipei, May 25–27, 1996, 10.

61. Zhang Ailing, "Qingcheng zhilian," 190; *Renditions*, 92.

62. Zhang Ailing, "Jingyu lu," 47; English translation by Oliver Stunt, *Renditions*, 51.

9. Shanghai Cosmopolitanism

1. Harold Isaacs, *Re-encounters in China: Notes from a Journey in a Time Capsule* (Armonk, N.Y.: M. E. Sharpe, 1985), 5.

2. Most books about the concessions tend to focus on their history and laws. For an in-depth study of municipal administration, see Christian Henriot, *Shanghai, 1927–1937: Municipal Power, Locality, and Modernization* (Berkeley: University of California Press, 1993). Fredric Wakeman's masterly study of the Shanghai police is approached from the "control" angle. See Fredric Wakeman, Jr., *Policing Shanghai, 1927–1937* (Berkeley: University of California Press, 1995). I have yet to check the voluminous police files for any accounts of my writers.

3. See Homi K. Bhabha, "Of Mimicry and Man: The Ambivalence of Colonial Discourse," in his *Location of Culture* (London: Routledge, 1994), 86–90.

4. Perhaps the first portrait of a genuine "mimic man" is to be found in Eileen Chang's fiction: for instance, George Qiao, the handsome hybrid charlatan in "Aloe Ashes—First Burning" with whom the heroine falls in love. But the story takes place entirely in Hong Kong, a setting of colonial mimicry in the extreme, not in Shanghai. Interestingly, of Chang's stories set in Shanghai in which Western foreigners do make an appearance, there is hardly a Chinese figure that fits Bhabha's prototype. The one exception may be the Chinese maid in "Shame, Amah," who serves her British master. Whether the maid subconsciously enacts her role as a "colonized" slave is still debatable, however, because her servant status is mediated by her other roles as a Chinese mother, wife, and working-class woman. It is her Chinese world which remains the center of her life.

5. Zhang Ailing, "Yangren kan jinxi ji qita" [A foreigner looks at Peking opera and other matters], in *Liuyan* [Gossip] (Taipei: Huangguan, 1984), 100–109.

6. This seems also to be the conclusion drawn by Tang Zhenchang, a leading scholar of Shanghai's social history, in "Shimin yishi yu Shanghai shehui" [Urbanite consciousness and Shanghai society], *Ershiyishiji* (Twenty-first century, Hong Kong) 11 (June 1992): 11–23.

7. Joseph Levenson, *Revolution and Cosmopolitanism: The Western Stage and the Chinese Stages* (Berkeley: University of California Press, 1971), 41.

8. Ibid., 31.

9. See also Chapter 7. These three volumes are included in *Lu Xun quanji* [Complete works of Lu Xun] (Beijing: Renmin wenxue chubanshe, 1973), vol. 13. The title of *Symbols of Suffering* is taken from a poetic line by Shelley: "They learn in suffering what they teach in song" (130).

10. Naoki Sakai, "Multi-ethnic Nation and Japanese Culturalism: On Cultural Studies and Internationalism," paper presented at the International Symposium, "Dialogue with Cultural Studies," at the University of Tokyo, March 17, 1996, 12.

11. *Yokomitsu Reiichi ki* [Collection of Yokomitsu Reiichi] (Tokyo: Kawadeshobo, 1977), 31:7; translated by Emanuel Pastreich in a paper submitted to my seminar at Harvard on Shanghai modernism, "Yokomitsu Reiichi's Shanghai" (Fall 1992), 15. I am most grateful to him for his permission to quote this translation and other insights from his paper.

12. Pastreich, "Yokomitsu Reiichi's Shanghai," 16.

13. The wave metaphor is used in Maeda Ai's analysis of the novel. See Maeda Ai, "Shanghai 1925," in *Toshi kukan no naka no bungaku* [Literature in city space] (Tokyo: Chikuma shōbo, 1983), 365–401. The relevance of Eisenstein's film is mentioned in Pastreich, "Yokomitsu Reiichi's Shanghai," 20.

14. Sakai, "Multi-ethnic Nation," 14.

15. Ibid.

16. Ibid., 1.

17. Martin Wilbur, "The Nationalist Revolution: From Canton to Nanking, 1923–28," in *The Cambridge History of China,* ed. John Fairbank, vol. 12, Pt. 1 (Cambridge: Cambridge University Press, 1983), 547.

18. Ibid., 548–549.

19. Translated in Pastreich, "Yokomitsu Reiichi's Shanghai," 10–11.

20. Sakai, "Multi-ethnic Nation," 30.

21. Maeda Ai, "Shanghai 1925," 376.

22. For Lu Xun's pathetic effort to keep up with what was going on in Soviet literary debates, see my book *Voices from the Iron House: A Study of Lu Xun* (Bloomington: Indiana University Press, 1987), chap. 8.

23. Isaacs, *Re-encountesr in China,* 21.

24. The particular poignancy of the Spanish civil war was brought home by Dai Wangshu as he translated a number of "Spanish anti-fascist ballads" in Hong Kong around 1940, on the eve of the Japanese takeover. See Shi Zhecun, ed., *Dai Wangshu yishi ji* [Poetry translations by Dai Wangshu] (Changsha: Hunan renmin chubanshe, 1983), 3. Shi included eight ballads in this collection by Vincente Alexandre and others (197–222).

10. Epilogue

1. Zhang Ailing, "Chenxiang xie—diyilu xiang" (Aloe ashes—first burning), in *Chuangqi* [Romances] (Shanghai: Shanhe tushu gongsi, 1946), 213, 224, 233–234.

2. Zhang Ailing, "Daodi shi Shanghai ren" [I am after all a Shanghai person], in *Liuyan* [Gossip] (Taipei: Huangguan, 1984), 57.

3. Lung Bingyi, *Xianggang gujin jianzhu* [Hong Kong architecture, ancient and modern] (Hong Kong: Sanlian shudian, 1992), 63.

4. Ibid., 119.

5. Ibid., 100.

6. He Ying, "Wo jiandao de Mu Shiying" [The Mu Shiying I saw], *Xin wenxue shiliao* [Historical materials on new literature] 3 (August 1989): 142–145. Lu Dun, "Yingtan de guoke" [A passer-by on the film scene], *Wenhui bao* (Hong Kong), December 7, 1987.

7. *Bungakkai* [Literary world] 7 (September 1940): 174–175. I am grateful to Philip Williams for providing me with this source.

8. The Hong Kong scholar Lu Weiluan has done thorough research on Dai's Hong Kong years and compiled a complete catalogue of his writings and translations published in Hong Kong, "Dai Wangshu zai Xianggang de zhuzuo yizuo mulu" (mimeographed), which come to a total of more than three hundred items. See also her book *Xianggang wenzong* [Hong Kong literary connections] (Hong Kong: Wah Hon Publishing Company, 1987), 176–211 (chapter on Dai Wangshu's years in Hong Kong).

9. Ye Lingfeng, "Wangshu he zainan de suiyue" [Wangshu and the years of suffering], *Wenyi shiji* [Literary century] (1957): 8. Zhao Cong, "Yuxiang shiren—Dai Wangshu" [The poet of the Rainy Alley—Dai Wangshu], *Wanren zazhi* [Multitude, Hong Kong] 164 (December 1970): 8. These and other reminiscences are included in a collection, *Dai Wangshu ziliao ji* [Materials on Dai Wangshu] (Hong Kong, n.d.).

10. Xu Chi, *Jiangnan xiaozhen* [A small town in the lower Yangtze] (Beijing: Zuojia chubanshe, 1993), 226.

11. Ibid., chaps. 14–18.

12. See the two prefaces to Ye Lingfeng, *Dushu suibi* [Random notes on reading] 3 vols. (Hong Kong: Sanlian, 1988), 1:1–22.

13. For a detailed account, see Lu Weiluan, *Xianggang wenzong*, 53–133.

14. Long Bingyi, *Xianggang gujin jianzhu*. 151.

15. Ibid., 154.

16. Ibid., 174–177.

17. One earlier series made in the mid-1970s was subsequently remade by Hong Kong TVB into a new series, *Xin Shanghai tan*. See Daisy Ng, "Back to

the Future: Imaginary Nostalgia and the Consumer Culture of Hong Kong," paper presented at the Annual Meeting of the New England Conference of the Association of Asian Studies, University of Vermont, October 19, 1996. I should also add that in 1997 I went shopping at Hong Kong's swanky new boutique Shanghai Tang, which carries merchandise with an Orientalist flavor.

18. Ibid., 10; quoted with the author's permission.
19. Ibid., 10–11.
20. Leung Ping-kwan, *City at the End of Time*, trans. Gordon T. Osing (Hong Kong: Twilight Books, 1992).
21. Ng, "Back to the Future," 11. Abbas's remark is from his article "The Last Emporium: Verse and Cultural Space," *Positions* 1.1 (1993): 1–17.
22. For a detailed account of horse racing in Hong Kong and Shanghai, see Austin Coates, *China Races* (Hong Kong: Oxford University Press, 1983).
23. Fredric Jameson, "Postmodernism and Consumer Society," in *The Anti-Aesthetic: Essays on Postmodern Culture*, ed. Hal Foster (Port Townsend, Wash.: Bay Press, 1983), 113–116.
24. Ibid., 116.
25. For a discussion of this film, see my article "Two Films from Hong Kong: Parody and Allegory," in *Contemporary Chinese Cinemas*, ed. Nick Browne et al. (Cambridge: Cambridge University Press, 1994), 206–209.
26. Joseph Levenson, *Revolution and Cosmopolitanism* (Berkeley: University of California Press, 1971), 55.
27. Gu Wei, "Ji Shi Zhecun xiansheng" [A record of Mr. Shi Zhecun], *Shanghai wenhua* [Shanghai culture] 1 (November 1993): 69–71.
28. Zhang Ailing, "Zhongghuo de riye," in *Chuanqi*, 390.

GLOSSARY

anshen 安身

Ba Jin 巴金

Bai Guang 白光

baihua 白話

Baihuali 百花里

Baijin de nüti suxiang 白金的女體塑像

Bai Juyi 白居易

Baike xiao congshu 百科小叢書

baike zhi xue 百科之學

Bai Liusu 白流蘇

Baimian shusheng 白面書生

Bansheng yuan 半生緣

Banyue 半月

Bao Tianxiao 包天笑

Bei dangzuo xiaoqianpin de nanzi 被當
作消遣品的男子

Beihai de ren 背海的人

beihuan lihe 悲歡離合

Beixin 北新

beizhuang 悲壯

bengbeng xi 蹦蹦戲

bisuan 筆算

bu'erqiaoya 布爾喬亞

Buliao qing 不了情

Bu Wancang 卜萬蒼

Cabi dancai hua 擦筆淡彩畫

Cai Chusheng 蔡楚生

Cai Yuanpei 蔡元培

caizi 才子

Canliu 殘留

cangliang 蒼涼

Cao Xueqin 曹雪芹

Cao Yu 曹禺

cenci de duizhao 參差的對照

Chahuanü 茶花女

changshi 常識

Chen Bailu 陳白露

Chen Bo'er 陳波兒

Chen Dieyi 陳蝶衣

Chen Duxiu 陳獨秀

Chen Huiyang　陳輝揚

Chen Mengjia　陳夢家

Chen Yanyan　陳燕燕

Chen Zhenling　陳珍玲

Chenxiangxie, di'erlu xiang　沉香屑，第
二爐香

Chenxiangxie, diyilu xiang　沉香屑，第
一爐香

Cheng Bugao　程步高

Cheng Jihua　程季華

Cheng Shewo　成舍我

Chiang Kai-shek　蔣介石

Chongqing　重慶

Chow Yuen-fat　周潤發

Chuanqi　傳奇

Chuangzao yuekan　創造月刊

chufengtou　出風頭

Chule xiangya zhi ta　出了象牙之塔

Chushi zhexue　處世哲學

Chuncan　春蠶

Chunyang　春陽

Cihai　辭海

ciji　刺激

congshu　叢書

Daguanyuan　大觀園

Daguangming　大光明

dajia guixiu　大家閨秀

Damalu　大馬路

Da Shanghai　大上海

Dashijie　大世界

da tuanyuan　大團圓

Daxin　大新

dazhong xiaoshuo　大眾小説

Dai Wangshu　戴望舒

dangfu　蕩婦

Di Chuqing　狄楚青

Dilao tianhuang buliao qing　地老天荒
不了情

dili　地理

Diyi xian　第一線

dian　電

Dianshizhai huabao　點石齋畫報

Diantong huabao　電通畫報

Dianying yuebao　電影月報

dongfang　東方

Dongfang wenku　東方文庫

Dongfang zazhi　東方雜誌

Du Heng　杜衡

Du Yaquan　杜亞泉

duhui de ciji　都會的刺激

Duhui jiaoxiangqu　都會交響曲

Dushi de nannü　都市的男女

Dushi fengjing xian　都市風景線

dushi yishi　都市意識

Duoshao hen　多少恨

Fan Liuyuan　范柳原

Fangcheng shi　方程式

Fang Guangtao　方光燾

Fang Qiulan　芳秋蘭

fangsi　放肆

Fei Mu　費穆

Fengjing　風景

Feng Naichao　馮乃超

Fengsuo　封鎖

Feng xiaoxiao　風蕭蕭

Feng Xuefeng　馮雪峰

Fengyang nü　鳳陽女

Fengyun er'nü　風雲兒女

Feng Zhi　馮至

Fu Lei　傅雷

Funü ribao　婦女日報

Funü zazhi　婦女雜誌

Furen huabao　婦人畫報

Fuxin sanbuqu　婦心三部曲

Fu Yanchang　傅彥長

Fuyuli　富裕里

Fuzhou lu　福州路

gangkou　港口

Gangnei xiaojing　港內小景

Ge Momei　葛莫美

Ge Weilong　葛薇龍

Gewu shengping　歌舞升平

Gengyi ji　更衣記

Gongheguo jiaokeshu　共和國教科書

Gonghe guomin duben　共和國民讀本

Gongmu　公墓

Gongyu shenghuo jiqu　公寓生活記趣

gongyuan　宮怨

gu　古

Gushi xinbian　故事新編

gushi xing　故事性

guang　光

Guangzhi　廣智

Guangzhou　廣州

guinü　閨女

Guo Jianying　郭建英

Guo Moruo　郭沫若

guochan dianying　國產電影

guohuo　國貨

guojia　國家

Guomindang　國民黨

Guotai　國泰

guowen　國文

Guoxue jiben congshu　國學基本叢書

hanyang　涵養

Hangzhou　杭州

helihua　合理化

Hei Ying　黑嬰

Hei Mudan　黑牡丹

Henhai　恨海

389

Hongfen kulou 紅粉骷髏

Hongmeigui yu baimeigui 紅玫瑰與
　白玫瑰

Hong Shen 洪深

Hu Die 胡蝶

Hu Lancheng 胡蘭成

huqin 胡琴

Hu Shi 胡適

hua 化

huahua gongzi 花花公子

huaju 話劇

huayang zachu 華洋雜處

Hua yiban de zui'e 花一般的罪惡

Huanzhou 幻洲

Huang Kewu 黃克武

Huang Liushuang 黃柳霜

Huangxin dashi 黃心大師

Huo yu rou 火與肉

jiqi wenming 機器文明

jiqiao 技巧

jishu 技术

Jia Baoyu 賈寶玉

jiachong 甲虫

jiaren 佳人

jiating lunli 家庭倫理

jiayangguizi 假洋鬼子

Jianming guowen jiaokeshu 簡明國文
　教科書

Jiangjun di tou 將軍底頭

Jiangnan 江南

Jiangsu 江蘇

Jiang Weiqiao 蔣維喬

jiaojihua 交際花

Jiaoyu bu shending 教育部審訂

Jiaoyu zazhi 教育雜誌

jiaozheng xisu 校正習俗

jiefu 節婦

jin 今

Jindai funü 近代婦女

Jindi 禁地

Jin Ping Mei 金瓶梅

Jinwu shudian 金屋書店

Jinwu yuekan 金屋月刊

Jinyu lu 爐餘錄

Jinyuan chunnong 禁苑春濃

jujiazhe 居家者

Ka'erdeng 卡爾登

Kafei guan de yiye 咖啡館的一夜

Kafei zuotan 咖啡座談

Kaiming 開明

Ke Ling 柯靈

Kexue xiao congshu 科學小叢書

Kumen de xiangzheng 苦悶的象徵

kumon no shocho 苦悶の象徵

kuaigan 快感

kunqu 昆曲

Langtaosha 浪淘沙

Lao She 老舍

Leung Ping-kwan 梁秉鈞

Libailiu 禮拜六

Libao 立報

Li Jinfa 李金髮

Li Jinhui 黎錦暉

Li Qingya 李青崖

lishi 歷史

Li Shizeng 李石曾

Lixian guomin duben 立憲國民讀本

Liyi yu weisheng 禮儀與衛生

Lianhua 聯華

Liangge shijian de buganzheng zhe 兩個
時間的不感症者

Liang Qichao 梁啓超

Liang Shiqiu 梁實秋

Liangyou 良友

Liangyou huabao 良友畫報

Liangyou tushu yinshua gongsi 良友圖
書印刷公司

Liangyou wenku 良友文庫

Liangyou wenxue congshu 良友文學
叢書

Liangyuan qiaohe 良緣巧合

Lin Biao 林彪

Lin Daiyu 林黛玉

Lin Niantong 林年同

Lin Shu 林紓

Lin Yutang 林語堂

Ling Changyan 凌昌言

Linglong 玲瓏

Linglong funü tuhua zazhi 玲瓏婦女圖畫
雜誌

Liu 流

Liu Na'ou 劉吶鷗

Liuqing 留情

Lu Mengshu 盧夢殊

Lu Shaofei 魯少飛

Lu Xiaoman 陸小曼

Lu Xun 魯迅

Luyishi 路易士

Lüshe 旅舍

Lunyu 論語

Luotuo, Nicaizhuyizhe yu nüren 駱駝，
尼采主義者與女人

Ma Guoliang 馬國亮

Malu tianshi 馬路天使

Ma Ning 馬寧

Ma Xu Weibang 馬徐維邦

manhua 漫畫

Mao Dun 茅盾

Meiqi 美琪

meiren 美人

Meiyu zhi xi 梅雨之夕

miaoling nülang 妙齡女郎

Miewang 滅亡

minzu 民族

Mingxing 明星

Modao 魔道

Modeng 摩登

motian dalou 摩天大樓

mubiao 幕表

Mudanting 牡丹亭

Mu Mutian 穆木天

Mu Shiying 穆時英

muwei 幕味

Nanbeiji 南北極

Nanguo 南國

Nanguo zhoukan 南國周刊

Nanjing lu (Nanking Road) 南京路

Ni Yide 倪貽德

Nie Er 聶耳

Niehai hua 孽海花

Ninong 妮孃

nongtang 弄堂

Nongxue zazhi 農學雜誌

nüxue 女學

Ou 鷗

Pangu 盤古

Pan Hannian 潘漢年

Pan Qiaoyun 潘巧雲

Paomating 跑馬廳

piyingxi 皮影戲

Pudong 浦東

qifa mengmei 啓發蒙昧

qifa sixiang 啓發思想

qimeng 啓蒙

qipao 旗袍

Qi zhi shengchen 妻之生辰

qianwei 前衛

Qian Xingcun 錢杏村

Qin Lili 秦莉莉

qing 情

Qingchang ru zhanchang 情場如戰場

Qingcheng zhi lian 傾城之戀

Qingdao 青島

qunyi 群益

Reqing zhi gu 熱情之骨

Richu 日出

Ruan Lingyu 阮玲玉

Sanbu 散步

Shan nüren xingpin 善女人行品

Shanshui, sixiang, renwu 山水，思想，人物

shangdi 上帝

Shanghai de hubuwu—yige pianduan
上海的狐步舞——一個片斷

Shanghai de jianglai 上海的將來

Shanghai menjing 上海門徑

Shanghai tan 上海灘

392

Shanghai wenhua　上海文化

Shanghai zhi ye　上海之夜

Shangwu yinshu guan　商務印書館

Shaonian zazhi　少年雜誌

Shao Xunmei　邵洵美

Shaoye　少爺

Shexie meiren　蛇蠍美人

shen　身

Shen bao　申報

Shen Congwen　沈從文

shenfen　身份

Shennü　神女

Shen Xilin　沈西麟

sheng　聲

Shenghuo　生活

sheng lao bing si　生老病死

Sheng Peiyu　盛佩玉

Sheng Xuanhuai　盛宣懷

shidai　時代

shidai guniang　時代姑娘

Shidai manhua　時代漫畫

Shi ershiwu shou　詩二十五首

Shihou　獅吼

Shi Hui　石揮

Shih Shu-mei　史書美

Shijing　詩經

shikumen　石庫門

shili yangchang　十里洋場

Shishi xinbao　時事新報

Shixiu　石秀

Shi Zhecun　施蟄存

shizhuang shinü tu　時裝仕女圖

Shizi jietou　十字街頭

Shizizuo liuxing　獅子座流星

Shuihu zhuan　水滸傳

shuili　水利

Shuimo　水沫

shuoming shu　説明書

Simalu　四馬路

Sixizi de shengyi　四喜子的生意

Song Qingling (Soong Ching-ling)　宋慶齡

Song Zhidi　宋之的

Subei　蘇北

Su Tong　蘇童

Su Wen　蘇汶

Tan Ying　談瑛

Taohua shan　桃花扇

Taoli jie　桃李劫

Teng Gang　滕剛

Teng Gu　滕固

Tiyu shijie　體育世界

Tian Han　田漢

Tianjin　天津

tingzijian　亭子間

tingzijian wenren　亭子間文人

tongmeng　童蒙

393

Tsui Hark　徐克

Tuibai xian de chandong　頹敗線的顫動

tuifei　頹廢

tui jia dang　頹加蕩

Tuijiadang de ai　頹加蕩的愛

tuitang　頹唐

wanku zidi　紈袴子弟

Wan Laiming　萬籟鳴

Wanxiang　萬象

Wanyou wenku　萬有文庫

Wang Dechang　王德昌

Wang Dingjiu　王定九

Wang Duqing　王獨清

Wang Jingwei　汪精衛

Wang Yunwu　王雲五

Weimei pai　唯美派

Weiwan de chanhuilu　未完的懺悔錄

weixin yundong　維新運動

Wenfan xiaopin　文飯小品

wenhua jie　文化街

wenku　文庫

wenming　文明

wenming xi　文明戲

wenren dianying　文人電影

Wenxue de zhenshixing　文學的真實性

Wenxue gongchan　文學工廠

wenyan　文言

wo　我

Wu　霧

wuchang　舞場

Wugui lieche　無軌列車

Wuhan　武漢

wuli kanhua　霧里看花

Wu Liande　吳聯德

wunü　舞女

wuting　舞廳

wutong　梧桐

Wu Woyao　吳沃堯

Wuxi　無錫

wuyin de yue　無音的樂

Wu Yonggang　吳永剛

Wuyue　五月

Wu Zhihui　吳稚暉

xifang　西方

xiren dianying　戲人電影

xizi　戲子

Xia Yan　夏衍

Xiandai biaoqingmei zaoxing　現代表
　　情美造型

Xiandai dianying　現代電影

Xiandai wenti congshu　現代問題叢書

Xiandai xiaoshuo　現代小說

xiandai xin　現代心

Xiandai zazhi　現代雜誌

Xianshi　先施

Xiaocheng zhichun　小城之春

Xiao Hong　蕭紅

Xiao Jun　蕭軍

xiao shimin　小市民

Xiaoshuo yuebao　小説月報

xiangcao meiren　香草美人

xin　新

Xin ganjue pai　新感覺派

Xinjing　心經

xinmin　新民

Xin pengyoumen　新朋友們

Xin Shanghai　新上海

xin shidai　新時代

Xinshidai shidi congshu　新時代史地
　叢書

xin wenhua　新文化

xin wenxue　新文學

Xin wenyi　新文藝

Xinxin　新新

xinxue　新學

xin zhishi　新知識

xinzheng　新政

Xinyue　新月

Xinyue shudian　新月書店

xinzhi　新知

Xingdao ribao　星島日報

Xingzuo　星座

Xiongzhai　凶宅

xiushen　修身

Xu Anhua (Ann Hui)　許鞍華

Xu Chi　徐遲

Xu Weinan　徐蔚南

Xu Xiacun　徐霞村

Xu Xu　徐訏

Xu Zhimo　徐志摩

Xuesheng zazhi　學生雜誌

xuetang　學堂

xuexiao　學校

Yan'an　延安

Yan Fu　嚴復

Yan Ruisheng　閻瑞生

yanjiu xueli　研究學理

Yan Ying　炎櫻

Yanzhi kou　胭脂扣

yanzhuang shaofu　艷裝少婦

Yang Aili　楊愛立

yangfang　洋房

Yang Guifei　楊貴妃

Yang Hansheng　楊翰笙

yanghua　洋化

yangnu　洋奴

Yangren kan jingxi ji qita　洋人看京戲
　及其他

Yang Xingfo　楊杏佛

Yang Xiong　楊雄

Yao yao yao, yaodao waipoqiao　搖搖搖, 搖
　到外婆橋

Yehan gesheng　夜半歌聲

Yecao 野草

Yecha 夜叉

yeji 野雞

Ye Lingfeng 葉靈鳳

Ye Qianyu 葉淺予

Yezonghui li de wuge ren 夜總會裡的
五個人

yiguo qingdiao 異國情調

Yipinxiang 一品香

Yishu jie 藝朮界

Yiwen qingbao 藝文情報

yiyifeng 譯意風

yizhi hua 一枝花

Yizhi lihua chun dai yu 一枝梨花春
帶雨

Yinxing 銀星

Yingluo 瓔珞

yingtan 影壇

Yingwen zazhi 英文雜誌

yingxi 影戲

Yingxi congbao 影戲叢報

Yingxi zazhi 影戲雜誌

Yingxiong er'nü 英雄兒女

Yingyu zhoukan 英語周刊

Ying Yunwei 應雲衛

Yong'an 永安

youwu 尤物

Youxi 游戲

Yu Dafu 郁達夫

Yuguangqu 漁光曲

Yu Jiayin 虞家茵

Yusi 語絲

Yuxiang 雨巷

Yuyuan lu (Yu Yuan Road) 愚園路

yuan 圓

Yuan Muzhi 袁牧之

Yuan Shikai 袁世凱

Zamen de shijie 咱們的世界

zahuo dian 雜貨店

zawen 雜文

Zai Bali daxiyuan 在巴黎大戲院

zai xiayishi zhong 在下意識中

Zeng Pu 曾朴

Zeng Xubai 曾虛白

Zhabei 閘北

Zhang Ailing (Eileen Chang) 張愛玲

Zhang Guangyu 張光宇

Zhang Jinglu 張靜廬

Zhang Jingyuan 張京媛

Zhang Kebiao 章克標

Zhang Leping 張樂平

Zhangmi 張迷

Zhang Ruogu 張若谷

Zhang Shichuan 張石川

Zhang Tianyi 張天翼

Zhang Yimou 張藝謀

Zhang Yingchao 張英超

Zhang Yingjin　張英進

Zhang Zhenyu　張振宇

Zhang Zhidong　張之洞

Zhang Ziping　張資平

Zhao Dan　趙丹

Zhao Jiabi　趙家璧

Zhao Jingshen　趙景深

Zhenbao　振保

Zhen Mei Shan　真美善

Zheng Boqi　鄭伯奇

Zheng Mantuo　鄭曼陀

Zheng Zhenduo　鄭振鐸

Zheng Zhengqiu　鄭正秋

zhiguai　志怪

Zhongguo de riye　中國的日夜

Zhongguo dianying fazhan shi　中國電影發展史

Zhongguo xinwenxue daxi　中國新文學大系

Zhongguo xuesheng　中國學生

Zhongguo yijiusanyi　中國一九三一

Zhongguo yingxi yanjiu she　中國影戲研究社

Zhonghua shuju　中華書局

zhongyang　中央

Zhou Furen　周夫人

Zhou Jianren　周建人

Zhou Shoujuan　周瘦鵑

Zhou Yang　周揚

Zhou Xuan　周璇

Zhou Zuoren　周作人

Zhu Hu Binxia　朱胡彬霞

zhufan dianlu　煮飯電爐

Zhu Yingpeng　朱應鵬

zhuanglie　壯烈

Zhui　追

Ziji de wenzhang　自己的文章

zilai huolu　自來火爐

Ziluolan　紫羅蘭

Ziye　子夜

zouhuo ru mo　走火入魔

Zou Taofen　鄒韜奮

INDEX